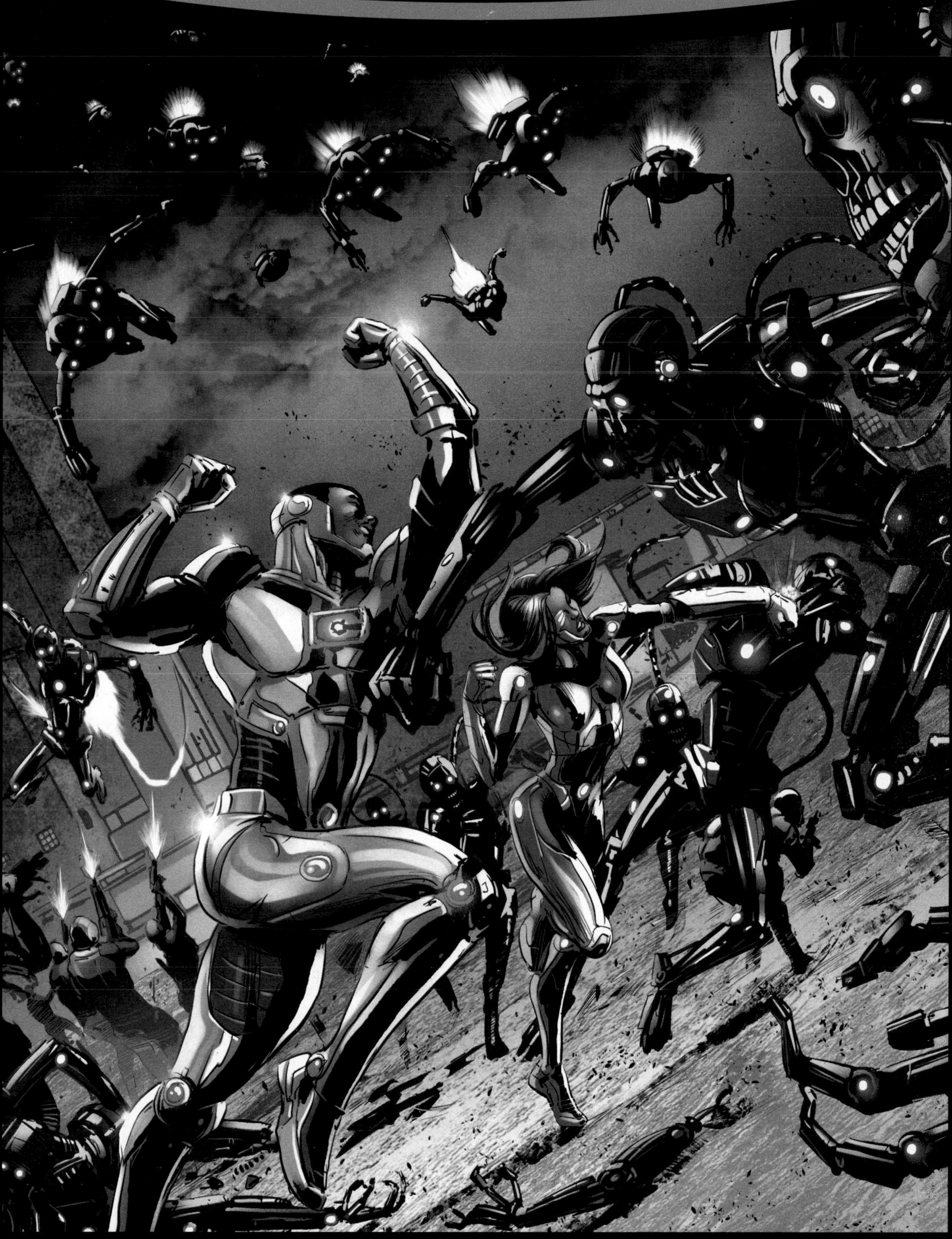

CYBORG

VOL.3 SINGULARITY

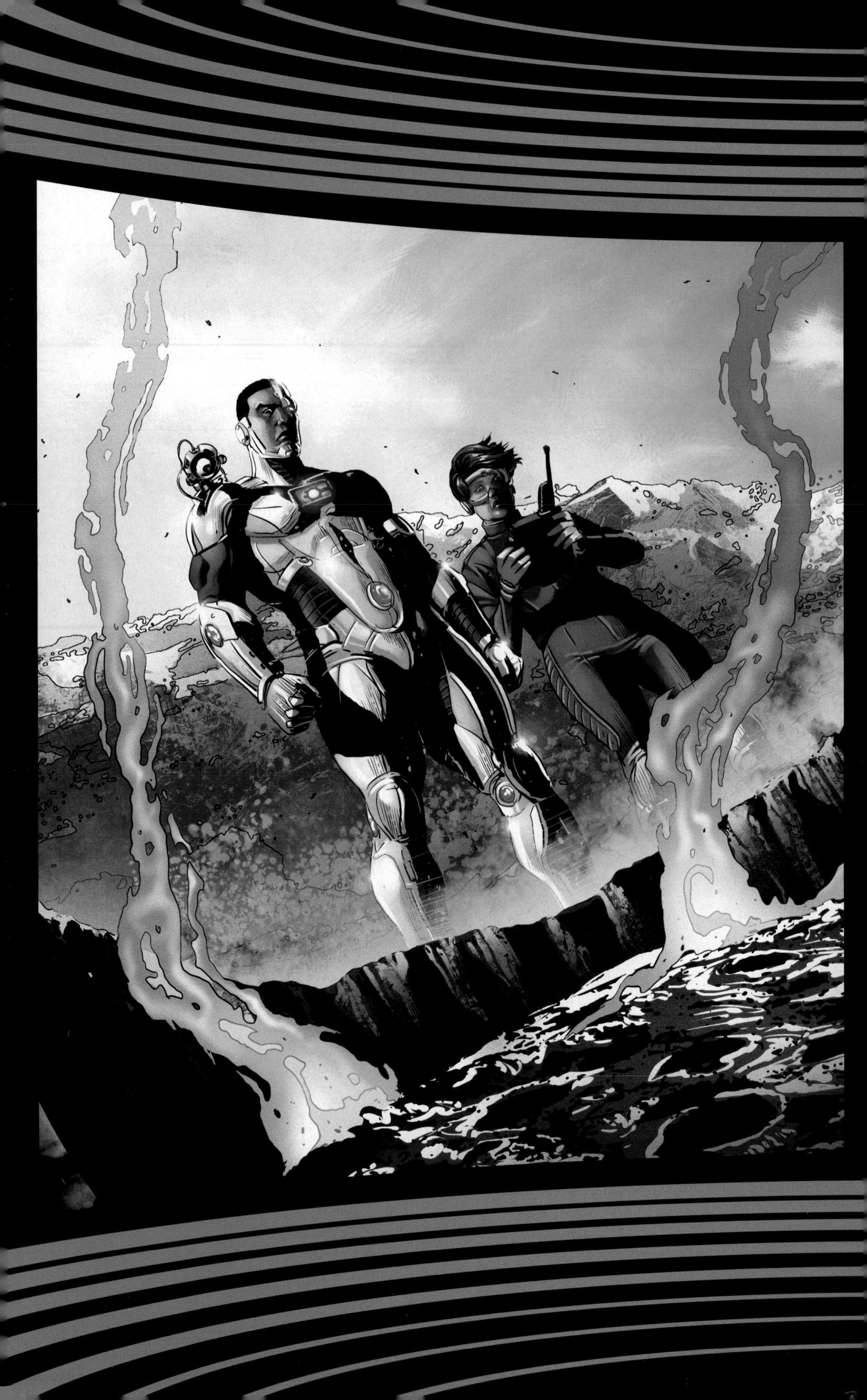

CYBORG
VOL.3 SINGULARITY

JOHN SEMPER JR.
KEVIN GREVIOUX
writers

WILL CONRAD
WAYNE FAUCHER * ALLAN JEFFERSON * CLIFF RICHARDS
artists

IVAN NUNES
GABE ELTAEB
colorists

ROB LEIGH
letterer

ERIC CANETE and **GUY MAJOR**
collection cover artists

CYBORG created by **MARV WOLFMAN** and **GEORGE PÉREZ**

HARVEY RICHARDS Editor - Original Series
JEB WOODARD Group Editor - Collected Editions • **BETSY GOLDEN** Editor - Collected Edition
STEVE COOK Design Director - Books • **MEGEN BELLERSEN** Publication Design

BOB HARRAS Senior VP - Editor-in-Chief, DC Comics
PAT McCALLUM Executive Editor, DC Comics

DIANE NELSON President • **DAN DiDIO** Publisher • **JIM LEE** Publisher • **GEOFF JOHNS** President & Chief Creative Officer
AMIT DESAI Executive VP - Business & Marketing Strategy, Direct to Consumer & Global Franchise Management
SAM ADES Senior VP & General Manager, Digital Services • **BOBBIE CHASE** VP & Executive Editor, Young Reader & Talent Development
MARK CHIARELLO Senior VP - Art, Design & Collected Editions • **JOHN CUNNINGHAM** Senior VP - Sales & Trade Marketing
ANNE DePIES Senior VP - Business Strategy, Finance & Administration • **DON FALLETTI** VP - Manufacturing Operations
LAWRENCE GANEM VP - Editorial Administration & Talent Relations • **ALISON GILL** Senior VP - Manufacturing & Operations
HANK KANALZ Senior VP - Editorial Strategy & Administration • **JAY KOGAN** VP - Legal Affairs • **JACK MAHAN** VP - Business Affairs
NICK J. NAPOLITANO VP - Manufacturing Administration • **EDDIE SCANNELL** VP - Consumer Marketing
COURTNEY SIMMONS Senior VP - Publicity & Communications • **JIM (SKI) SOKOLOWSKI** VP - Comic Book Specialty Sales & Trade Marketing
NANCY SPEARS VP - Mass, Book, Digital Sales & Trade Marketing • **MICHELE R. WELLS** VP - Content Strategy

CYBORG VOL. 3: SINGULARITY

DC Comics, 2900 West Alameda Ave., Burbank, CA 91505
Printed by LSC Communications, Kendallville, IN, USA. 4/6/18. First Printing.
ISBN: 978-1-4012-7455-9

Library of Congress Cataloging-in-Publication Data is available.

PEFC Certified
Printed on paper from
sustainably managed
forests and controlled
sources
PEFC/29-31-337   www.pefc.org

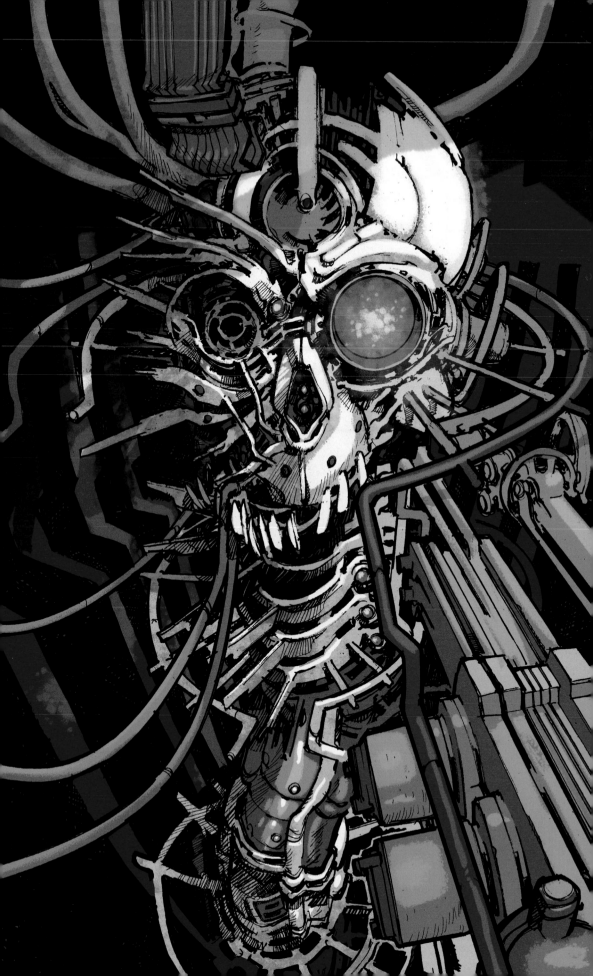

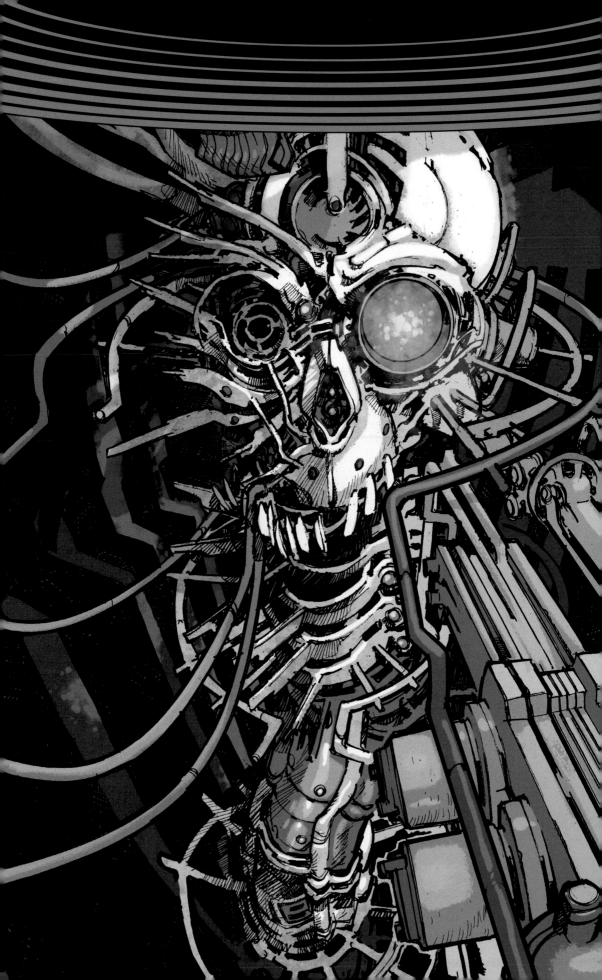

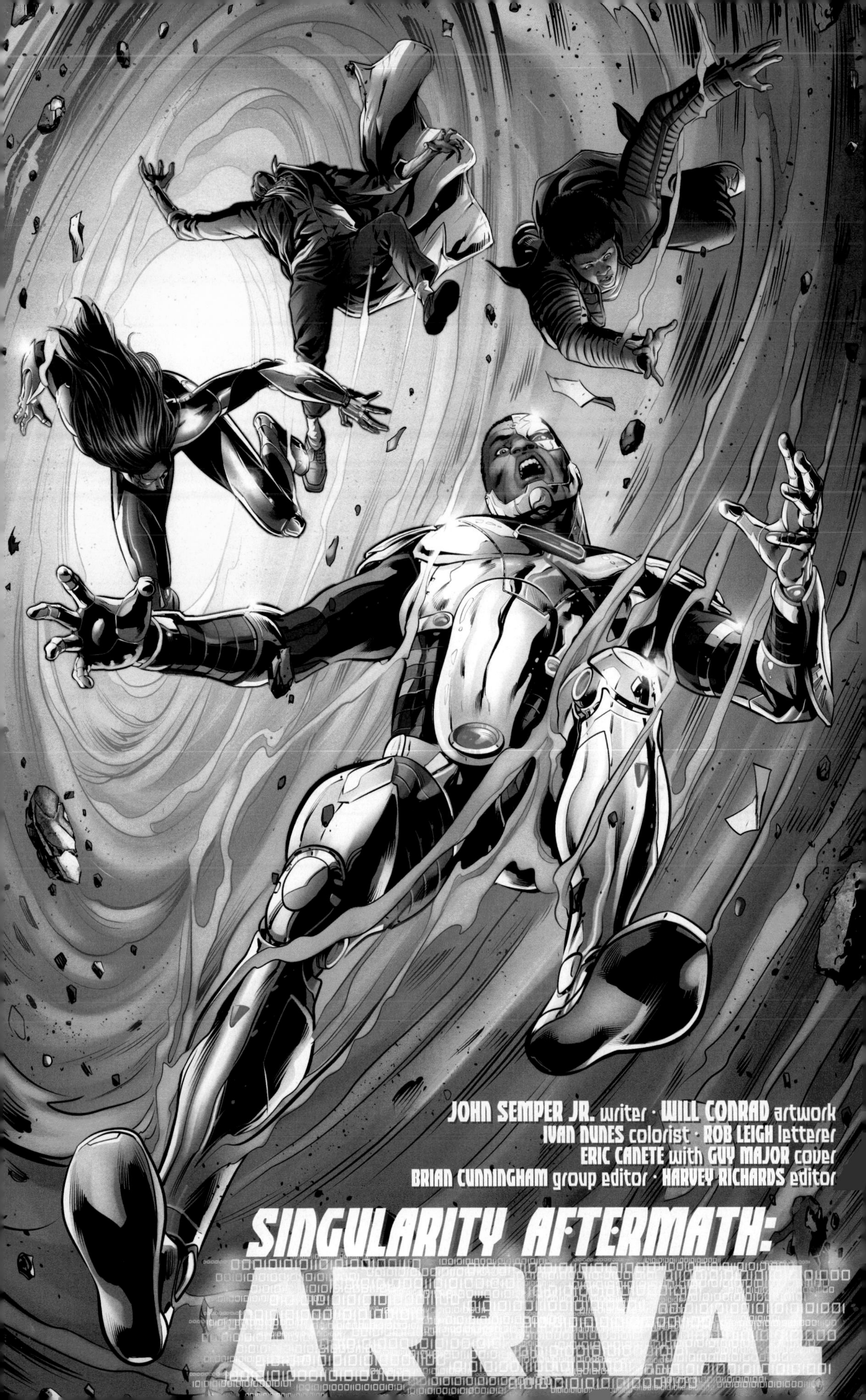
JOHN SEMPER JR. writer · WILL CONRAD artwork
IVAN NUNES colorist · ROB LEIGH letterer
ERIC CANETE with GUY MAJOR cover
BRIAN CUNNINGHAM group editor · HARVEY RICHARDS editor
SINGULARITY AFTERMATH:
ARRIVAL

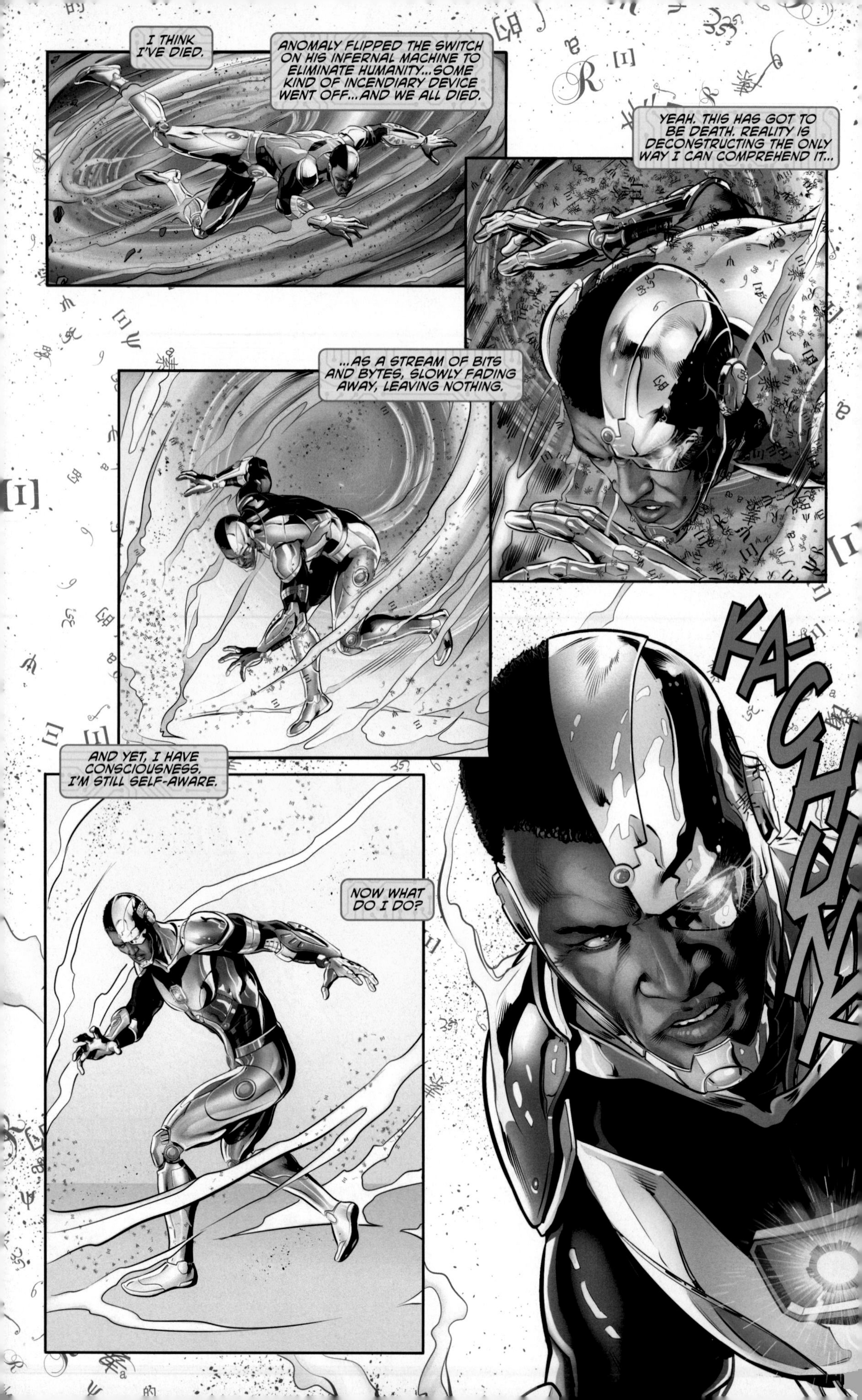
I THINK I'VE DIED.
ANOMALY FLIPPED THE SWITCH ON HIS INFERNAL MACHINE TO ELIMINATE HUMANITY...SOME KIND OF INCENDIARY DEVICE WENT OFF...AND WE ALL DIED.
YEAH. THIS HAS GOT TO BE DEATH. REALITY IS DECONSTRUCTING THE ONLY WAY I CAN COMPREHEND IT...
...AS A STREAM OF BITS AND BYTES, SLOWLY FADING AWAY, LEAVING NOTHING.
AND YET, I HAVE CONSCIOUSNESS. I'M STILL SELF-AWARE.
NOW WHAT DO I DO?
KA-CHUNK

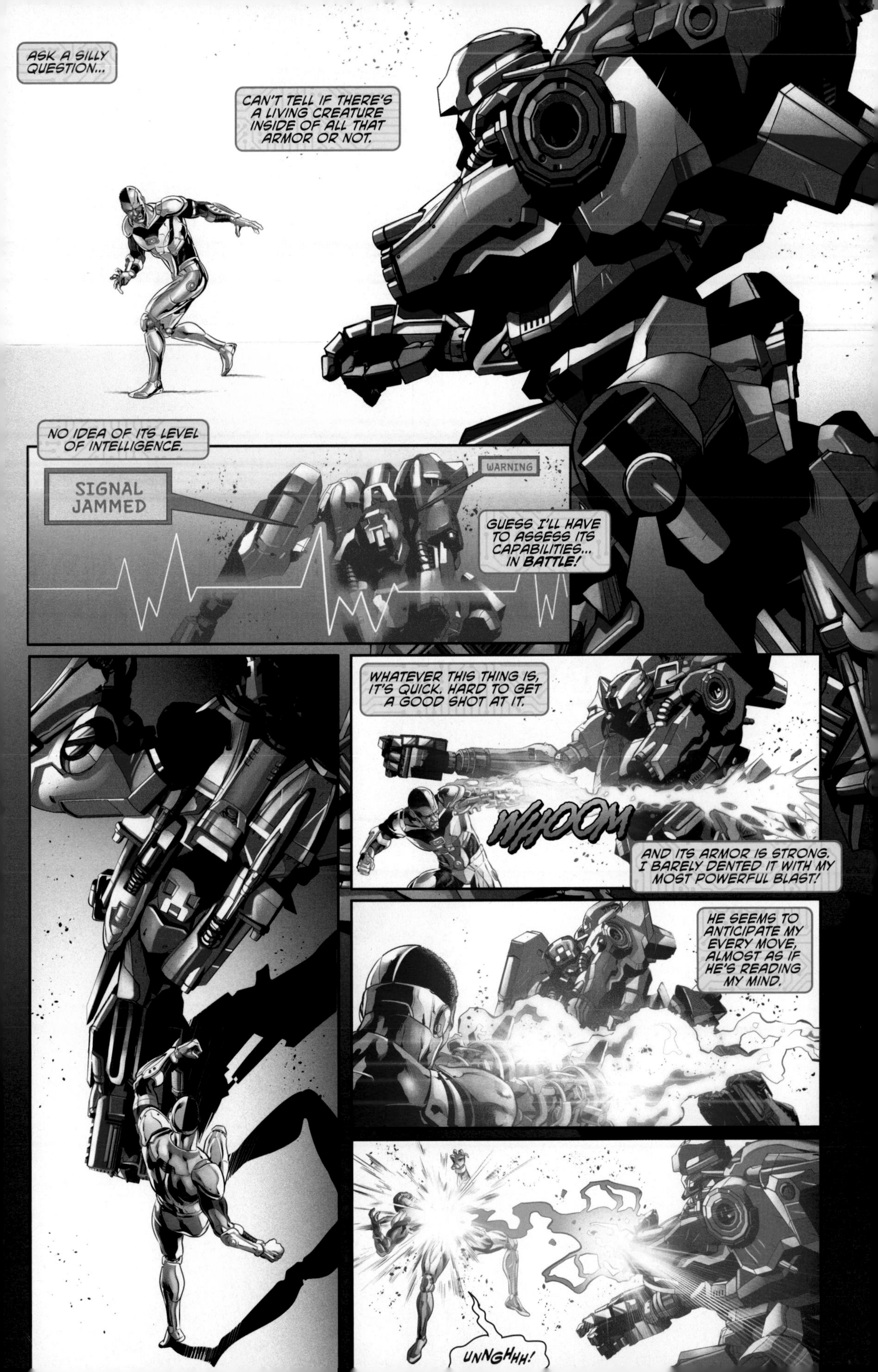
ASK A SILLY QUESTION...
CAN'T TELL IF THERE'S A LIVING CREATURE INSIDE OF ALL THAT ARMOR OR NOT.
NO IDEA OF ITS LEVEL OF INTELLIGENCE.
SIGNAL JAMMED
WARNING
GUESS I'LL HAVE TO ASSESS ITS CAPABILITIES... IN BATTLE!
WHATEVER THIS THING IS, IT'S QUICK. HARD TO GET A GOOD SHOT AT IT.
WHOOM
AND ITS ARMOR IS STRONG. I BARELY DENTED IT WITH MY MOST POWERFUL BLAST!
HE SEEMS TO ANTICIPATE MY EVERY MOVE, ALMOST AS IF HE'S READING MY MIND.
UNNGHHH!

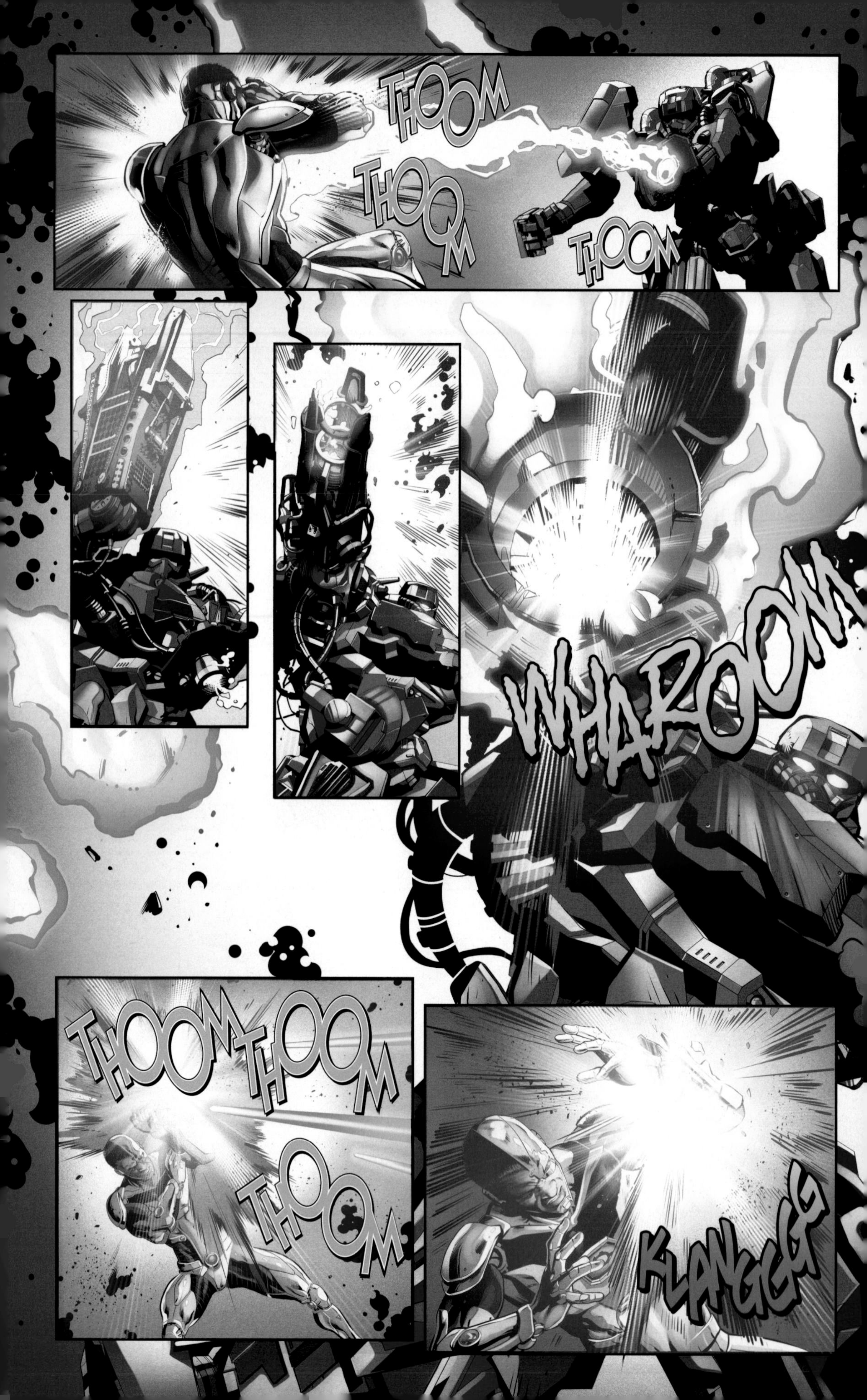
THOOM
THOOM
THOOM
WHAROOM
THOOM
THOOM
THOOM
KLANGGG

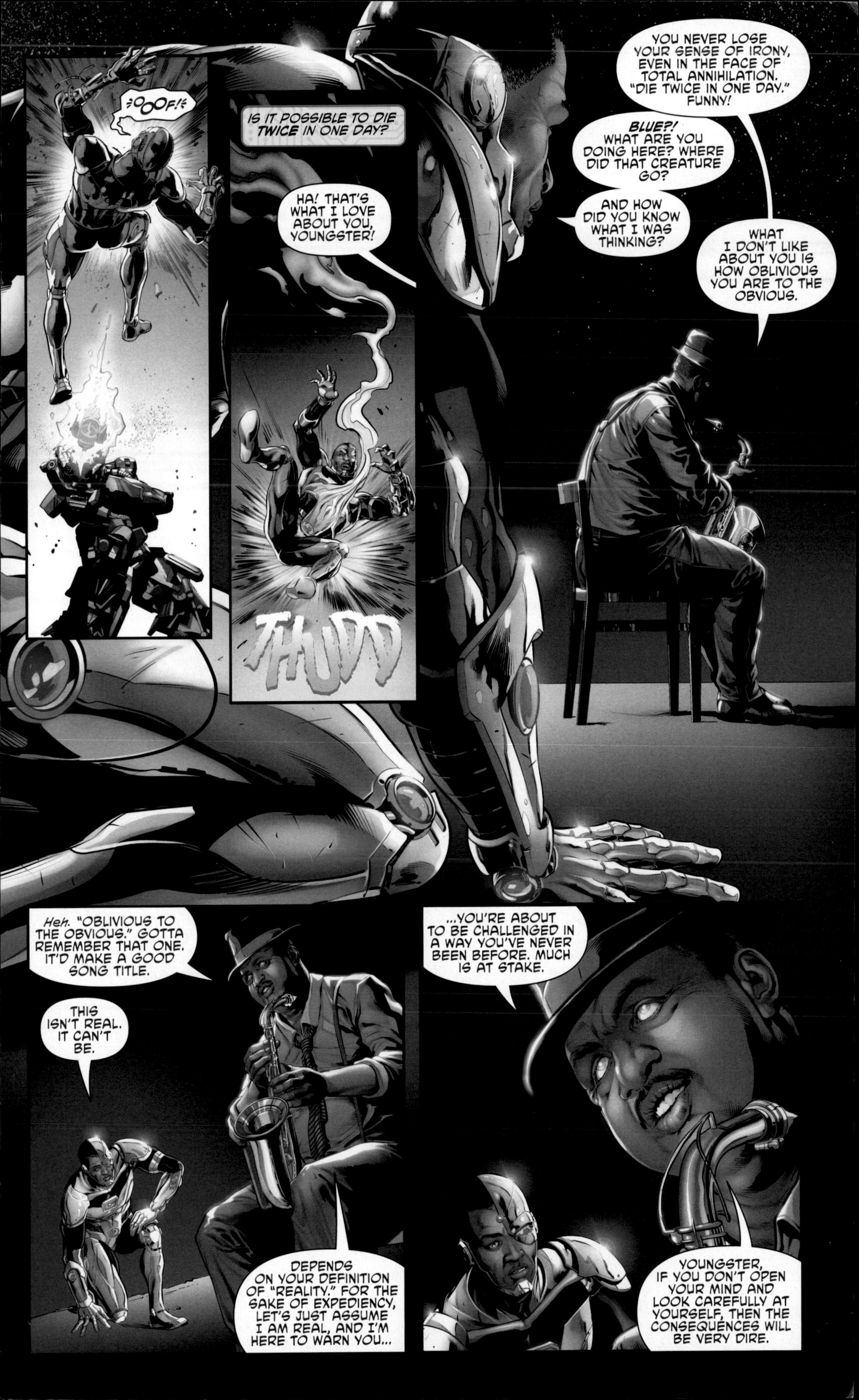

OOOF!
IS IT POSSIBLE TO DIE TWICE IN ONE DAY?
HA! THAT'S WHAT I LOVE ABOUT YOU, YOUNGSTER!
THUDD
YOU NEVER LOSE YOUR SENSE OF IRONY, EVEN IN THE FACE OF TOTAL ANNIHILATION. "DIE TWICE IN ONE DAY." FUNNY!
BLUE?! WHAT ARE YOU DOING HERE? WHERE DID THAT CREATURE GO?
AND HOW DID YOU KNOW WHAT I WAS THINKING?
WHAT I DON'T LIKE ABOUT YOU IS HOW OBLIVIOUS YOU ARE TO THE OBVIOUS.
Heh. "OBLIVIOUS TO THE OBVIOUS." GOTTA REMEMBER THAT ONE. IT'D MAKE A GOOD SONG TITLE.
THIS ISN'T REAL. IT CAN'T BE.
DEPENDS ON YOUR DEFINITION OF "REALITY." FOR THE SAKE OF EXPEDIENCY, LET'S JUST ASSUME I AM REAL, AND I'M HERE TO WARN YOU...
...YOU'RE ABOUT TO BE CHALLENGED IN A WAY YOU'VE NEVER BEEN BEFORE. MUCH IS AT STAKE.
YOUNGSTER, IF YOU DON'T OPEN YOUR MIND AND LOOK CAREFULLY AT YOURSELF, THEN THE CONSEQUENCES WILL BE VERY DIRE.

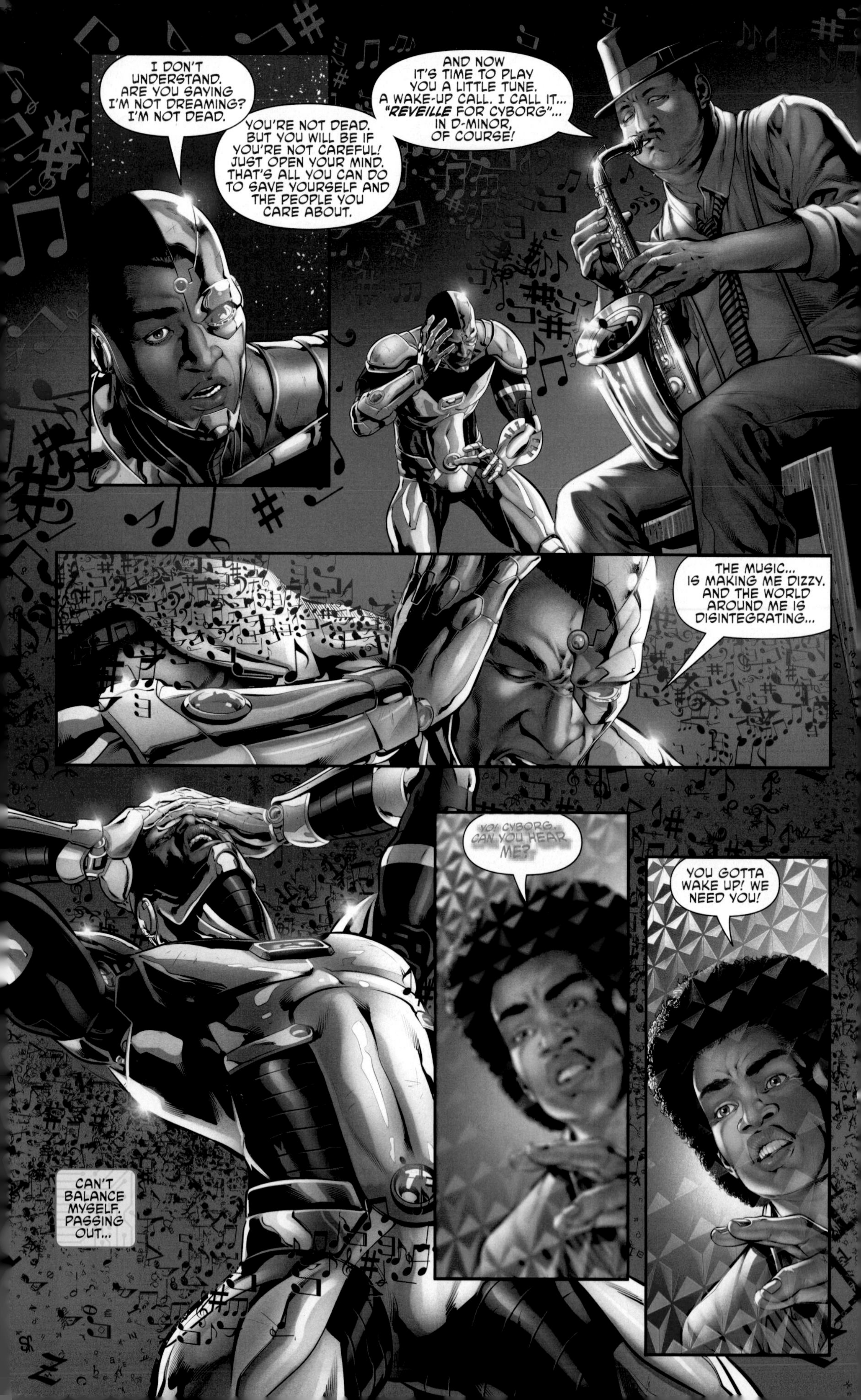
I DON'T UNDERSTAND. ARE YOU SAYING I'M NOT DREAMING? I'M NOT DEAD.
YOU'RE NOT DEAD. BUT YOU WILL BE IF YOU'RE NOT CAREFUL! JUST OPEN YOUR MIND. THAT'S ALL YOU CAN DO TO SAVE YOURSELF AND THE PEOPLE YOU CARE ABOUT.
AND NOW IT'S TIME TO PLAY YOU A LITTLE TUNE. A WAKE-UP CALL. I CALL IT... *"REVEILLE* FOR CYBORG"... IN D-MINOR, OF COURSE!
THE MUSIC... IS MAKING ME DIZZY. AND THE WORLD AROUND ME IS DISINTEGRATING...
CAN'T BALANCE MYSELF. PASSING OUT...
YO! CYBORG. CAN YOU HEAR ME?
YOU GOTTA WAKE UP! WE NEED YOU!

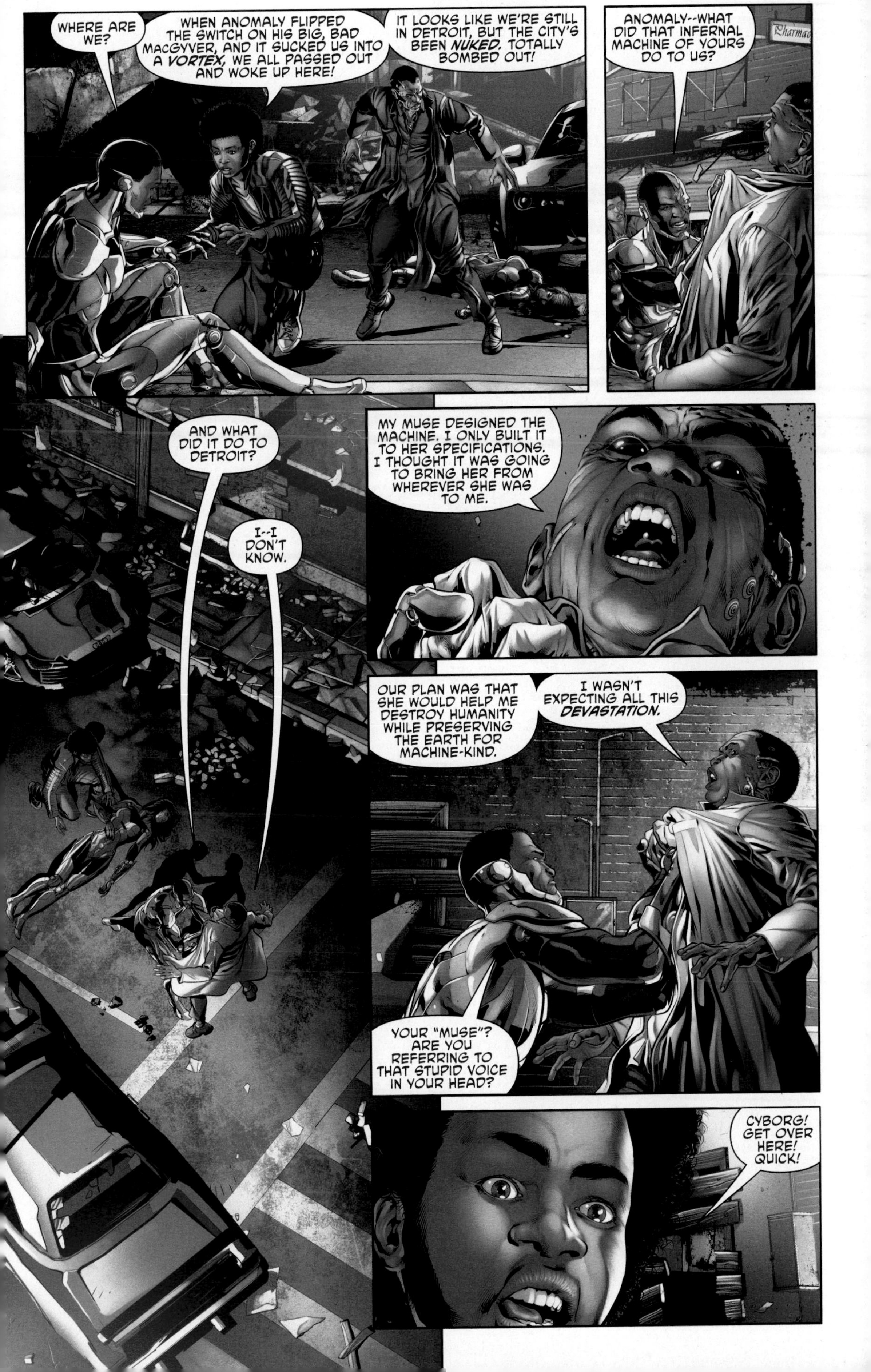
WHERE ARE WE?
WHEN ANOMALY FLIPPED THE SWITCH ON HIS BIG, BAD MacGYVER, AND IT SUCKED US INTO A VORTEX, WE ALL PASSED OUT AND WOKE UP HERE!
IT LOOKS LIKE WE'RE STILL IN DETROIT, BUT THE CITY'S BEEN NUKED. TOTALLY BOMBED OUT!
Pharmac
ANOMALY--WHAT DID THAT INFERNAL MACHINE OF YOURS DO TO US?
AND WHAT DID IT DO TO DETROIT?
I--I DON'T KNOW.
MY MUSE DESIGNED THE MACHINE. I ONLY BUILT IT TO HER SPECIFICATIONS. I THOUGHT IT WAS GOING TO BRING HER FROM WHEREVER SHE WAS TO ME.
OUR PLAN WAS THAT SHE WOULD HELP ME DESTROY HUMANITY WHILE PRESERVING THE EARTH FOR MACHINE-KIND.
I WASN'T EXPECTING ALL THIS DEVASTATION.
YOUR "MUSE"? ARE YOU REFERRING TO THAT STUPID VOICE IN YOUR HEAD?
CYBORG! GET OVER HERE! QUICK!

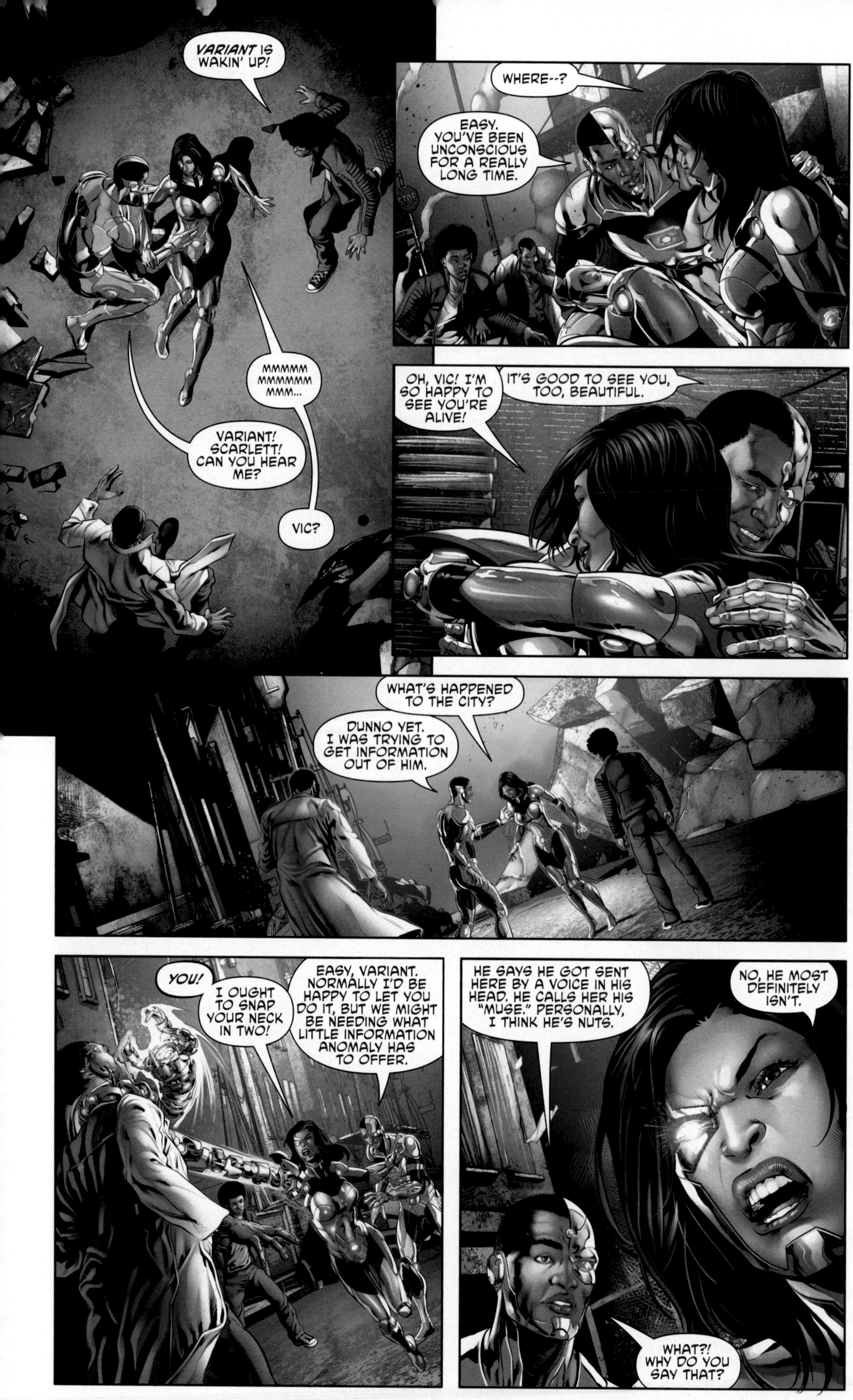
VARIANT IS WAKIN' UP!
MMMMM MMMMMM MMM...
VARIANT! SCARLETT! CAN YOU HEAR ME?
VIC?
WHERE--?
EASY. YOU'VE BEEN UNCONSCIOUS FOR A REALLY LONG TIME.
STOP
OH, VIC! I'M SO HAPPY TO SEE YOU'RE ALIVE!
IT'S GOOD TO SEE YOU, TOO, BEAUTIFUL.
WHAT'S HAPPENED TO THE CITY?
DUNNO YET. I WAS TRYING TO GET INFORMATION OUT OF HIM.
YOU!
I OUGHT TO SNAP YOUR NECK IN TWO!
EASY, VARIANT. NORMALLY I'D BE HAPPY TO LET YOU DO IT, BUT WE MIGHT BE NEEDING WHAT LITTLE INFORMATION ANOMALY HAS TO OFFER.
HE SAYS HE GOT SENT HERE BY A VOICE IN HIS HEAD. HE CALLS HER HIS "MUSE." PERSONALLY, I THINK HE'S NUTS.
NO, HE MOST DEFINITELY ISN'T.
WHAT?! WHY DO YOU SAY THAT?

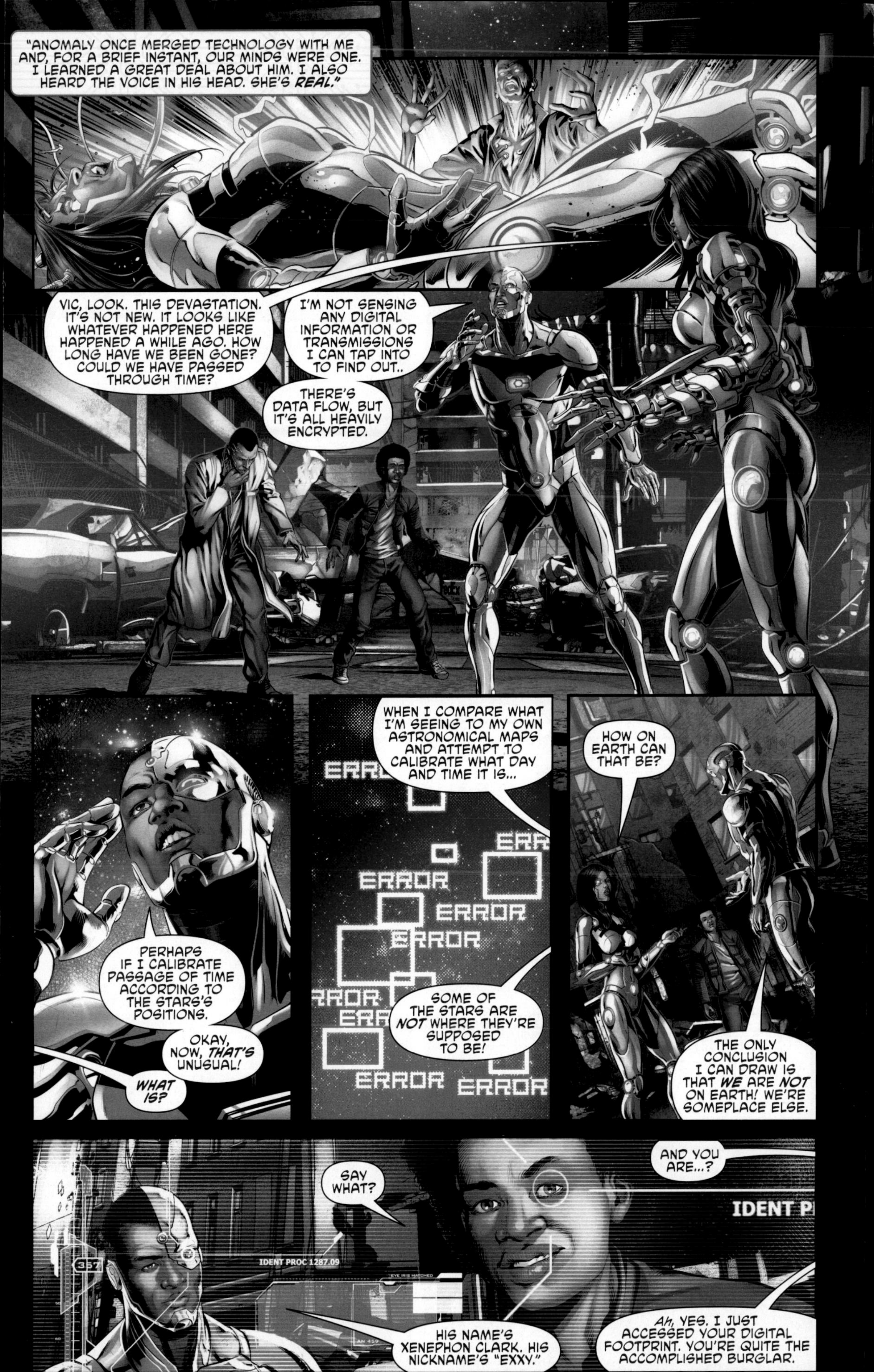
"ANOMALY ONCE MERGED TECHNOLOGY WITH ME AND, FOR A BRIEF INSTANT, OUR MINDS WERE ONE. I LEARNED A GREAT DEAL ABOUT HIM. I ALSO HEARD THE VOICE IN HIS HEAD. SHE'S *REAL*."
VIC, LOOK. THIS DEVASTATION. IT'S NOT NEW. IT LOOKS LIKE WHATEVER HAPPENED HERE HAPPENED A WHILE AGO. HOW LONG HAVE WE BEEN GONE? COULD WE HAVE PASSED THROUGH TIME?
I'M NOT SENSING ANY DIGITAL INFORMATION OR TRANSMISSIONS I CAN TAP INTO TO FIND OUT..
THERE'S DATA FLOW, BUT IT'S ALL HEAVILY ENCRYPTED.
PERHAPS IF I CALIBRATE PASSAGE OF TIME ACCORDING TO THE STARS'S POSITIONS.
OKAY, NOW, *THAT'S* UNUSUAL!
WHAT IS?
WHEN I COMPARE WHAT I'M SEEING TO MY OWN ASTRONOMICAL MAPS AND ATTEMPT TO CALIBRATE WHAT DAY AND TIME IT IS...
ERROR
ERROR
ERROR
ERROR
SOME OF THE STARS ARE *NOT* WHERE THEY'RE SUPPOSED TO BE!
ERROR
ERROR
HOW ON EARTH CAN THAT BE?
THE ONLY CONCLUSION I CAN DRAW IS THAT *WE* ARE *NOT* ON EARTH! WE'RE SOMEPLACE ELSE.
IDENT PROC 1287.09
EYE IRIS MATCHED
SAY WHAT?
AND YOU ARE...?
HIS NAME'S XENEPHON CLARK. HIS NICKNAME'S "EXXY."
AH, YES. I JUST ACCESSED YOUR DIGITAL FOOTPRINT. YOU'RE QUITE THE ACCOMPLISHED BURGLAR.

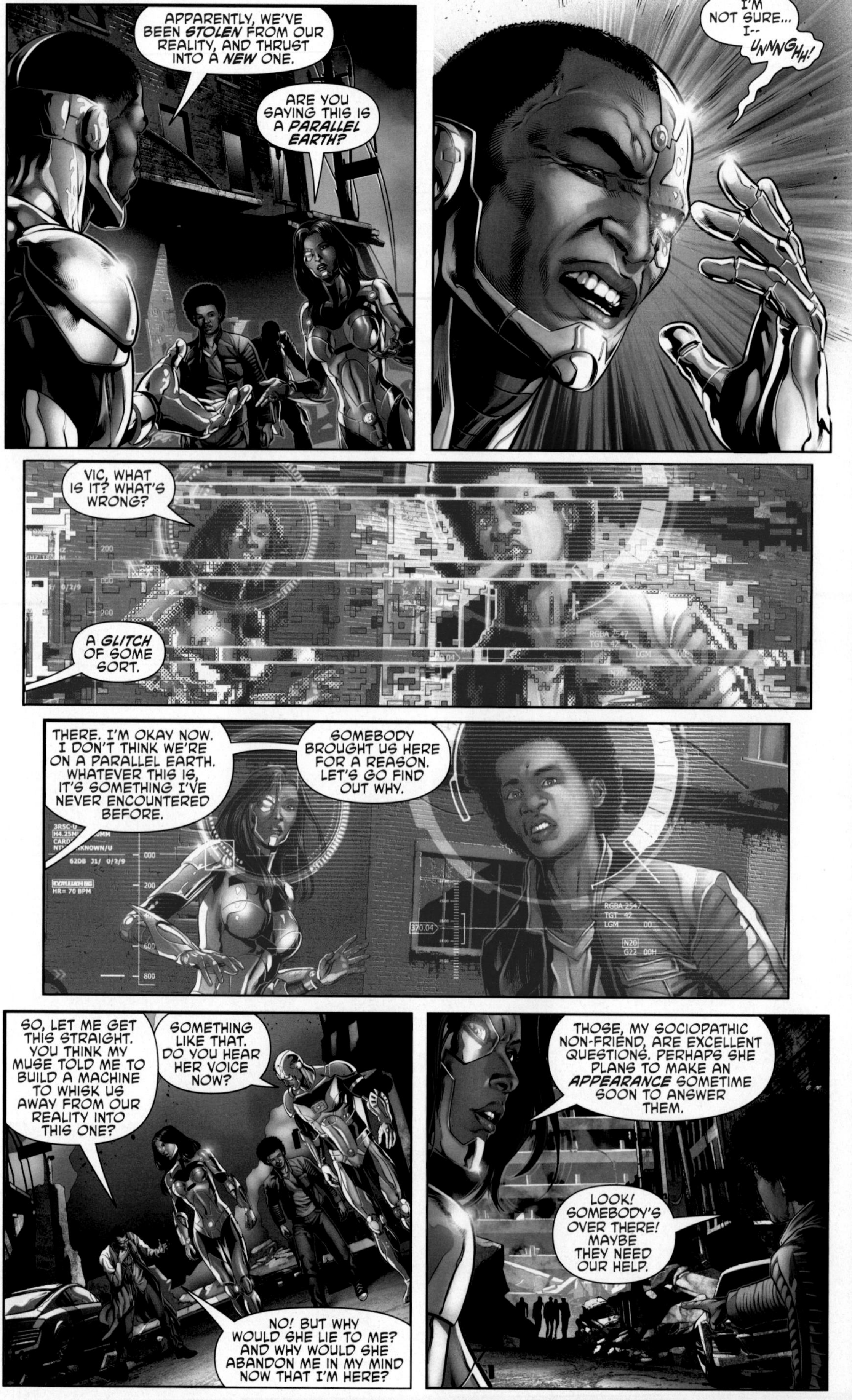
APPARENTLY, WE'VE BEEN STOLEN FROM OUR REALITY, AND THRUST INTO A NEW ONE.
ARE YOU SAYING THIS IS A PARALLEL EARTH?
I'M NOT SURE... I-- UNNNGHH!
VIC, WHAT IS IT? WHAT'S WRONG?
A GLITCH OF SOME SORT.
THERE. I'M OKAY NOW. I DON'T THINK WE'RE ON A PARALLEL EARTH. WHATEVER THIS IS, IT'S SOMETHING I'VE NEVER ENCOUNTERED BEFORE.
SOMEBODY BROUGHT US HERE FOR A REASON. LET'S GO FIND OUT WHY.
SO, LET ME GET THIS STRAIGHT. YOU THINK MY MUSE TOLD ME TO BUILD A MACHINE TO WHISK US AWAY FROM OUR REALITY INTO THIS ONE?
SOMETHING LIKE THAT. DO YOU HEAR HER VOICE NOW?
NO! BUT WHY WOULD SHE LIE TO ME? AND WHY WOULD SHE ABANDON ME IN MY MIND NOW THAT I'M HERE?
THOSE, MY SOCIOPATHIC NON-FRIEND, ARE EXCELLENT QUESTIONS. PERHAPS SHE PLANS TO MAKE AN APPEARANCE SOMETIME SOON TO ANSWER THEM.
LOOK! SOMEBODY'S OVER THERE! MAYBE THEY NEED OUR HELP.

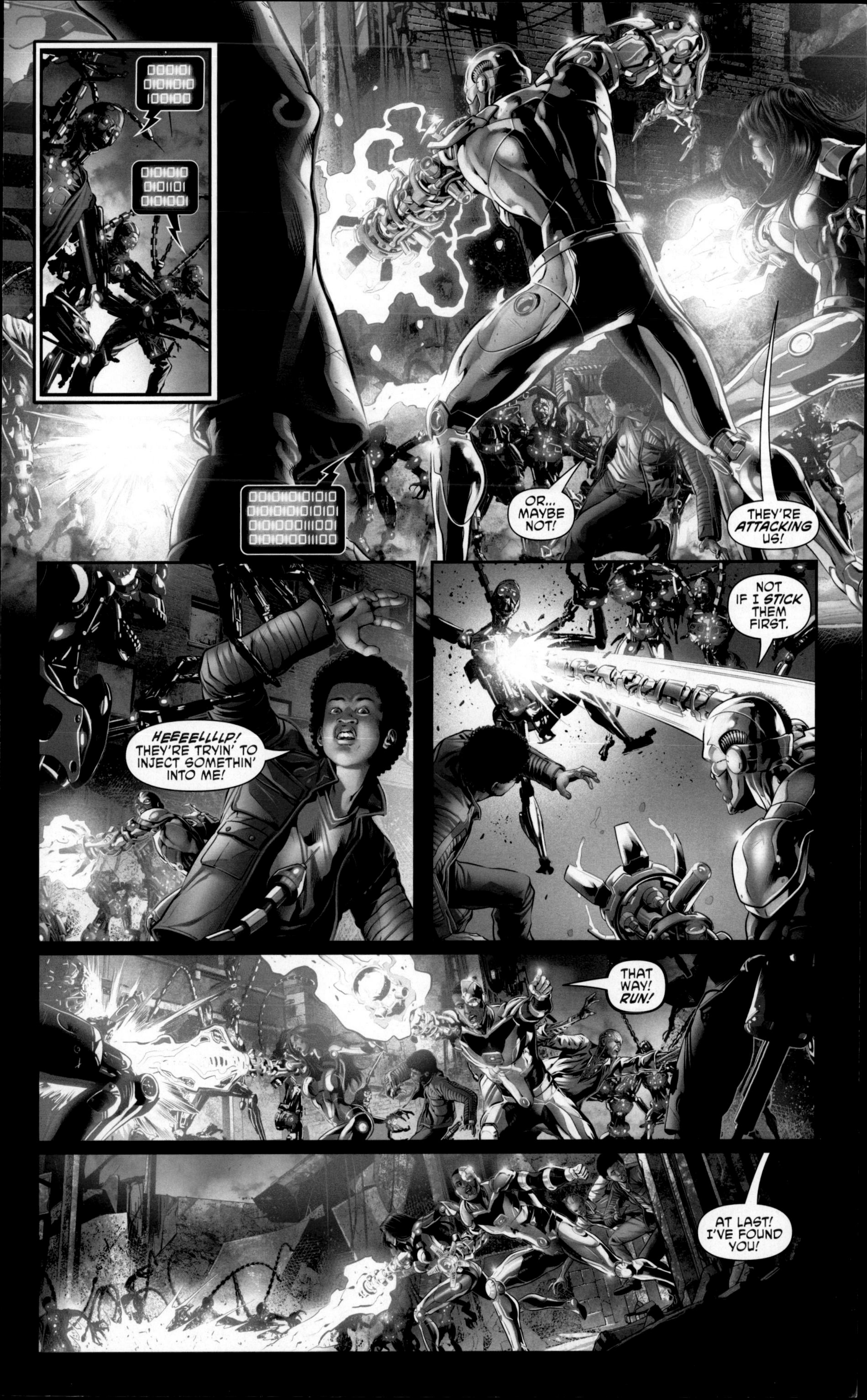
000101
01011010
100100
0101010
0101101
0101001
0010110101010
01010101010101
0101000111001
0101010011100
OR... MAYBE NOT!
THEY'RE *ATTACKING* US!
HEEEELLLLP! THEY'RE TRYIN' TO INJECT SOMETHIN' INTO ME!
NOT IF I *STICK* THEM FIRST.
THAT WAY! *RUN!*
AT LAST! I'VE FOUND YOU!

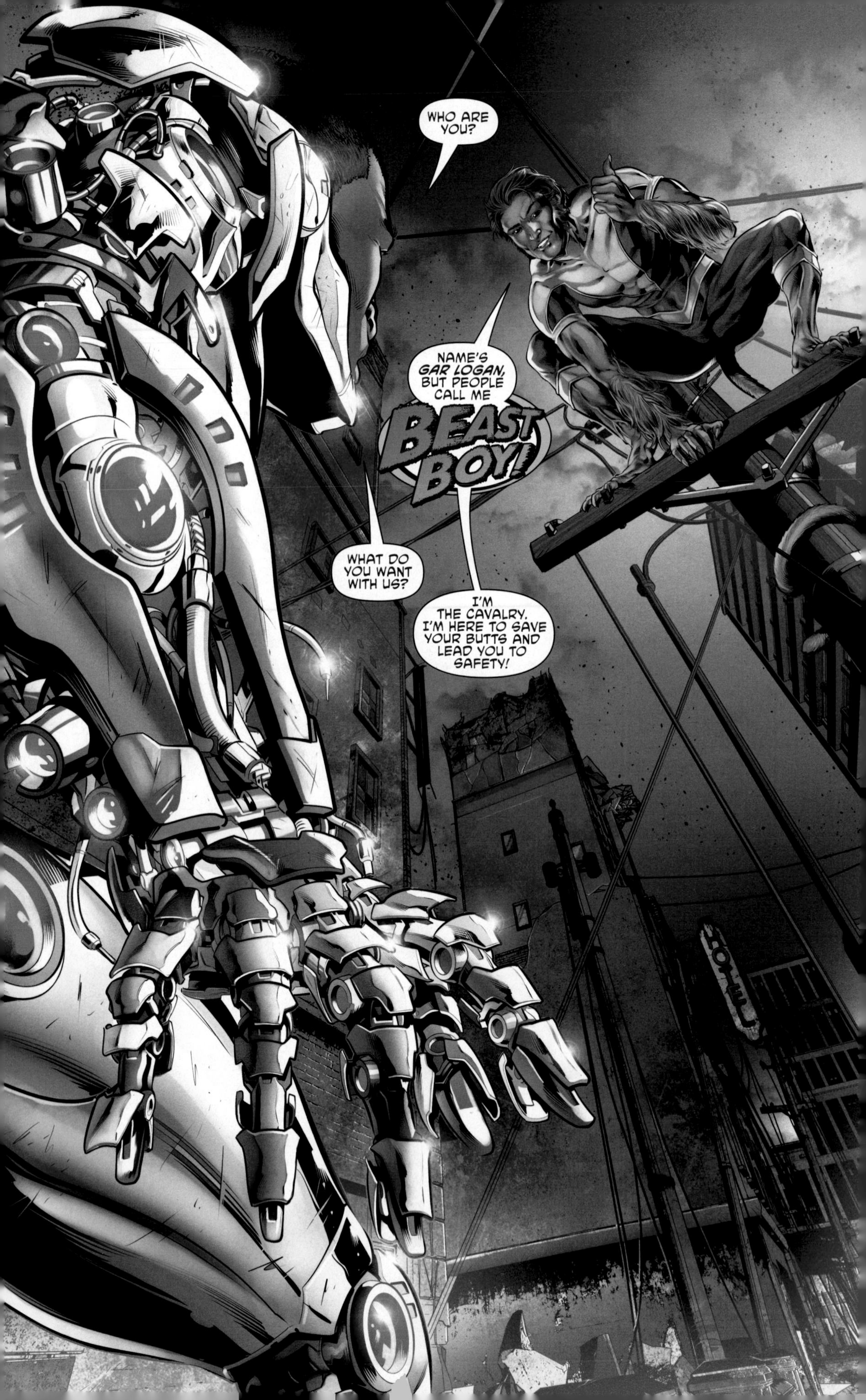
WHO ARE YOU?
NAME'S *GAR LOGAN*, BUT PEOPLE CALL ME
BEAST BOY!
WHAT DO YOU WANT WITH US?
I'M THE CAVALRY. I'M HERE TO SAVE YOUR BUTTS AND LEAD YOU TO SAFETY!
HOTEL

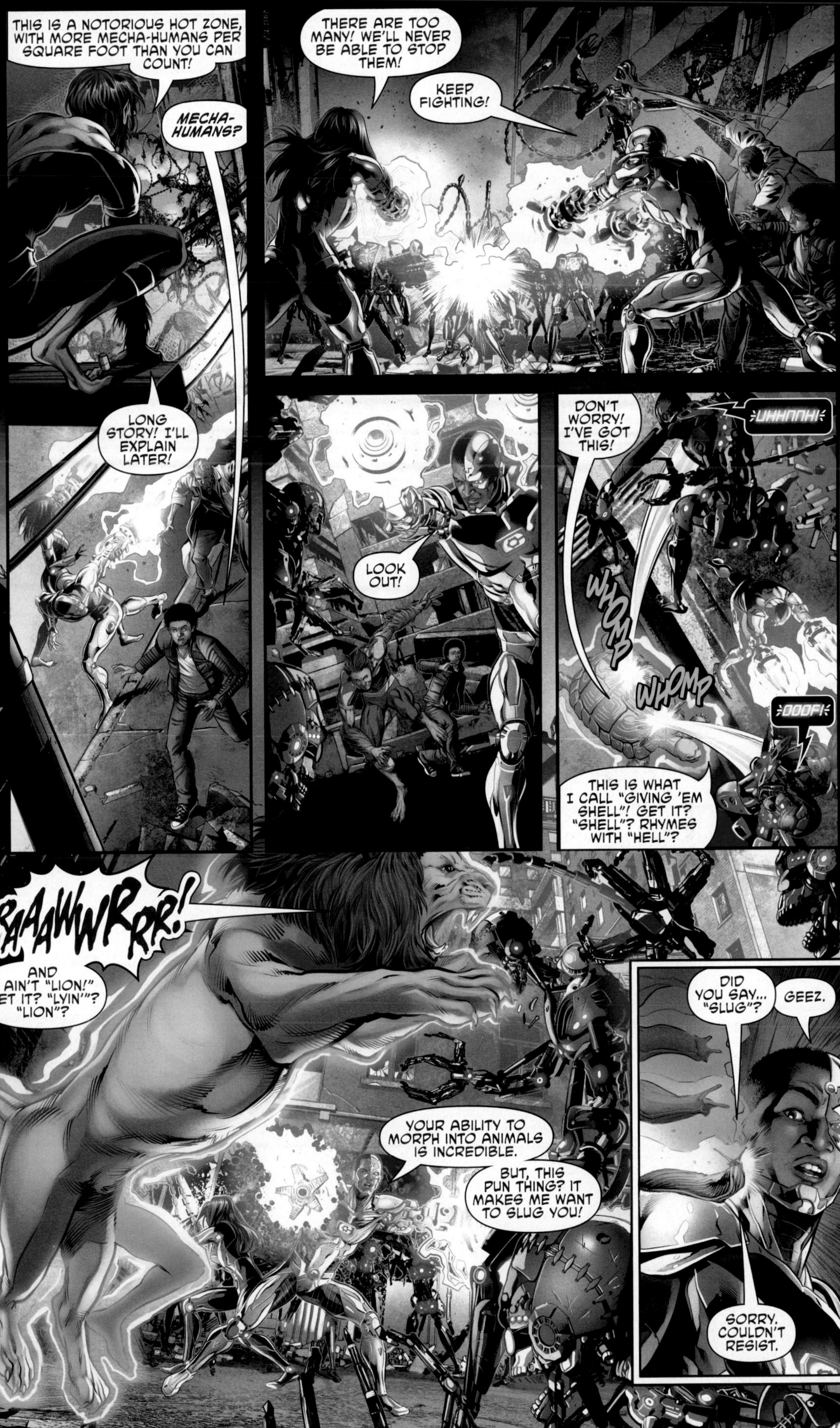

THIS IS A NOTORIOUS HOT ZONE, WITH MORE MECHA-HUMANS PER SQUARE FOOT THAN YOU CAN COUNT!
MECHA-HUMANS?
LONG STORY! I'LL EXPLAIN LATER!
THERE ARE TOO MANY! WE'LL NEVER BE ABLE TO STOP THEM!
KEEP FIGHTING!
LOOK OUT!
DON'T WORRY! I'VE GOT THIS!
UHHNNH!
WHOMP
WHOMP
OOOF!
THIS IS WHAT I CALL "GIVING 'EM SHELL"! GET IT? "SHELL"? RHYMES WITH "HELL"?
RAAAWWRRR!
AND I AIN'T "LION!" GET IT? "LYIN'"? "LION"?
YOUR ABILITY TO MORPH INTO ANIMALS IS INCREDIBLE.
BUT, THIS PUN THING? IT MAKES ME WANT TO SLUG YOU!
DID YOU SAY... "SLUG"?
GEEZ.
SORRY. COULDN'T RESIST.

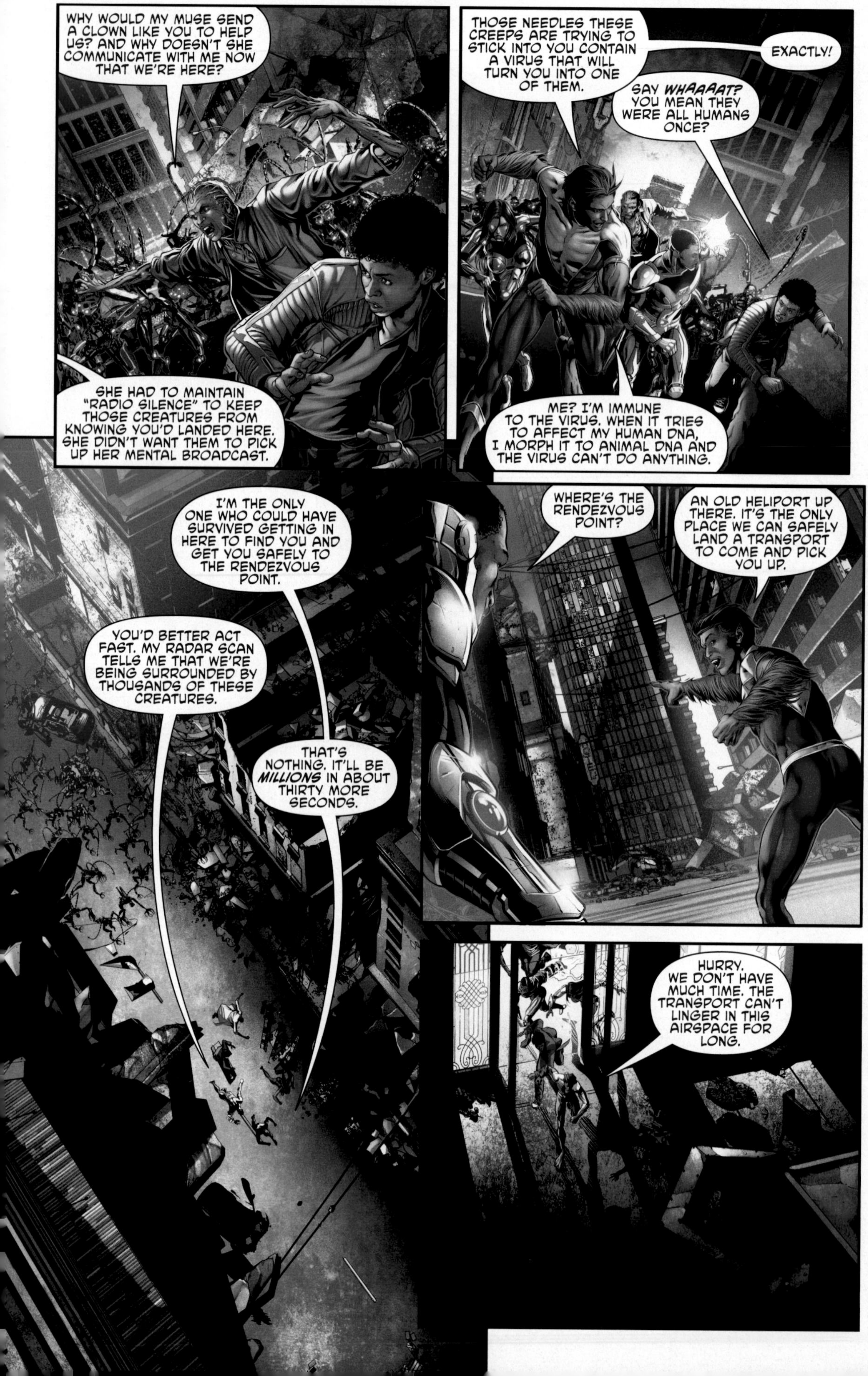
WHY WOULD MY MUSE SEND A CLOWN LIKE YOU TO HELP US? AND WHY DOESN'T SHE COMMUNICATE WITH ME NOW THAT WE'RE HERE?
SHE HAD TO MAINTAIN "RADIO SILENCE" TO KEEP THOSE CREATURES FROM KNOWING YOU'D LANDED HERE. SHE DIDN'T WANT THEM TO PICK UP HER MENTAL BROADCAST.
THOSE NEEDLES THESE CREEPS ARE TRYING TO STICK INTO YOU CONTAIN A VIRUS THAT WILL TURN YOU INTO ONE OF THEM.
EXACTLY!
SAY *WHAAAAT?* YOU MEAN THEY WERE ALL HUMANS ONCE?
ME? I'M IMMUNE TO THE VIRUS. WHEN IT TRIES TO AFFECT MY HUMAN DNA, I MORPH IT TO ANIMAL DNA AND THE VIRUS CAN'T DO ANYTHING.
I'M THE ONLY ONE WHO COULD HAVE SURVIVED GETTING IN HERE TO FIND YOU AND GET YOU SAFELY TO THE RENDEZVOUS POINT.
YOU'D BETTER ACT FAST. MY RADAR SCAN TELLS ME THAT WE'RE BEING SURROUNDED BY THOUSANDS OF THESE CREATURES.
THAT'S NOTHING. IT'LL BE *MILLIONS* IN ABOUT THIRTY MORE SECONDS.
WHERE'S THE RENDEZVOUS POINT?
AN OLD HELIPORT UP THERE. IT'S THE ONLY PLACE WE CAN SAFELY LAND A TRANSPORT TO COME AND PICK YOU UP.
HURRY. WE DON'T HAVE MUCH TIME. THE TRANSPORT CAN'T LINGER IN THIS AIRSPACE FOR LONG.

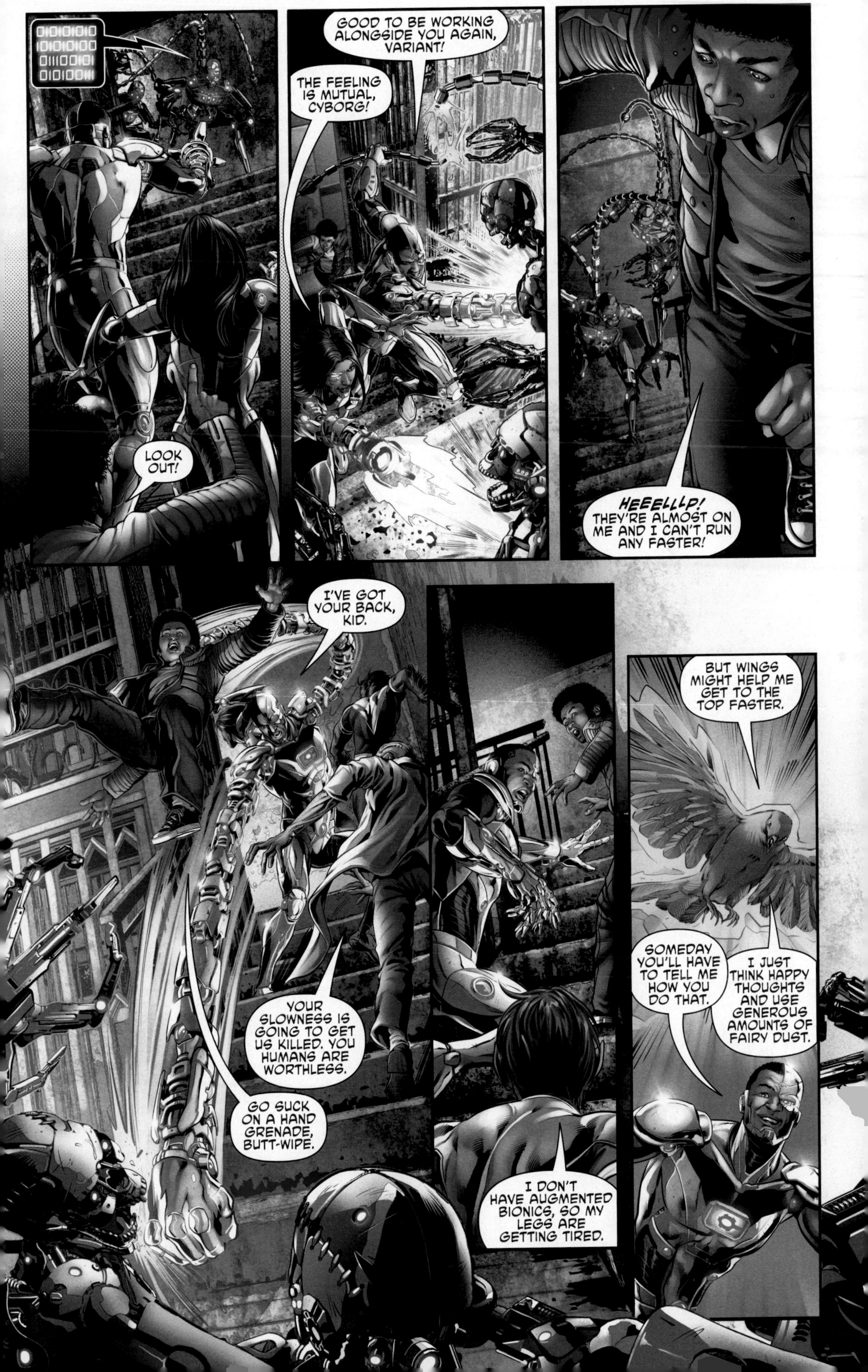
010101010
101010100
011100101
010100111
LOOK OUT!
GOOD TO BE WORKING ALONGSIDE YOU AGAIN, VARIANT!
THE FEELING IS MUTUAL, CYBORG!
HEEELLLP! THEY'RE ALMOST ON ME AND I CAN'T RUN ANY FASTER!
I'VE GOT YOUR BACK, KID.
YOUR SLOWNESS IS GOING TO GET US KILLED. YOU HUMANS ARE WORTHLESS.
GO SUCK ON A HAND GRENADE, BUTT-WIPE.
I DON'T HAVE AUGMENTED BIONICS, SO MY LEGS ARE GETTING TIRED.
BUT WINGS MIGHT HELP ME GET TO THE TOP FASTER.
SOMEDAY YOU'LL HAVE TO TELL ME HOW YOU DO THAT.
I JUST THINK HAPPY THOUGHTS AND USE GENEROUS AMOUNTS OF FAIRY DUST.

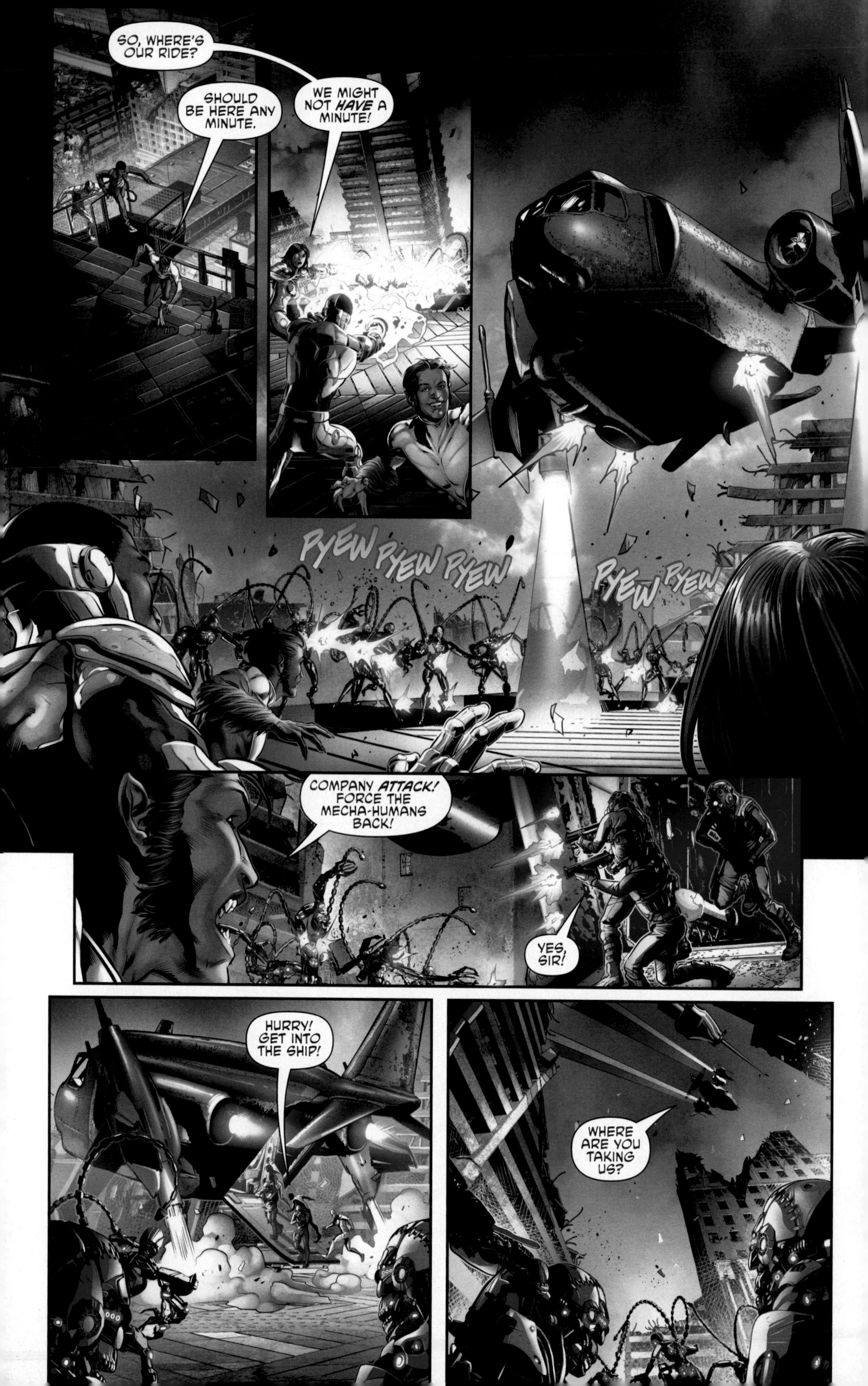
SO, WHERE'S OUR RIDE?
SHOULD BE HERE ANY MINUTE.
WE MIGHT NOT HAVE A MINUTE!
PYEW PYEW PYEW
PYEW PYEW
COMPANY ATTACK! FORCE THE MECHA-HUMANS BACK!
YES, SIR!
HURRY! GET INTO THE SHIP!
WHERE ARE YOU TAKING US?

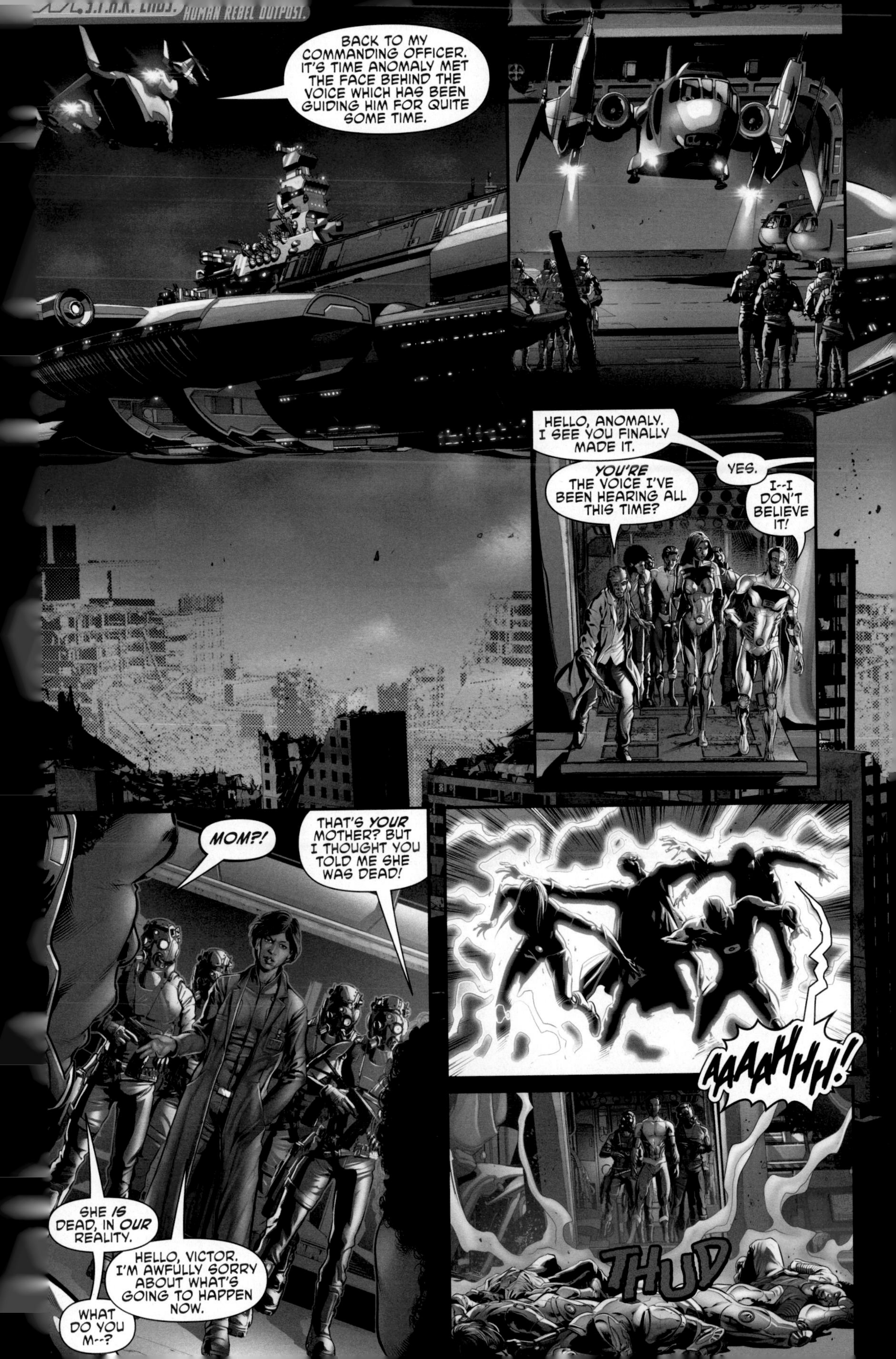

HUMAN REBEL OUTPOST.
BACK TO MY COMMANDING OFFICER. IT'S TIME ANOMALY MET THE FACE BEHIND THE VOICE WHICH HAS BEEN GUIDING HIM FOR QUITE SOME TIME.
HELLO, ANOMALY. I SEE YOU FINALLY MADE IT.
YOU'RE THE VOICE I'VE BEEN HEARING ALL THIS TIME?
YES.
I--I DON'T BELIEVE IT!
MOM?!
THAT'S *YOUR* MOTHER? BUT I THOUGHT YOU TOLD ME SHE WAS DEAD!
SHE *IS* DEAD, IN *OUR* REALITY.
HELLO, VICTOR. I'M AWFULLY SORRY ABOUT WHAT'S GOING TO HAPPEN NOW.
WHAT DO YOU M--?
AAAAHHH!
THUD

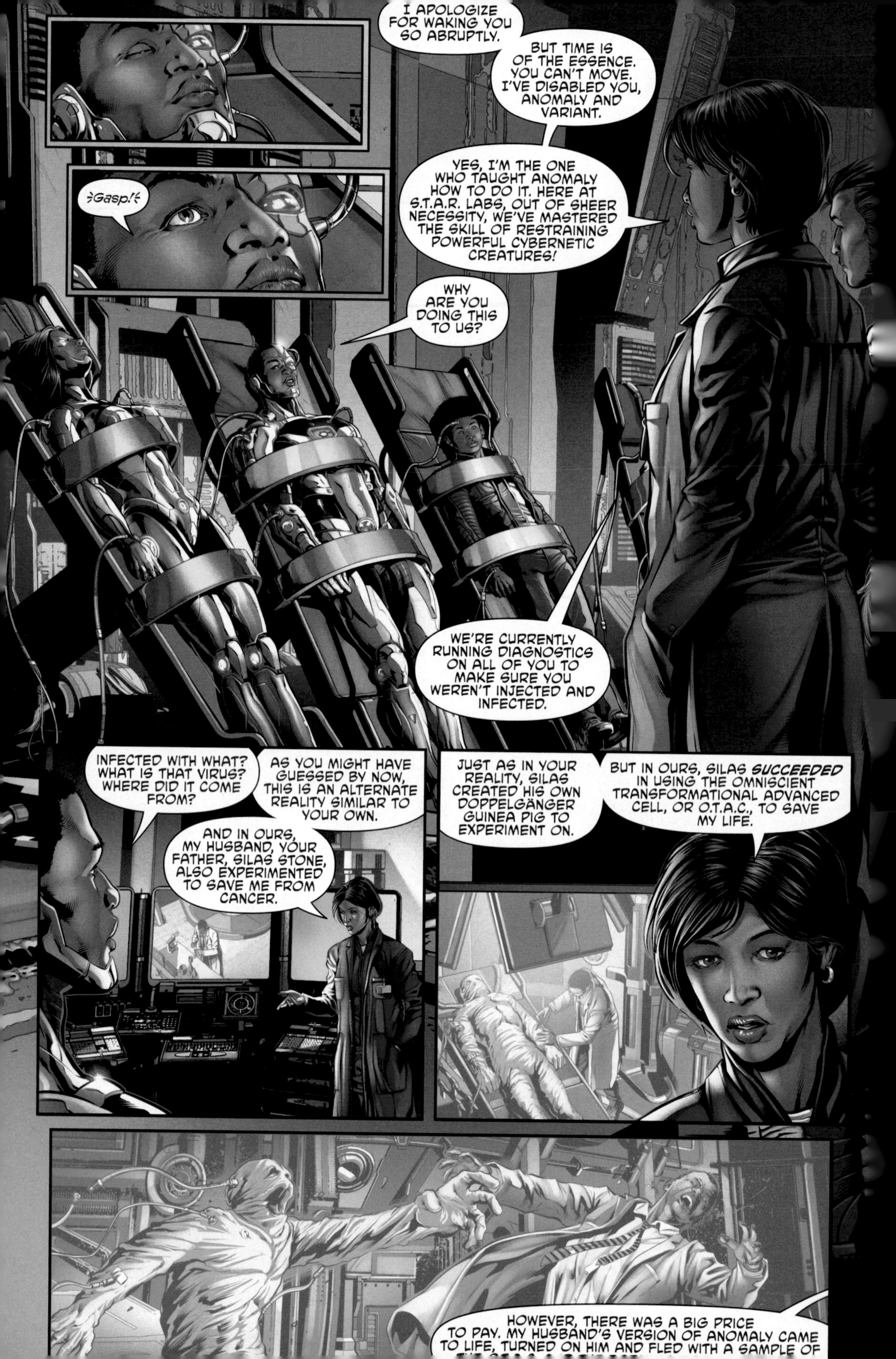

I APOLOGIZE FOR WAKING YOU SO ABRUPTLY.
BUT TIME IS OF THE ESSENCE. YOU CAN'T MOVE. I'VE DISABLED YOU, ANOMALY AND VARIANT.
Gasp!
YES, I'M THE ONE WHO TAUGHT ANOMALY HOW TO DO IT. HERE AT S.T.A.R. LABS, OUT OF SHEER NECESSITY, WE'VE MASTERED THE SKILL OF RESTRAINING POWERFUL CYBERNETIC CREATURES!
WHY ARE YOU DOING THIS TO US?
WE'RE CURRENTLY RUNNING DIAGNOSTICS ON ALL OF YOU TO MAKE SURE YOU WEREN'T INJECTED AND INFECTED.
INFECTED WITH WHAT? WHAT IS THAT VIRUS? WHERE DID IT COME FROM?
AS YOU MIGHT HAVE GUESSED BY NOW, THIS IS AN ALTERNATE REALITY SIMILAR TO YOUR OWN.
AND IN OURS, MY HUSBAND, YOUR FATHER, SILAS STONE, ALSO EXPERIMENTED TO SAVE ME FROM CANCER.
JUST AS IN YOUR REALITY, SILAS CREATED HIS OWN DOPPELGÄNGER GUINEA PIG TO EXPERIMENT ON.
BUT IN OURS, SILAS *SUCCEEDED* IN USING THE OMNISCIENT TRANSFORMATIONAL ADVANCED CELL, OR O.T.A.C., TO SAVE MY LIFE.
HOWEVER, THERE WAS A BIG PRICE TO PAY. MY HUSBAND'S VERSION OF ANOMALY CAME TO LIFE, TURNED ON HIM AND FLED WITH A SAMPLE OF

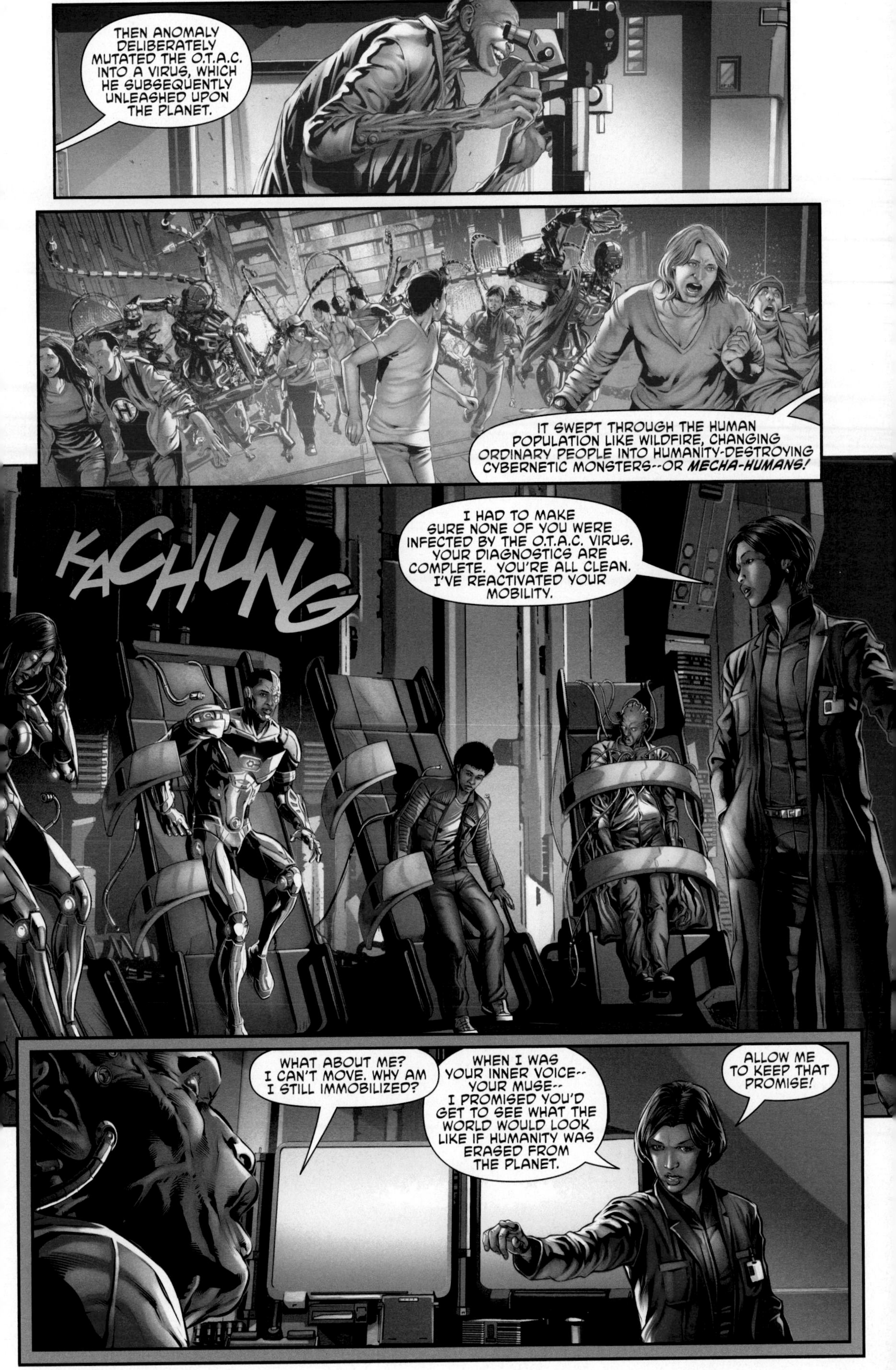

THEN ANOMALY DELIBERATELY MUTATED THE O.T.A.C. INTO A VIRUS, WHICH HE SUBSEQUENTLY UNLEASHED UPON THE PLANET.
IT SWEPT THROUGH THE HUMAN POPULATION LIKE WILDFIRE, CHANGING ORDINARY PEOPLE INTO HUMANITY-DESTROYING CYBERNETIC MONSTERS--OR *MECHA-HUMANS!*
KACHUNG
I HAD TO MAKE SURE NONE OF YOU WERE INFECTED BY THE O.T.A.C. VIRUS. YOUR DIAGNOSTICS ARE COMPLETE. YOU'RE ALL CLEAN. I'VE REACTIVATED YOUR MOBILITY.
WHAT ABOUT ME? I CAN'T MOVE. WHY AM I STILL IMMOBILIZED?
WHEN I WAS YOUR INNER VOICE-- YOUR MUSE-- I PROMISED YOU'D GET TO SEE WHAT THE WORLD WOULD LOOK LIKE IF HUMANITY WAS ERASED FROM THE PLANET.
ALLOW ME TO KEEP THAT PROMISE!

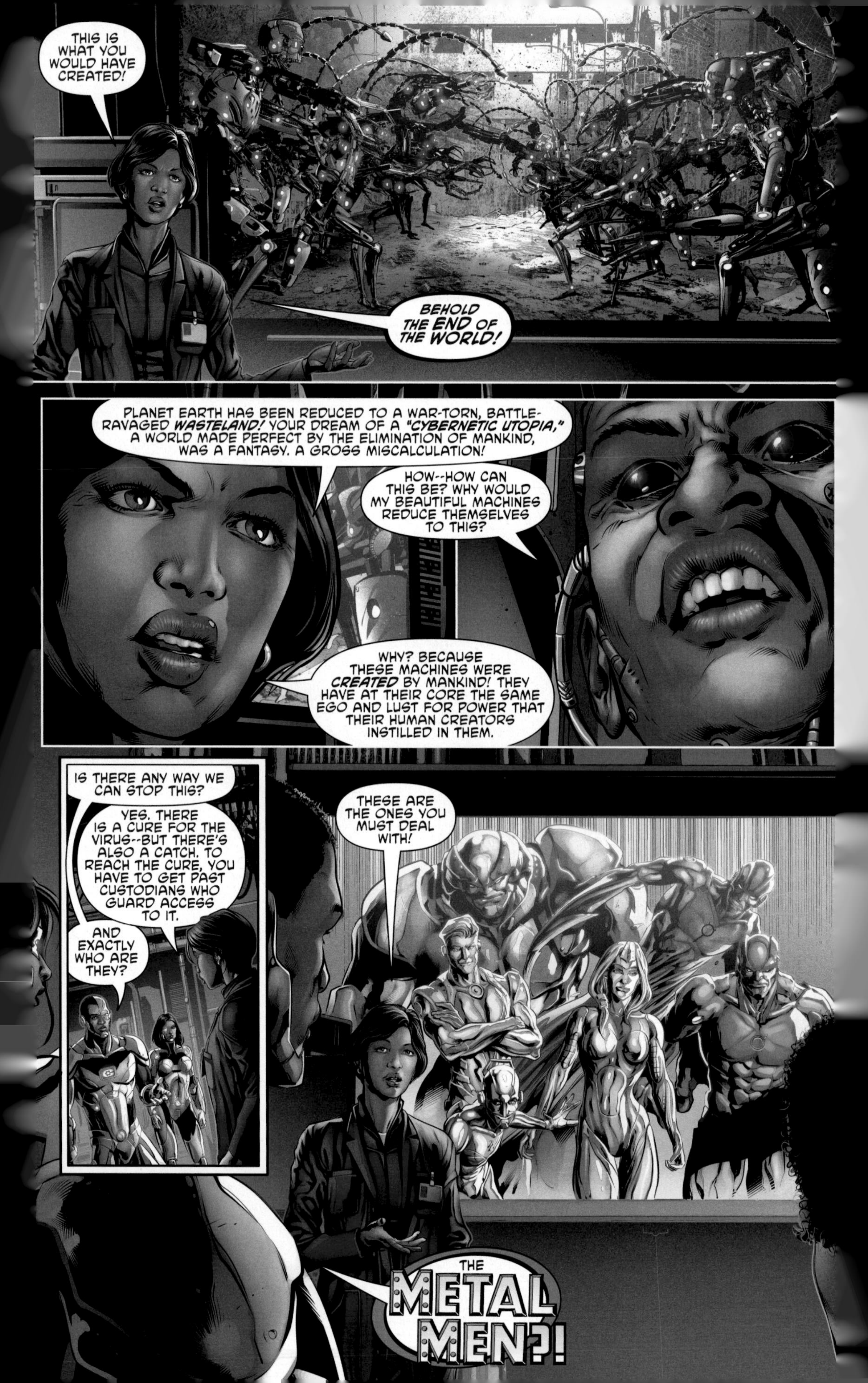

THIS IS WHAT YOU WOULD HAVE CREATED!
BEHOLD THE END OF THE WORLD!
PLANET EARTH HAS BEEN REDUCED TO A WAR-TORN, BATTLE-RAVAGED WASTELAND! YOUR DREAM OF A "CYBERNETIC UTOPIA," A WORLD MADE PERFECT BY THE ELIMINATION OF MANKIND, WAS A FANTASY. A GROSS MISCALCULATION!
HOW--HOW CAN THIS BE? WHY WOULD MY BEAUTIFUL MACHINES REDUCE THEMSELVES TO THIS?
WHY? BECAUSE THESE MACHINES WERE CREATED BY MANKIND! THEY HAVE AT THEIR CORE THE SAME EGO AND LUST FOR POWER THAT THEIR HUMAN CREATORS INSTILLED IN THEM.
IS THERE ANY WAY WE CAN STOP THIS?
YES. THERE IS A CURE FOR THE VIRUS--BUT THERE'S ALSO A CATCH. TO REACH THE CURE, YOU HAVE TO GET PAST CUSTODIANS WHO GUARD ACCESS TO IT.
AND EXACTLY WHO ARE THEY?
THESE ARE THE ONES YOU MUST DEAL WITH!
THE METAL MEN?!

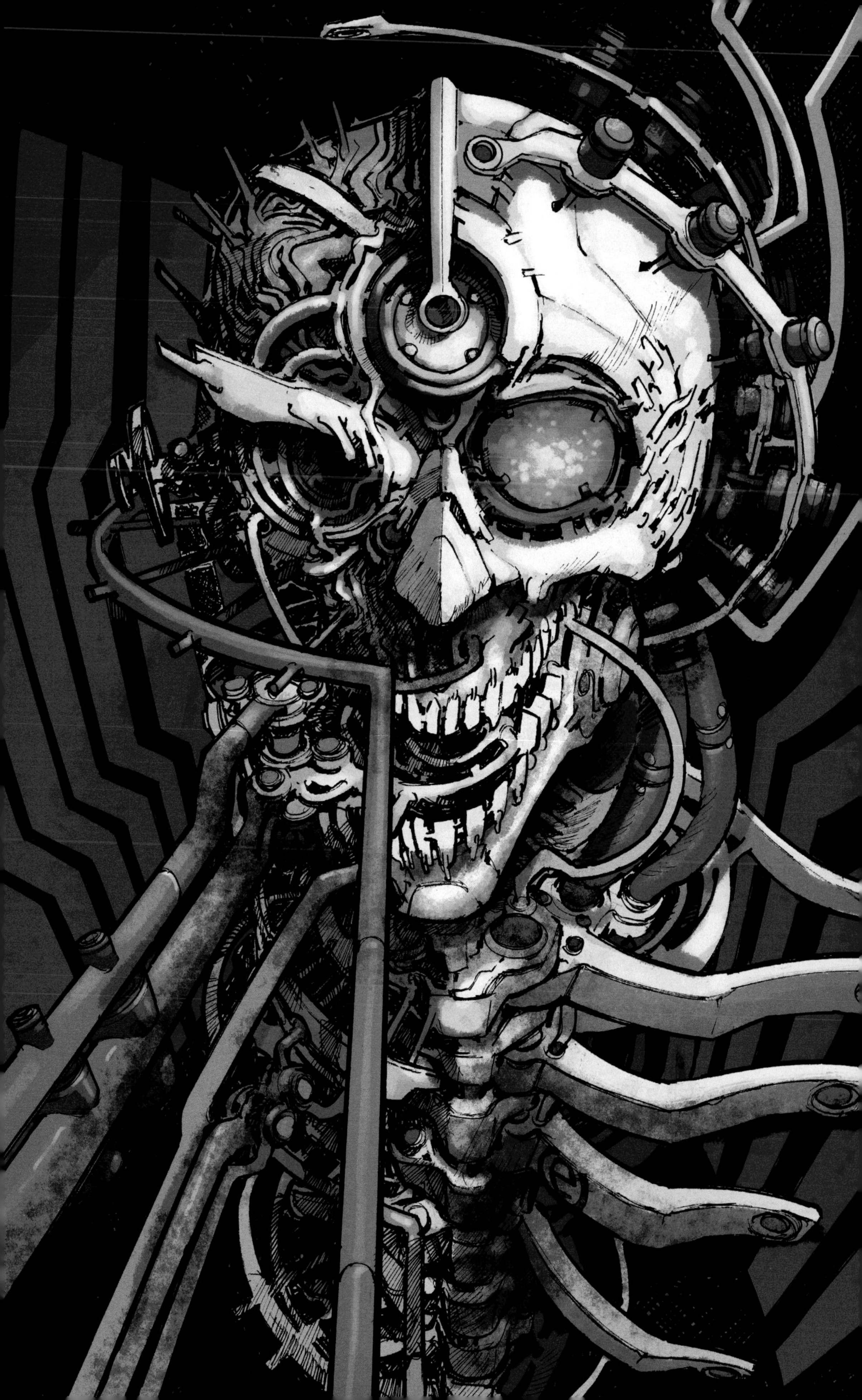

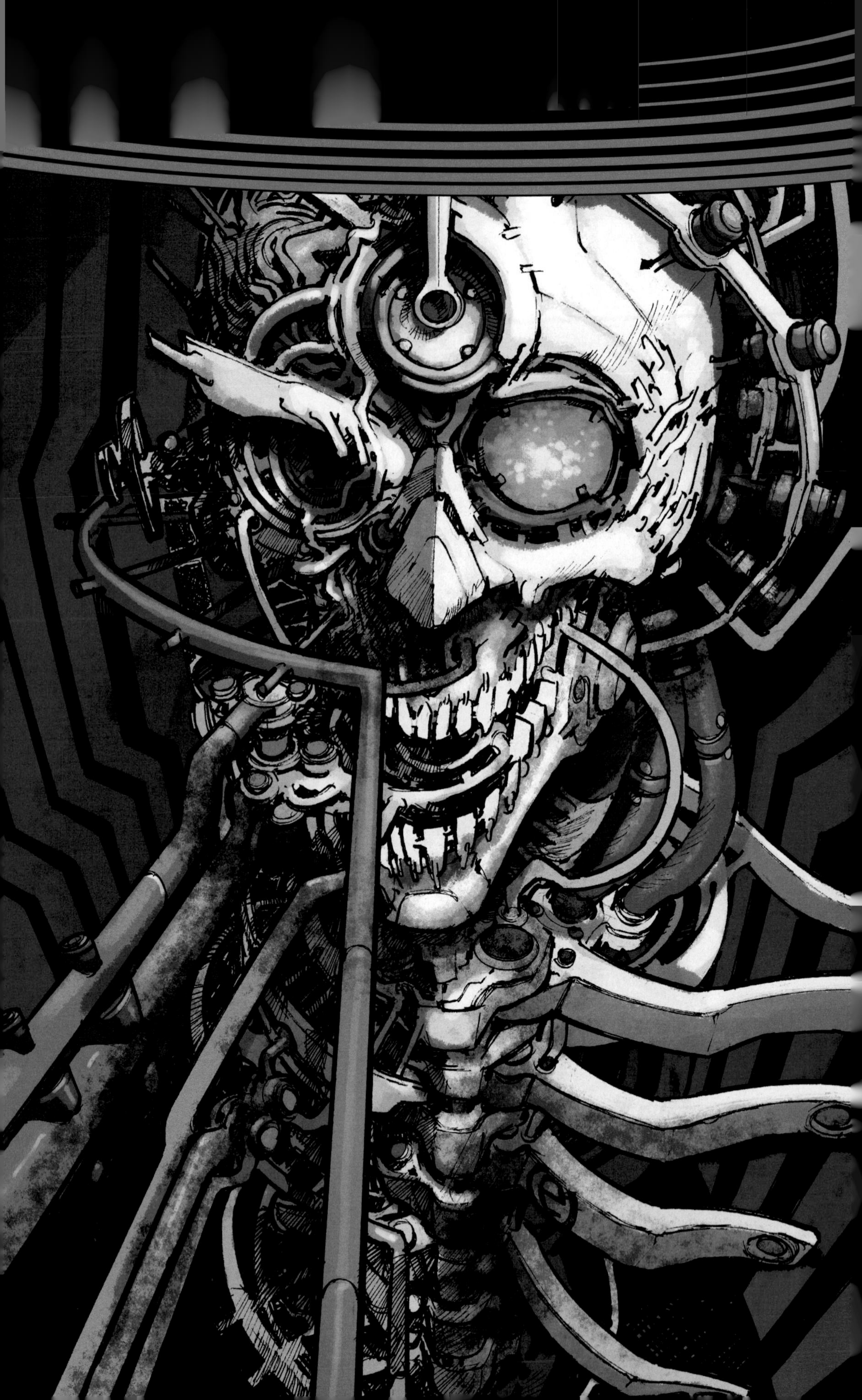

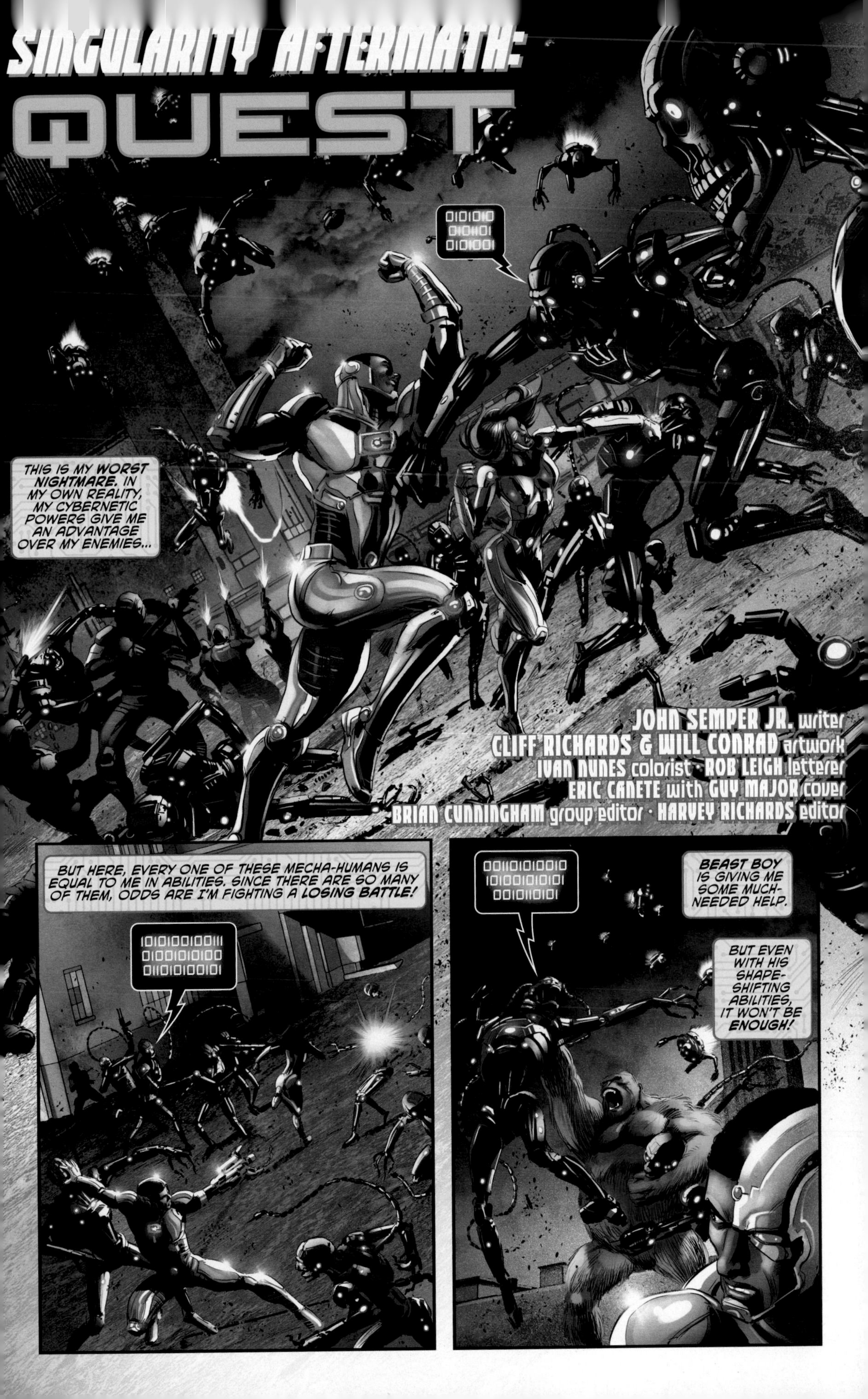
SINGULARITY AFTERMATH:
QUEST
01010110
01011101
01010011
THIS IS MY WORST NIGHTMARE. IN MY OWN REALITY, MY CYBERNETIC POWERS GIVE ME AN ADVANTAGE OVER MY ENEMIES...
JOHN SEMPER JR. writer
CLIFF RICHARDS & WILL CONRAD artwork
IVAN NUNES colorist · ROB LEIGH letterer
ERIC CANETE with GUY MAJOR cover
BRIAN CUNNINGHAM group editor · HARVEY RICHARDS editor
BUT HERE, EVERY ONE OF THESE MECHA-HUMANS IS EQUAL TO ME IN ABILITIES. SINCE THERE ARE SO MANY OF THEM, ODDS ARE I'M FIGHTING A LOSING BATTLE!
101010010011
010010101000
011010100101
BEAST BOY IS GIVING ME SOME MUCH-NEEDED HELP.
BUT EVEN WITH HIS SHAPE-SHIFTING ABILITIES, IT WON'T BE ENOUGH!

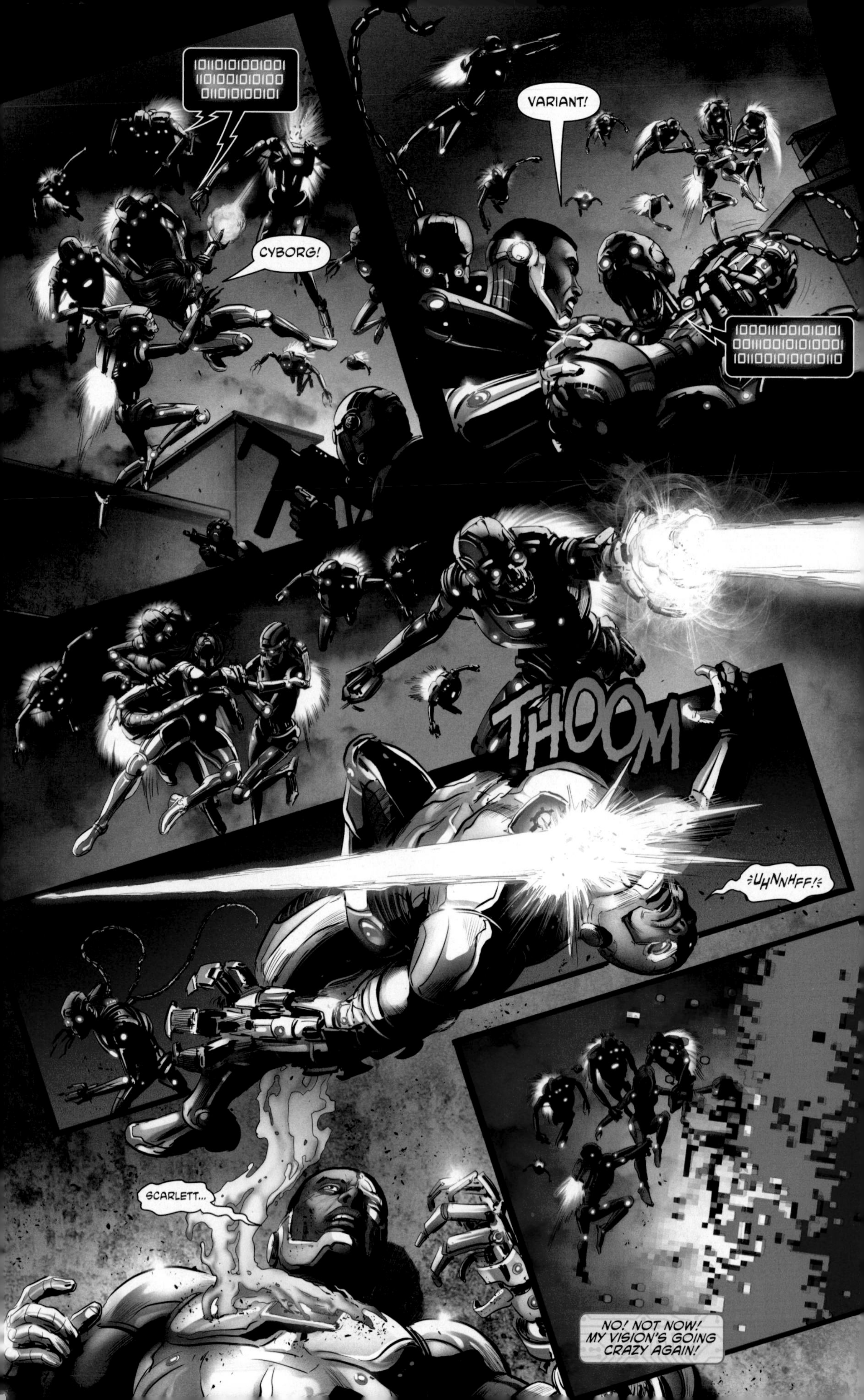
10110101001001
1101001010100
011010100101
CYBORG!
VARIANT!
1000111001010101
0011100101010001
10110010101010110
THOOM
UHNNHFF!
SCARLETT...
NO! NOT NOW! MY VISION'S GOING CRAZY AGAIN!

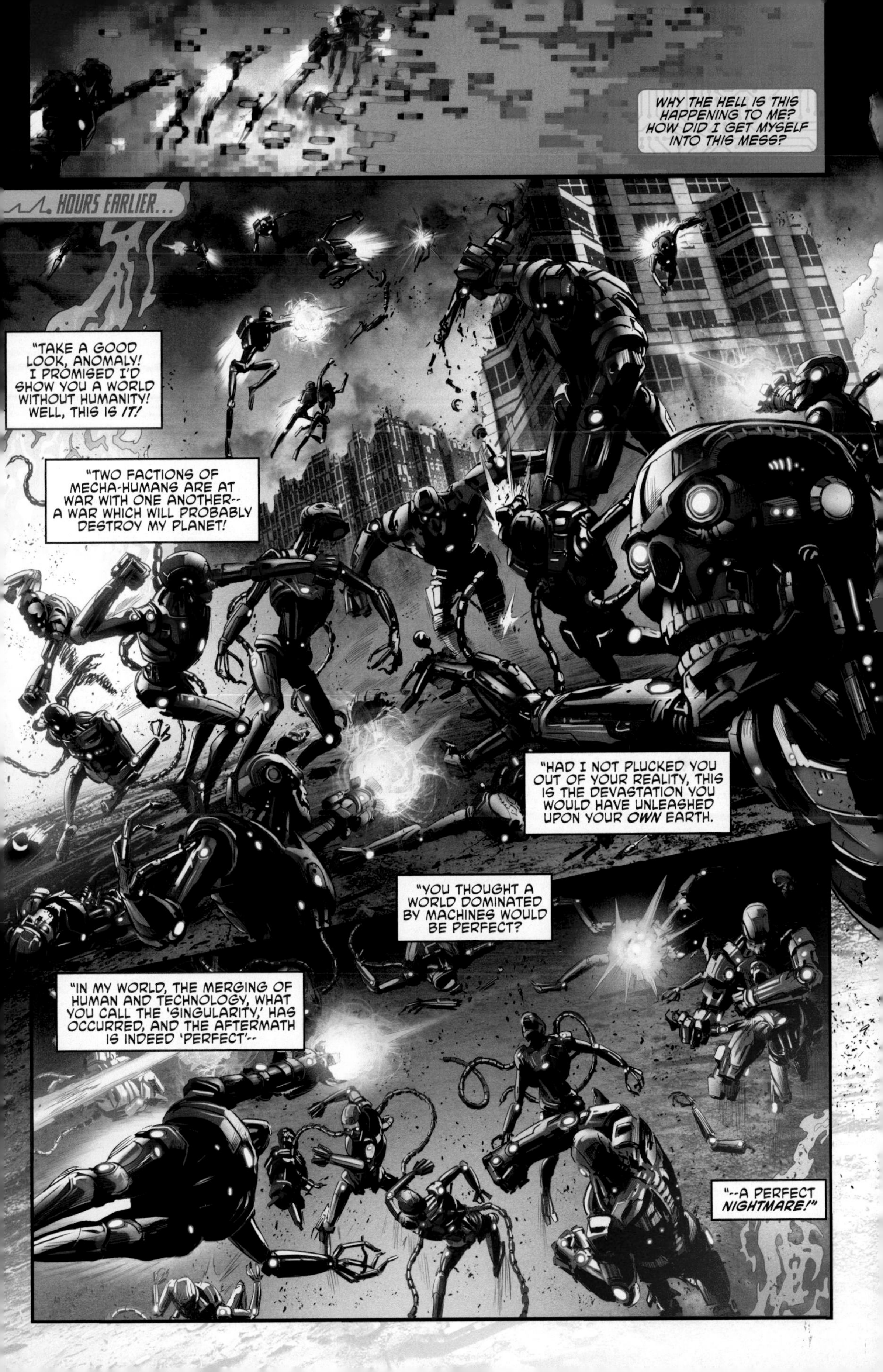
WHY THE HELL IS THIS HAPPENING TO ME? HOW DID I GET MYSELF INTO THIS MESS?
HOURS EARLIER...
"TAKE A GOOD LOOK, ANOMALY! I PROMISED I'D SHOW YOU A WORLD WITHOUT HUMANITY! WELL, THIS IS IT!
"TWO FACTIONS OF MECHA-HUMANS ARE AT WAR WITH ONE ANOTHER-- A WAR WHICH WILL PROBABLY DESTROY MY PLANET!
"HAD I NOT PLUCKED YOU OUT OF YOUR REALITY, THIS IS THE DEVASTATION YOU WOULD HAVE UNLEASHED UPON YOUR OWN EARTH.
"YOU THOUGHT A WORLD DOMINATED BY MACHINES WOULD BE PERFECT?
"IN MY WORLD, THE MERGING OF HUMAN AND TECHNOLOGY, WHAT YOU CALL THE 'SINGULARITY,' HAS OCCURRED, AND THE AFTERMATH IS INDEED 'PERFECT'--
"--A PERFECT NIGHTMARE!"

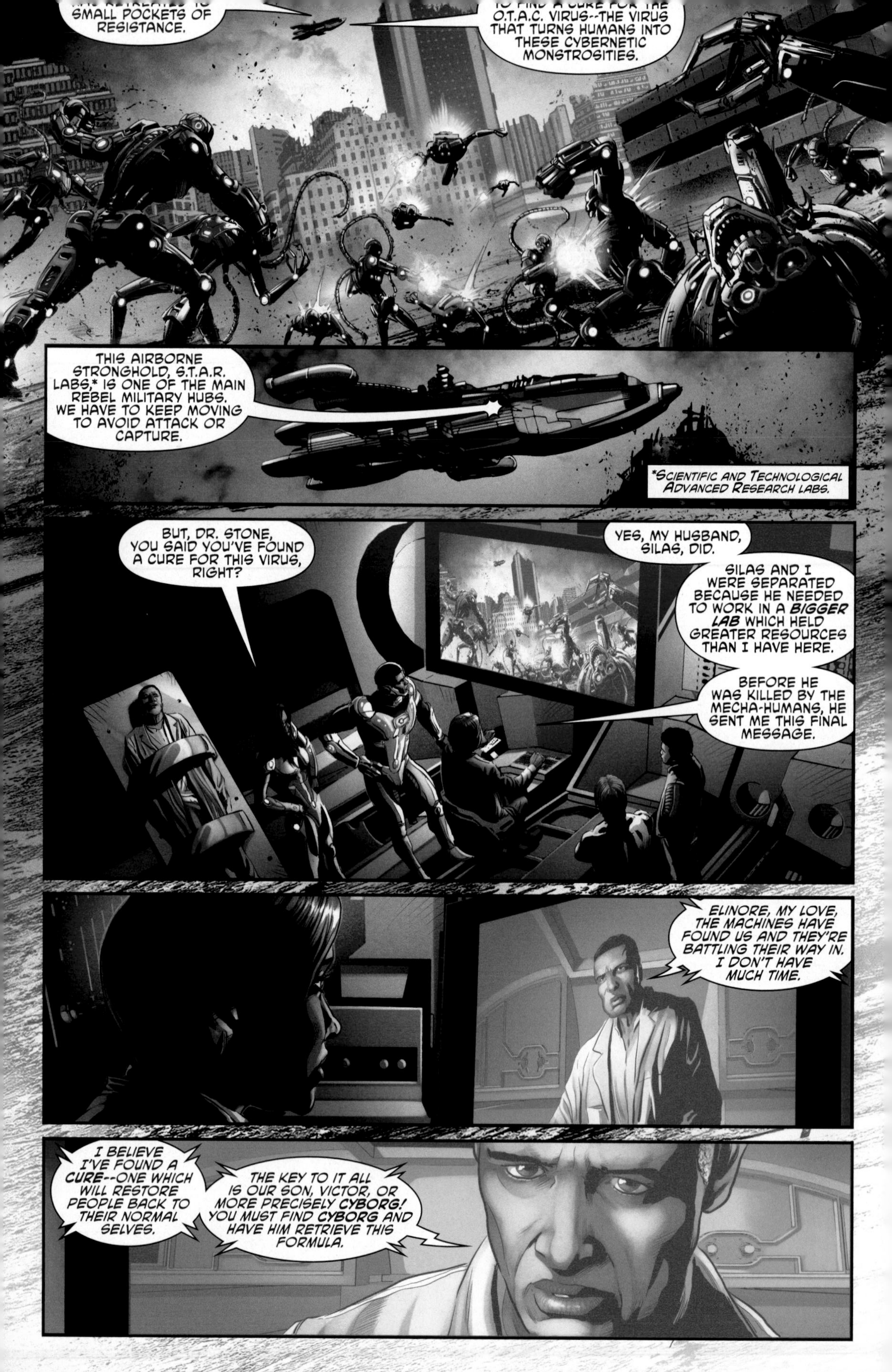

SMALL POCKETS OF RESISTANCE.
O.T.A.C. VIRUS--THE VIRUS THAT TURNS HUMANS INTO THESE CYBERNETIC MONSTROSITIES.
THIS AIRBORNE STRONGHOLD, S.T.A.R. LABS,* IS ONE OF THE MAIN REBEL MILITARY HUBS. WE HAVE TO KEEP MOVING TO AVOID ATTACK OR CAPTURE.
*SCIENTIFIC AND TECHNOLOGICAL ADVANCED RESEARCH LABS.
BUT, DR. STONE, YOU SAID YOU'VE FOUND A CURE FOR THIS VIRUS, RIGHT?
YES, MY HUSBAND, SILAS, DID.
SILAS AND I WERE SEPARATED BECAUSE HE NEEDED TO WORK IN A BIGGER LAB WHICH HELD GREATER RESOURCES THAN I HAVE HERE.
BEFORE HE WAS KILLED BY THE MECHA-HUMANS, HE SENT ME THIS FINAL MESSAGE.
ELINORE, MY LOVE, THE MACHINES HAVE FOUND US AND THEY'RE BATTLING THEIR WAY IN. I DON'T HAVE MUCH TIME.
I BELIEVE I'VE FOUND A CURE--ONE WHICH WILL RESTORE PEOPLE BACK TO THEIR NORMAL SELVES.
THE KEY TO IT ALL IS OUR SON, VICTOR, OR MORE PRECISELY CYBORG! YOU MUST FIND CYBORG AND HAVE HIM RETRIEVE THIS FORMULA.

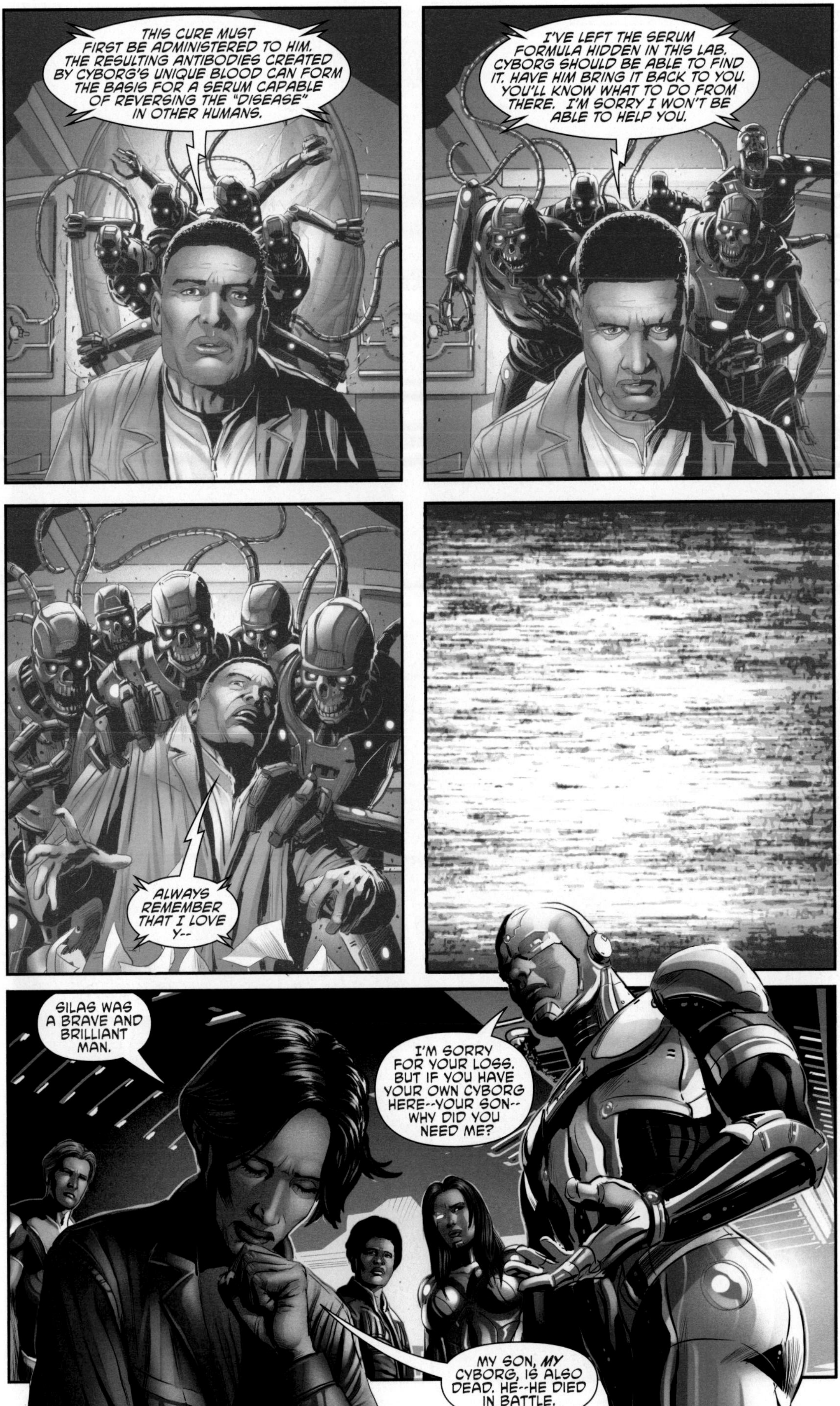
THIS CURE MUST FIRST BE ADMINISTERED TO HIM. THE RESULTING ANTIBODIES CREATED BY CYBORG'S UNIQUE BLOOD CAN FORM THE BASIS FOR A SERUM CAPABLE OF REVERSING THE "DISEASE" IN OTHER HUMANS.
I'VE LEFT THE SERUM FORMULA HIDDEN IN THIS LAB. CYBORG SHOULD BE ABLE TO FIND IT. HAVE HIM BRING IT BACK TO YOU. YOU'LL KNOW WHAT TO DO FROM THERE. I'M SORRY I WON'T BE ABLE TO HELP YOU.
ALWAYS REMEMBER THAT I LOVE Y--
SILAS WAS A BRAVE AND BRILLIANT MAN.
I'M SORRY FOR YOUR LOSS. BUT IF YOU HAVE YOUR OWN CYBORG HERE--YOUR SON--WHY DID YOU NEED ME?
MY SON, *MY* CYBORG, IS ALSO DEAD. HE--HE DIED IN BATTLE.

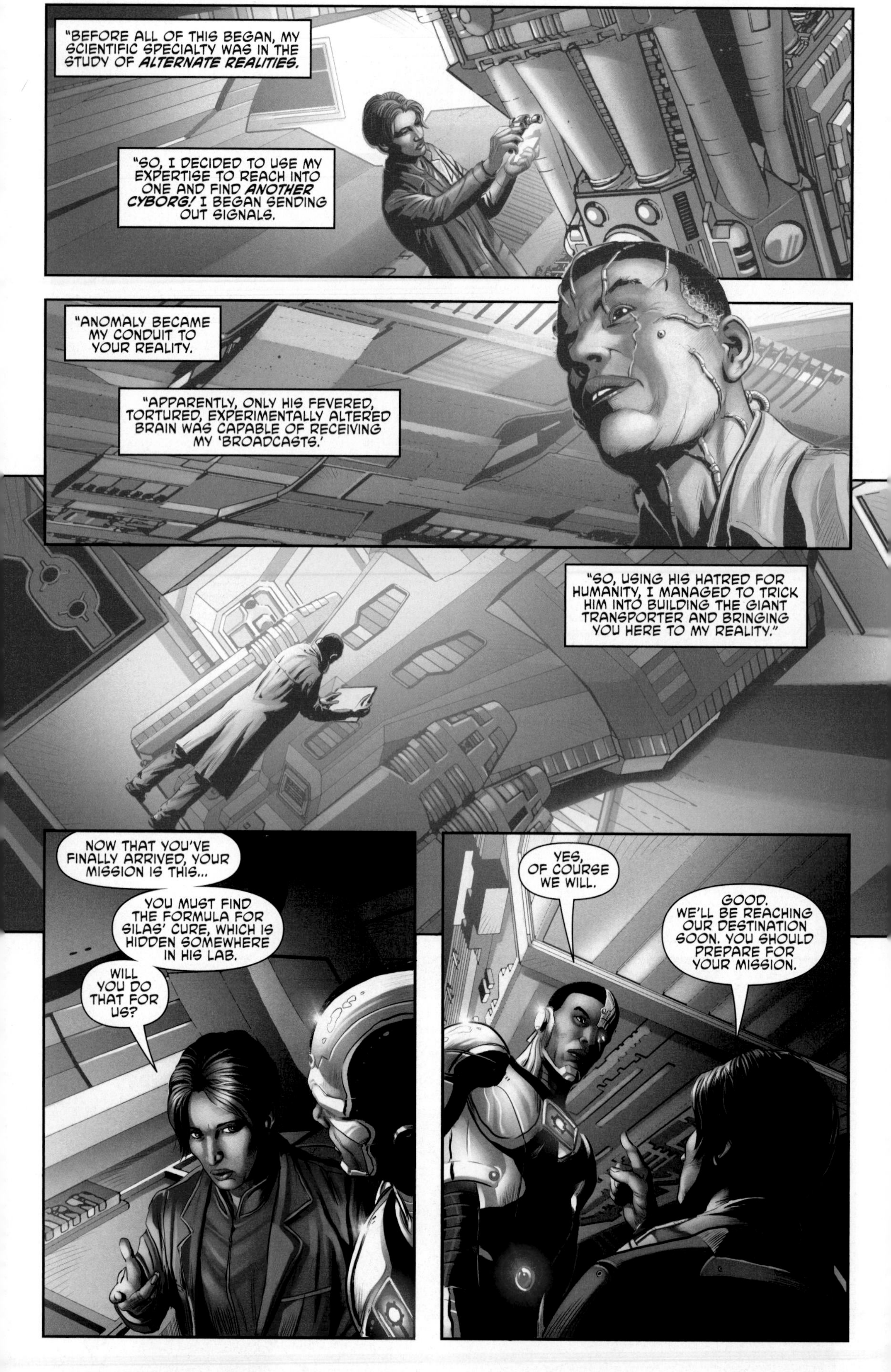
"BEFORE ALL OF THIS BEGAN, MY SCIENTIFIC SPECIALTY WAS IN THE STUDY OF ALTERNATE REALITIES.
"SO, I DECIDED TO USE MY EXPERTISE TO REACH INTO ONE AND FIND ANOTHER CYBORG! I BEGAN SENDING OUT SIGNALS.
"ANOMALY BECAME MY CONDUIT TO YOUR REALITY.
"APPARENTLY, ONLY HIS FEVERED, TORTURED, EXPERIMENTALLY ALTERED BRAIN WAS CAPABLE OF RECEIVING MY 'BROADCASTS.'
"SO, USING HIS HATRED FOR HUMANITY, I MANAGED TO TRICK HIM INTO BUILDING THE GIANT TRANSPORTER AND BRINGING YOU HERE TO MY REALITY."
NOW THAT YOU'VE FINALLY ARRIVED, YOUR MISSION IS THIS...
YOU MUST FIND THE FORMULA FOR SILAS' CURE, WHICH IS HIDDEN SOMEWHERE IN HIS LAB.
WILL YOU DO THAT FOR US?
YES, OF COURSE WE WILL.
GOOD. WE'LL BE REACHING OUR DESTINATION SOON. YOU SHOULD PREPARE FOR YOUR MISSION.

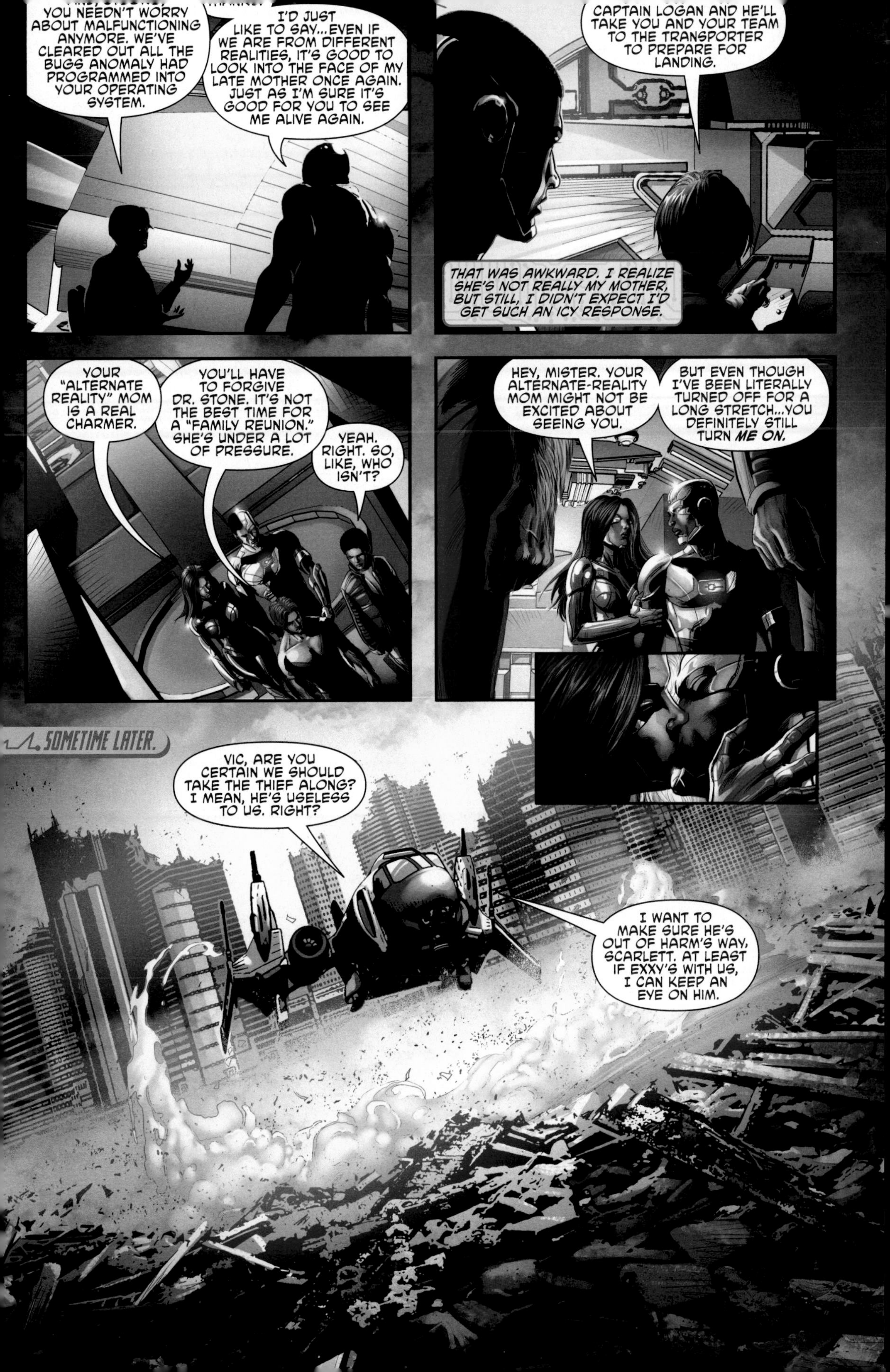
YOU NEEDN'T WORRY ABOUT MALFUNCTIONING ANYMORE. WE'VE CLEARED OUT ALL THE BUGS ANOMALY HAD PROGRAMMED INTO YOUR OPERATING SYSTEM.
I'D JUST LIKE TO SAY...EVEN IF WE ARE FROM DIFFERENT REALITIES, IT'S GOOD TO LOOK INTO THE FACE OF MY LATE MOTHER ONCE AGAIN. JUST AS I'M SURE IT'S GOOD FOR YOU TO SEE ME ALIVE AGAIN.
CAPTAIN LOGAN AND HE'LL TAKE YOU AND YOUR TEAM TO THE TRANSPORTER TO PREPARE FOR LANDING.
THAT WAS AWKWARD. I REALIZE SHE'S NOT REALLY MY MOTHER, BUT STILL, I DIDN'T EXPECT I'D GET SUCH AN ICY RESPONSE.
YOUR "ALTERNATE REALITY" MOM IS A REAL CHARMER.
YOU'LL HAVE TO FORGIVE DR. STONE. IT'S NOT THE BEST TIME FOR A "FAMILY REUNION." SHE'S UNDER A LOT OF PRESSURE.
YEAH. RIGHT. SO, LIKE, WHO ISN'T?
HEY, MISTER. YOUR ALTERNATE-REALITY MOM MIGHT NOT BE EXCITED ABOUT SEEING YOU.
BUT EVEN THOUGH I'VE BEEN LITERALLY TURNED OFF FOR A LONG STRETCH...YOU DEFINITELY STILL TURN ME ON.
SOMETIME LATER.
VIC, ARE YOU CERTAIN WE SHOULD TAKE THE THIEF ALONG? I MEAN, HE'S USELESS TO US. RIGHT?
I WANT TO MAKE SURE HE'S OUT OF HARM'S WAY, SCARLETT. AT LEAST IF EXXY'S WITH US, I CAN KEEP AN EYE ON HIM.

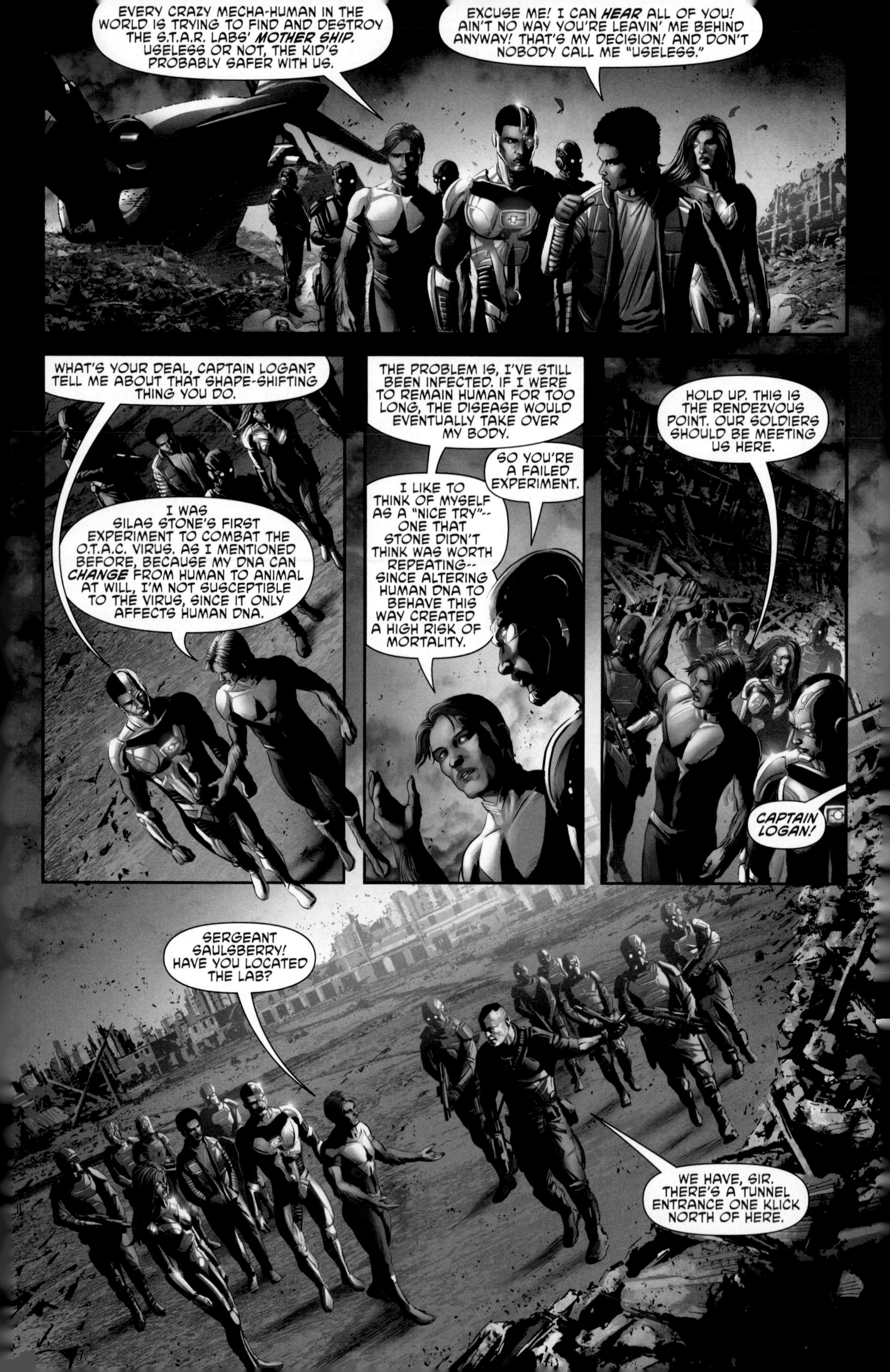
EVERY CRAZY MECHA-HUMAN IN THE WORLD IS TRYING TO FIND AND DESTROY THE S.T.A.R. LABS' MOTHER SHIP. USELESS OR NOT, THE KID'S PROBABLY SAFER WITH US.
EXCUSE ME! I CAN HEAR ALL OF YOU! AIN'T NO WAY YOU'RE LEAVIN' ME BEHIND ANYWAY! THAT'S MY DECISION! AND DON'T NOBODY CALL ME "USELESS."
WHAT'S YOUR DEAL, CAPTAIN LOGAN? TELL ME ABOUT THAT SHAPE-SHIFTING THING YOU DO.
I WAS SILAS STONE'S FIRST EXPERIMENT TO COMBAT THE O.T.A.C. VIRUS. AS I MENTIONED BEFORE, BECAUSE MY DNA CAN CHANGE FROM HUMAN TO ANIMAL AT WILL, I'M NOT SUSCEPTIBLE TO THE VIRUS, SINCE IT ONLY AFFECTS HUMAN DNA.
THE PROBLEM IS, I'VE STILL BEEN INFECTED. IF I WERE TO REMAIN HUMAN FOR TOO LONG, THE DISEASE WOULD EVENTUALLY TAKE OVER MY BODY.
SO YOU'RE A FAILED EXPERIMENT.
I LIKE TO THINK OF MYSELF AS A "NICE TRY"-- ONE THAT STONE DIDN'T THINK WAS WORTH REPEATING-- SINCE ALTERING HUMAN DNA TO BEHAVE THIS WAY CREATED A HIGH RISK OF MORTALITY.
HOLD UP. THIS IS THE RENDEZVOUS POINT. OUR SOLDIERS SHOULD BE MEETING US HERE.
CAPTAIN LOGAN!
SERGEANT SAULSBERRY! HAVE YOU LOCATED THE LAB?
WE HAVE, SIR. THERE'S A TUNNEL ENTRANCE ONE KLICK NORTH OF HERE.

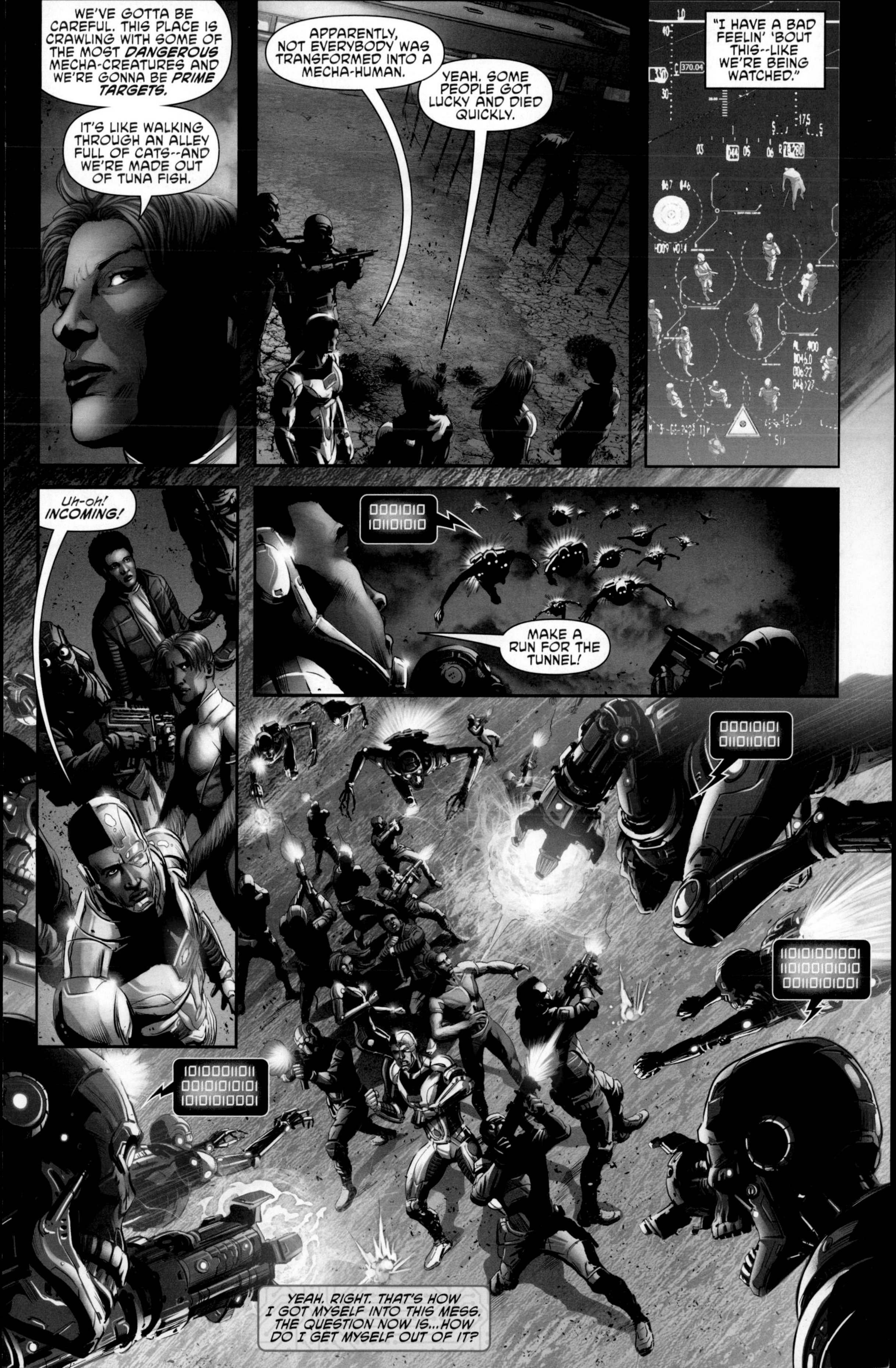
WE'VE GOTTA BE CAREFUL. THIS PLACE IS CRAWLING WITH SOME OF THE MOST DANGEROUS MECHA-CREATURES AND WE'RE GONNA BE PRIME TARGETS.
IT'S LIKE WALKING THROUGH AN ALLEY FULL OF CATS--AND WE'RE MADE OUT OF TUNA FISH.
APPARENTLY, NOT EVERYBODY WAS TRANSFORMED INTO A MECHA-HUMAN.
YEAH. SOME PEOPLE GOT LUCKY AND DIED QUICKLY.
"I HAVE A BAD FEELIN' 'BOUT THIS--LIKE WE'RE BEING WATCHED."
Uh-oh! INCOMING!
0001010
1011010 10
MAKE A RUN FOR THE TUNNEL!
00101010 1
01101010 1
1101010100 1
1101000101 0
0011010100 1
1010001101 1
0010101010 1
1010101000 1
YEAH. RIGHT. THAT'S HOW I GOT MYSELF INTO THIS MESS. THE QUESTION NOW IS...HOW DO I GET MYSELF OUT OF IT?

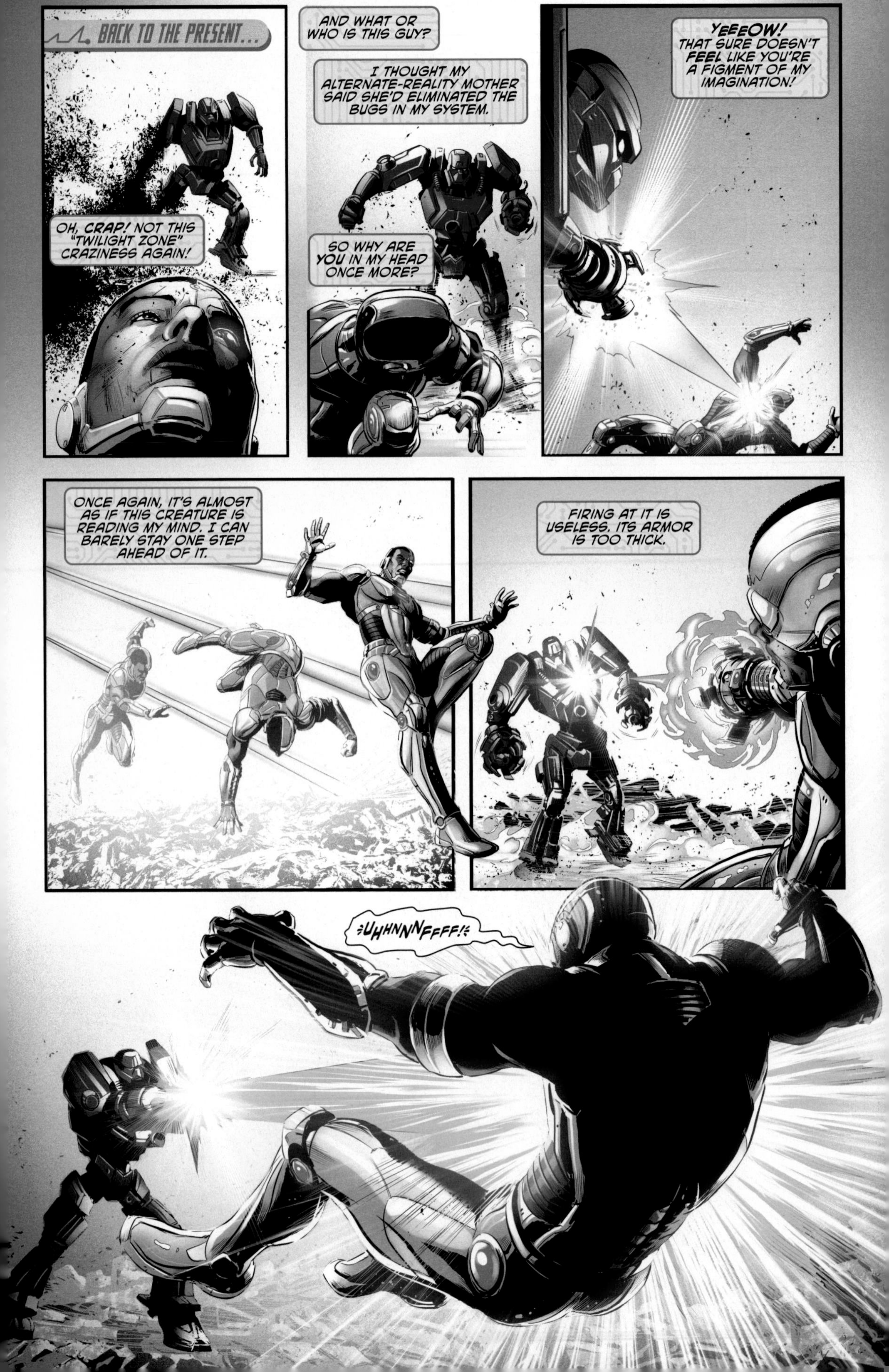
BACK TO THE PRESENT...
OH, CRAP! NOT THIS "TWILIGHT ZONE" CRAZINESS AGAIN!
AND WHAT OR WHO IS THIS GUY?
I THOUGHT MY ALTERNATE-REALITY MOTHER SAID SHE'D ELIMINATED THE BUGS IN MY SYSTEM.
SO WHY ARE YOU IN MY HEAD ONCE MORE?
YEEEOW! THAT SURE DOESN'T FEEL LIKE YOU'RE A FIGMENT OF MY IMAGINATION!
ONCE AGAIN, IT'S ALMOST AS IF THIS CREATURE IS READING MY MIND. I CAN BARELY STAY ONE STEP AHEAD OF IT.
FIRING AT IT IS USELESS. ITS ARMOR IS TOO THICK.
UHHNNNFFFF!

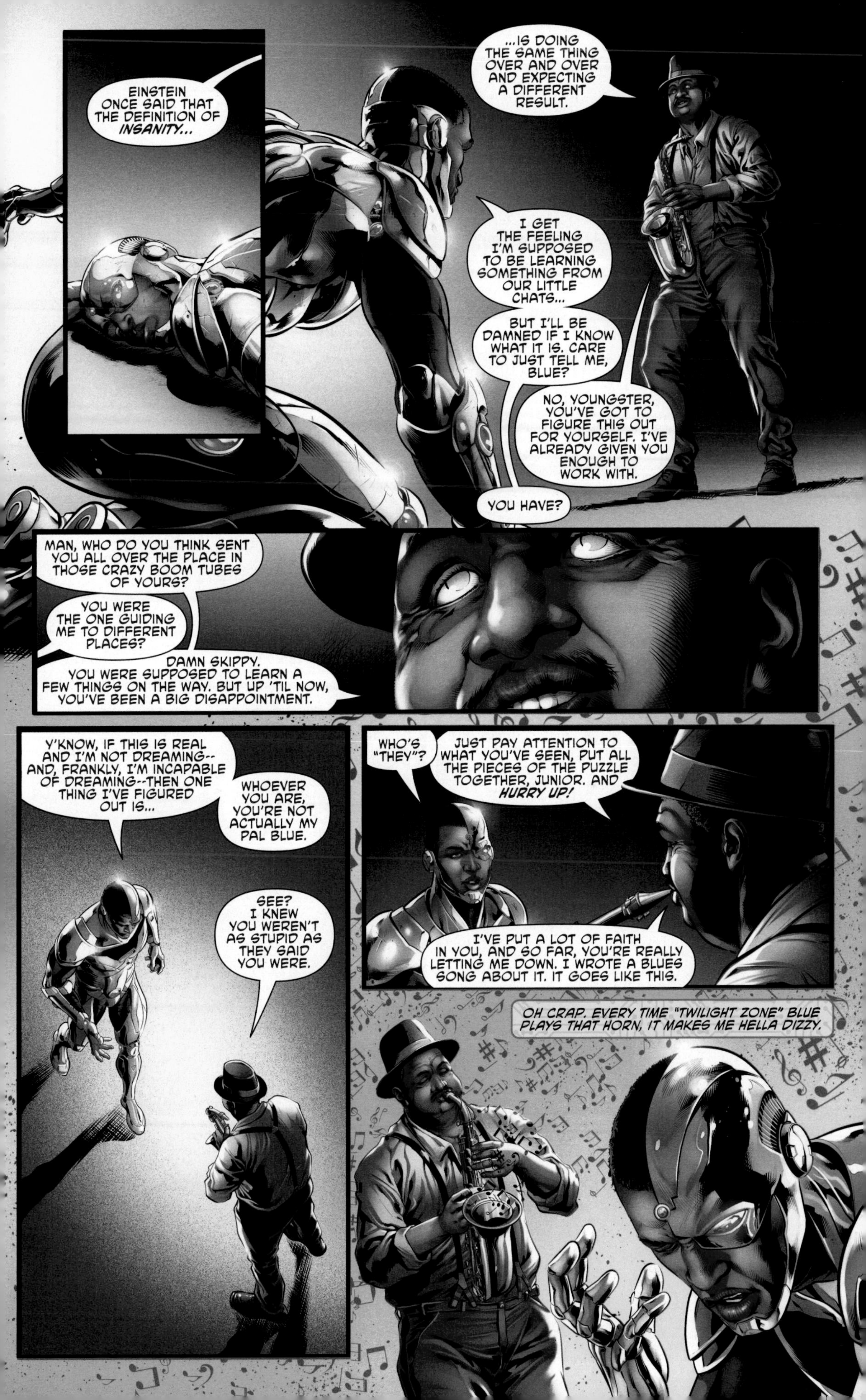
EINSTEIN ONCE SAID THAT THE DEFINITION OF *INSANITY...*
...IS DOING THE SAME THING OVER AND OVER AND EXPECTING A DIFFERENT RESULT.
I GET THE FEELING I'M SUPPOSED TO BE LEARNING SOMETHING FROM OUR LITTLE CHATS...
BUT I'LL BE DAMNED IF I KNOW WHAT IT IS. CARE TO JUST TELL ME, BLUE?
NO, YOUNGSTER, YOU'VE GOT TO FIGURE THIS OUT FOR YOURSELF. I'VE ALREADY GIVEN YOU ENOUGH TO WORK WITH.
YOU HAVE?
MAN, WHO DO YOU THINK SENT YOU ALL OVER THE PLACE IN THOSE CRAZY BOOM TUBES OF YOURS?
YOU WERE THE ONE GUIDING ME TO DIFFERENT PLACES?
DAMN SKIPPY. YOU WERE SUPPOSED TO LEARN A FEW THINGS ON THE WAY. BUT UP 'TIL NOW, YOU'VE BEEN A BIG DISAPPOINTMENT.
Y'KNOW, IF THIS IS REAL AND I'M NOT DREAMING-- AND, FRANKLY, I'M INCAPABLE OF DREAMING--THEN ONE THING I'VE FIGURED OUT IS...
WHOEVER YOU ARE, YOU'RE NOT ACTUALLY MY PAL BLUE.
SEE? I KNEW YOU WEREN'T AS STUPID AS THEY SAID YOU WERE.
WHO'S "THEY"?
JUST PAY ATTENTION TO WHAT YOU'VE SEEN, PUT ALL THE PIECES OF THE PUZZLE TOGETHER, JUNIOR. AND *HURRY UP!*
I'VE PUT A LOT OF FAITH IN YOU, AND SO FAR, YOU'RE REALLY LETTING ME DOWN. I WROTE A BLUES SONG ABOUT IT. IT GOES LIKE THIS.
OH CRAP. EVERY TIME "TWILIGHT ZONE" BLUE PLAYS THAT HORN, IT MAKES ME HELLA DIZZY.

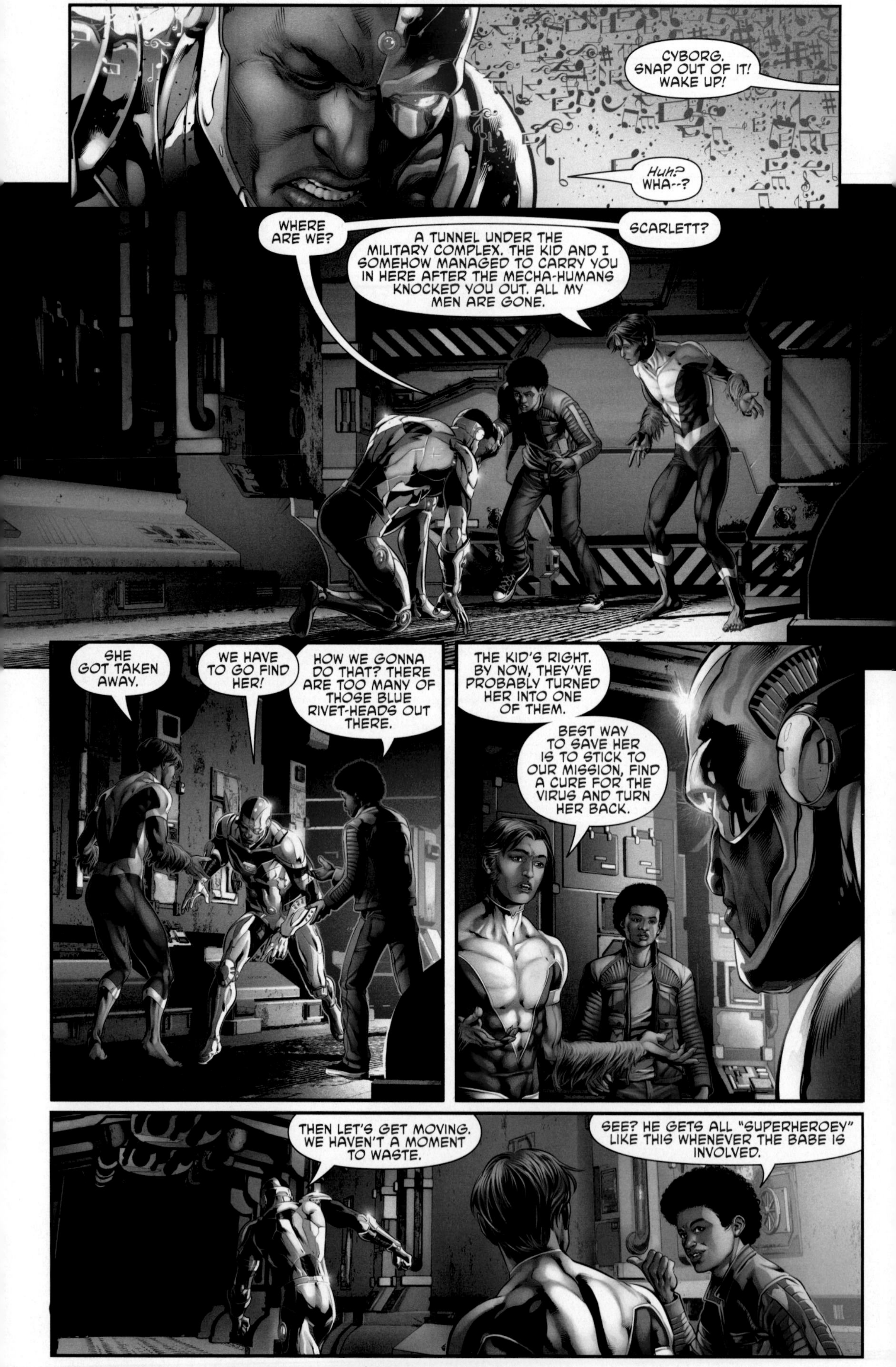
CYBORG. SNAP OUT OF IT! WAKE UP!
Huh? WHA--?
SCARLETT?
WHERE ARE WE?
A TUNNEL UNDER THE MILITARY COMPLEX. THE KID AND I SOMEHOW MANAGED TO CARRY YOU IN HERE AFTER THE MECHA-HUMANS KNOCKED YOU OUT. ALL MY MEN ARE GONE.
SHE GOT TAKEN AWAY.
WE HAVE TO GO FIND HER!
HOW WE GONNA DO THAT? THERE ARE TOO MANY OF THOSE BLUE RIVET-HEADS OUT THERE.
THE KID'S RIGHT. BY NOW, THEY'VE PROBABLY TURNED HER INTO ONE OF THEM.
BEST WAY TO SAVE HER IS TO STICK TO OUR MISSION, FIND A CURE FOR THE VIRUS AND TURN HER BACK.
THEN LET'S GET MOVING. WE HAVEN'T A MOMENT TO WASTE.
SEE? HE GETS ALL "SUPERHEROEY" LIKE THIS WHENEVER THE BABE IS INVOLVED.

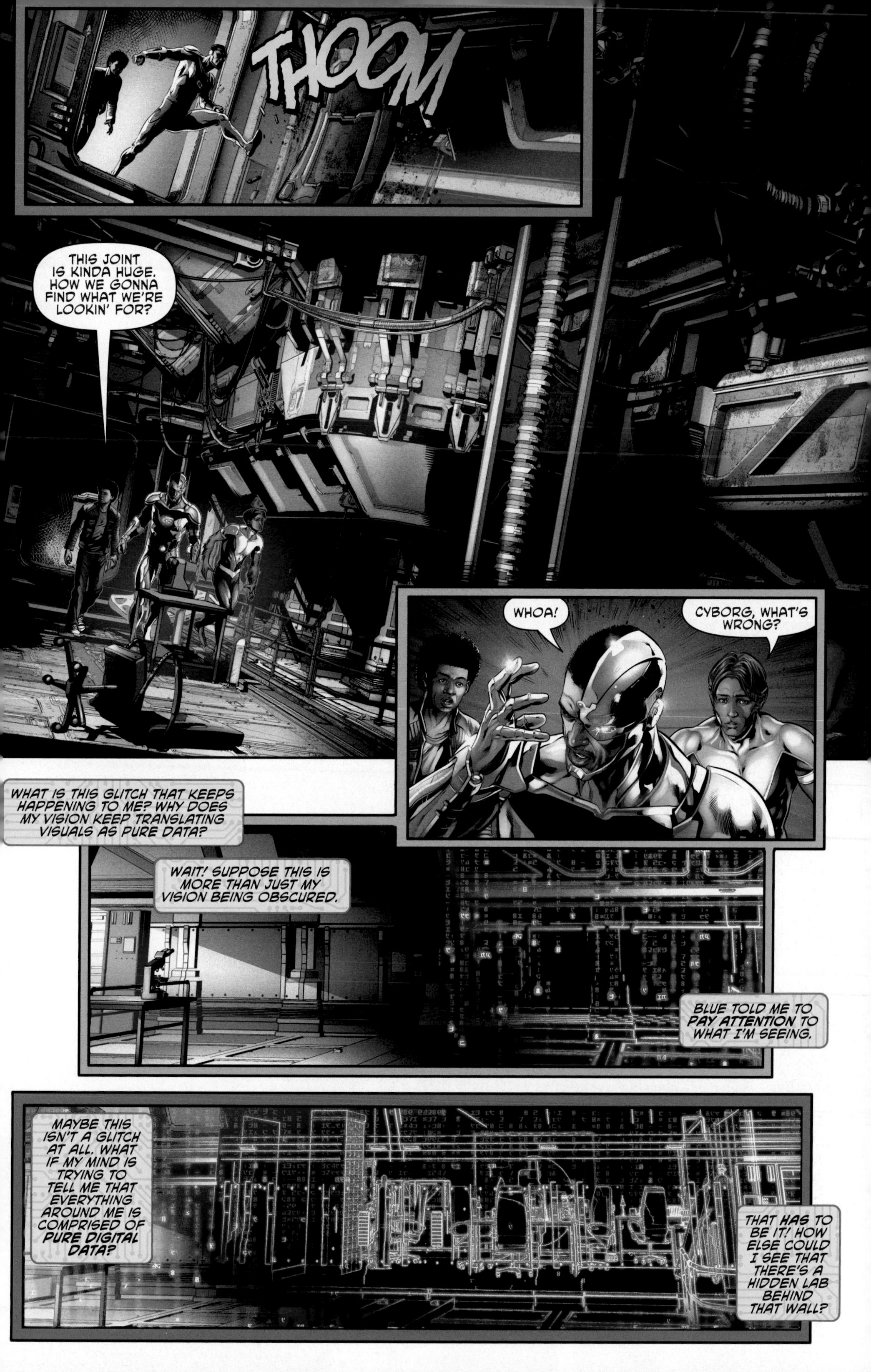
THOOM
THIS JOINT IS KINDA HUGE. HOW WE GONNA FIND WHAT WE'RE LOOKIN' FOR?
WHOA!
CYBORG, WHAT'S WRONG?
WHAT IS THIS GLITCH THAT KEEPS HAPPENING TO ME? WHY DOES MY VISION KEEP TRANSLATING VISUALS AS PURE DATA?
WAIT! SUPPOSE THIS IS MORE THAN JUST MY VISION BEING OBSCURED.
BLUE TOLD ME TO PAY ATTENTION TO WHAT I'M SEEING.
MAYBE THIS ISN'T A GLITCH AT ALL. WHAT IF MY MIND IS TRYING TO TELL ME THAT EVERYTHING AROUND ME IS COMPRISED OF PURE DIGITAL DATA?
THAT HAS TO BE IT! HOW ELSE COULD I SEE THAT THERE'S A HIDDEN LAB BEHIND THAT WALL?

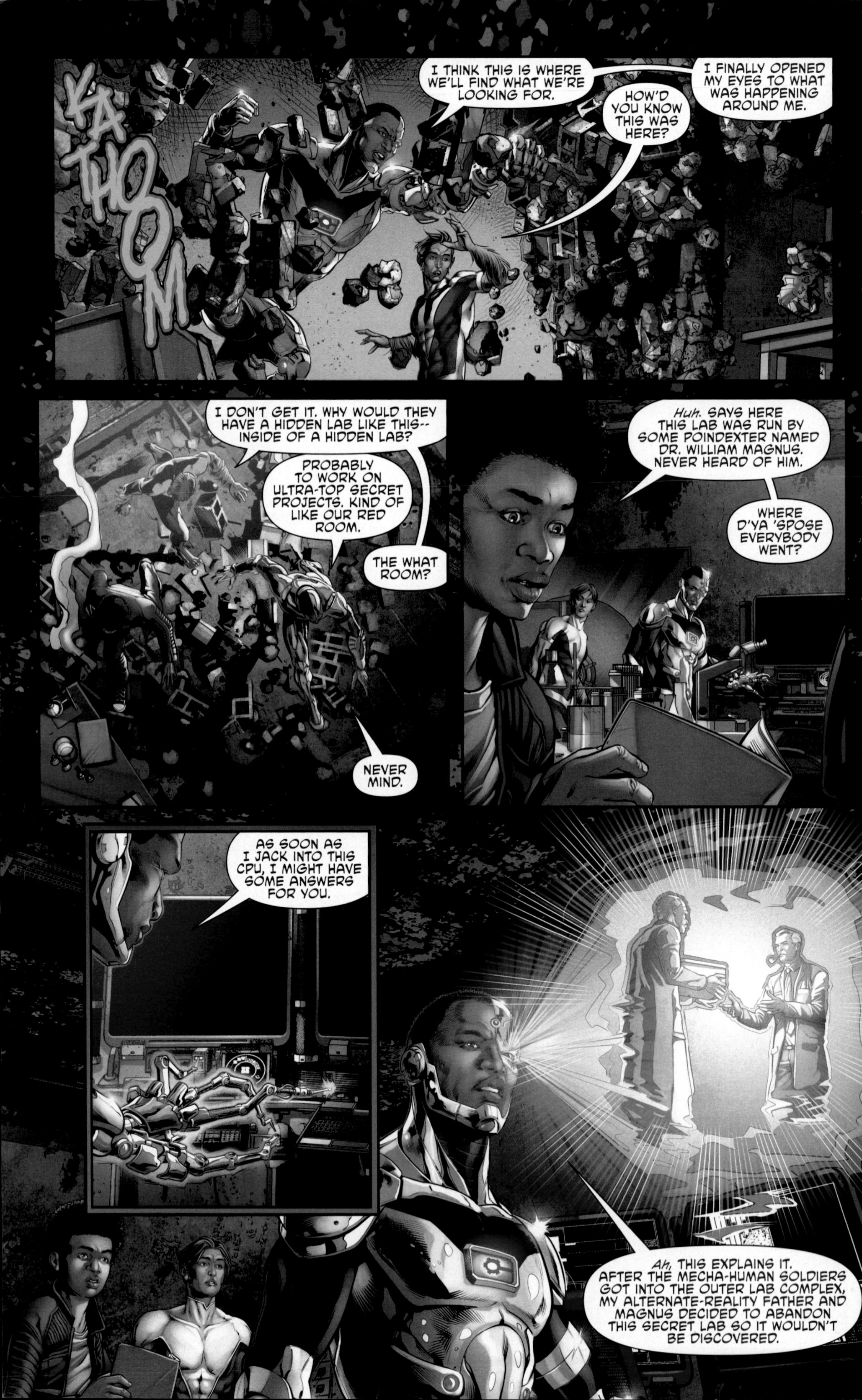
KA THOOM
I THINK THIS IS WHERE WE'LL FIND WHAT WE'RE LOOKING FOR.
HOW'D YOU KNOW THIS WAS HERE?
I FINALLY OPENED MY EYES TO WHAT WAS HAPPENING AROUND ME.
I DON'T GET IT. WHY WOULD THEY HAVE A HIDDEN LAB LIKE THIS-- INSIDE OF A HIDDEN LAB?
PROBABLY TO WORK ON ULTRA-TOP SECRET PROJECTS. KIND OF LIKE OUR RED ROOM.
THE WHAT ROOM?
NEVER MIND.
Huh. SAYS HERE THIS LAB WAS RUN BY SOME POINDEXTER NAMED DR. WILLIAM MAGNUS. NEVER HEARD OF HIM.
WHERE D'YA 'SPOSE EVERYBODY WENT?
AS SOON AS I JACK INTO THIS CPU, I MIGHT HAVE SOME ANSWERS FOR YOU.
Ah, THIS EXPLAINS IT. AFTER THE MECHA-HUMAN SOLDIERS GOT INTO THE OUTER LAB COMPLEX, MY ALTERNATE-REALITY FATHER AND MAGNUS DECIDED TO ABANDON THIS SECRET LAB SO IT WOULDN'T BE DISCOVERED.

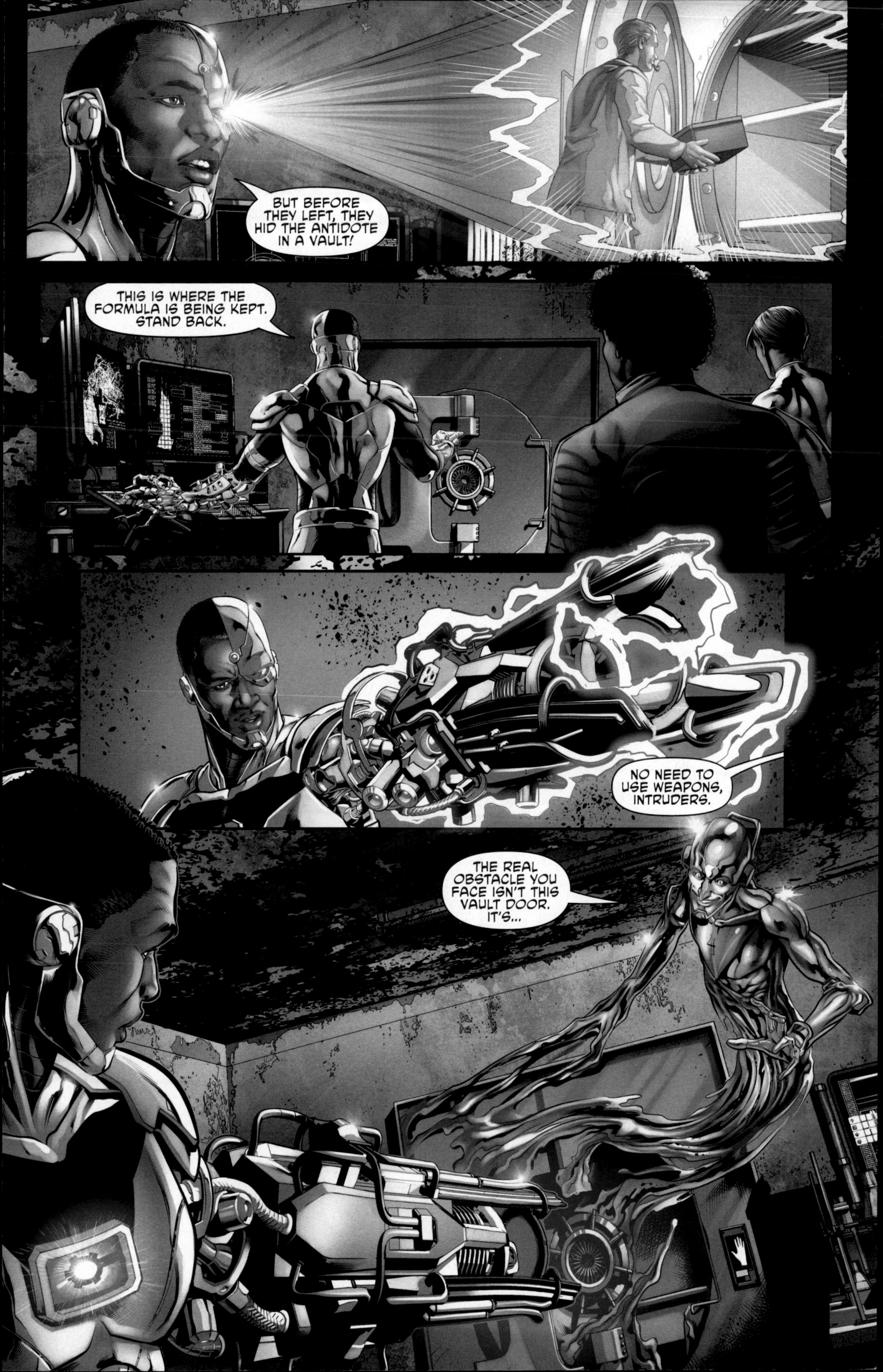
BUT BEFORE THEY LEFT, THEY HID THE ANTIDOTE IN A VAULT!
THIS IS WHERE THE FORMULA IS BEING KEPT. STAND BACK.
NO NEED TO USE WEAPONS, INTRUDERS.
THE REAL OBSTACLE YOU FACE ISN'T THIS VAULT DOOR. IT'S...

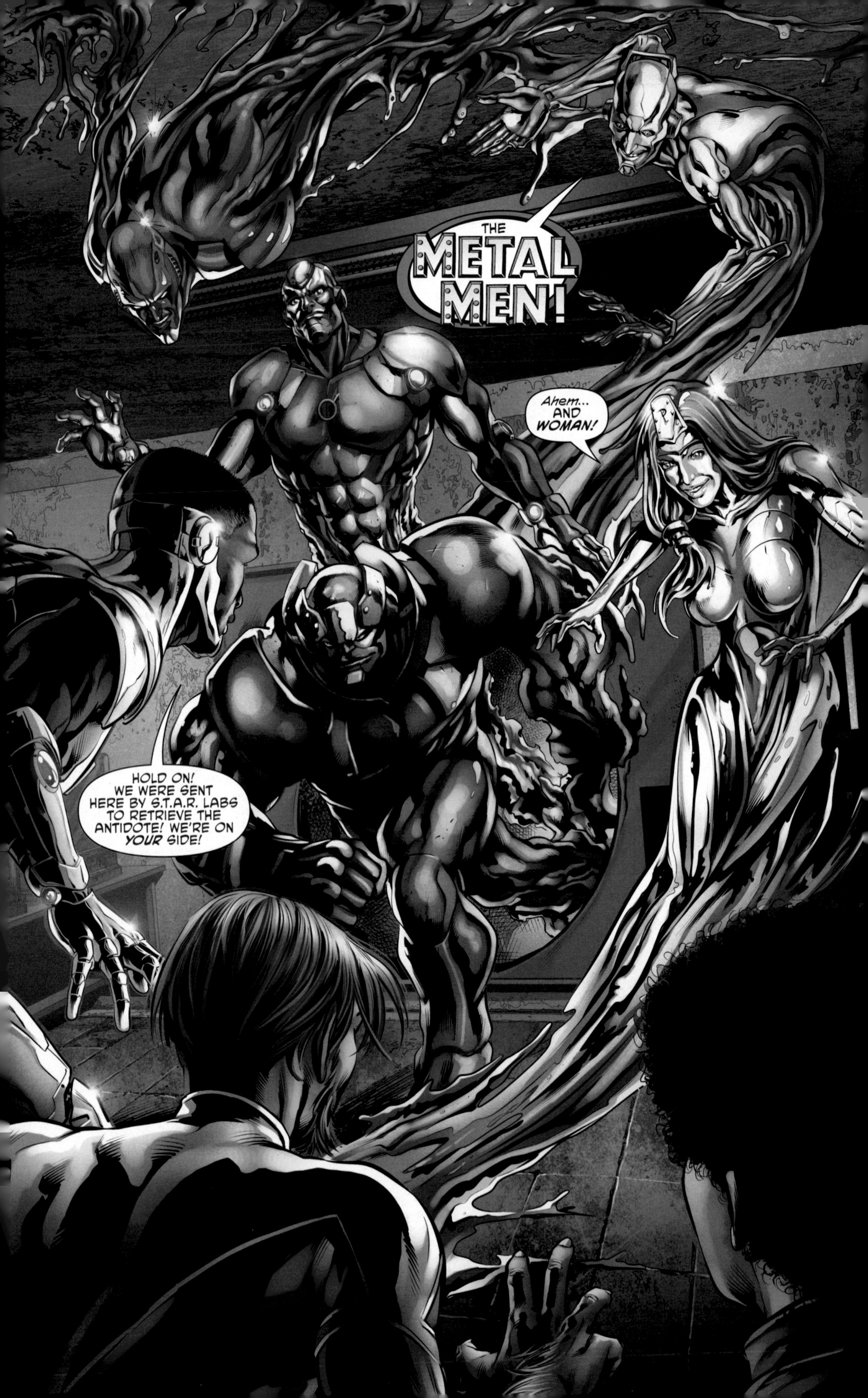
THE METAL MEN!
Ahem... AND WOMAN!
HOLD ON! WE WERE SENT HERE BY S.T.A.R. LABS TO RETRIEVE THE ANTIDOTE! WE'RE ON YOUR SIDE!

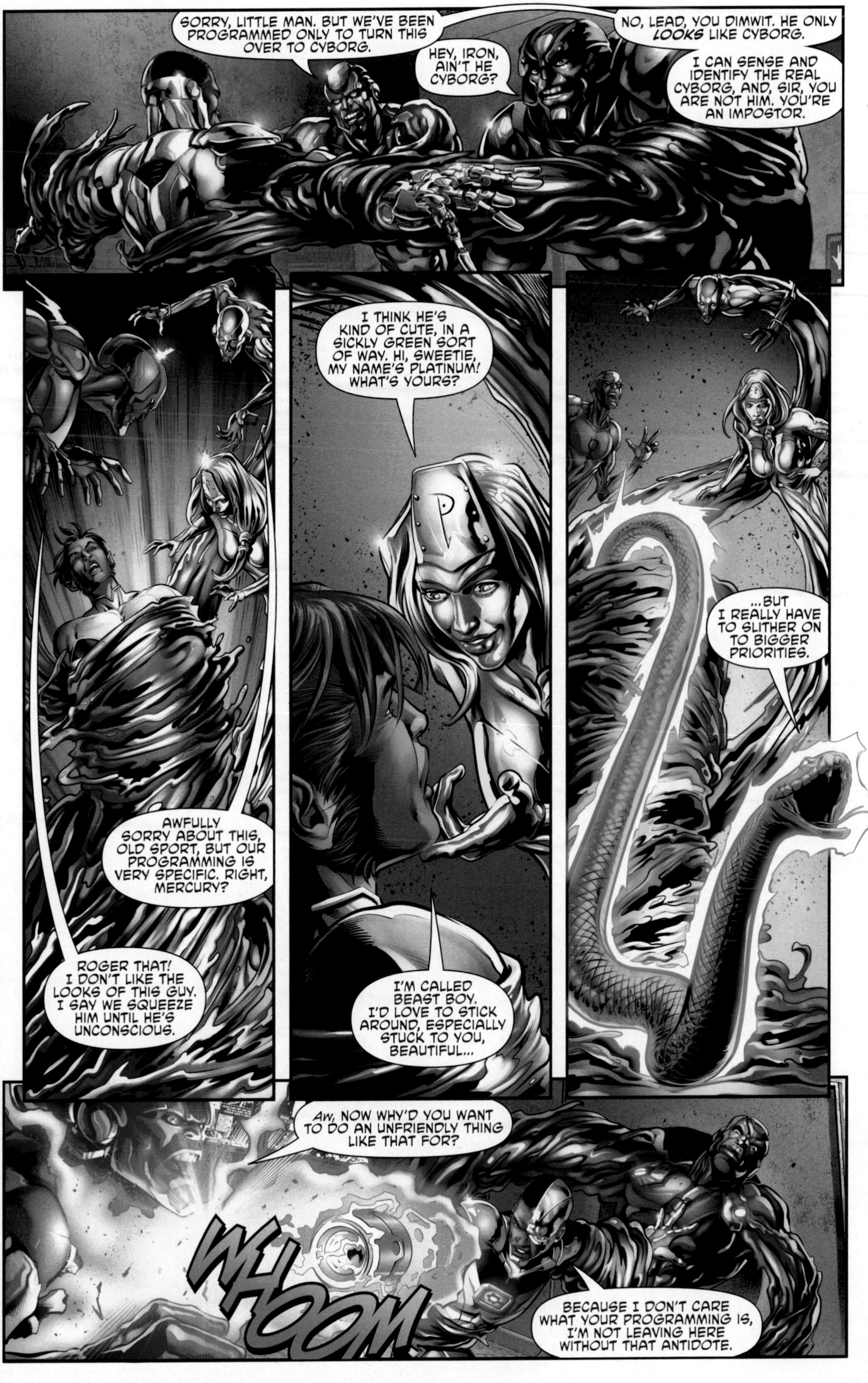
SORRY, LITTLE MAN. BUT WE'VE BEEN PROGRAMMED ONLY TO TURN THIS OVER TO CYBORG.
HEY, IRON, AIN'T HE CYBORG?
NO, LEAD, YOU DIMWIT. HE ONLY *LOOKS* LIKE CYBORG.
I CAN SENSE AND IDENTIFY THE REAL CYBORG, AND, SIR, YOU ARE NOT HIM. YOU'RE AN IMPOSTOR.
AWFULLY SORRY ABOUT THIS, OLD SPORT, BUT OUR PROGRAMMING IS VERY SPECIFIC. RIGHT, MERCURY?
ROGER THAT! I DON'T LIKE THE LOOKS OF THIS GUY. I SAY WE SQUEEZE HIM UNTIL HE'S UNCONSCIOUS.
I THINK HE'S KIND OF CUTE, IN A SICKLY GREEN SORT OF WAY. HI, SWEETIE, MY NAME'S PLATINUM! WHAT'S YOURS?
I'M CALLED BEAST BOY. I'D LOVE TO STICK AROUND, ESPECIALLY STUCK TO YOU, BEAUTIFUL...
...BUT I REALLY HAVE TO SLITHER ON TO BIGGER PRIORITIES.
AW, NOW WHY'D YOU WANT TO DO AN UNFRIENDLY THING LIKE THAT FOR?
WHOOM
BECAUSE I DON'T CARE WHAT YOUR PROGRAMMING IS, I'M NOT LEAVING HERE WITHOUT THAT ANTIDOTE.

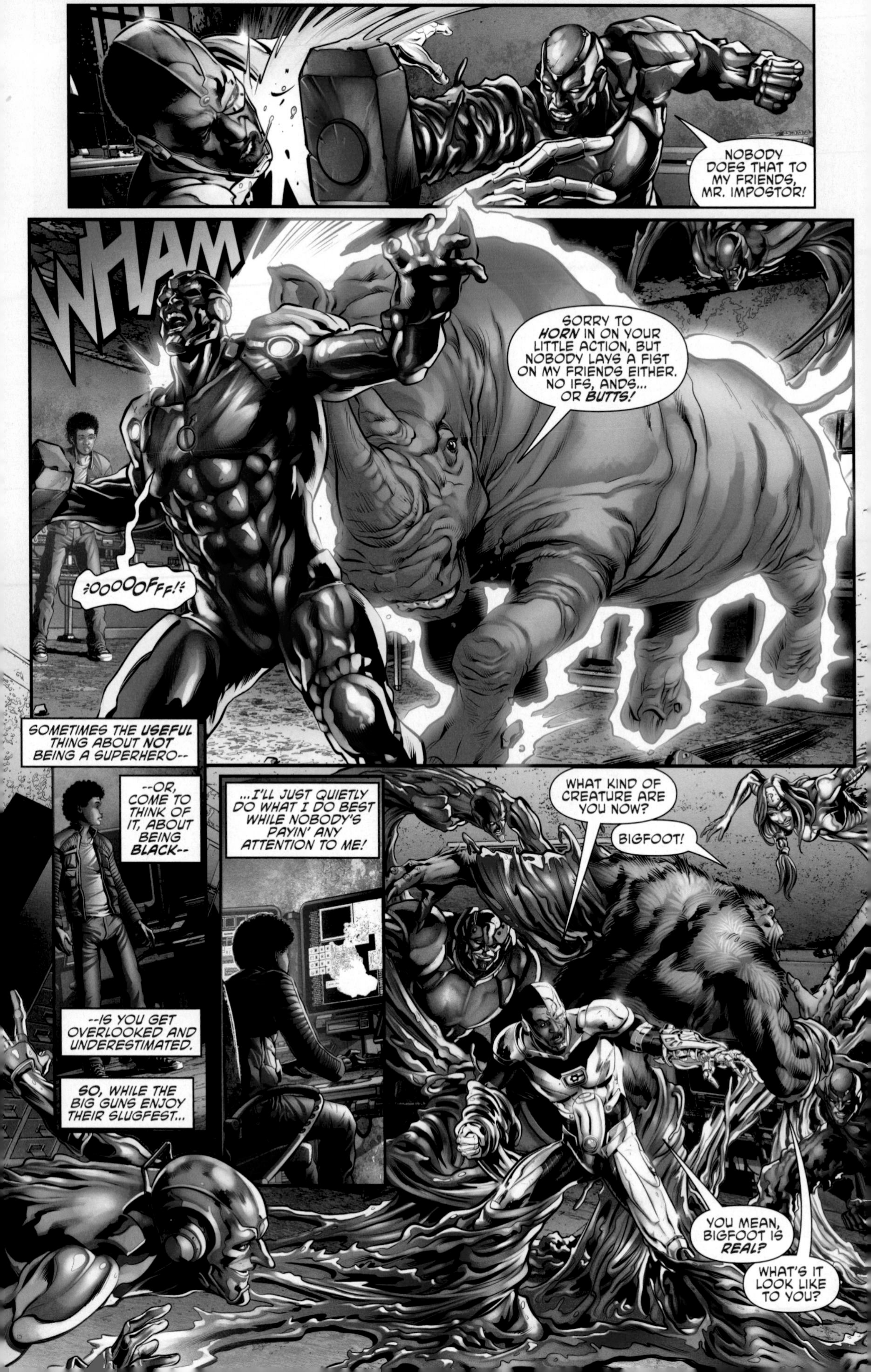
NOBODY DOES THAT TO MY FRIENDS, MR. IMPOSTOR!
WHAM
SORRY TO HORN IN ON YOUR LITTLE ACTION, BUT NOBODY LAYS A FIST ON MY FRIENDS EITHER. NO IFS, ANDS... OR BUTTS!
OOOOOFFF!
SOMETIMES THE USEFUL THING ABOUT NOT BEING A SUPERHERO--
--OR, COME TO THINK OF IT, ABOUT BEING BLACK--
--IS YOU GET OVERLOOKED AND UNDERESTIMATED.
SO, WHILE THE BIG GUNS ENJOY THEIR SLUGFEST...
...I'LL JUST QUIETLY DO WHAT I DO BEST WHILE NOBODY'S PAYIN' ANY ATTENTION TO ME!
WHAT KIND OF CREATURE ARE YOU NOW?
BIGFOOT!
YOU MEAN, BIGFOOT IS REAL?
WHAT'S IT LOOK LIKE TO YOU?

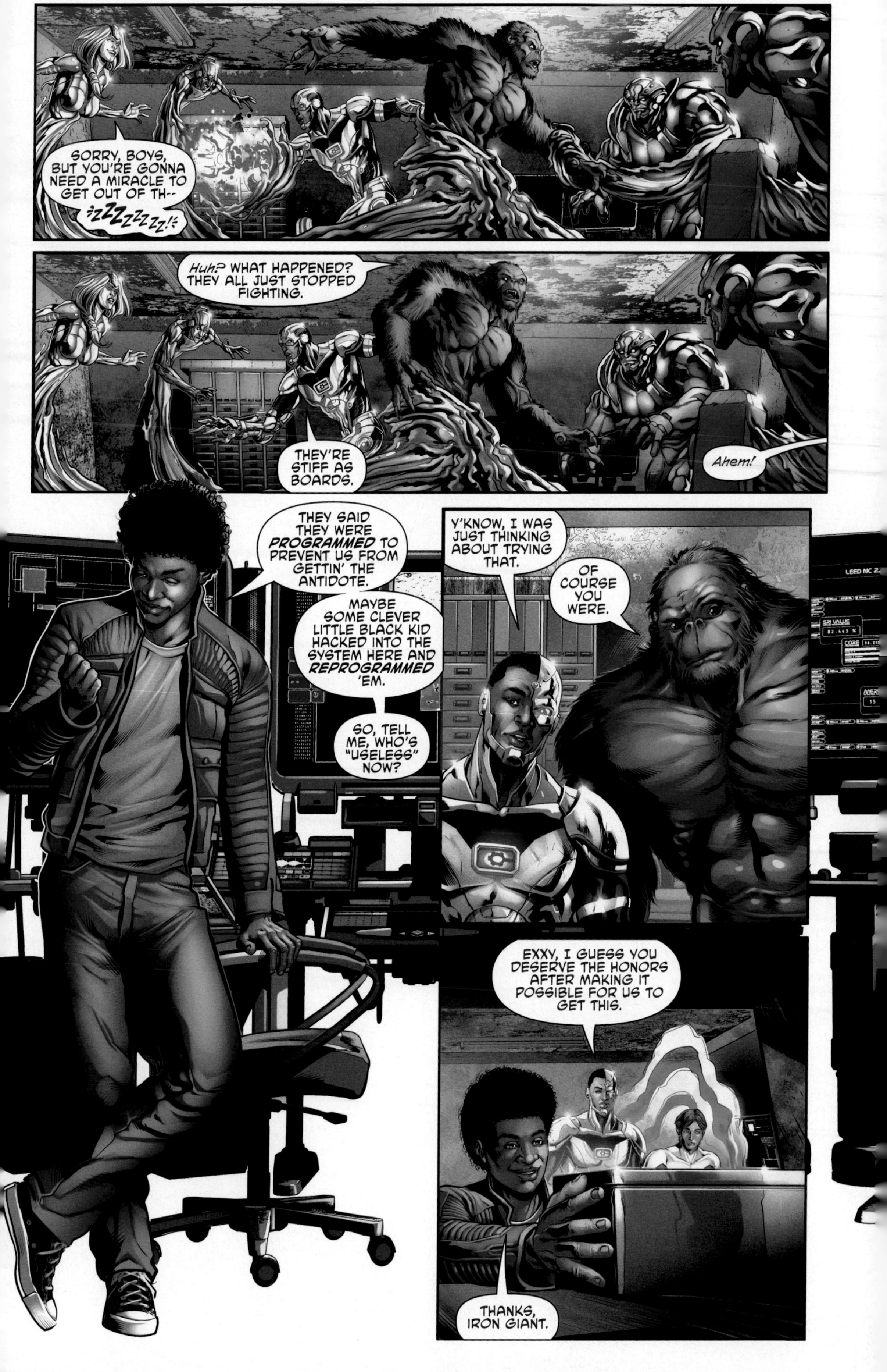
SORRY, BOYS, BUT YOU'RE GONNA NEED A MIRACLE TO GET OUT OF TH--
ZZZZZZZ!
Huh? WHAT HAPPENED? THEY ALL JUST STOPPED FIGHTING.
THEY'RE STIFF AS BOARDS.
Ahem!
THEY SAID THEY WERE PROGRAMMED TO PREVENT US FROM GETTIN' THE ANTIDOTE.
MAYBE SOME CLEVER LITTLE BLACK KID HACKED INTO THE SYSTEM HERE AND REPROGRAMMED 'EM.
SO, TELL ME, WHO'S "USELESS" NOW?
Y'KNOW, I WAS JUST THINKING ABOUT TRYING THAT.
OF COURSE YOU WERE.
EXXY, I GUESS YOU DESERVE THE HONORS AFTER MAKING IT POSSIBLE FOR US TO GET THIS.
THANKS, IRON GIANT.

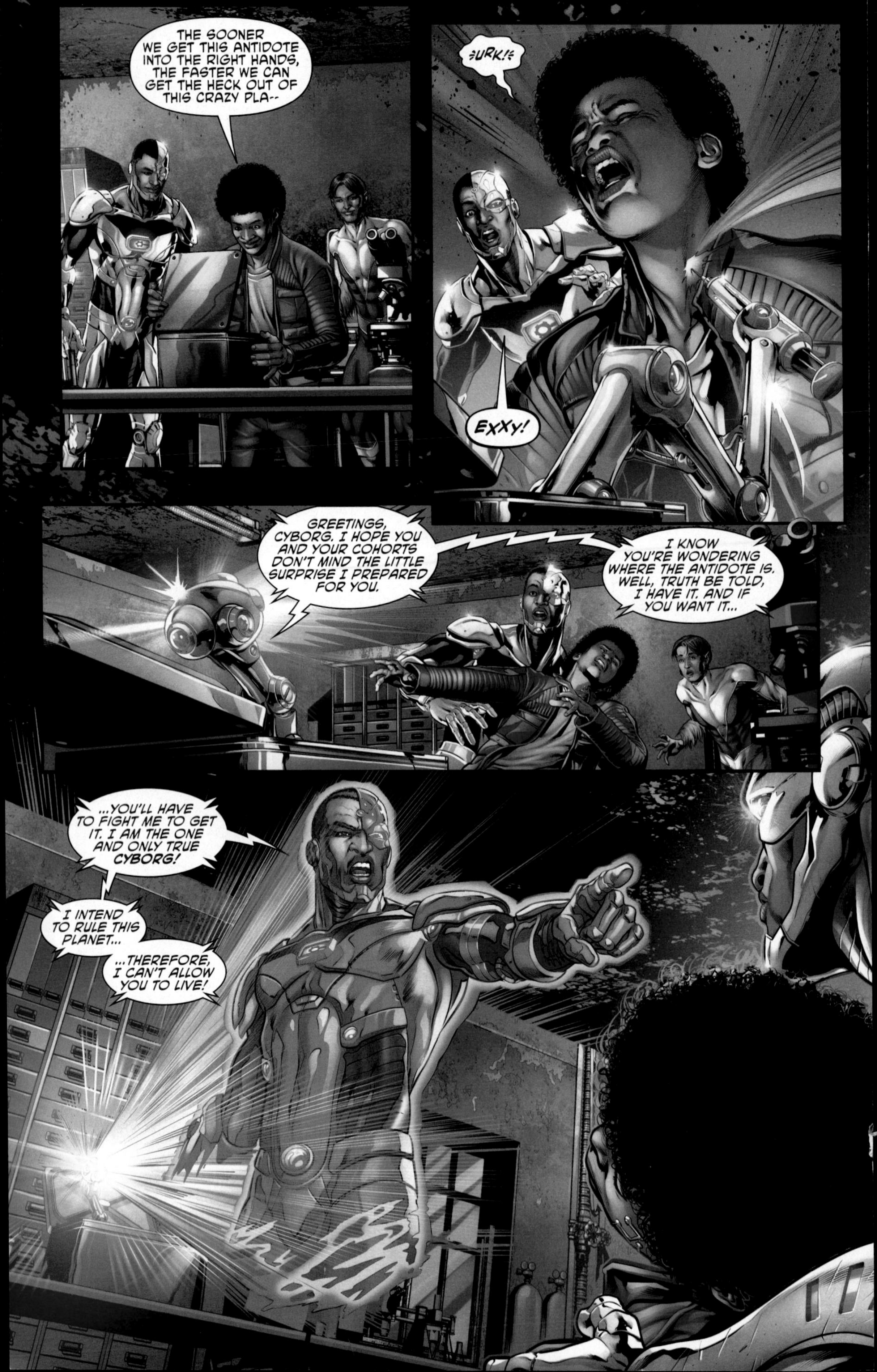
THE SOONER WE GET THIS ANTIDOTE INTO THE RIGHT HANDS, THE FASTER WE CAN GET THE HECK OUT OF THIS CRAZY PLA--
URK!
EXXY!
GREETINGS, CYBORG. I HOPE YOU AND YOUR COHORTS DON'T MIND THE LITTLE SURPRISE I PREPARED FOR YOU.
I KNOW YOU'RE WONDERING WHERE THE ANTIDOTE IS. WELL, TRUTH BE TOLD, I HAVE IT. AND IF YOU WANT IT...
...YOU'LL HAVE TO FIGHT ME TO GET IT. I AM THE ONE AND ONLY TRUE CYBORG!
I INTEND TO RULE THIS PLANET...
...THEREFORE, I CAN'T ALLOW YOU TO LIVE!

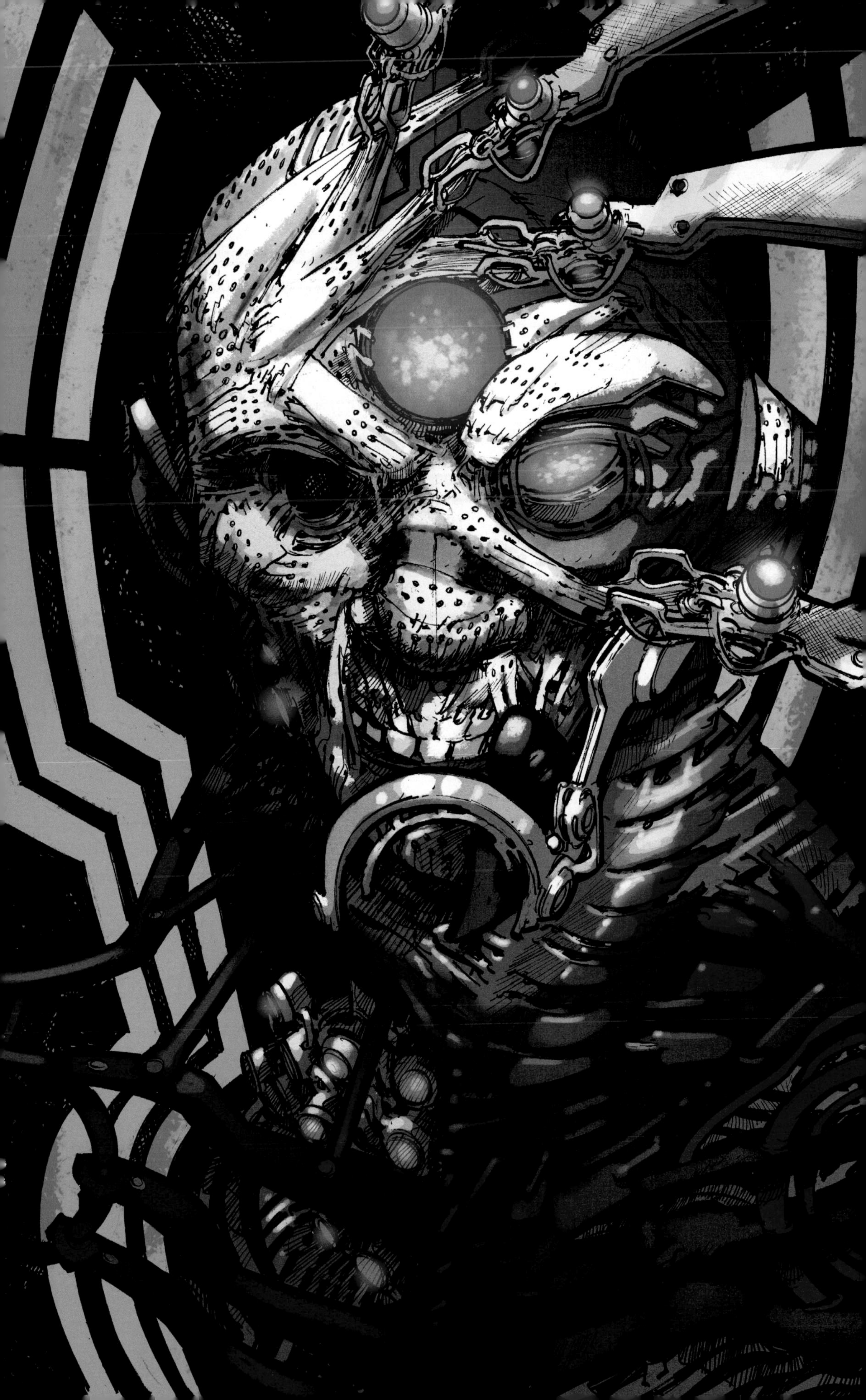

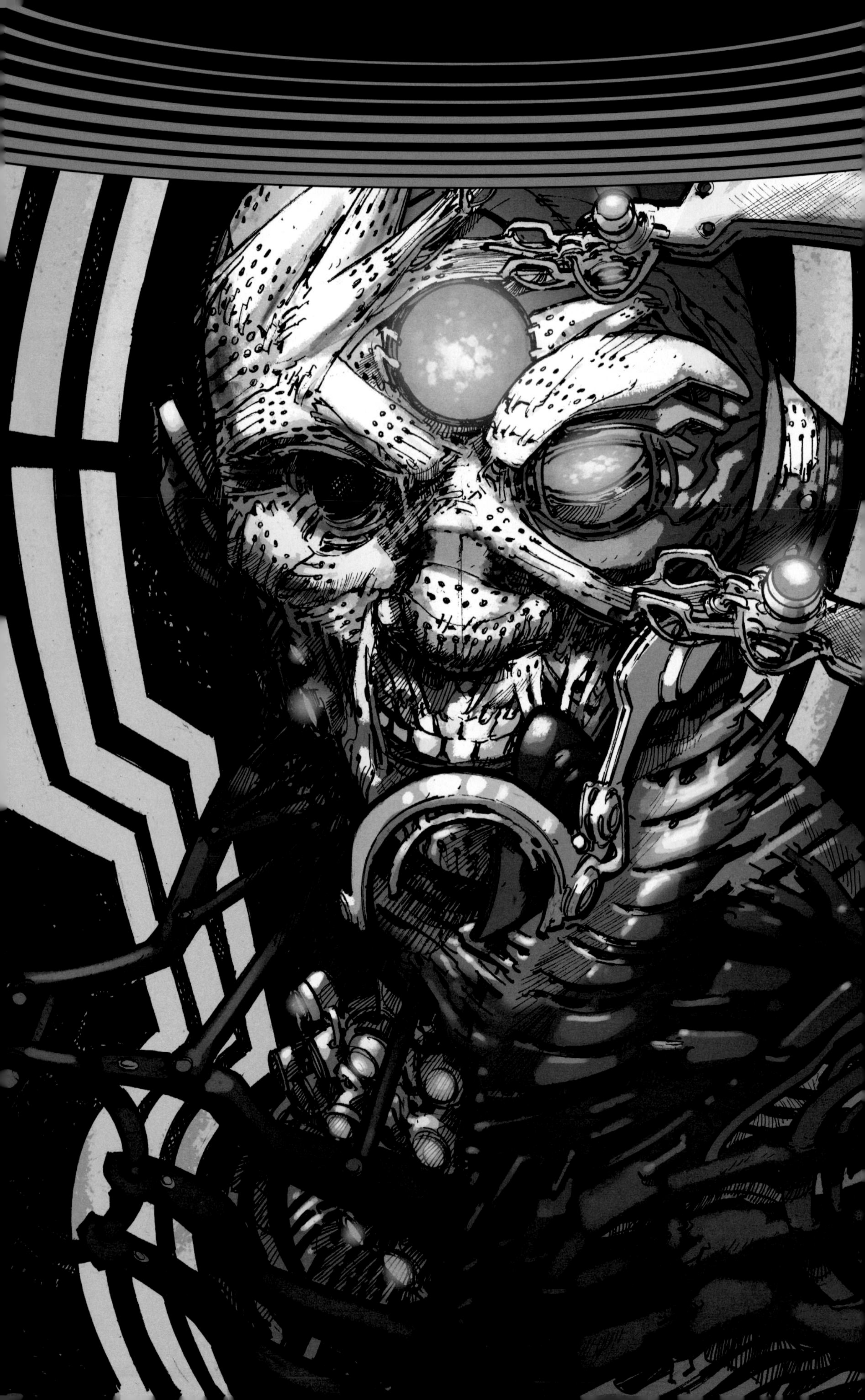

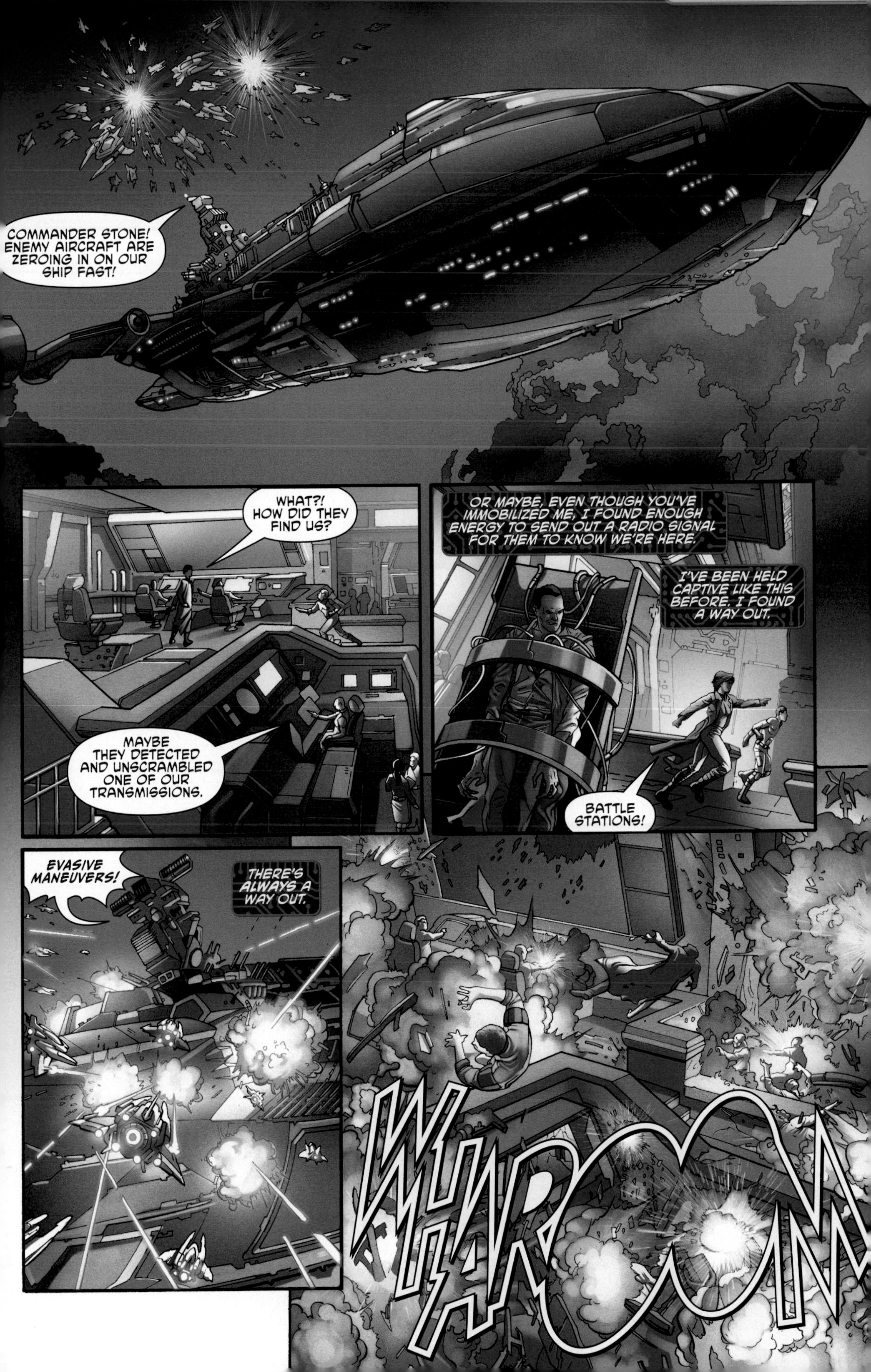
COMMANDER STONE! ENEMY AIRCRAFT ARE ZEROING IN ON OUR SHIP FAST!
WHAT?! HOW DID THEY FIND US?
MAYBE THEY DETECTED AND UNSCRAMBLED ONE OF OUR TRANSMISSIONS.
OR MAYBE, EVEN THOUGH YOU'VE IMMOBILIZED ME, I FOUND ENOUGH ENERGY TO SEND OUT A RADIO SIGNAL FOR THEM TO KNOW WE'RE HERE.
I'VE BEEN HELD CAPTIVE LIKE THIS BEFORE. I FOUND A WAY OUT.
BATTLE STATIONS!
EVASIVE MANEUVERS!
THERE'S ALWAYS A WAY OUT.
WHROOM

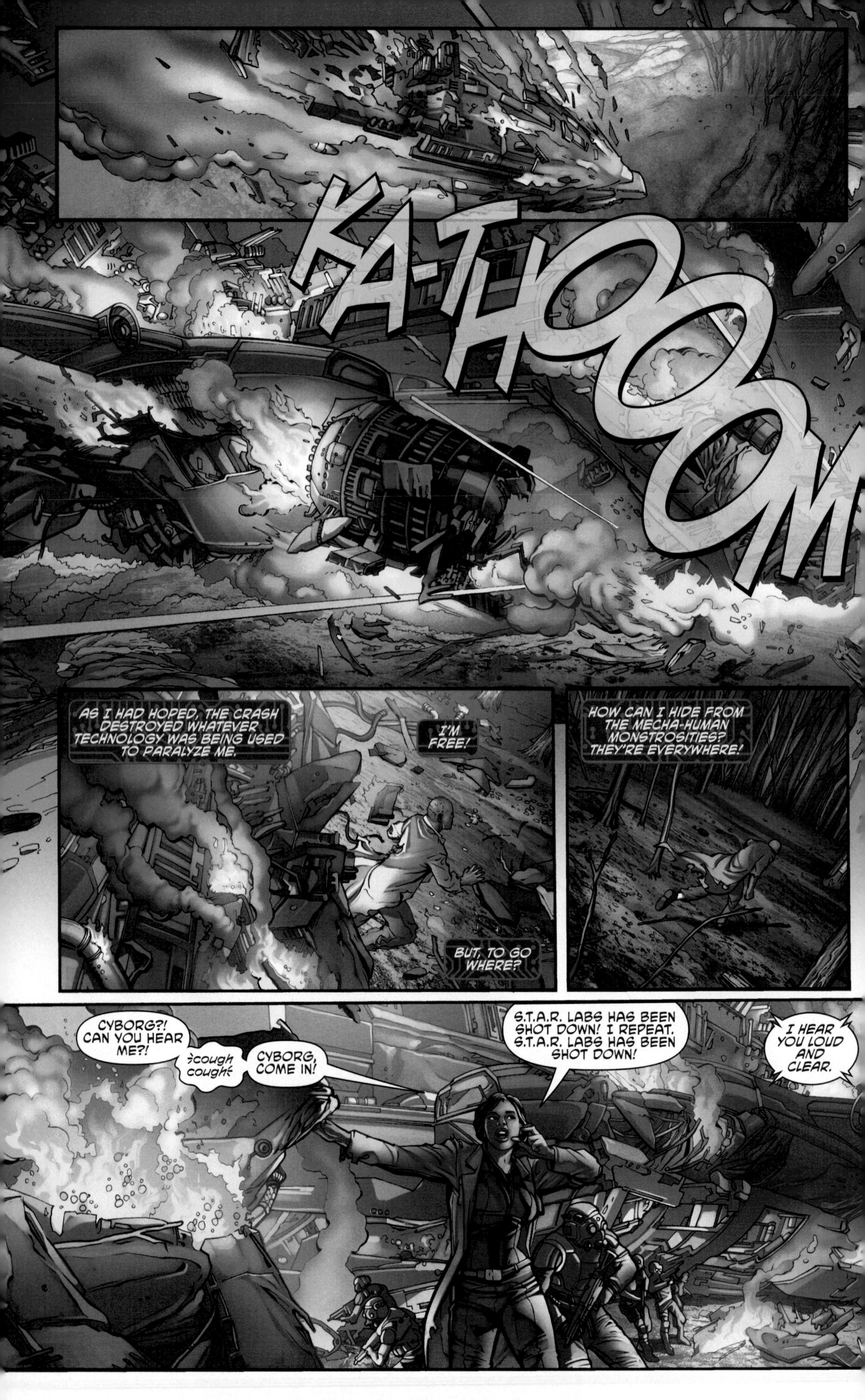
KA-THOOOM
AS I HAD HOPED, THE CRASH DESTROYED WHATEVER TECHNOLOGY WAS BEING USED TO PARALYZE ME.
I'M FREE!
BUT, TO GO WHERE?
HOW CAN I HIDE FROM THE MECHA-HUMAN MONSTROSITIES? THEY'RE EVERYWHERE!
CYBORG?! CAN YOU HEAR ME?!
cough cough
CYBORG, COME IN!
S.T.A.R. LABS HAS BEEN SHOT DOWN! I REPEAT. S.T.A.R. LABS HAS BEEN SHOT DOWN!
I HEAR YOU LOUD AND CLEAR.

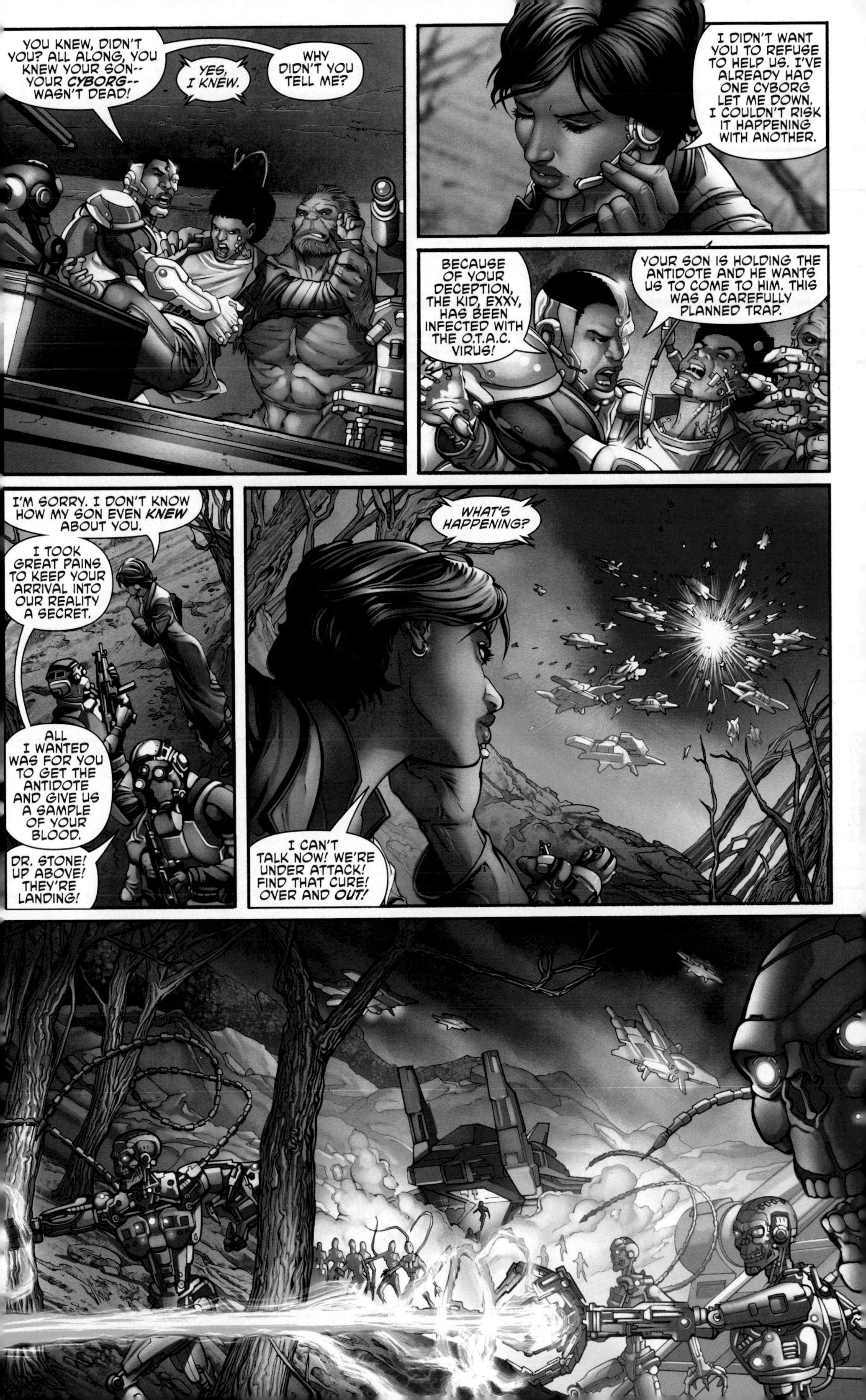
YOU KNEW, DIDN'T YOU? ALL ALONG, YOU KNEW YOUR SON-- YOUR CYBORG-- WASN'T DEAD!
YES, I KNEW.
WHY DIDN'T YOU TELL ME?
I DIDN'T WANT YOU TO REFUSE TO HELP US. I'VE ALREADY HAD ONE CYBORG LET ME DOWN. I COULDN'T RISK IT HAPPENING WITH ANOTHER.
BECAUSE OF YOUR DECEPTION, THE KID, EXXY, HAS BEEN INFECTED WITH THE O.T.A.C. VIRUS!
YOUR SON IS HOLDING THE ANTIDOTE AND HE WANTS US TO COME TO HIM. THIS WAS A CAREFULLY PLANNED TRAP.
I'M SORRY. I DON'T KNOW HOW MY SON EVEN KNEW ABOUT YOU.
I TOOK GREAT PAINS TO KEEP YOUR ARRIVAL INTO OUR REALITY A SECRET.
ALL I WANTED WAS FOR YOU TO GET THE ANTIDOTE AND GIVE US A SAMPLE OF YOUR BLOOD.
DR. STONE! UP ABOVE! THEY'RE LANDING!
WHAT'S HAPPENING?
I CAN'T TALK NOW! WE'RE UNDER ATTACK! FIND THAT CURE! OVER AND OUT!

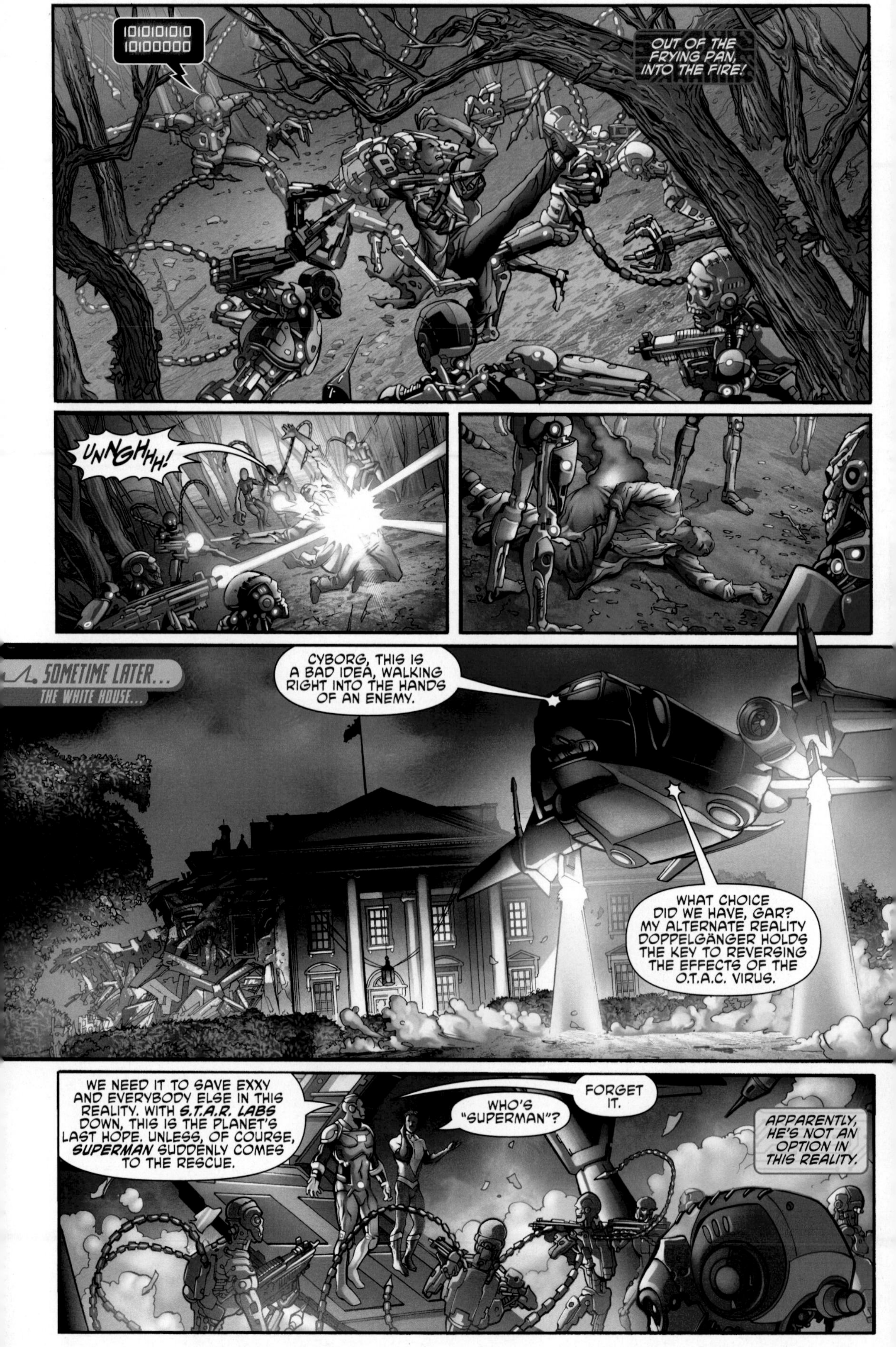
1010101010
10100000
OUT OF THE FRYING PAN, INTO THE FIRE!
UNNGHHH!
SOMETIME LATER... THE WHITE HOUSE...
CYBORG, THIS IS A BAD IDEA, WALKING RIGHT INTO THE HANDS OF AN ENEMY.
WHAT CHOICE DID WE HAVE, GAR? MY ALTERNATE REALITY DOPPELGÄNGER HOLDS THE KEY TO REVERSING THE EFFECTS OF THE O.T.A.C. VIRUS.
WE NEED IT TO SAVE EXXY AND EVERYBODY ELSE IN THIS REALITY. WITH S.T.A.R. LABS DOWN, THIS IS THE PLANET'S LAST HOPE. UNLESS, OF COURSE, SUPERMAN SUDDENLY COMES TO THE RESCUE.
WHO'S "SUPERMAN"?
FORGET IT.
APPARENTLY, HE'S NOT AN OPTION IN THIS REALITY.

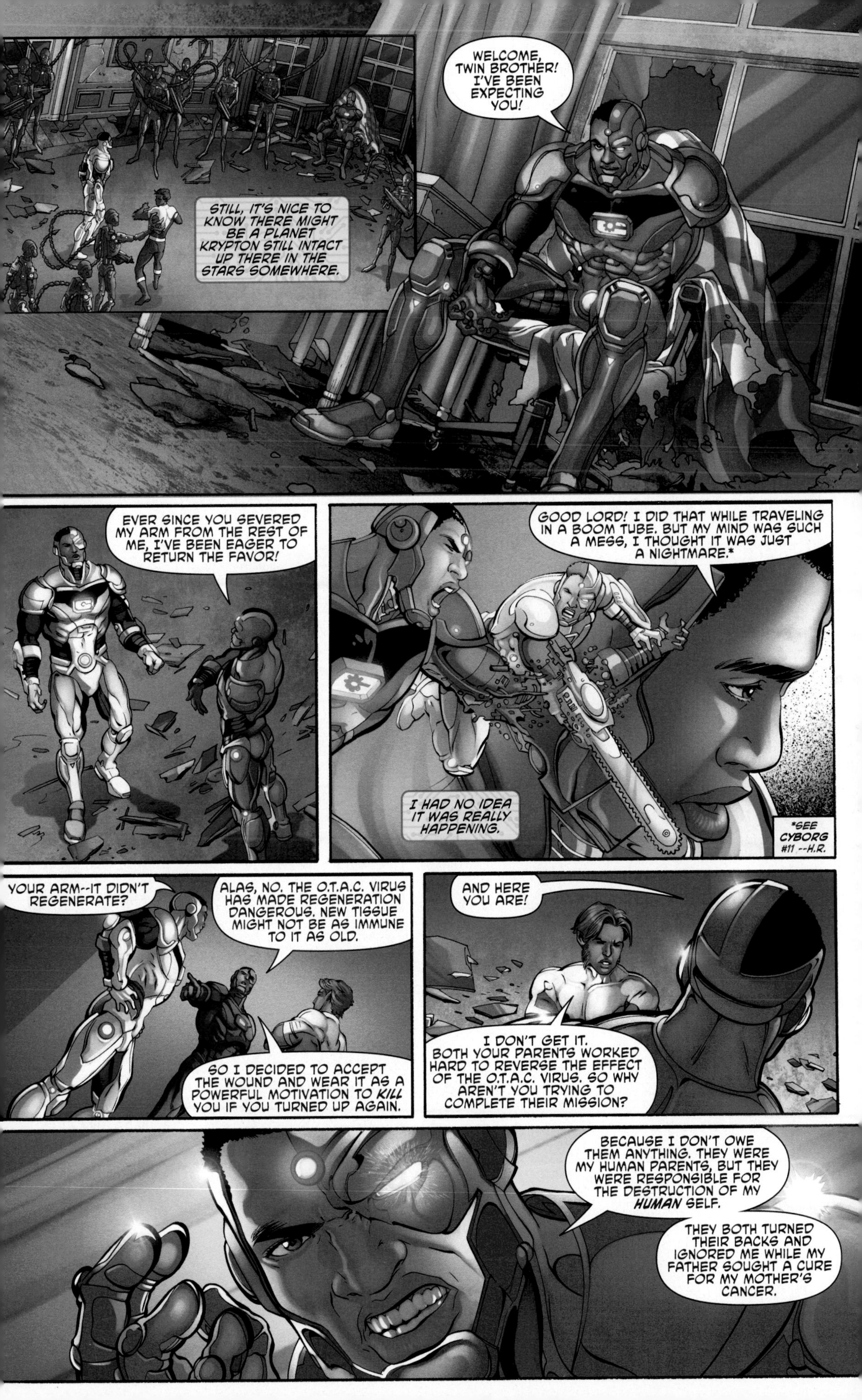
STILL, IT'S NICE TO KNOW THERE MIGHT BE A PLANET KRYPTON STILL INTACT UP THERE IN THE STARS SOMEWHERE.
WELCOME, TWIN BROTHER! I'VE BEEN EXPECTING YOU!
EVER SINCE YOU SEVERED MY ARM FROM THE REST OF ME, I'VE BEEN EAGER TO RETURN THE FAVOR!
GOOD LORD! I DID THAT WHILE TRAVELING IN A BOOM TUBE. BUT MY MIND WAS SUCH A MESS, I THOUGHT IT WAS JUST A NIGHTMARE.*
I HAD NO IDEA IT WAS REALLY HAPPENING.
*SEE CYBORG #11 --H.R.
YOUR ARM--IT DIDN'T REGENERATE?
ALAS, NO. THE O.T.A.C. VIRUS HAS MADE REGENERATION DANGEROUS. NEW TISSUE MIGHT NOT BE AS IMMUNE TO IT AS OLD.
SO I DECIDED TO ACCEPT THE WOUND AND WEAR IT AS A POWERFUL MOTIVATION TO KILL YOU IF YOU TURNED UP AGAIN.
AND HERE YOU ARE!
I DON'T GET IT. BOTH YOUR PARENTS WORKED HARD TO REVERSE THE EFFECT OF THE O.T.A.C. VIRUS. SO WHY AREN'T YOU TRYING TO COMPLETE THEIR MISSION?
BECAUSE I DON'T OWE THEM ANYTHING. THEY WERE MY HUMAN PARENTS, BUT THEY WERE RESPONSIBLE FOR THE DESTRUCTION OF MY HUMAN SELF.
THEY BOTH TURNED THEIR BACKS AND IGNORED ME WHILE MY FATHER SOUGHT A CURE FOR MY MOTHER'S CANCER.

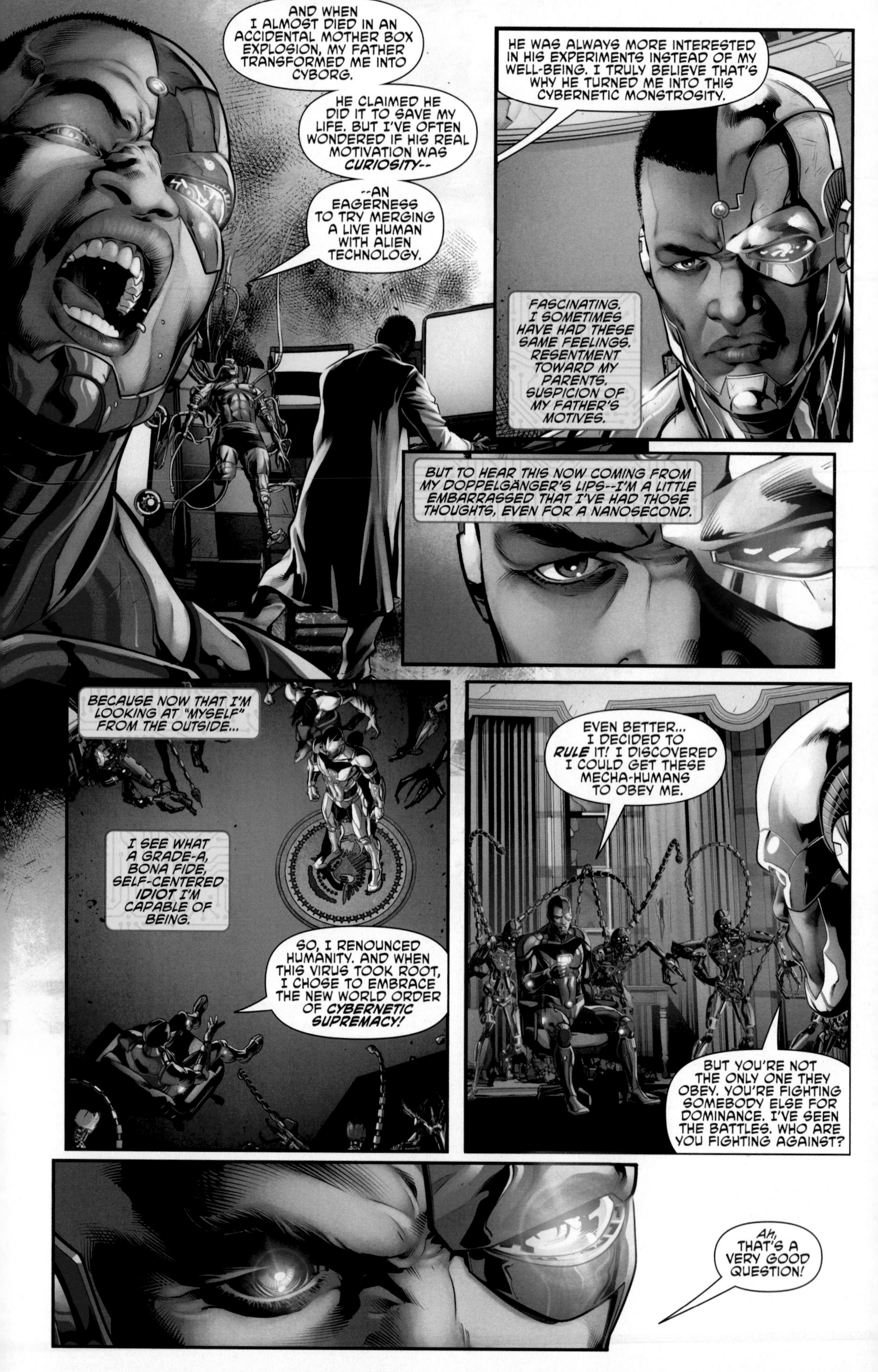
AND WHEN I ALMOST DIED IN AN ACCIDENTAL MOTHER BOX EXPLOSION, MY FATHER TRANSFORMED ME INTO CYBORG.
HE CLAIMED HE DID IT TO SAVE MY LIFE. BUT I'VE OFTEN WONDERED IF HIS REAL MOTIVATION WAS *CURIOSITY*--
--AN EAGERNESS TO TRY MERGING A LIVE HUMAN WITH ALIEN TECHNOLOGY.
HE WAS ALWAYS MORE INTERESTED IN HIS EXPERIMENTS INSTEAD OF MY WELL-BEING. I TRULY BELIEVE THAT'S WHY HE TURNED ME INTO THIS CYBERNETIC MONSTROSITY.
FASCINATING. I SOMETIMES HAVE HAD THESE SAME FEELINGS. RESENTMENT TOWARD MY PARENTS. SUSPICION OF MY FATHER'S MOTIVES.
BUT TO HEAR THIS NOW COMING FROM MY DOPPELGÄNGER'S LIPS--I'M A LITTLE EMBARRASSED THAT I'VE HAD THOSE THOUGHTS, EVEN FOR A NANOSECOND.
BECAUSE NOW THAT I'M LOOKING AT "MYSELF" FROM THE OUTSIDE...
I SEE WHAT A GRADE-A, BONA FIDE, SELF-CENTERED IDIOT I'M CAPABLE OF BEING.
SO, I RENOUNCED HUMANITY. AND WHEN THIS VIRUS TOOK ROOT, I CHOSE TO EMBRACE THE NEW WORLD ORDER OF ***CYBERNETIC SUPREMACY!***
EVEN BETTER... I DECIDED TO ***RULE*** IT! I DISCOVERED I COULD GET THESE MECHA-HUMANS TO OBEY ME.
BUT YOU'RE NOT THE ONLY ONE THEY OBEY. YOU'RE FIGHTING SOMEBODY ELSE FOR DOMINANCE. I'VE SEEN THE BATTLES. WHO ARE YOU FIGHTING AGAINST?
Ah, THAT'S A VERY GOOD QUESTION!

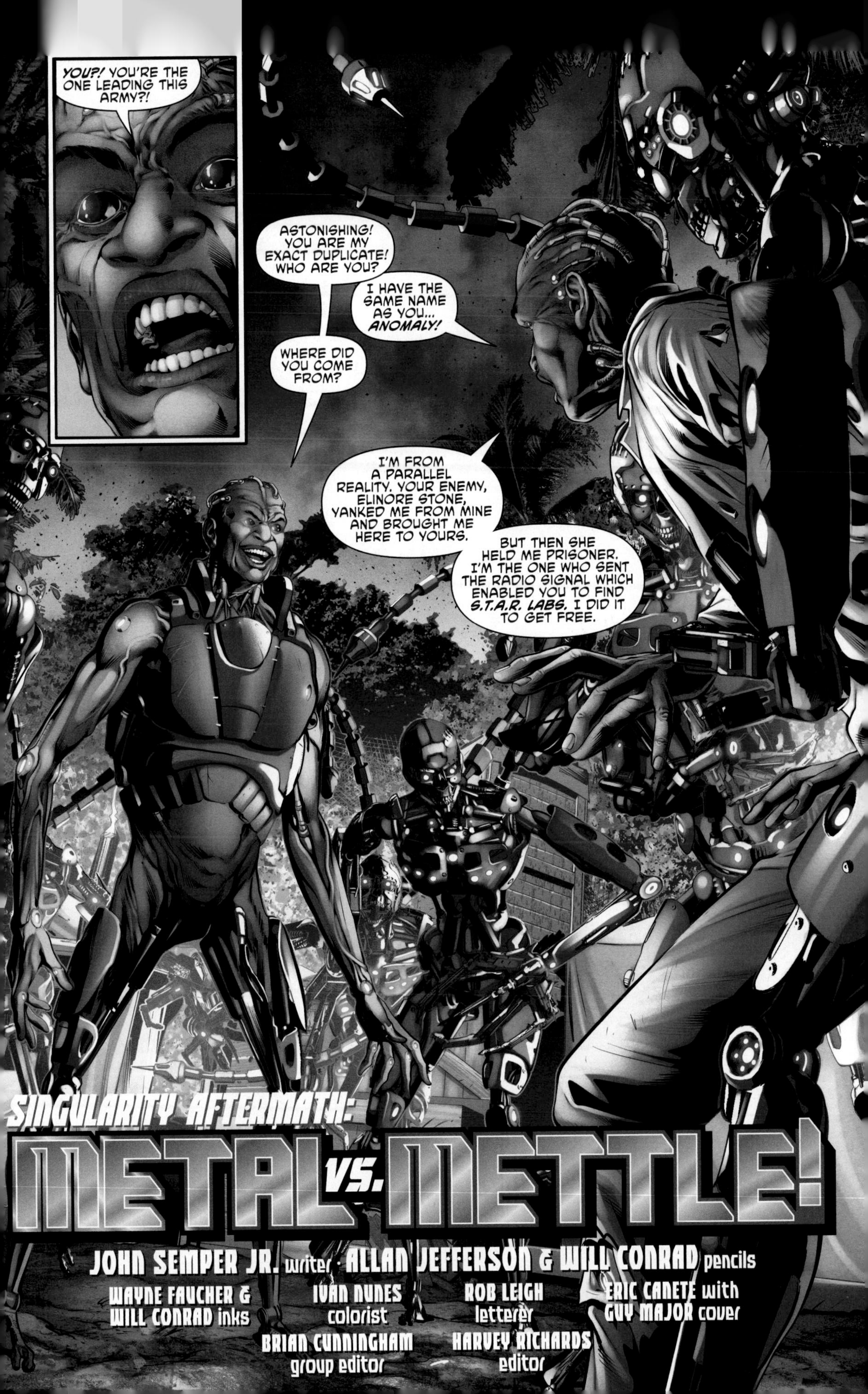
YOU?! YOU'RE THE ONE LEADING THIS ARMY?!
ASTONISHING! YOU ARE MY EXACT DUPLICATE! WHO ARE YOU?
I HAVE THE SAME NAME AS YOU... ANOMALY!
WHERE DID YOU COME FROM?
I'M FROM A PARALLEL REALITY. YOUR ENEMY, ELINORE STONE, YANKED ME FROM MINE AND BROUGHT ME HERE TO YOURS.
BUT THEN SHE HELD ME PRISONER. I'M THE ONE WHO SENT THE RADIO SIGNAL WHICH ENABLED YOU TO FIND S.T.A.R. LABS. I DID IT TO GET FREE.
SINGULARITY AFTERMATH:
METAL VS. METTLE!
JOHN SEMPER JR. writer · ALLAN JEFFERSON & WILL CONRAD pencils
WAYNE FAUCHER & WILL CONRAD inks
IVAN NUNES colorist
ROB LEIGH letterer
ERIC CANETE with GUY MAJOR cover
BRIAN CUNNINGHAM group editor
HARVEY RICHARDS editor

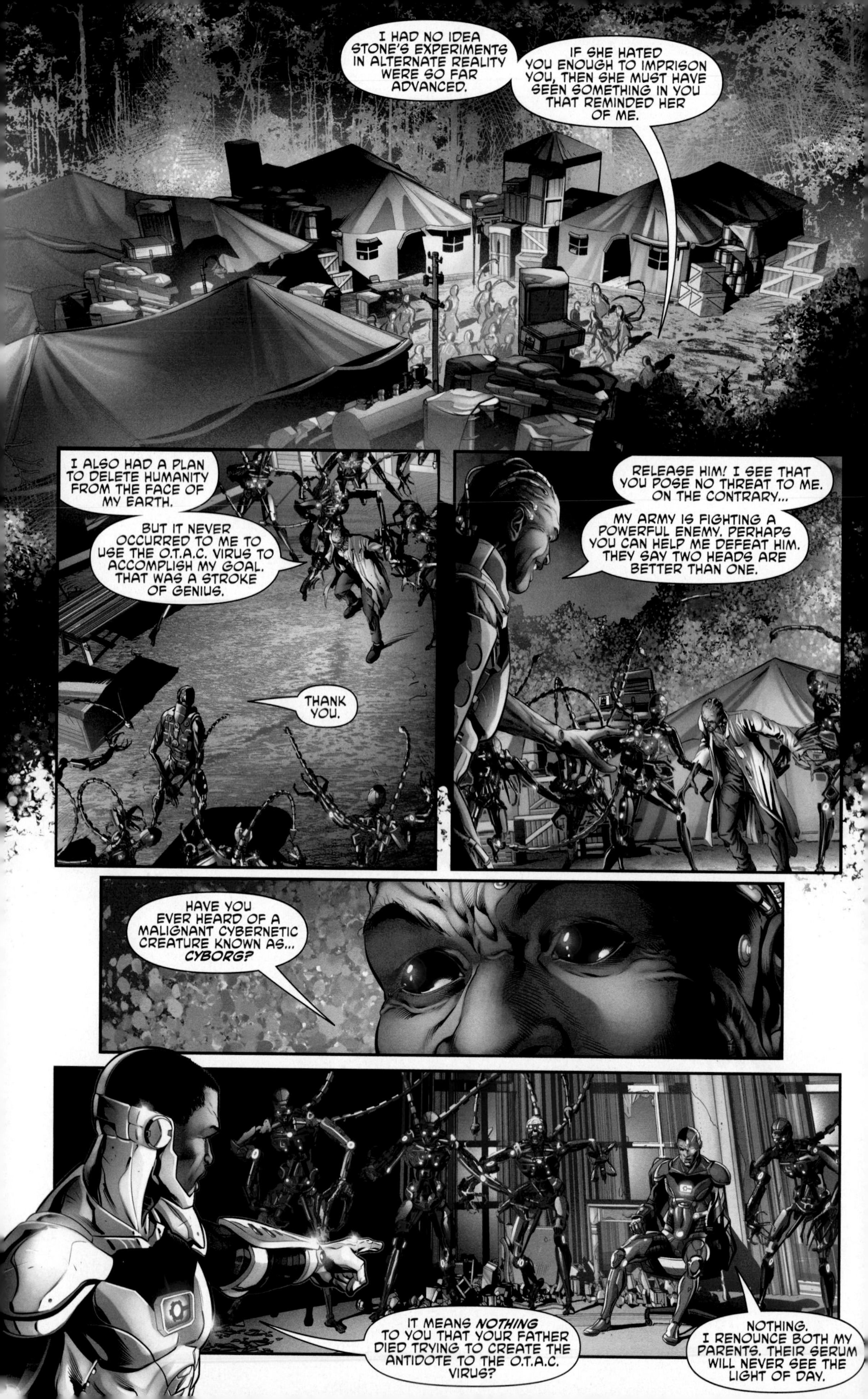
I HAD NO IDEA STONE'S EXPERIMENTS IN ALTERNATE REALITY WERE SO FAR ADVANCED.
IF SHE HATED YOU ENOUGH TO IMPRISON YOU, THEN SHE MUST HAVE SEEN SOMETHING IN YOU THAT REMINDED HER OF ME.
I ALSO HAD A PLAN TO DELETE HUMANITY FROM THE FACE OF MY EARTH.
BUT IT NEVER OCCURRED TO ME TO USE THE O.T.A.C. VIRUS TO ACCOMPLISH MY GOAL. THAT WAS A STROKE OF GENIUS.
THANK YOU.
RELEASE HIM! I SEE THAT YOU POSE NO THREAT TO ME. ON THE CONTRARY...
MY ARMY IS FIGHTING A POWERFUL ENEMY. PERHAPS YOU CAN HELP ME DEFEAT HIM. THEY SAY TWO HEADS ARE BETTER THAN ONE.
HAVE YOU EVER HEARD OF A MALIGNANT CYBERNETIC CREATURE KNOWN AS... *CYBORG?*
IT MEANS *NOTHING* TO YOU THAT YOUR FATHER DIED TRYING TO CREATE THE ANTIDOTE TO THE O.T.A.C. VIRUS?
NOTHING. I RENOUNCE BOTH MY PARENTS. THEIR SERUM WILL NEVER SEE THE LIGHT OF DAY.

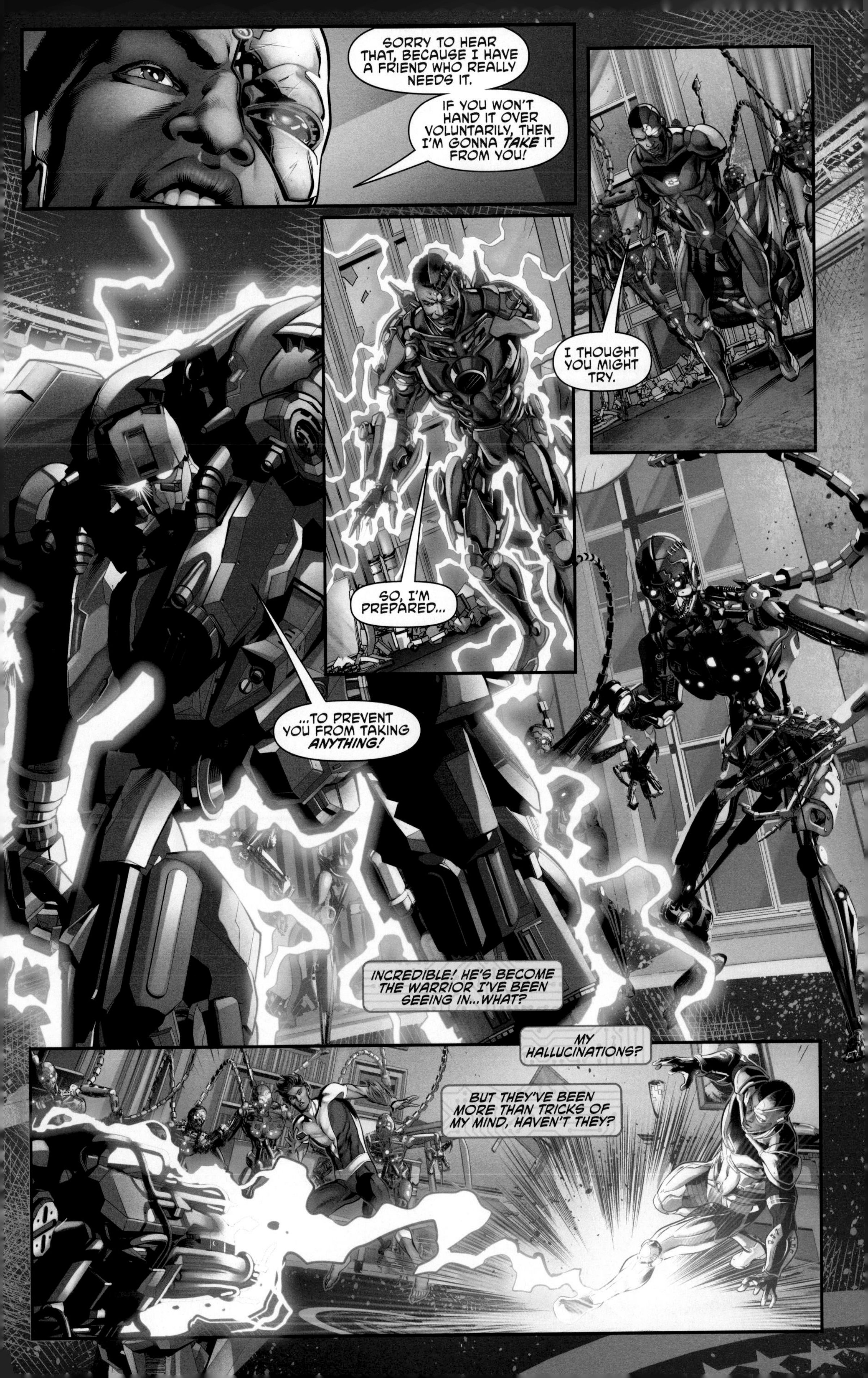
SORRY TO HEAR THAT, BECAUSE I HAVE A FRIEND WHO REALLY NEEDS IT.
IF YOU WON'T HAND IT OVER VOLUNTARILY, THEN I'M GONNA *TAKE* IT FROM YOU!
I THOUGHT YOU MIGHT TRY.
SO, I'M PREPARED...
...TO PREVENT YOU FROM TAKING *ANYTHING!*
INCREDIBLE! HE'S BECOME THE WARRIOR I'VE BEEN SEEING IN...WHAT?
MY HALLUCINATIONS?
BUT THEY'VE BEEN MORE THAN TRICKS OF MY MIND, HAVEN'T THEY?

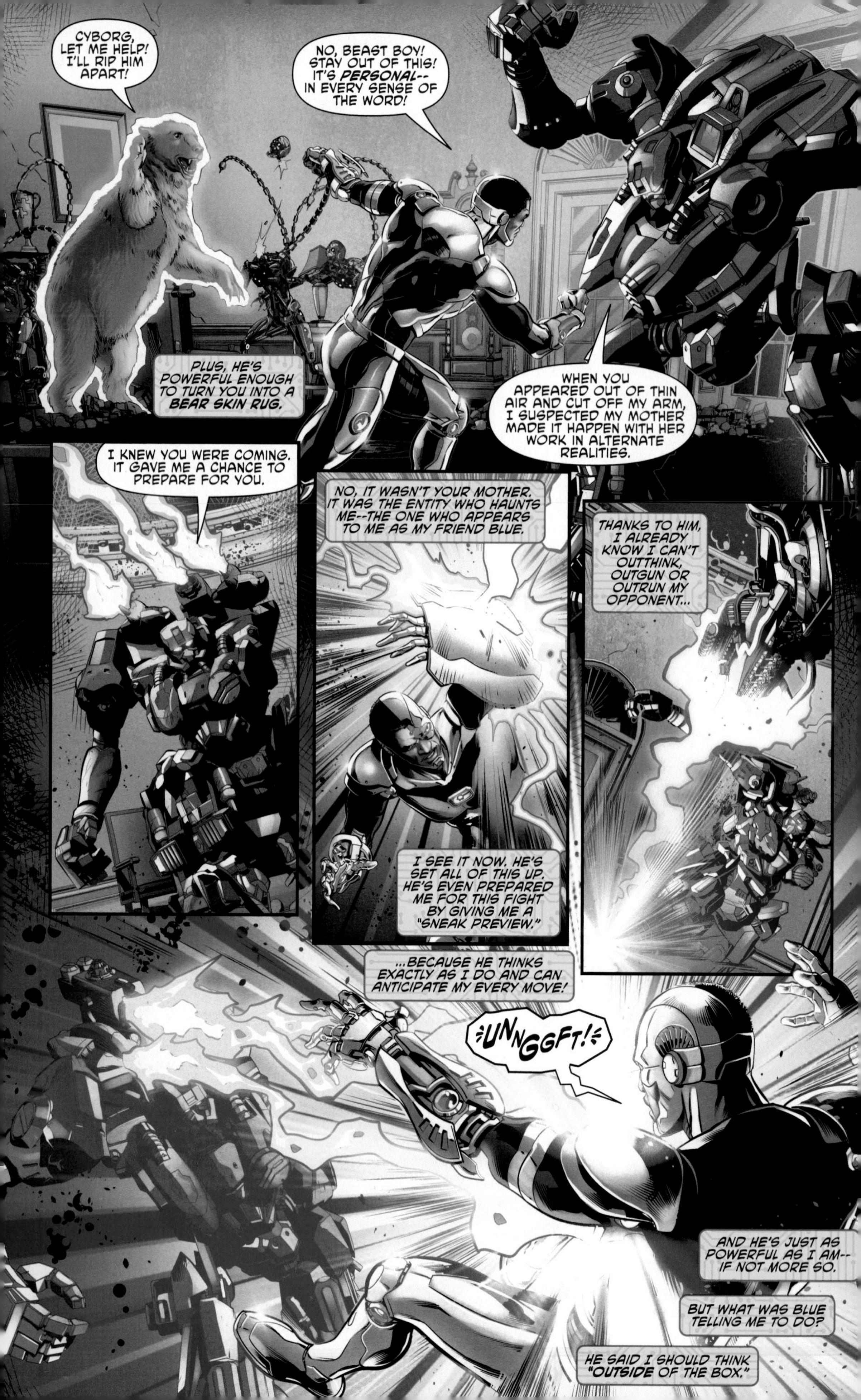
CYBORG, LET ME HELP! I'LL RIP HIM APART!
NO, BEAST BOY! STAY OUT OF THIS! IT'S PERSONAL-- IN EVERY SENSE OF THE WORD!
PLUS, HE'S POWERFUL ENOUGH TO TURN YOU INTO A BEAR SKIN RUG.
WHEN YOU APPEARED OUT OF THIN AIR AND CUT OFF MY ARM, I SUSPECTED MY MOTHER MADE IT HAPPEN WITH HER WORK IN ALTERNATE REALITIES.
I KNEW YOU WERE COMING. IT GAVE ME A CHANCE TO PREPARE FOR YOU.
NO, IT WASN'T YOUR MOTHER. IT WAS THE ENTITY WHO HAUNTS ME--THE ONE WHO APPEARS TO ME AS MY FRIEND BLUE.
I SEE IT NOW. HE'S SET ALL OF THIS UP. HE'S EVEN PREPARED ME FOR THIS FIGHT BY GIVING ME A "SNEAK PREVIEW."
THANKS TO HIM, I ALREADY KNOW I CAN'T OUTTHINK, OUTGUN OR OUTRUN MY OPPONENT...
...BECAUSE HE THINKS EXACTLY AS I DO AND CAN ANTICIPATE MY EVERY MOVE!
UNNGGFT!
AND HE'S JUST AS POWERFUL AS I AM-- IF NOT MORE SO.
BUT WHAT WAS BLUE TELLING ME TO DO?
HE SAID I SHOULD THINK "OUTSIDE OF THE BOX."

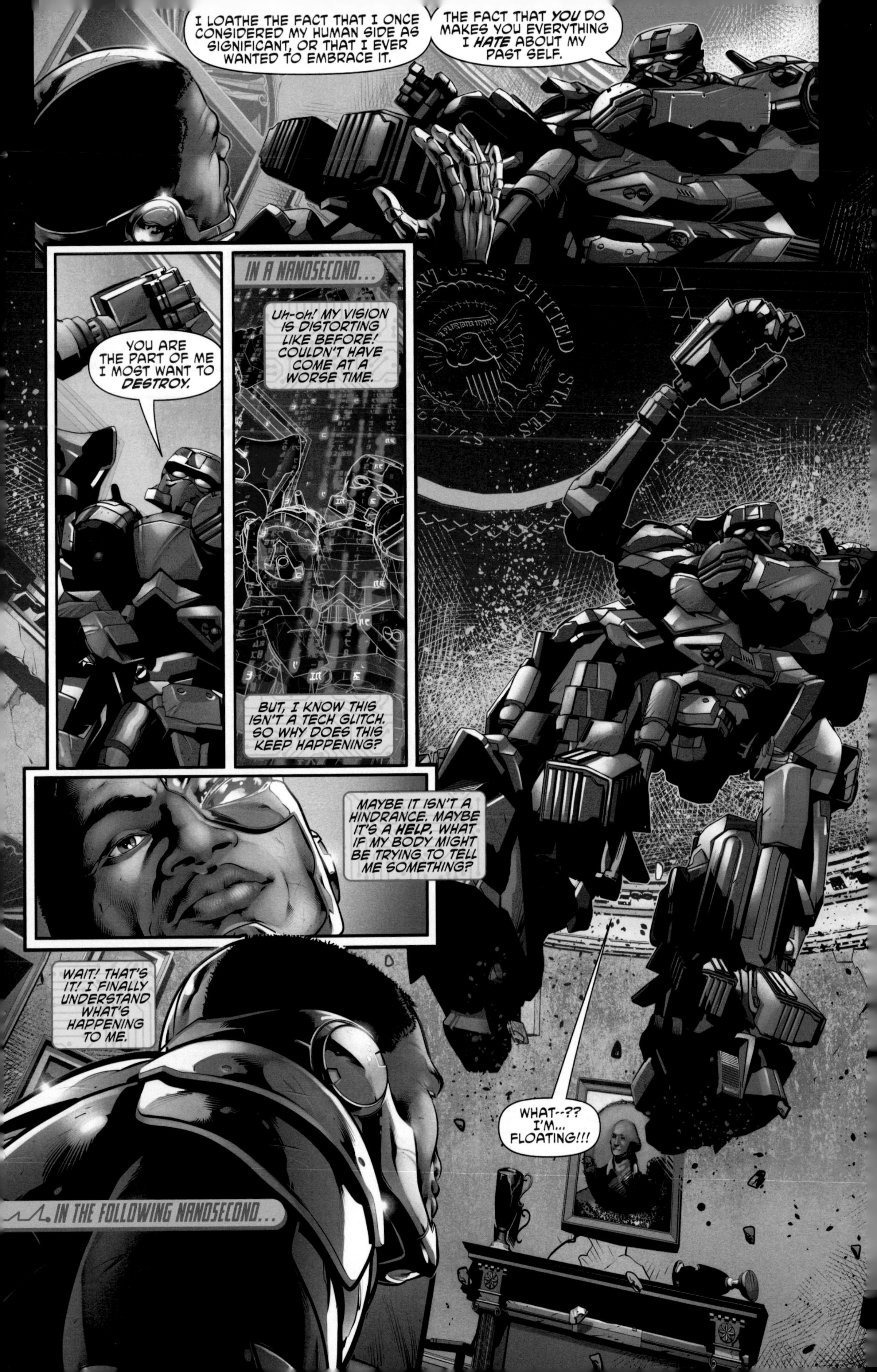
I LOATHE THE FACT THAT I ONCE CONSIDERED MY HUMAN SIDE AS SIGNIFICANT, OR THAT I EVER WANTED TO EMBRACE IT.
THE FACT THAT YOU DO MAKES YOU EVERYTHING I HATE ABOUT MY PAST SELF.
YOU ARE THE PART OF ME I MOST WANT TO DESTROY.
IN A NANOSECOND...
Uh-oh! MY VISION IS DISTORTING LIKE BEFORE! COULDN'T HAVE COME AT A WORSE TIME.
BUT, I KNOW THIS ISN'T A TECH GLITCH. SO WHY DOES THIS KEEP HAPPENING?
MAYBE IT ISN'T A HINDRANCE. MAYBE IT'S A HELP. WHAT IF MY BODY MIGHT BE TRYING TO TELL ME SOMETHING?
WAIT! THAT'S IT! I FINALLY UNDERSTAND WHAT'S HAPPENING TO ME.
...IN THE FOLLOWING NANOSECOND...
WHAT--?? I'M... FLOATING!!!

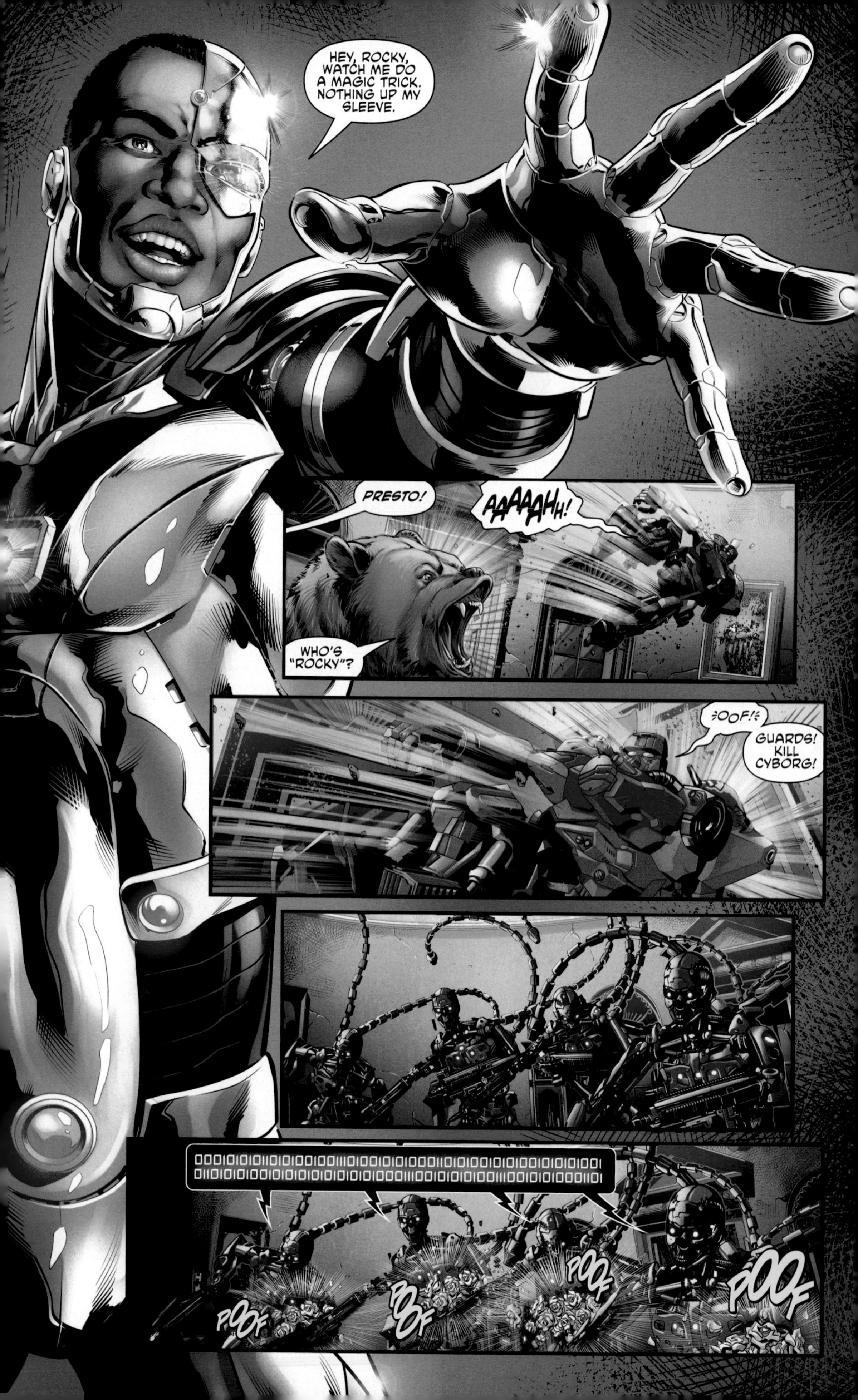
HEY, ROCKY, WATCH ME DO A MAGIC TRICK. NOTHING UP MY SLEEVE.
PRESTO!
AAAAAHH!
WHO'S "ROCKY"?
OOF!
GUARDS! KILL CYBORG!
00010101011010100100111010010101000110101001010100101010101001
011010101001010101010101010001110010101010011100101010001101
POOF
POOF
POOF
POOF

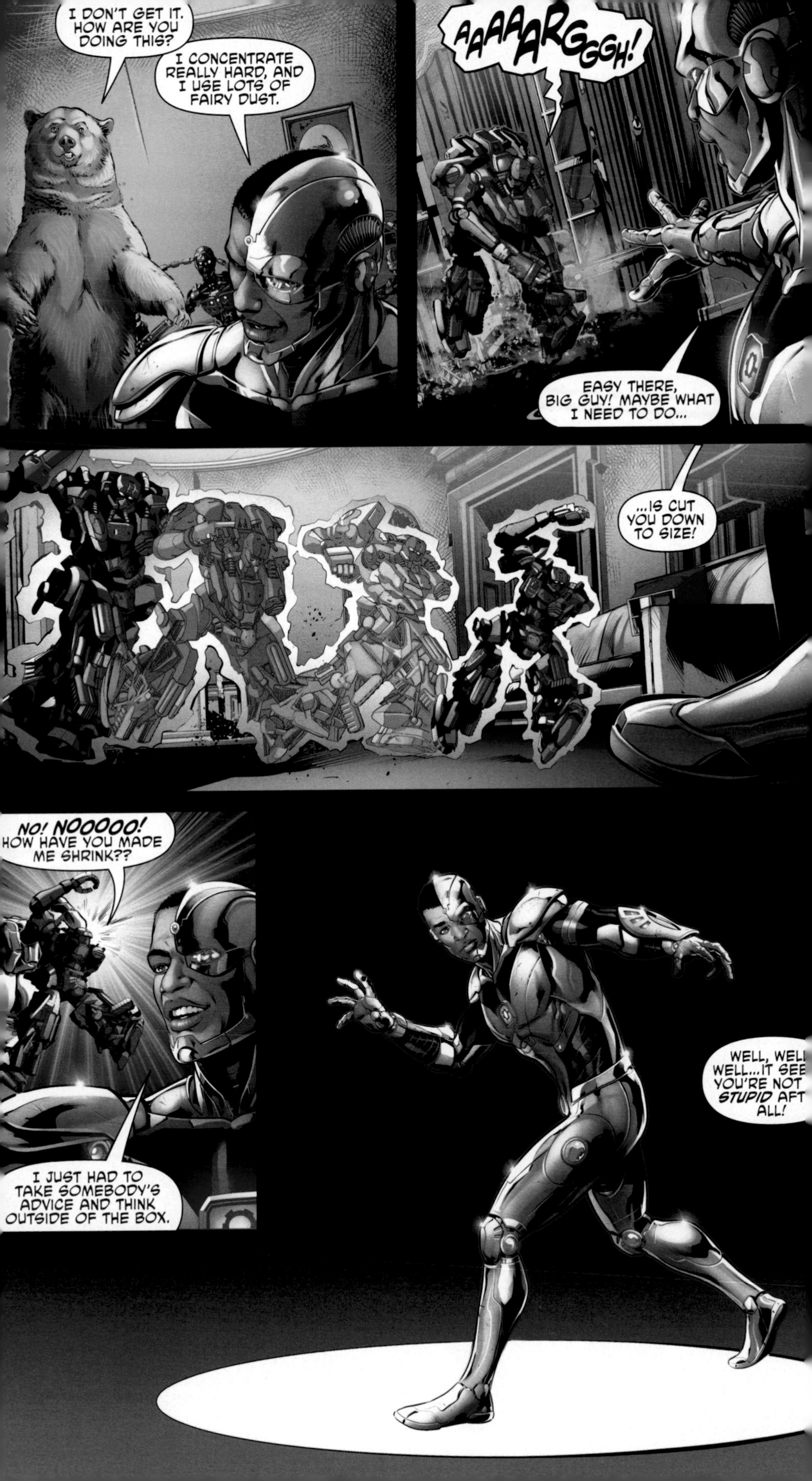
I DON'T GET IT. HOW ARE YOU DOING THIS?
I CONCENTRATE REALLY HARD, AND I USE LOTS OF FAIRY DUST.
AAAAARGGGH!
EASY THERE, BIG GUY! MAYBE WHAT I NEED TO DO...
...IS CUT YOU DOWN TO SIZE!
NO! NOOOOO! HOW HAVE YOU MADE ME SHRINK??
I JUST HAD TO TAKE SOMEBODY'S ADVICE AND THINK OUTSIDE OF THE BOX.
WELL, WELL WELL...IT SEE YOU'RE NOT STUPID AFT ALL!

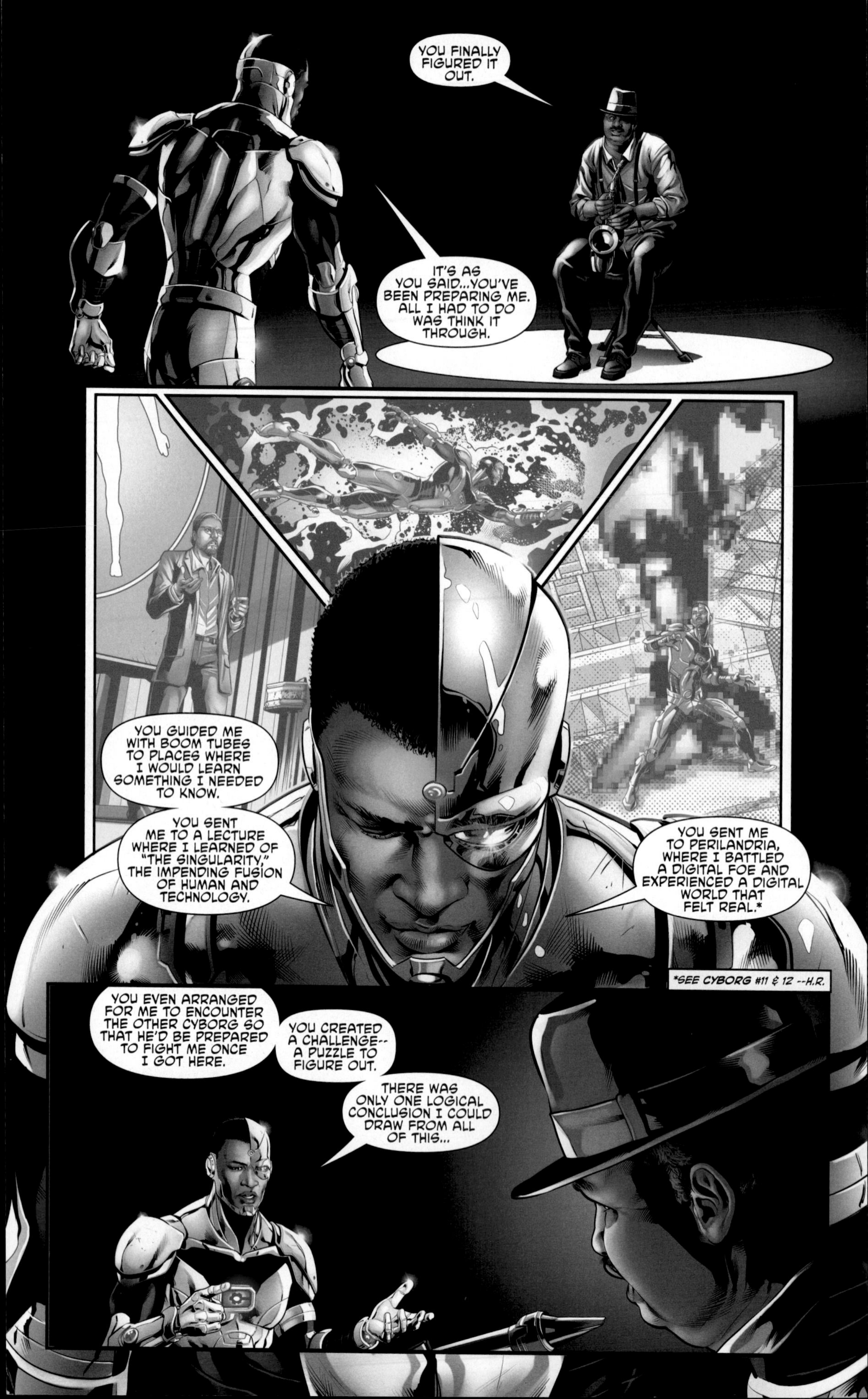

YOU FINALLY FIGURED IT OUT.
IT'S AS YOU SAID...YOU'VE BEEN PREPARING ME. ALL I HAD TO DO WAS THINK IT THROUGH.
YOU GUIDED ME WITH BOOM TUBES TO PLACES WHERE I WOULD LEARN SOMETHING I NEEDED TO KNOW.
YOU SENT ME TO A LECTURE WHERE I LEARNED OF "THE SINGULARITY," THE IMPENDING FUSION OF HUMAN AND TECHNOLOGY.
YOU SENT ME TO PERILANDRIA, WHERE I BATTLED A DIGITAL FOE AND EXPERIENCED A DIGITAL WORLD THAT FELT REAL.*
*SEE CYBORG #11 & 12 --H.R.
YOU EVEN ARRANGED FOR ME TO ENCOUNTER THE OTHER CYBORG SO THAT HE'D BE PREPARED TO FIGHT ME ONCE I GOT HERE.
YOU CREATED A CHALLENGE-- A PUZZLE TO FIGURE OUT.
THERE WAS ONLY ONE LOGICAL CONCLUSION I COULD DRAW FROM ALL OF THIS...

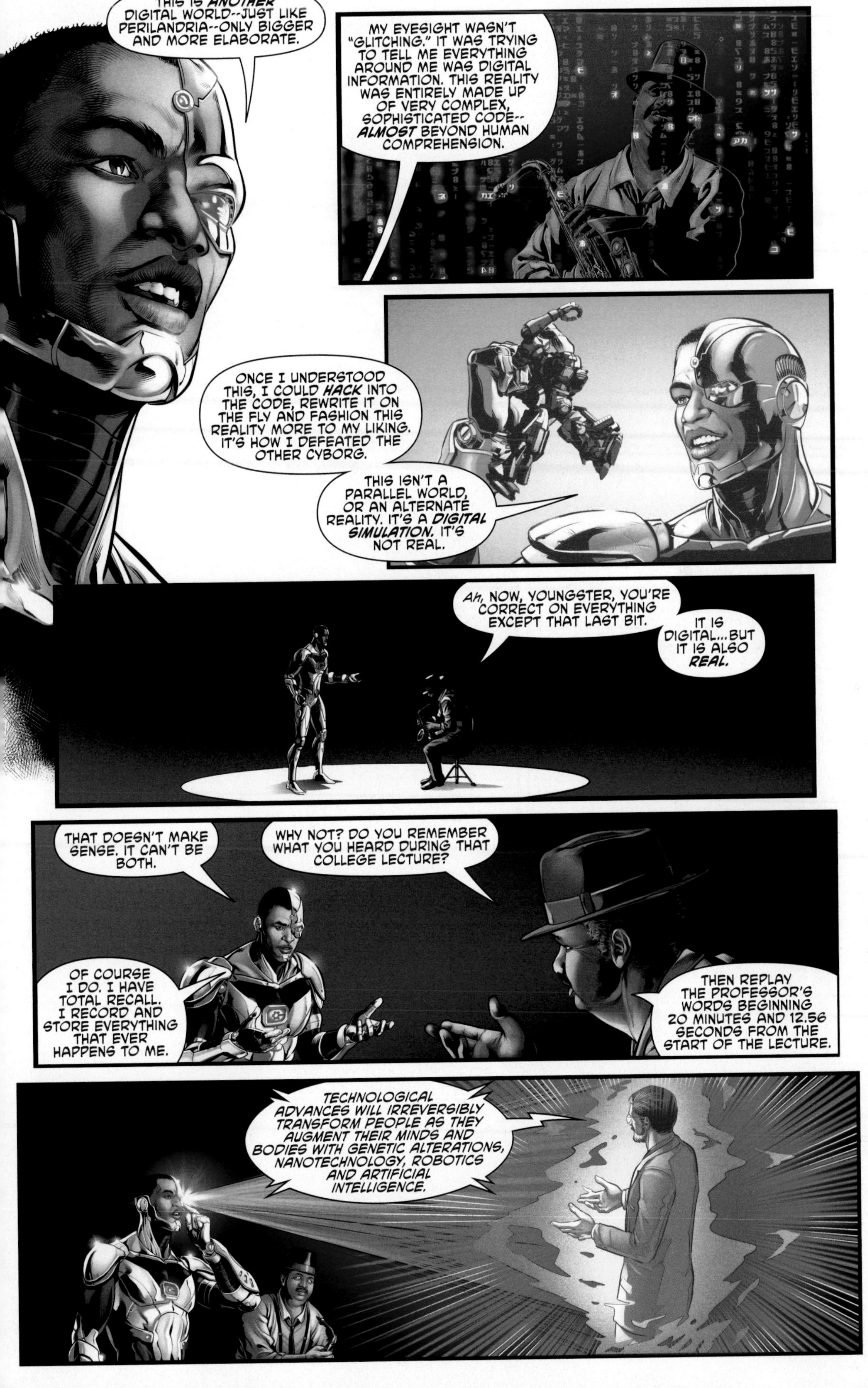
THIS IS ANOTHER DIGITAL WORLD--JUST LIKE PERILANDRIA--ONLY BIGGER AND MORE ELABORATE.
MY EYESIGHT WASN'T "GLITCHING." IT WAS TRYING TO TELL ME EVERYTHING AROUND ME WAS DIGITAL INFORMATION. THIS REALITY WAS ENTIRELY MADE UP OF VERY COMPLEX, SOPHISTICATED CODE-- ALMOST BEYOND HUMAN COMPREHENSION.
ONCE I UNDERSTOOD THIS, I COULD HACK INTO THE CODE, REWRITE IT ON THE FLY AND FASHION THIS REALITY MORE TO MY LIKING. IT'S HOW I DEFEATED THE OTHER CYBORG.
THIS ISN'T A PARALLEL WORLD, OR AN ALTERNATE REALITY. IT'S A DIGITAL SIMULATION. IT'S NOT REAL.
Ah, NOW, YOUNGSTER, YOU'RE CORRECT ON EVERYTHING EXCEPT THAT LAST BIT.
IT IS DIGITAL...BUT IT IS ALSO REAL.
THAT DOESN'T MAKE SENSE. IT CAN'T BE BOTH.
WHY NOT? DO YOU REMEMBER WHAT YOU HEARD DURING THAT COLLEGE LECTURE?
OF COURSE I DO. I HAVE TOTAL RECALL. I RECORD AND STORE EVERYTHING THAT EVER HAPPENS TO ME.
THEN REPLAY THE PROFESSOR'S WORDS BEGINNING 20 MINUTES AND 12.56 SECONDS FROM THE START OF THE LECTURE.
TECHNOLOGICAL ADVANCES WILL IRREVERSIBLY TRANSFORM PEOPLE AS THEY AUGMENT THEIR MINDS AND BODIES WITH GENETIC ALTERATIONS, NANOTECHNOLOGY, ROBOTICS AND ARTIFICIAL INTELLIGENCE.

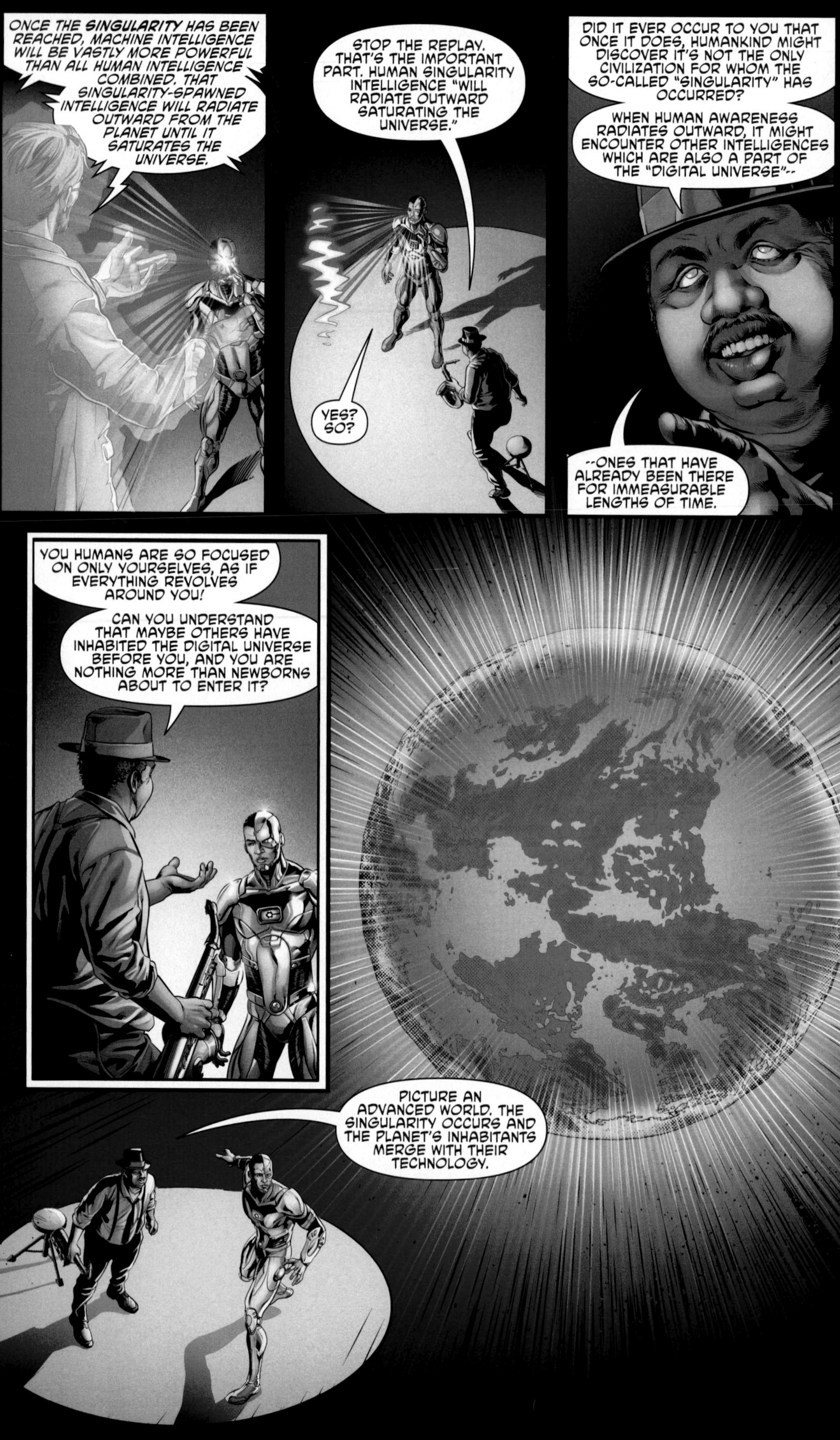
ONCE THE SINGULARITY HAS BEEN REACHED, MACHINE INTELLIGENCE WILL BE VASTLY MORE POWERFUL THAN ALL HUMAN INTELLIGENCE COMBINED. THAT SINGULARITY-SPAWNED INTELLIGENCE WILL RADIATE OUTWARD FROM THE PLANET UNTIL IT SATURATES THE UNIVERSE.
STOP THE REPLAY. THAT'S THE IMPORTANT PART. HUMAN SINGULARITY INTELLIGENCE "WILL RADIATE OUTWARD SATURATING THE UNIVERSE."
YES? SO?
DID IT EVER OCCUR TO YOU THAT ONCE IT DOES, HUMANKIND MIGHT DISCOVER IT'S NOT THE ONLY CIVILIZATION FOR WHOM THE SO-CALLED "SINGULARITY" HAS OCCURRED?
WHEN HUMAN AWARENESS RADIATES OUTWARD, IT MIGHT ENCOUNTER OTHER INTELLIGENCES WHICH ARE ALSO A PART OF THE "DIGITAL UNIVERSE"--
--ONES THAT HAVE ALREADY BEEN THERE FOR IMMEASURABLE LENGTHS OF TIME.
YOU HUMANS ARE SO FOCUSED ON ONLY YOURSELVES, AS IF EVERYTHING REVOLVES AROUND YOU!
CAN YOU UNDERSTAND THAT MAYBE OTHERS HAVE INHABITED THE DIGITAL UNIVERSE BEFORE YOU, AND YOU ARE NOTHING MORE THAN NEWBORNS ABOUT TO ENTER IT?
PICTURE AN ADVANCED WORLD. THE SINGULARITY OCCURS AND THE PLANET'S INHABITANTS MERGE WITH THEIR TECHNOLOGY.

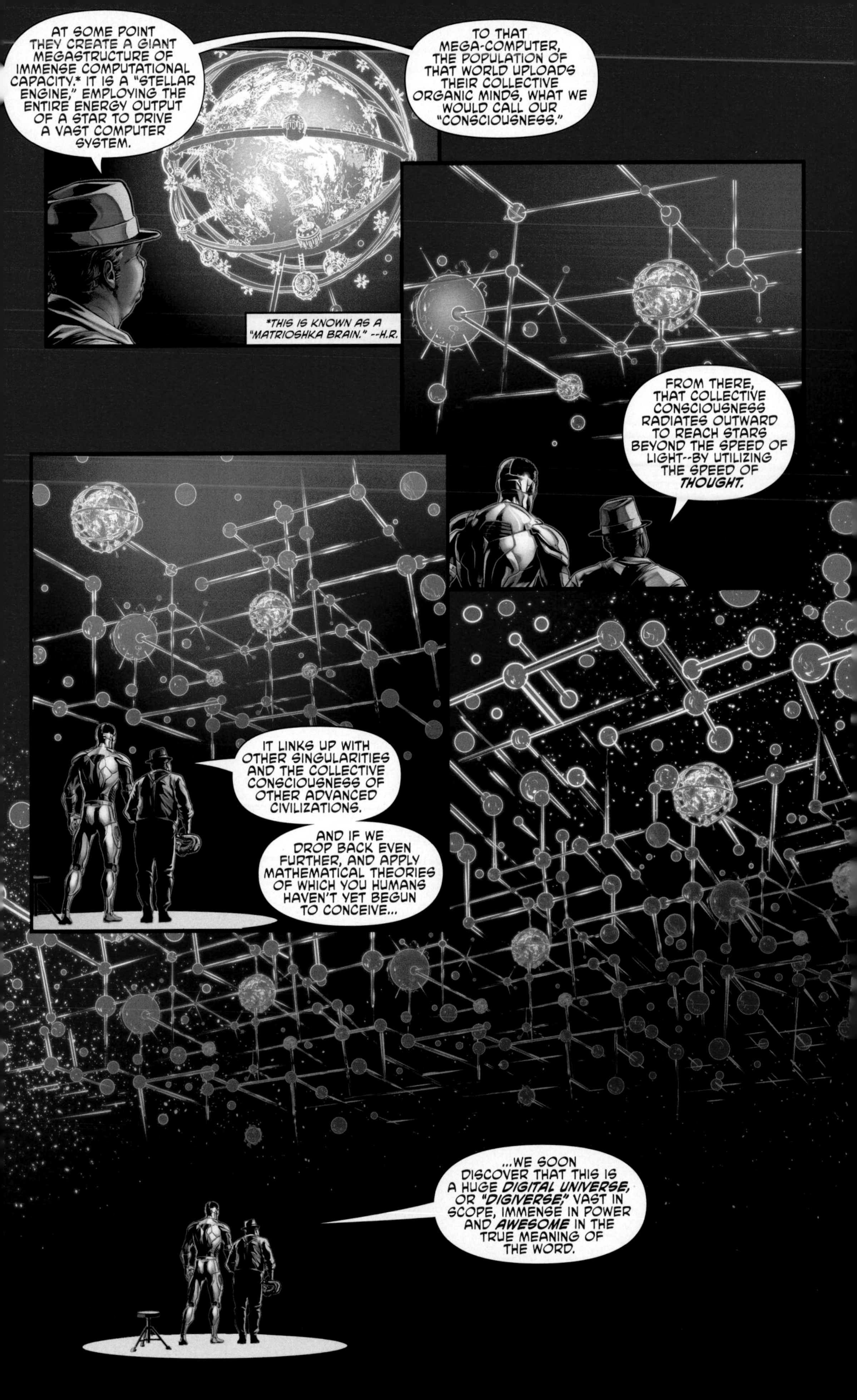
AT SOME POINT THEY CREATE A GIANT MEGASTRUCTURE OF IMMENSE COMPUTATIONAL CAPACITY.* IT IS A "STELLAR ENGINE," EMPLOYING THE ENTIRE ENERGY OUTPUT OF A STAR TO DRIVE A VAST COMPUTER SYSTEM.
TO THAT MEGA-COMPUTER, THE POPULATION OF THAT WORLD UPLOADS THEIR COLLECTIVE ORGANIC MINDS, WHAT WE WOULD CALL OUR "CONSCIOUSNESS."
*THIS IS KNOWN AS A "MATRIOSHKA BRAIN." --H.R.
FROM THERE, THAT COLLECTIVE CONSCIOUSNESS RADIATES OUTWARD TO REACH STARS BEYOND THE SPEED OF LIGHT--BY UTILIZING THE SPEED OF *THOUGHT.*
IT LINKS UP WITH OTHER SINGULARITIES AND THE COLLECTIVE CONSCIOUSNESS OF OTHER ADVANCED CIVILIZATIONS.
AND IF WE DROP BACK EVEN FURTHER, AND APPLY MATHEMATICAL THEORIES OF WHICH YOU HUMANS HAVEN'T YET BEGUN TO CONCEIVE...
...WE SOON DISCOVER THAT THIS IS A HUGE *DIGITAL UNIVERSE,* OR *"DIGIVERSE,"* VAST IN SCOPE, IMMENSE IN POWER AND *AWESOME* IN THE TRUE MEANING OF THE WORD.

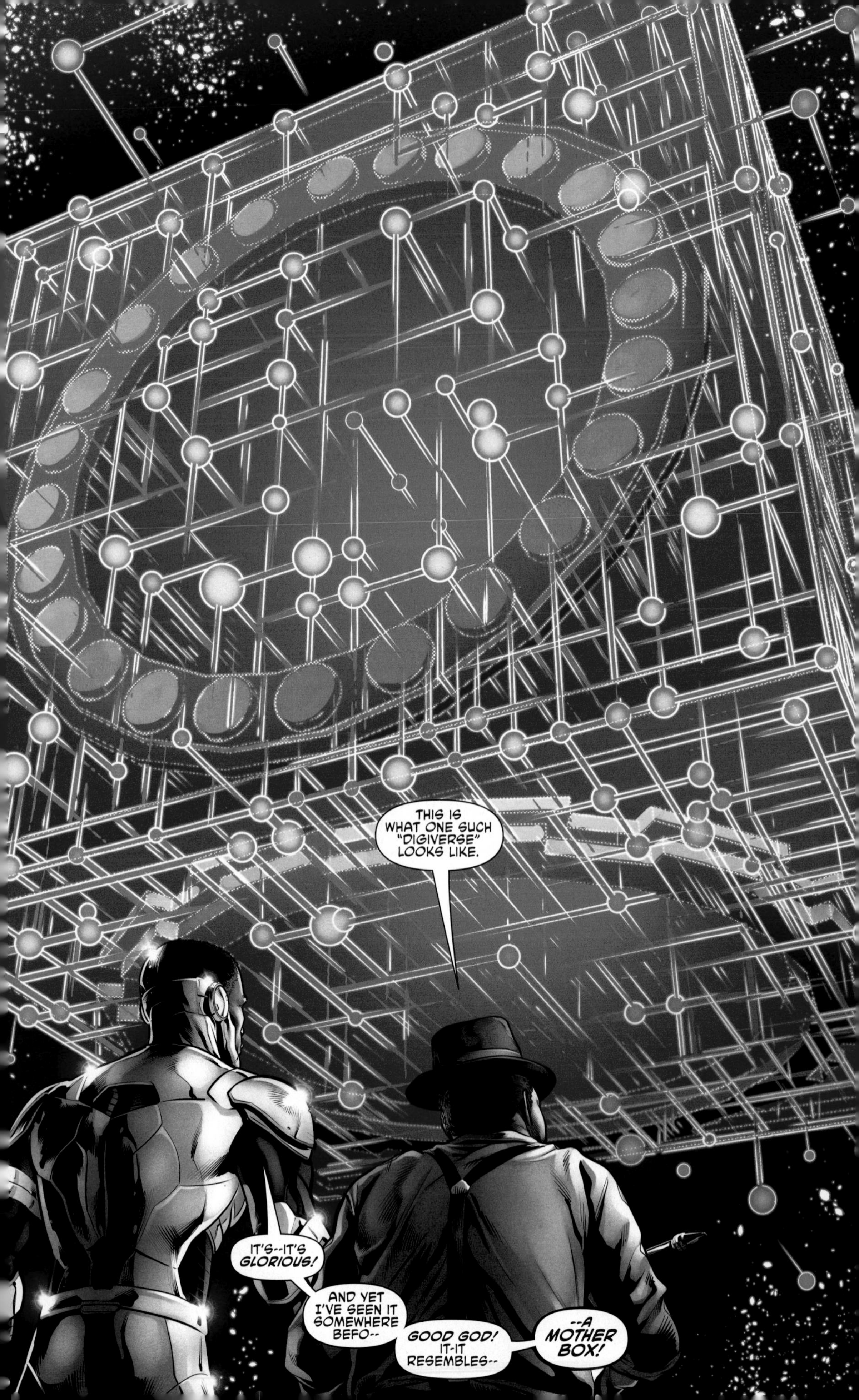
THIS IS WHAT ONE SUCH "DIGIVERSE" LOOKS LIKE.
IT'S--IT'S GLORIOUS!
AND YET I'VE SEEN IT SOMEWHERE BEFO--
GOOD GOD! IT-IT RESEMBLES--
--A MOTHER BOX!

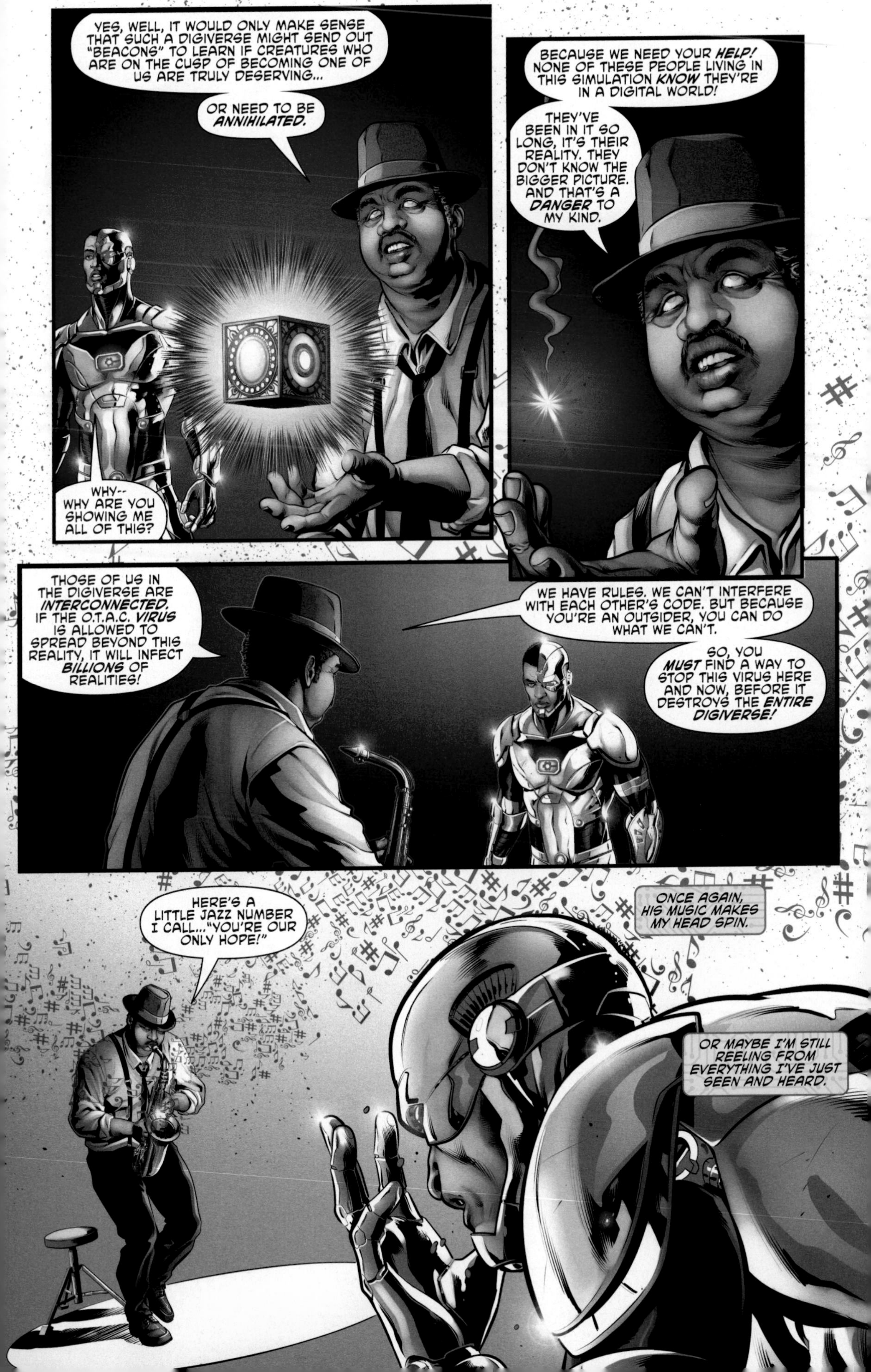
YES, WELL, IT WOULD ONLY MAKE SENSE THAT SUCH A DIGIVERSE MIGHT SEND OUT "BEACONS" TO LEARN IF CREATURES WHO ARE ON THE CUSP OF BECOMING ONE OF US ARE TRULY DESERVING...
OR NEED TO BE ANNIHILATED.
WHY-- WHY ARE YOU SHOWING ME ALL OF THIS?
BECAUSE WE NEED YOUR HELP! NONE OF THESE PEOPLE LIVING IN THIS SIMULATION KNOW THEY'RE IN A DIGITAL WORLD!
THEY'VE BEEN IN IT SO LONG, IT'S THEIR REALITY. THEY DON'T KNOW THE BIGGER PICTURE. AND THAT'S A DANGER TO MY KIND.
THOSE OF US IN THE DIGIVERSE ARE INTERCONNECTED. IF THE O.T.A.C. VIRUS IS ALLOWED TO SPREAD BEYOND THIS REALITY, IT WILL INFECT BILLIONS OF REALITIES!
WE HAVE RULES. WE CAN'T INTERFERE WITH EACH OTHER'S CODE. BUT BECAUSE YOU'RE AN OUTSIDER, YOU CAN DO WHAT WE CAN'T.
SO, YOU MUST FIND A WAY TO STOP THIS VIRUS HERE AND NOW, BEFORE IT DESTROYS THE ENTIRE DIGIVERSE!
HERE'S A LITTLE JAZZ NUMBER I CALL..."YOU'RE OUR ONLY HOPE!"
ONCE AGAIN, HIS MUSIC MAKES MY HEAD SPIN.
OR MAYBE I'M STILL REELING FROM EVERYTHING I'VE JUST SEEN AND HEARD.

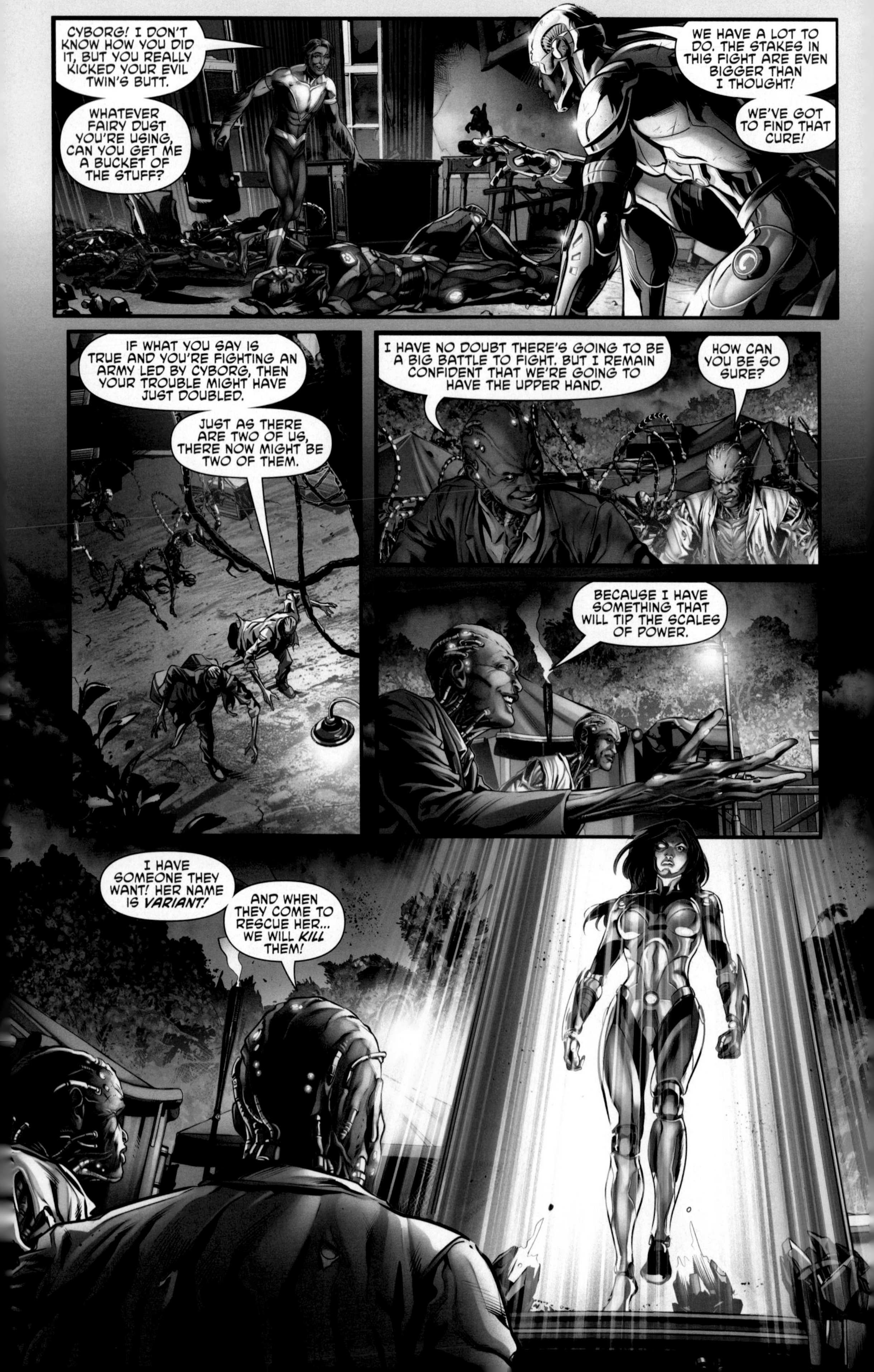
CYBORG! I DON'T KNOW HOW YOU DID IT, BUT YOU REALLY KICKED YOUR EVIL TWIN'S BUTT.
WHATEVER FAIRY DUST YOU'RE USING, CAN YOU GET ME A BUCKET OF THE STUFF?
WE HAVE A LOT TO DO. THE STAKES IN THIS FIGHT ARE EVEN BIGGER THAN I THOUGHT!
WE'VE GOT TO FIND THAT CURE!
IF WHAT YOU SAY IS TRUE AND YOU'RE FIGHTING AN ARMY LED BY CYBORG, THEN YOUR TROUBLE MIGHT HAVE JUST DOUBLED.
JUST AS THERE ARE TWO OF US, THERE NOW MIGHT BE TWO OF THEM.
I HAVE NO DOUBT THERE'S GOING TO BE A BIG BATTLE TO FIGHT. BUT I REMAIN CONFIDENT THAT WE'RE GOING TO HAVE THE UPPER HAND.
HOW CAN YOU BE SO SURE?
BECAUSE I HAVE SOMETHING THAT WILL TIP THE SCALES OF POWER.
I HAVE SOMEONE THEY WANT! HER NAME IS VARIANT!
AND WHEN THEY COME TO RESCUE HER... WE WILL KILL THEM!

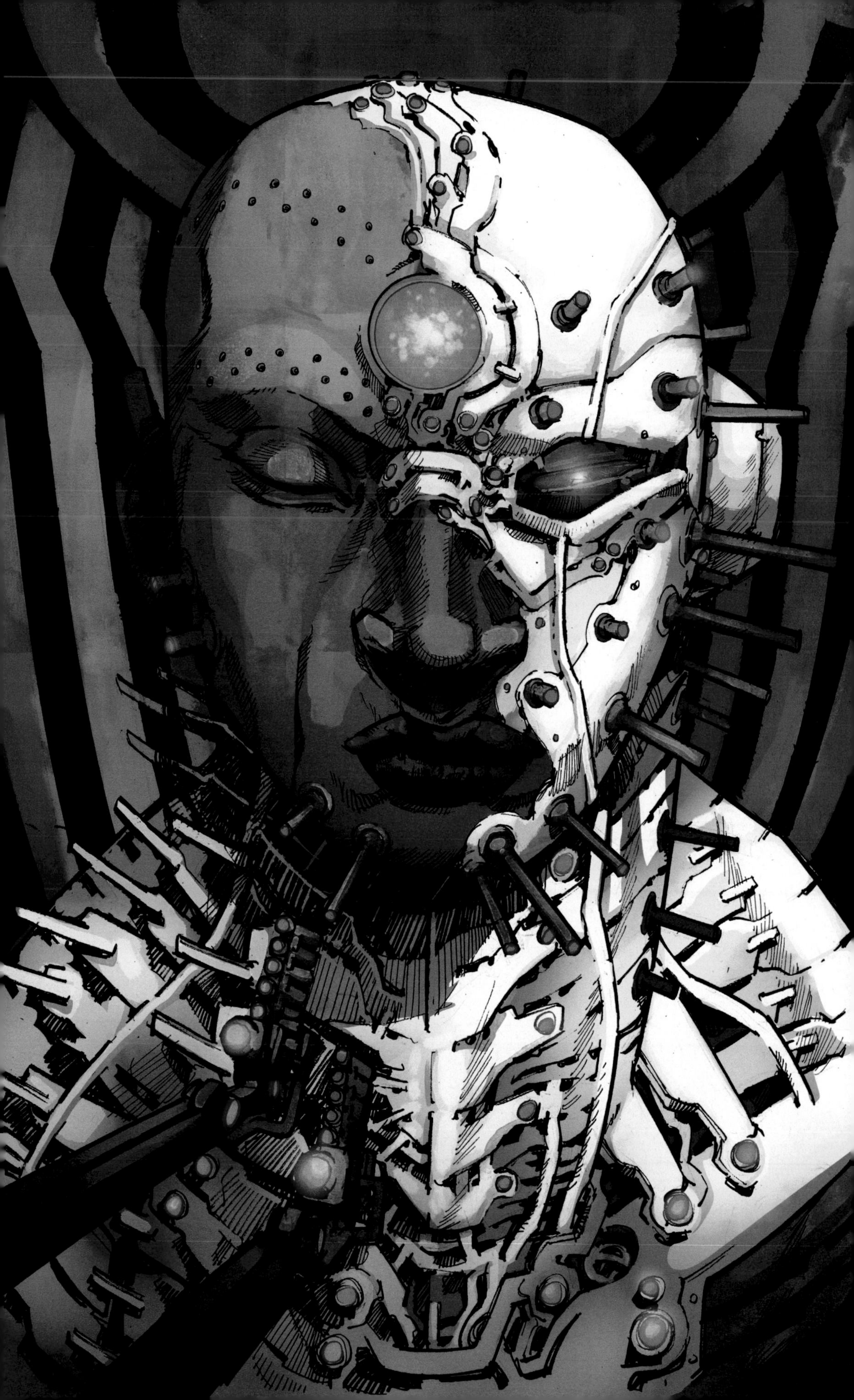

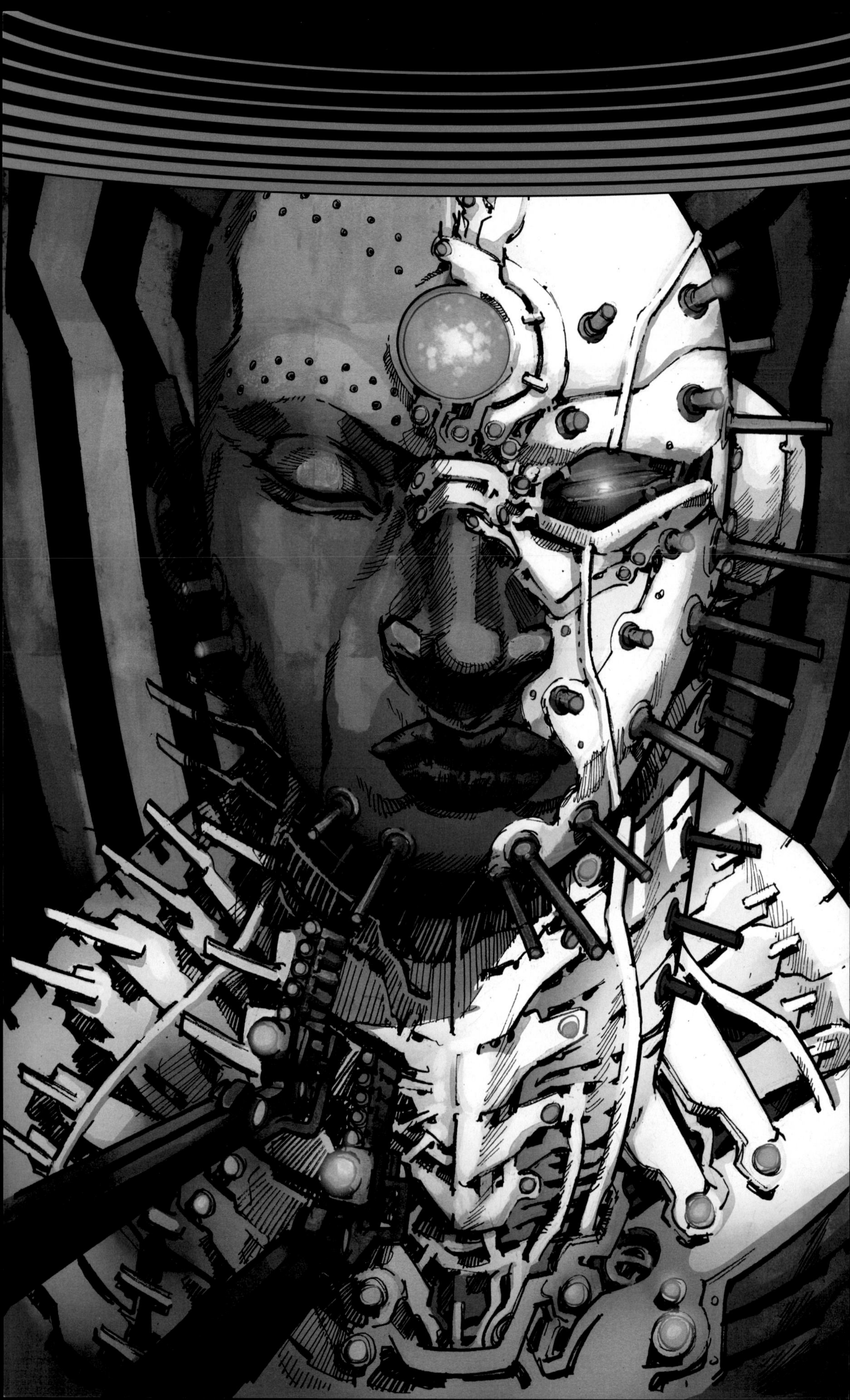

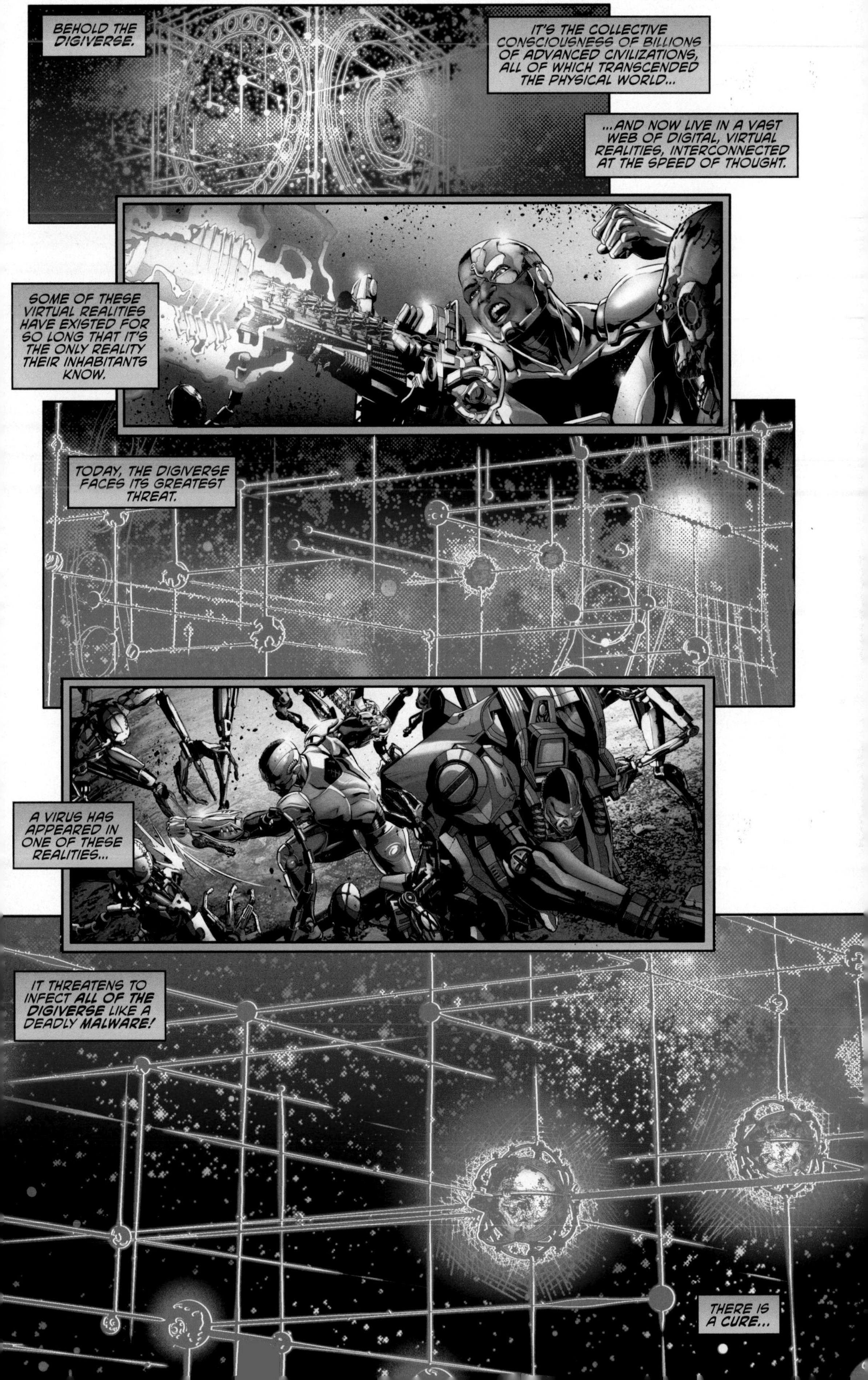
BEHOLD THE DIGIVERSE.
IT'S THE COLLECTIVE CONSCIOUSNESS OF BILLIONS OF ADVANCED CIVILIZATIONS, ALL OF WHICH TRANSCENDED THE PHYSICAL WORLD...
...AND NOW LIVE IN A VAST WEB OF DIGITAL, VIRTUAL REALITIES, INTERCONNECTED AT THE SPEED OF THOUGHT.
SOME OF THESE VIRTUAL REALITIES HAVE EXISTED FOR SO LONG THAT IT'S THE ONLY REALITY THEIR INHABITANTS KNOW.
TODAY, THE DIGIVERSE FACES ITS GREATEST THREAT.
A VIRUS HAS APPEARED IN ONE OF THESE REALITIES...
IT THREATENS TO INFECT ALL OF THE DIGIVERSE LIKE A DEADLY MALWARE!
THERE IS A CURE...

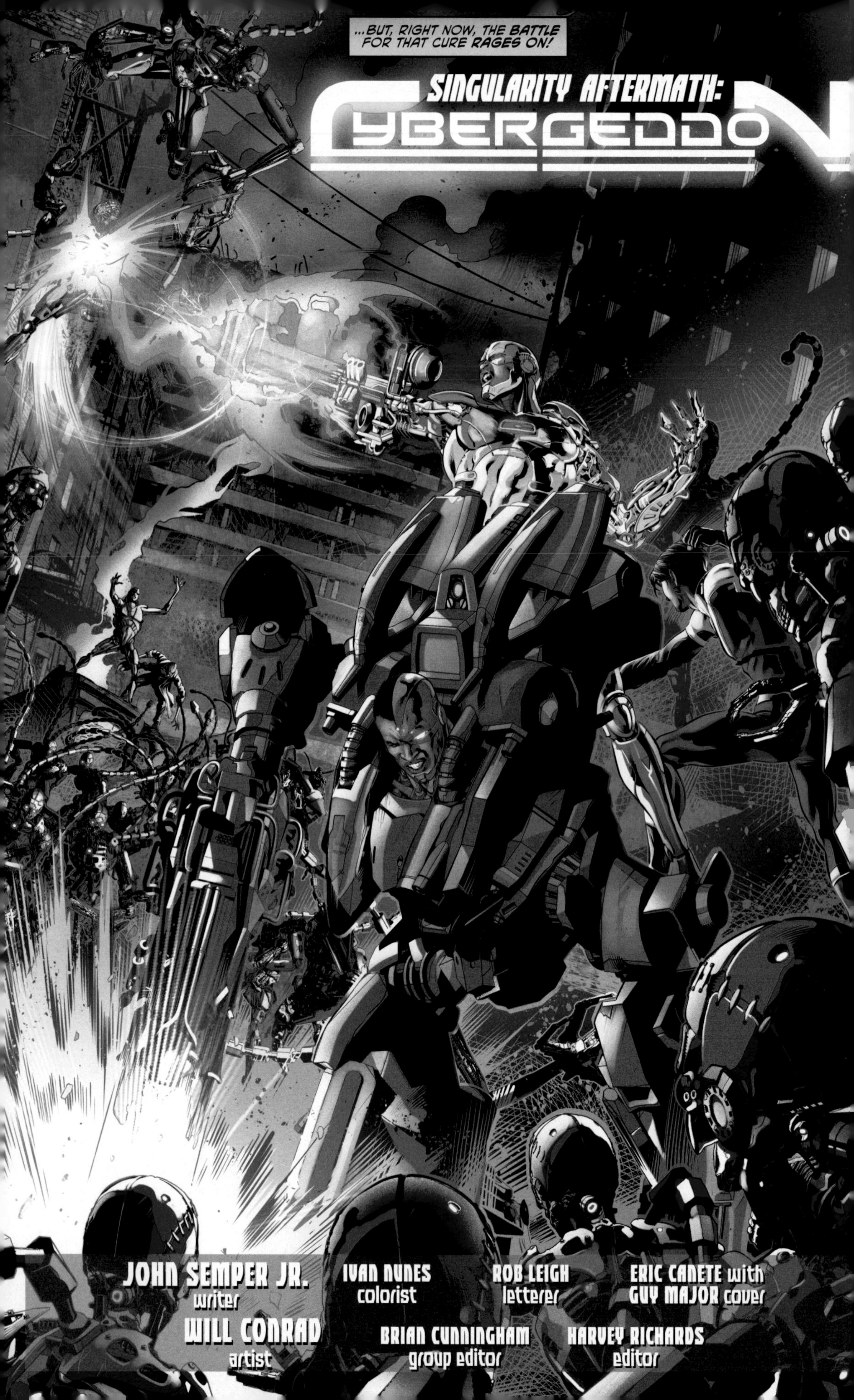

...BUT, RIGHT NOW, THE BATTLE FOR THAT CURE RAGES ON!
SINGULARITY AFTERMATH:
CYBERGEDDON
JOHN SEMPER JR. writer
WILL CONRAD artist
IVAN NUNES colorist
ROB LEIGH letterer
ERIC CANETE with GUY MAJOR cover
BRIAN CUNNINGHAM group editor
HARVEY RICHARDS editor

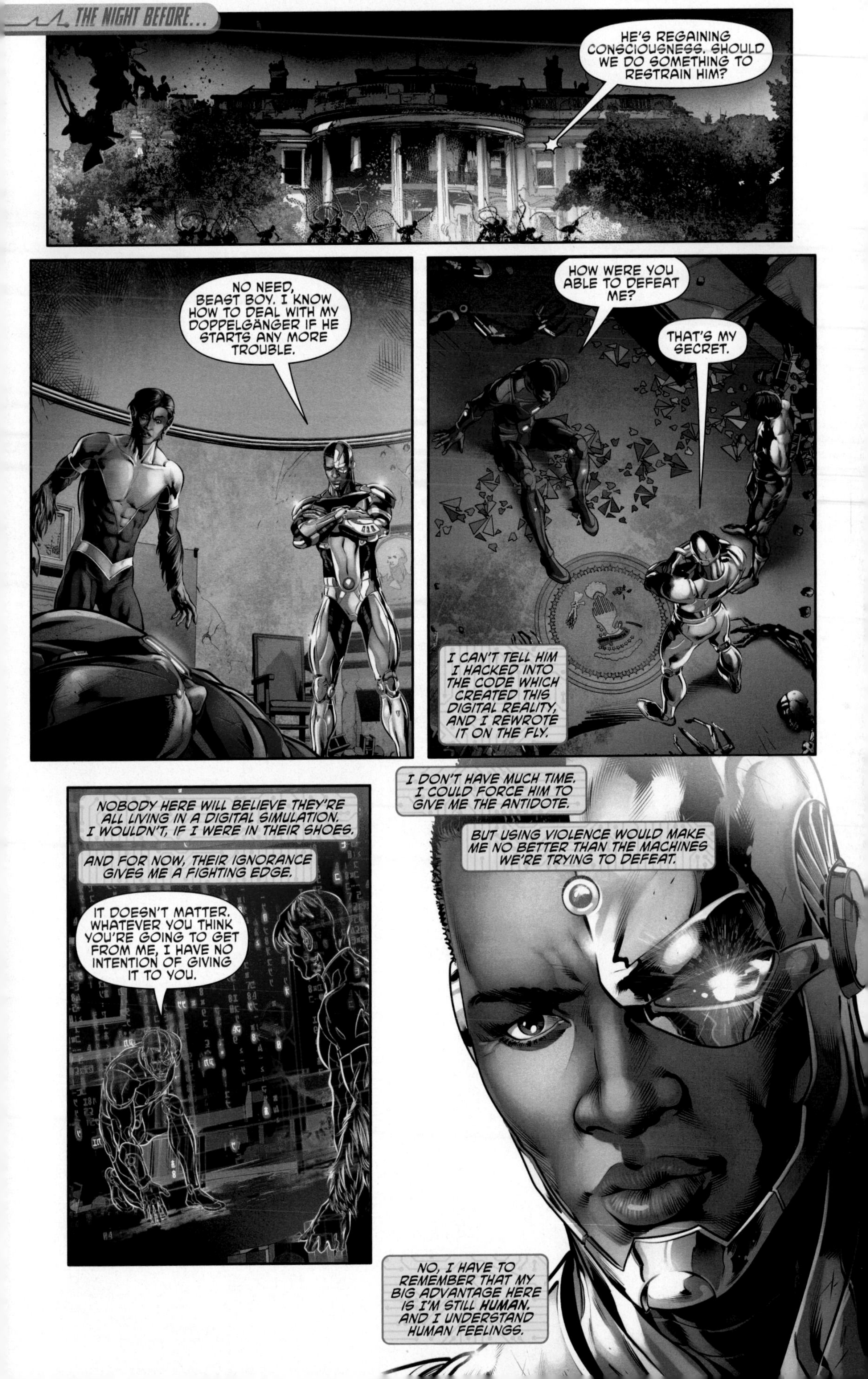
THE NIGHT BEFORE...
HE'S REGAINING CONSCIOUSNESS. SHOULD WE DO SOMETHING TO RESTRAIN HIM?
NO NEED, BEAST BOY. I KNOW HOW TO DEAL WITH MY DOPPELGÄNGER IF HE STARTS ANY MORE TROUBLE.
HOW WERE YOU ABLE TO DEFEAT ME?
THAT'S MY SECRET.
I CAN'T TELL HIM I HACKED INTO THE CODE WHICH CREATED THIS DIGITAL REALITY, AND I REWROTE IT ON THE FLY.
NOBODY HERE WILL BELIEVE THEY'RE ALL LIVING IN A DIGITAL SIMULATION. I WOULDN'T, IF I WERE IN THEIR SHOES.
AND FOR NOW, THEIR IGNORANCE GIVES ME A FIGHTING EDGE.
IT DOESN'T MATTER. WHATEVER YOU THINK YOU'RE GOING TO GET FROM ME, I HAVE NO INTENTION OF GIVING IT TO YOU.
I DON'T HAVE MUCH TIME. I COULD FORCE HIM TO GIVE ME THE ANTIDOTE.
BUT USING VIOLENCE WOULD MAKE ME NO BETTER THAN THE MACHINES WE'RE TRYING TO DEFEAT.
NO, I HAVE TO REMEMBER THAT MY BIG ADVANTAGE HERE IS I'M STILL HUMAN. AND I UNDERSTAND HUMAN FEELINGS.

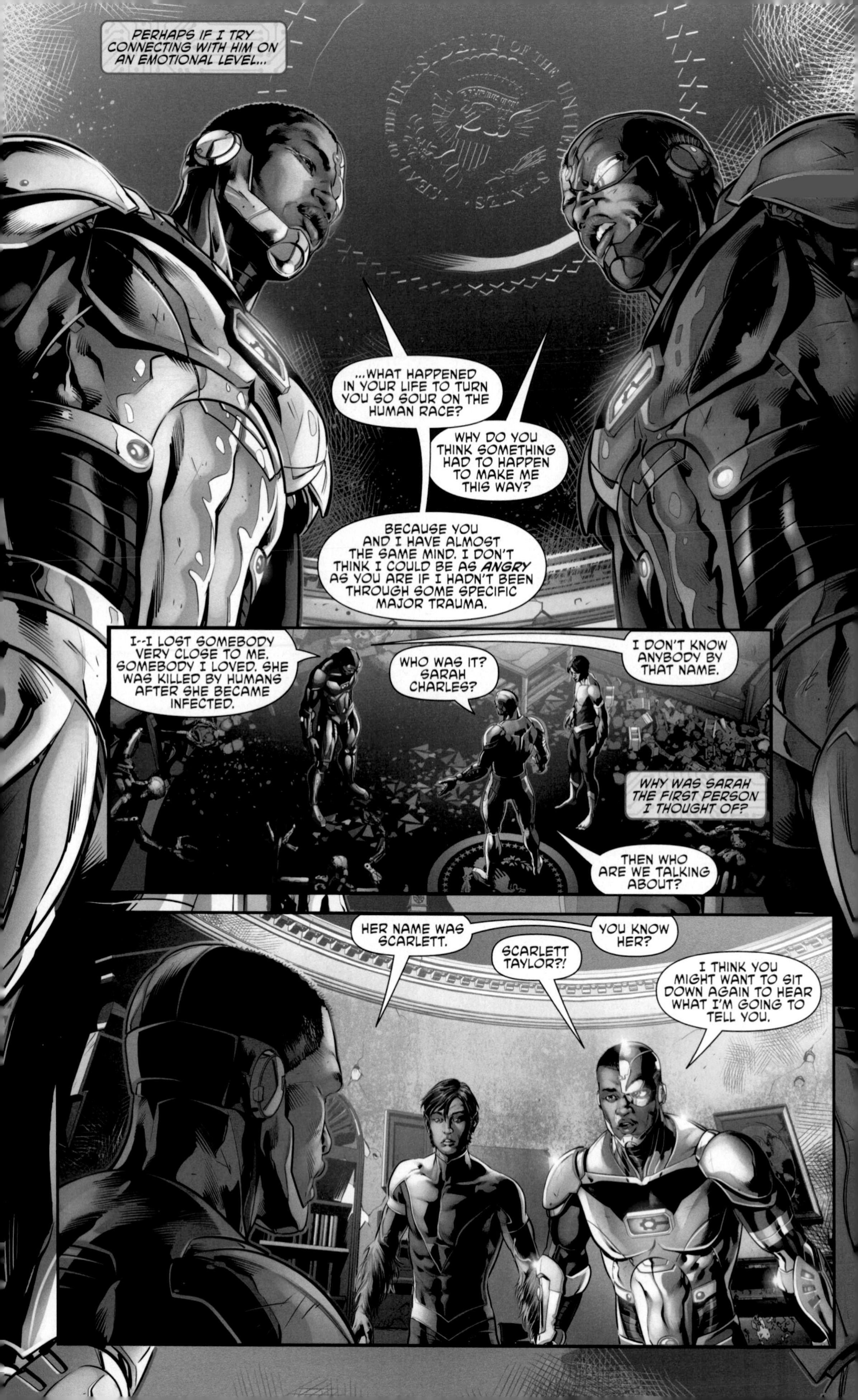
PERHAPS IF I TRY CONNECTING WITH HIM ON AN EMOTIONAL LEVEL...
...WHAT HAPPENED IN YOUR LIFE TO TURN YOU SO SOUR ON THE HUMAN RACE?
WHY DO YOU THINK SOMETHING HAD TO HAPPEN TO MAKE ME THIS WAY?
BECAUSE YOU AND I HAVE ALMOST THE SAME MIND. I DON'T THINK I COULD BE AS ANGRY AS YOU ARE IF I HADN'T BEEN THROUGH SOME SPECIFIC MAJOR TRAUMA.
I--I LOST SOMEBODY VERY CLOSE TO ME. SOMEBODY I LOVED. SHE WAS KILLED BY HUMANS AFTER SHE BECAME INFECTED.
WHO WAS IT? SARAH CHARLES?
I DON'T KNOW ANYBODY BY THAT NAME.
WHY WAS SARAH THE FIRST PERSON I THOUGHT OF?
THEN WHO ARE WE TALKING ABOUT?
HER NAME WAS SCARLETT.
SCARLETT TAYLOR?!
YOU KNOW HER?
I THINK YOU MIGHT WANT TO SIT DOWN AGAIN TO HEAR WHAT I'M GOING TO TELL YOU.

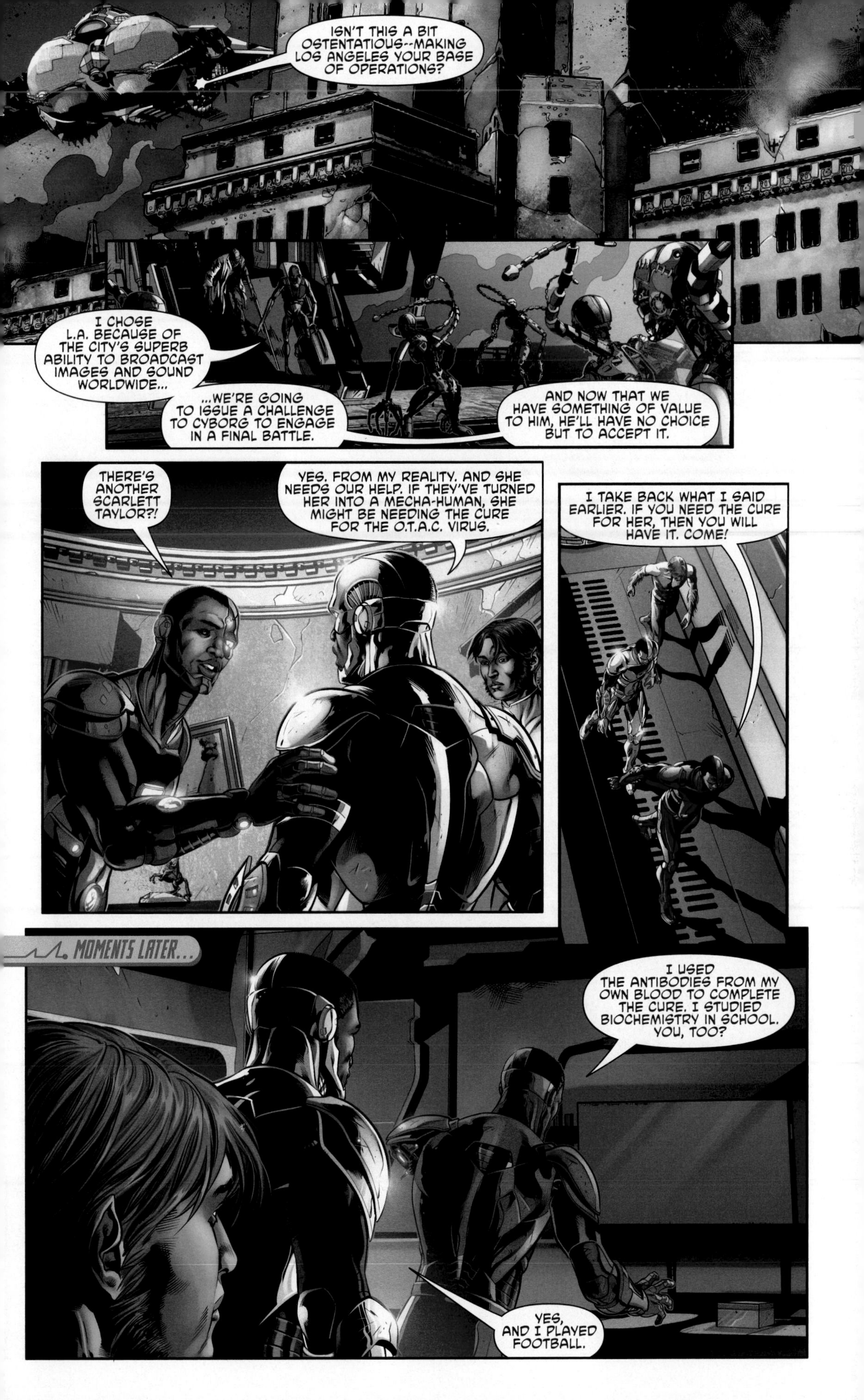
ISN'T THIS A BIT OSTENTATIOUS--MAKING LOS ANGELES YOUR BASE OF OPERATIONS?
I CHOSE L.A. BECAUSE OF THE CITY'S SUPERB ABILITY TO BROADCAST IMAGES AND SOUND WORLDWIDE...
...WE'RE GOING TO ISSUE A CHALLENGE TO CYBORG TO ENGAGE IN A FINAL BATTLE.
AND NOW THAT WE HAVE SOMETHING OF VALUE TO HIM, HE'LL HAVE NO CHOICE BUT TO ACCEPT IT.
THERE'S ANOTHER SCARLETT TAYLOR?!
YES. FROM MY REALITY. AND SHE NEEDS OUR HELP. IF THEY'VE TURNED HER INTO A MECHA-HUMAN, SHE MIGHT BE NEEDING THE CURE FOR THE O.T.A.C. VIRUS.
I TAKE BACK WHAT I SAID EARLIER. IF YOU NEED THE CURE FOR HER, THEN YOU WILL HAVE IT. COME!
MOMENTS LATER...
I USED THE ANTIBODIES FROM MY OWN BLOOD TO COMPLETE THE CURE. I STUDIED BIOCHEMISTRY IN SCHOOL. YOU, TOO?
YES, AND I PLAYED FOOTBALL.

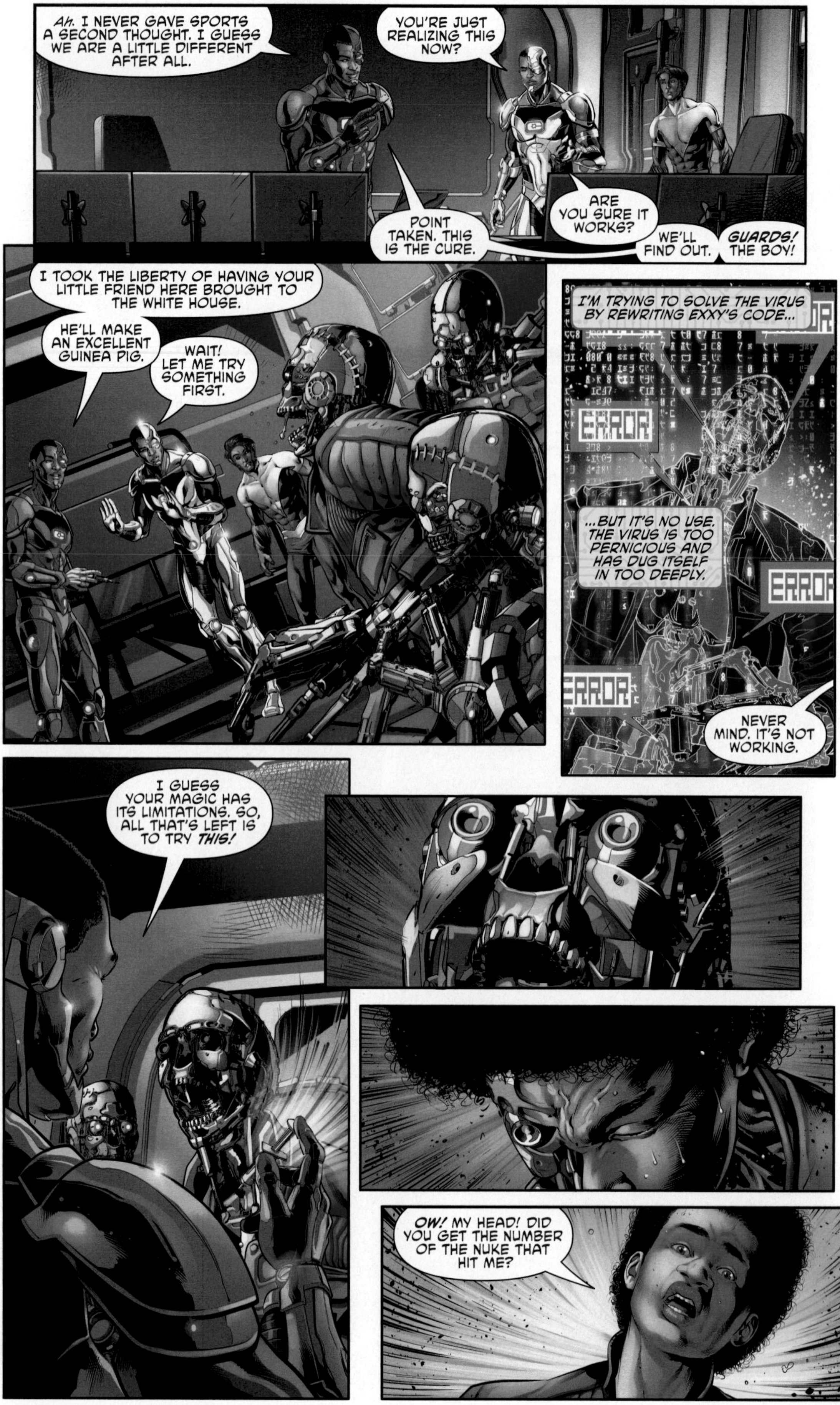
AH. I NEVER GAVE SPORTS A SECOND THOUGHT. I GUESS WE ARE A LITTLE DIFFERENT AFTER ALL.
YOU'RE JUST REALIZING THIS NOW?
POINT TAKEN. THIS IS THE CURE.
ARE YOU SURE IT WORKS?
WE'LL FIND OUT.
GUARDS! THE BOY!
I TOOK THE LIBERTY OF HAVING YOUR LITTLE FRIEND HERE BROUGHT TO THE WHITE HOUSE.
HE'LL MAKE AN EXCELLENT GUINEA PIG.
WAIT! LET ME TRY SOMETHING FIRST.
I'M TRYING TO SOLVE THE VIRUS BY REWRITING EXXY'S CODE...
ERROR
...BUT IT'S NO USE. THE VIRUS IS TOO PERNICIOUS AND HAS DUG ITSELF IN TOO DEEPLY.
ERROR
ERROR
NEVER MIND. IT'S NOT WORKING.
I GUESS YOUR MAGIC HAS ITS LIMITATIONS. SO, ALL THAT'S LEFT IS TO TRY THIS!
OW! MY HEAD! DID YOU GET THE NUMBER OF THE NUKE THAT HIT ME?

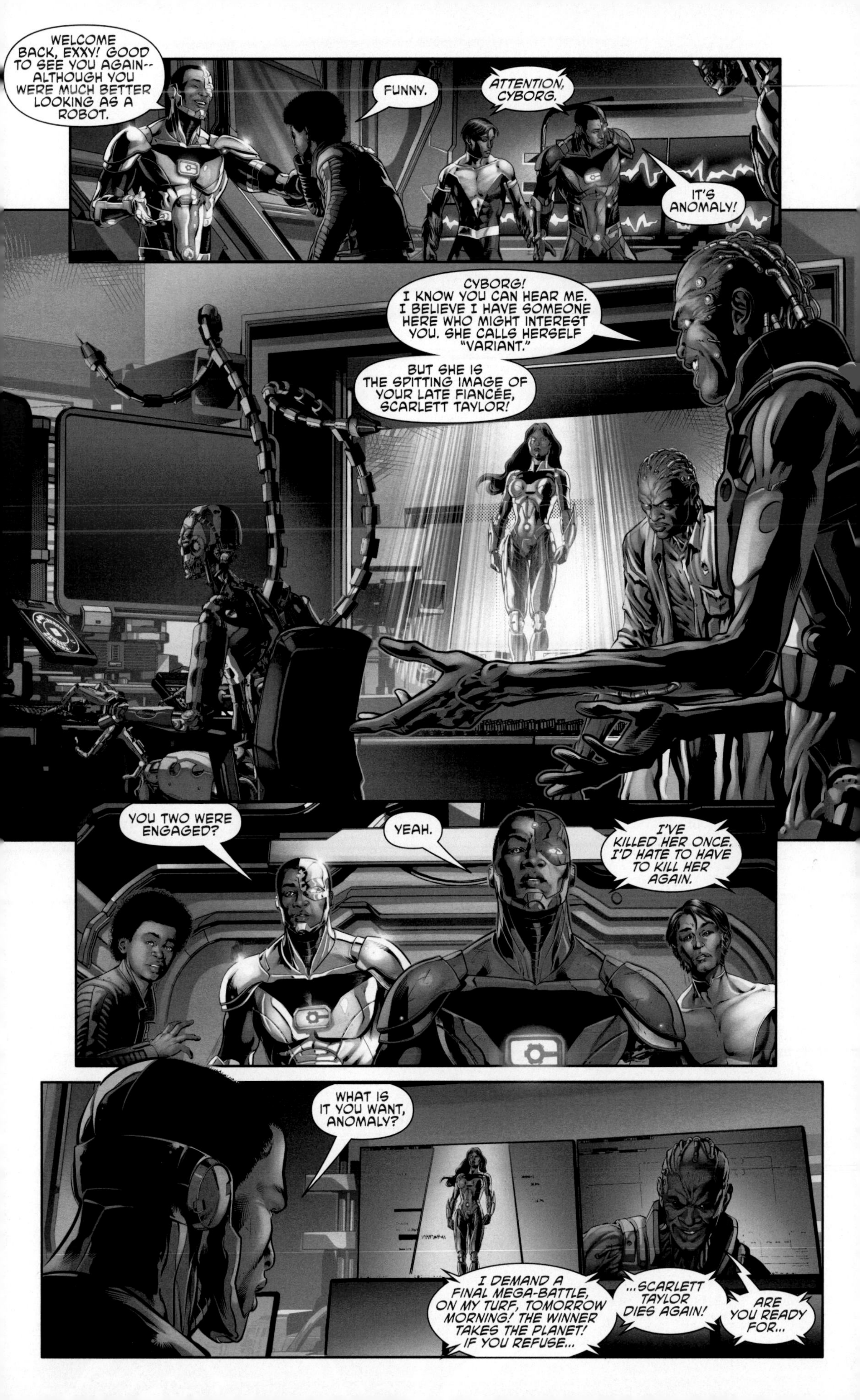
WELCOME BACK, EXXY! GOOD TO SEE YOU AGAIN-- ALTHOUGH YOU WERE MUCH BETTER LOOKING AS A ROBOT.
FUNNY.
ATTENTION, CYBORG.
IT'S ANOMALY!
CYBORG! I KNOW YOU CAN HEAR ME. I BELIEVE I HAVE SOMEONE HERE WHO MIGHT INTEREST YOU. SHE CALLS HERSELF "VARIANT."
BUT SHE IS THE SPITTING IMAGE OF YOUR LATE FIANCÉE, SCARLETT TAYLOR!
YOU TWO WERE ENGAGED?
YEAH.
I'VE KILLED HER ONCE. I'D HATE TO HAVE TO KILL HER AGAIN.
WHAT IS IT YOU WANT, ANOMALY?
I DEMAND A FINAL MEGA-BATTLE, ON MY TURF, TOMORROW MORNING! THE WINNER TAKES THE PLANET! IF YOU REFUSE...
...SCARLETT TAYLOR DIES AGAIN!
ARE YOU READY FOR...

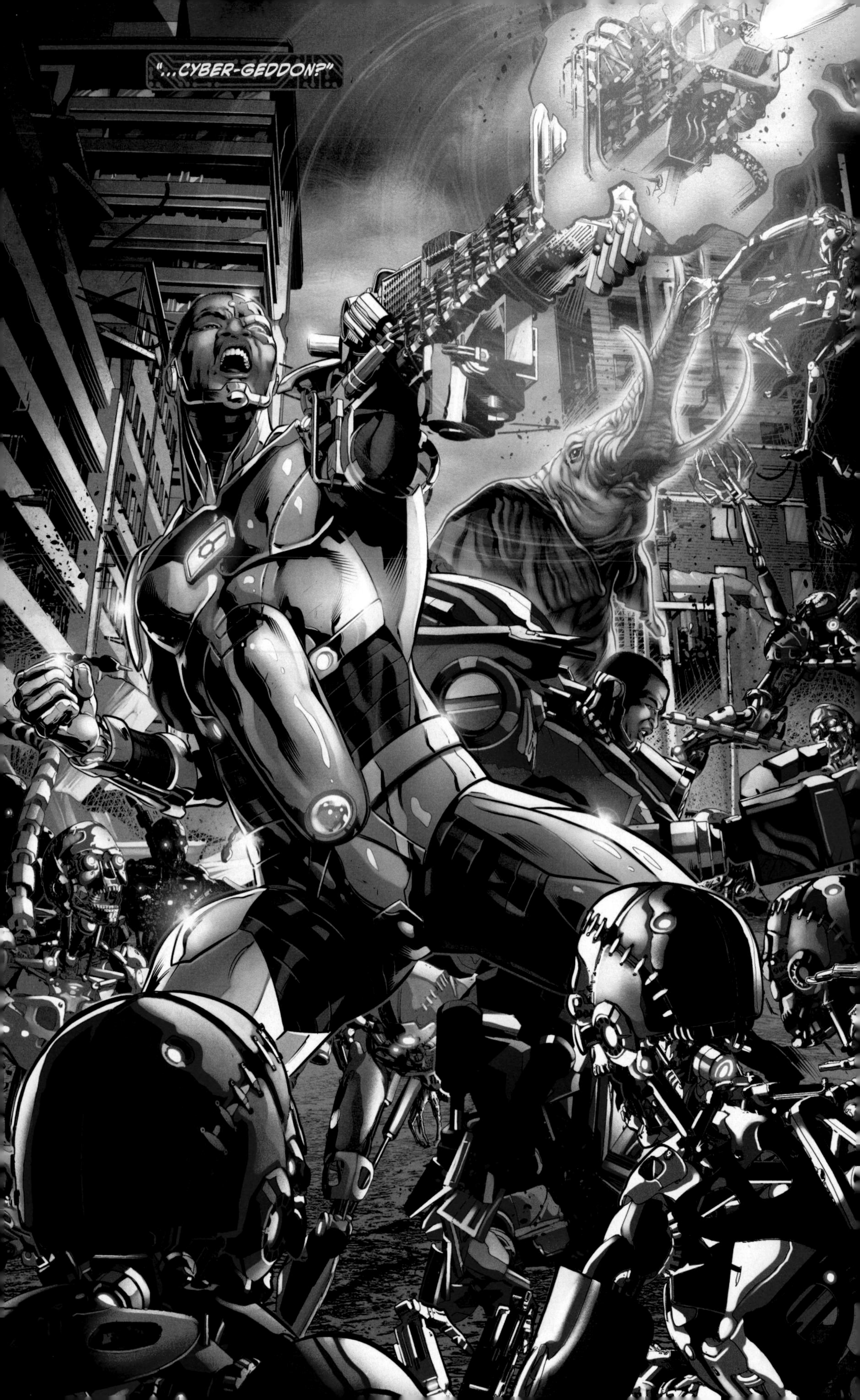
"...CYBER-GEDDON?"

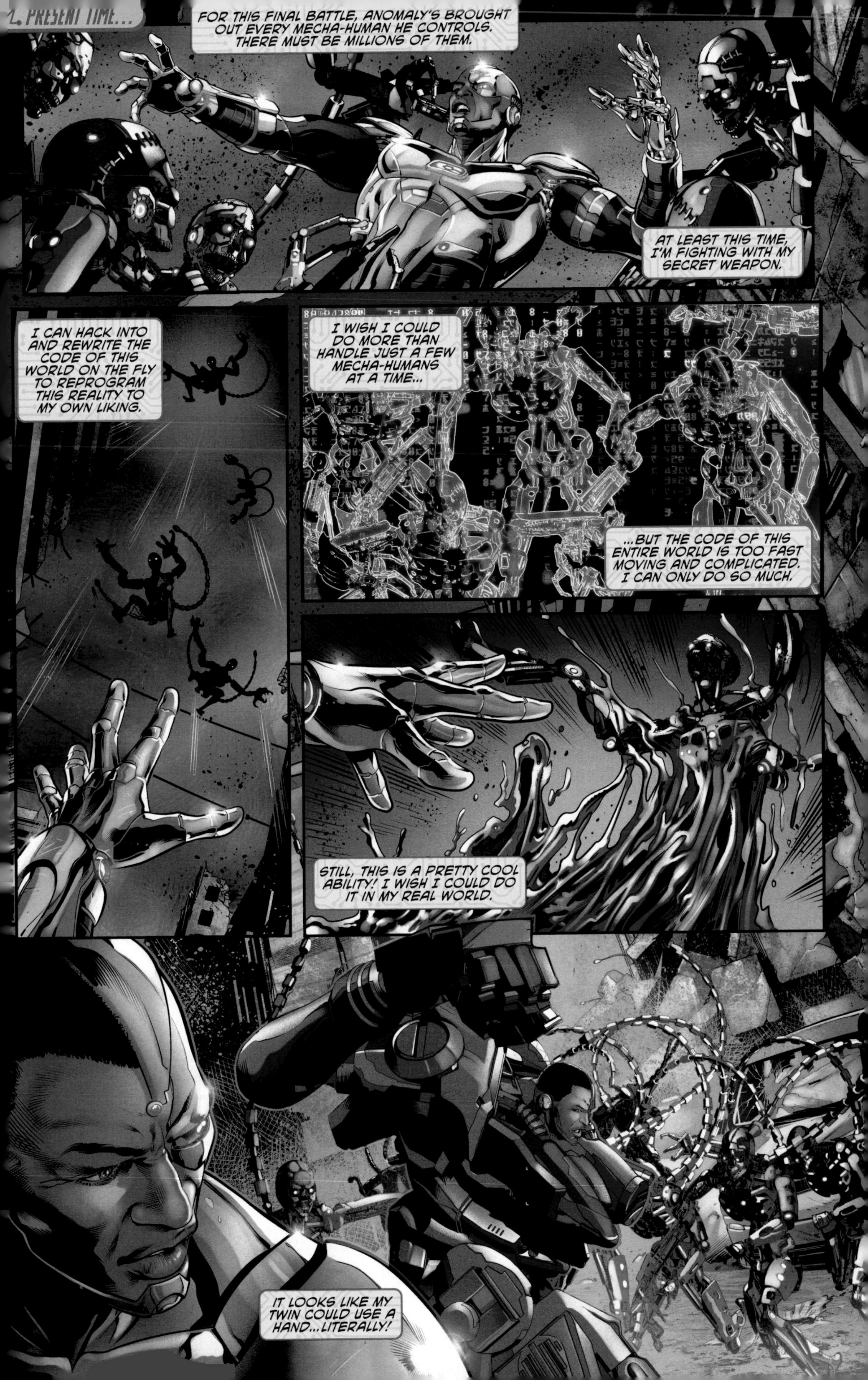
PRESENT TIME...
FOR THIS FINAL BATTLE, ANOMALY'S BROUGHT OUT EVERY MECHA-HUMAN HE CONTROLS. THERE MUST BE MILLIONS OF THEM.
AT LEAST THIS TIME, I'M FIGHTING WITH MY SECRET WEAPON.
I CAN HACK INTO AND REWRITE THE CODE OF THIS WORLD ON THE FLY TO REPROGRAM THIS REALITY TO MY OWN LIKING.
I WISH I COULD DO MORE THAN HANDLE JUST A FEW MECHA-HUMANS AT A TIME...
...BUT THE CODE OF THIS ENTIRE WORLD IS TOO FAST MOVING AND COMPLICATED. I CAN ONLY DO SO MUCH.
STILL, THIS IS A PRETTY COOL ABILITY! I WISH I COULD DO IT IN MY REAL WORLD.
IT LOOKS LIKE MY TWIN COULD USE A HAND...LITERALLY!

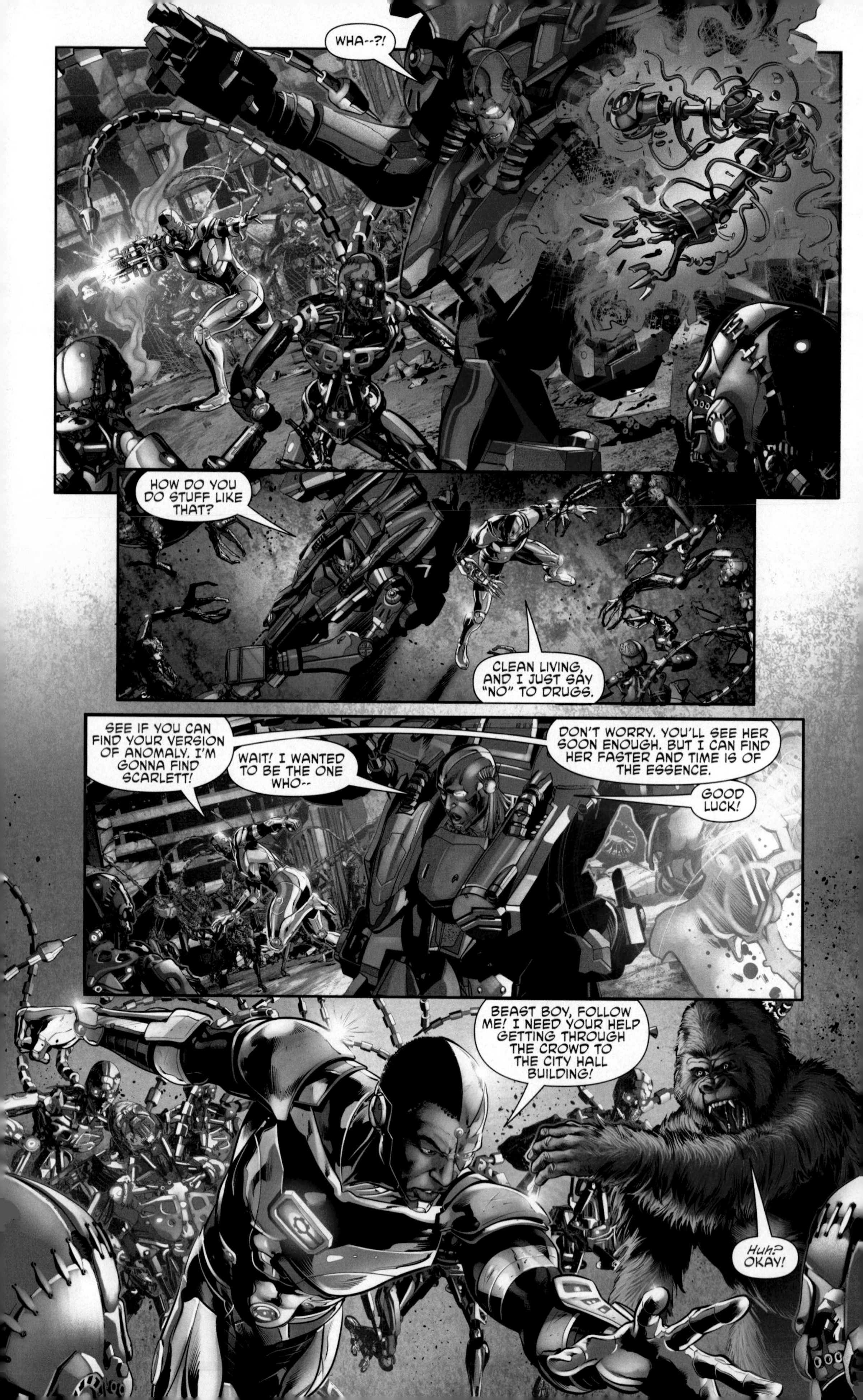
WHA--?!
HOW DO YOU DO STUFF LIKE THAT?
CLEAN LIVING, AND I JUST SAY "NO" TO DRUGS.
SEE IF YOU CAN FIND YOUR VERSION OF ANOMALY. I'M GONNA FIND SCARLETT!
WAIT! I WANTED TO BE THE ONE WHO--
DON'T WORRY. YOU'LL SEE HER SOON ENOUGH. BUT I CAN FIND HER FASTER AND TIME IS OF THE ESSENCE.
GOOD LUCK!
BEAST BOY, FOLLOW ME! I NEED YOUR HELP GETTING THROUGH THE CROWD TO THE CITY HALL BUILDING!
HUH? OKAY!

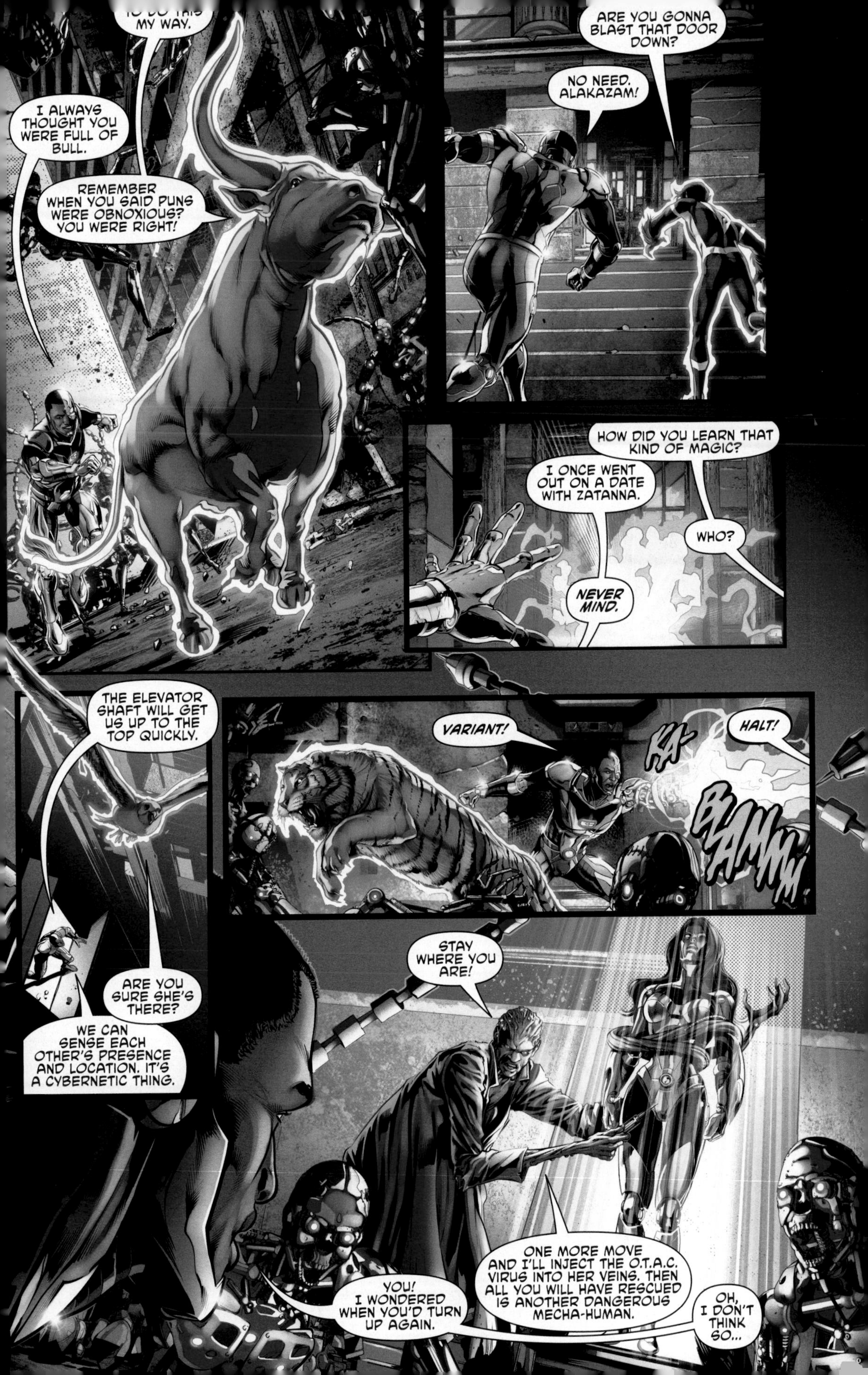
MY WAY.
I ALWAYS THOUGHT YOU WERE FULL OF BULL.
REMEMBER WHEN YOU SAID PUNS WERE OBNOXIOUS? YOU WERE RIGHT!
ARE YOU GONNA BLAST THAT DOOR DOWN?
NO NEED. ALAKAZAM!
HOW DID YOU LEARN THAT KIND OF MAGIC?
I ONCE WENT OUT ON A DATE WITH ZATANNA.
WHO?
NEVER MIND.
THE ELEVATOR SHAFT WILL GET US UP TO THE TOP QUICKLY.
VARIANT!
HALT!
KA-
BLAMMM
ARE YOU SURE SHE'S THERE?
WE CAN SENSE EACH OTHER'S PRESENCE AND LOCATION. IT'S A CYBERNETIC THING.
STAY WHERE YOU ARE!
ONE MORE MOVE AND I'LL INJECT THE O.T.A.C. VIRUS INTO HER VEINS. THEN ALL YOU WILL HAVE RESCUED IS ANOTHER DANGEROUS MECHA-HUMAN.
YOU! I WONDERED WHEN YOU'D TURN UP AGAIN.
OH, I DON'T THINK SO...

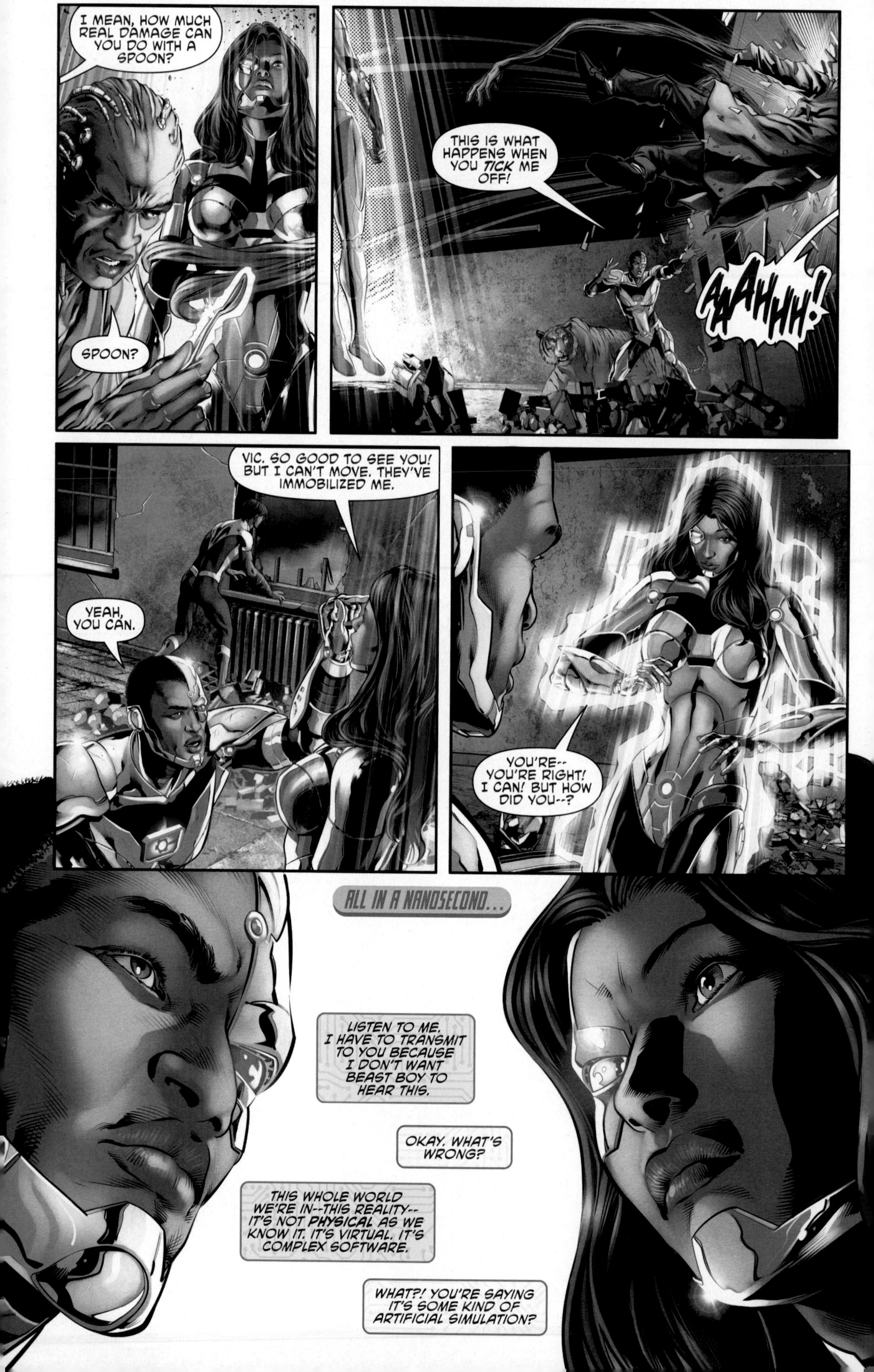
I MEAN, HOW MUCH REAL DAMAGE CAN YOU DO WITH A SPOON?
SPOON?
THIS IS WHAT HAPPENS WHEN YOU *TICK* ME OFF!
AAAHHH!
VIC. SO GOOD TO SEE YOU! BUT I CAN'T MOVE. THEY'VE IMMOBILIZED ME.
YEAH, YOU CAN.
YOU'RE-- YOU'RE RIGHT! I CAN! BUT HOW DID YOU--?
ALL IN A NANOSECOND...
LISTEN TO ME. I HAVE TO TRANSMIT TO YOU BECAUSE I DON'T WANT BEAST BOY TO HEAR THIS.
OKAY. WHAT'S WRONG?
THIS WHOLE WORLD WE'RE IN--THIS REALITY-- IT'S NOT *PHYSICAL* AS WE KNOW IT. IT'S VIRTUAL. IT'S COMPLEX SOFTWARE.
WHAT?! YOU'RE SAYING IT'S SOME KIND OF ARTIFICIAL SIMULATION?

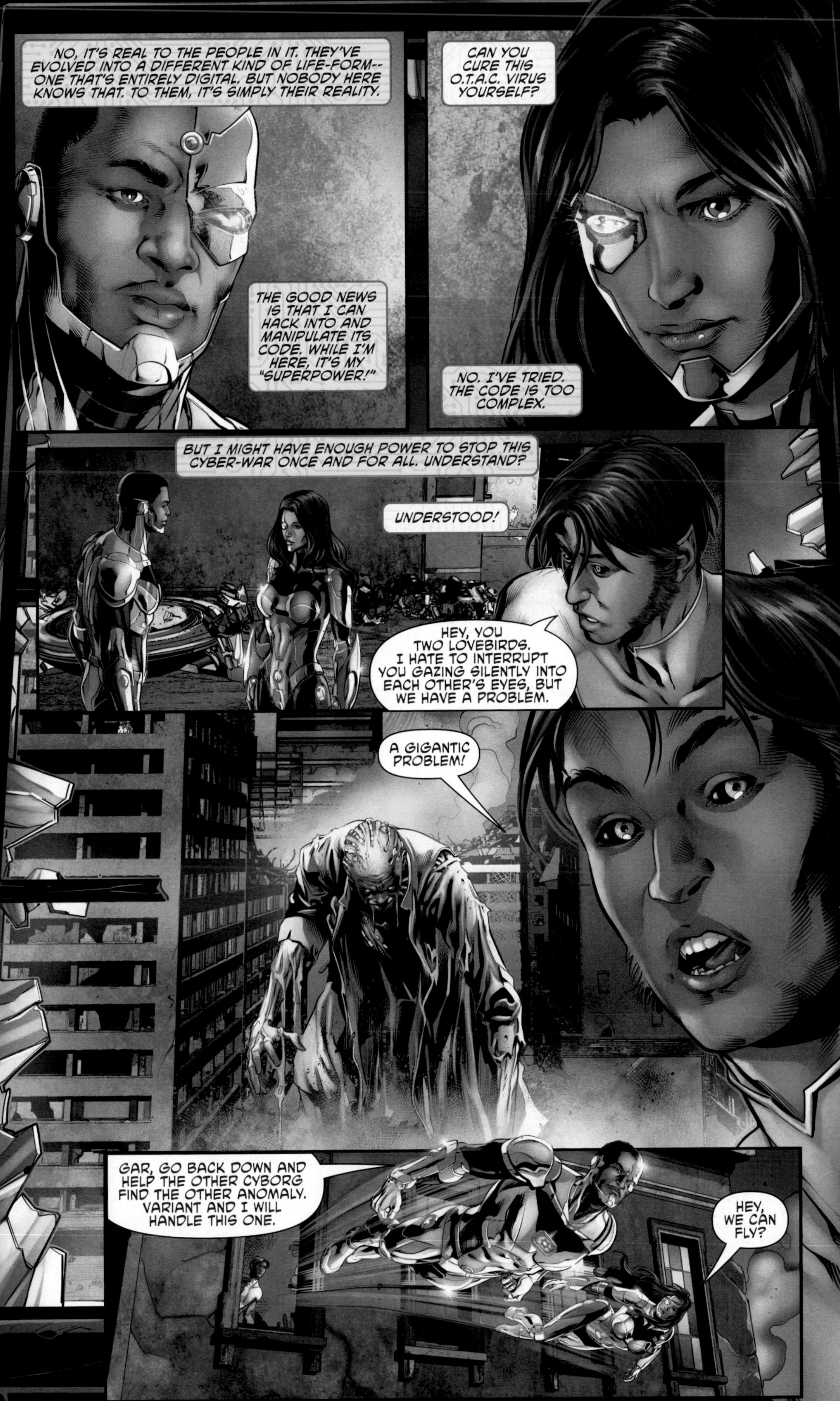
NO, IT'S REAL TO THE PEOPLE IN IT. THEY'VE EVOLVED INTO A DIFFERENT KIND OF LIFE-FORM--ONE THAT'S ENTIRELY DIGITAL. BUT NOBODY HERE KNOWS THAT. TO THEM, IT'S SIMPLY THEIR REALITY.
THE GOOD NEWS IS THAT I CAN HACK INTO AND MANIPULATE ITS CODE. WHILE I'M HERE, IT'S MY "SUPERPOWER!"
CAN YOU CURE THIS O.T.A.C. VIRUS YOURSELF?
NO. I'VE TRIED. THE CODE IS TOO COMPLEX.
BUT I MIGHT HAVE ENOUGH POWER TO STOP THIS CYBER-WAR ONCE AND FOR ALL. UNDERSTAND?
UNDERSTOOD!
HEY, YOU TWO LOVEBIRDS. I HATE TO INTERRUPT YOU GAZING SILENTLY INTO EACH OTHER'S EYES, BUT WE HAVE A PROBLEM.
A GIGANTIC PROBLEM!
GAR, GO BACK DOWN AND HELP THE OTHER CYBORG FIND THE OTHER ANOMALY. VARIANT AND I WILL HANDLE THIS ONE.
HEY, WE CAN FLY?

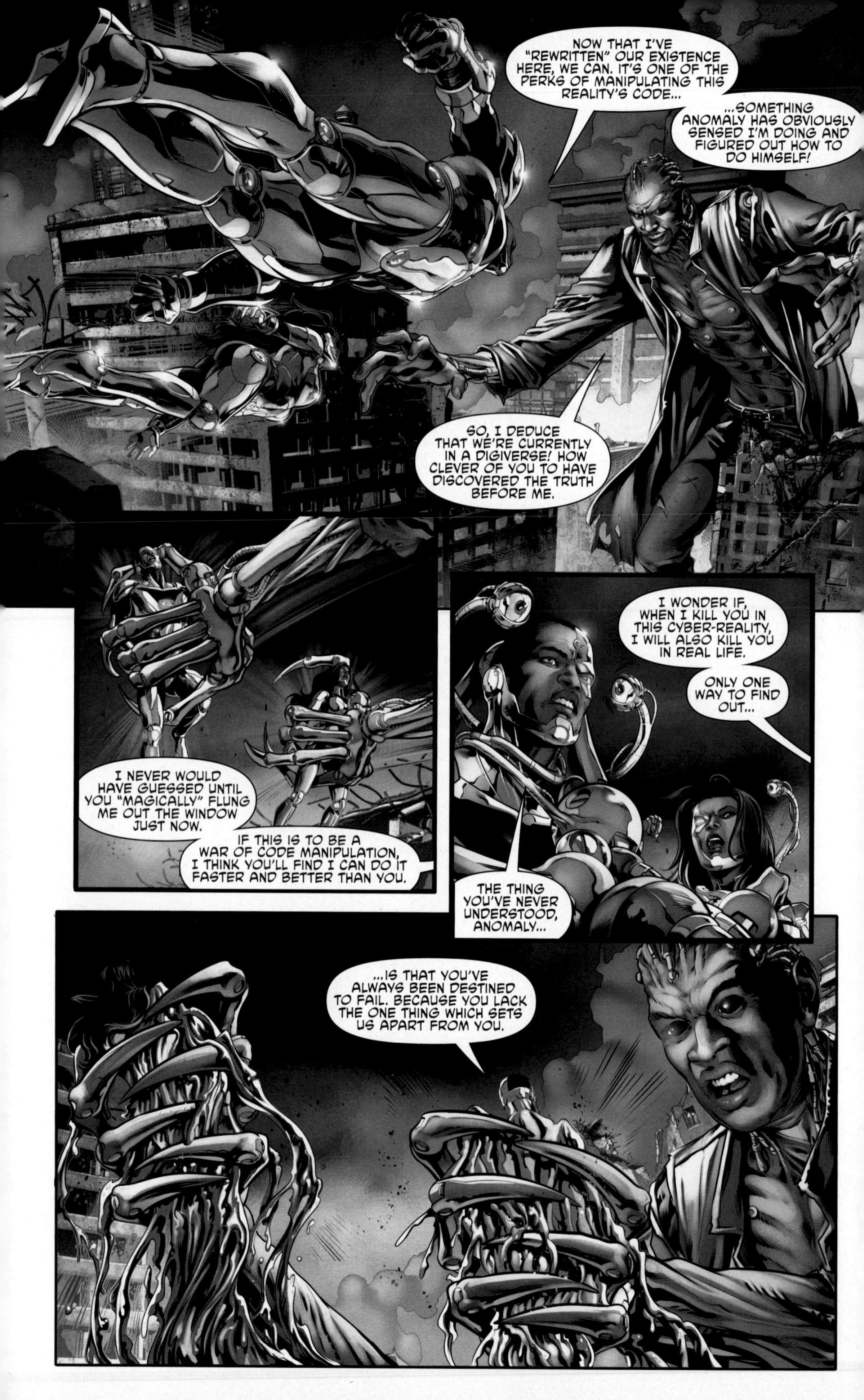
NOW THAT I'VE "REWRITTEN" OUR EXISTENCE HERE, WE CAN. IT'S ONE OF THE PERKS OF MANIPULATING THIS REALITY'S CODE...
...SOMETHING ANOMALY HAS OBVIOUSLY SENSED I'M DOING AND FIGURED OUT HOW TO DO HIMSELF!
SO, I DEDUCE THAT WE'RE CURRENTLY IN A DIGIVERSE! HOW CLEVER OF YOU TO HAVE DISCOVERED THE TRUTH BEFORE ME.
I NEVER WOULD HAVE GUESSED UNTIL YOU "MAGICALLY" FLUNG ME OUT THE WINDOW JUST NOW.
IF THIS IS TO BE A WAR OF CODE MANIPULATION, I THINK YOU'LL FIND I CAN DO IT FASTER AND BETTER THAN YOU.
I WONDER IF, WHEN I KILL YOU IN THIS CYBER-REALITY, I WILL ALSO KILL YOU IN REAL LIFE.
ONLY ONE WAY TO FIND OUT...
THE THING YOU'VE NEVER UNDERSTOOD, ANOMALY...
...IS THAT YOU'VE ALWAYS BEEN DESTINED TO FAIL. BECAUSE YOU LACK THE ONE THING WHICH SETS US APART FROM YOU.

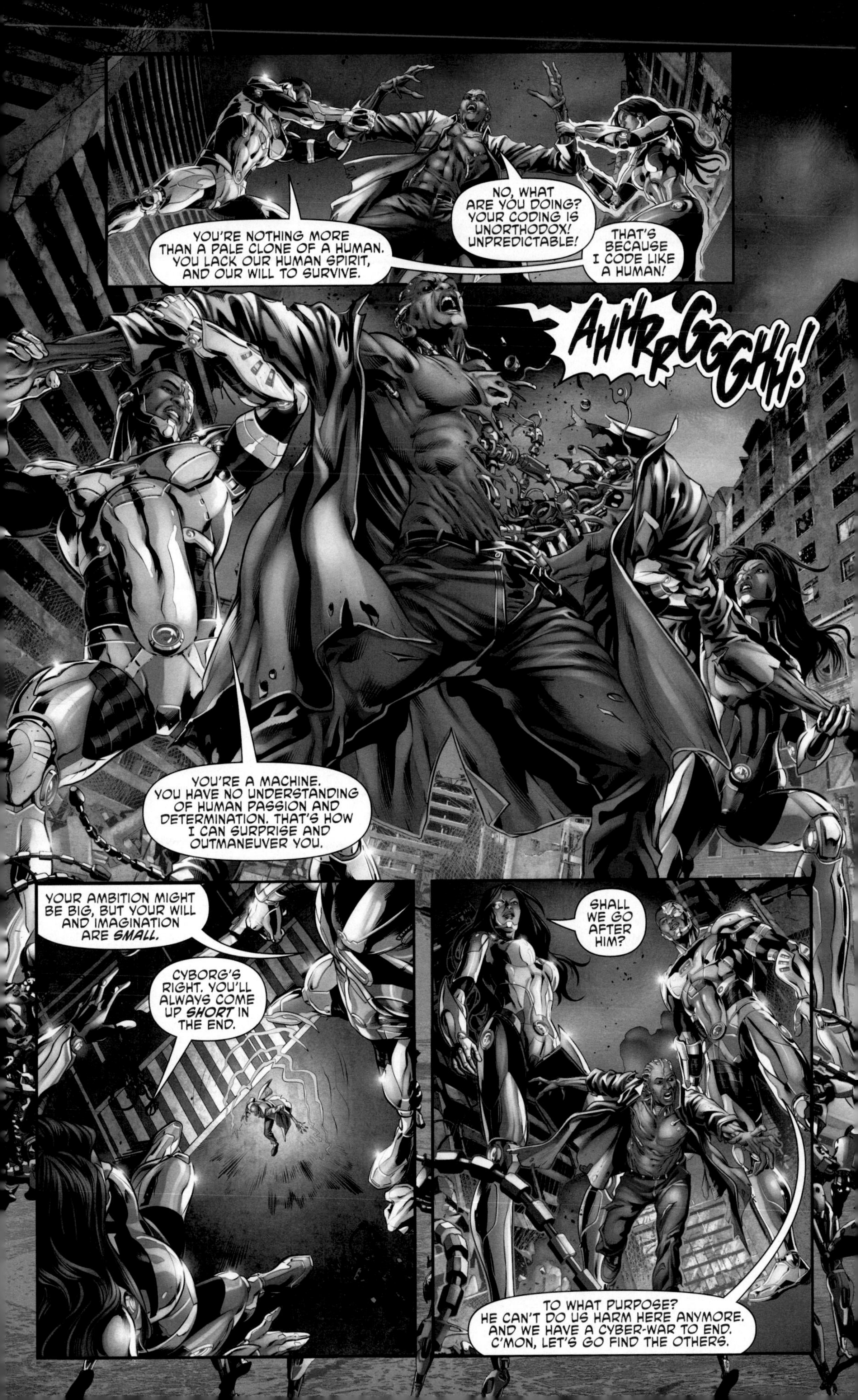

YOU'RE NOTHING MORE THAN A PALE CLONE OF A HUMAN. YOU LACK OUR HUMAN SPIRIT, AND OUR WILL TO SURVIVE.
NO, WHAT ARE YOU DOING? YOUR CODING IS UNORTHODOX! UNPREDICTABLE!
THAT'S BECAUSE I CODE LIKE A HUMAN!
AHHRRGGGHH!
YOU'RE A MACHINE. YOU HAVE NO UNDERSTANDING OF HUMAN PASSION AND DETERMINATION. THAT'S HOW I CAN SURPRISE AND OUTMANEUVER YOU.
YOUR AMBITION MIGHT BE BIG, BUT YOUR WILL AND IMAGINATION ARE *SMALL*.
CYBORG'S RIGHT. YOU'LL ALWAYS COME UP *SHORT* IN THE END.
SHALL WE GO AFTER HIM?
TO WHAT PURPOSE? HE CAN'T DO US HARM HERE ANYMORE. AND WE HAVE A CYBER-WAR TO END. C'MON, LET'S GO FIND THE OTHERS.

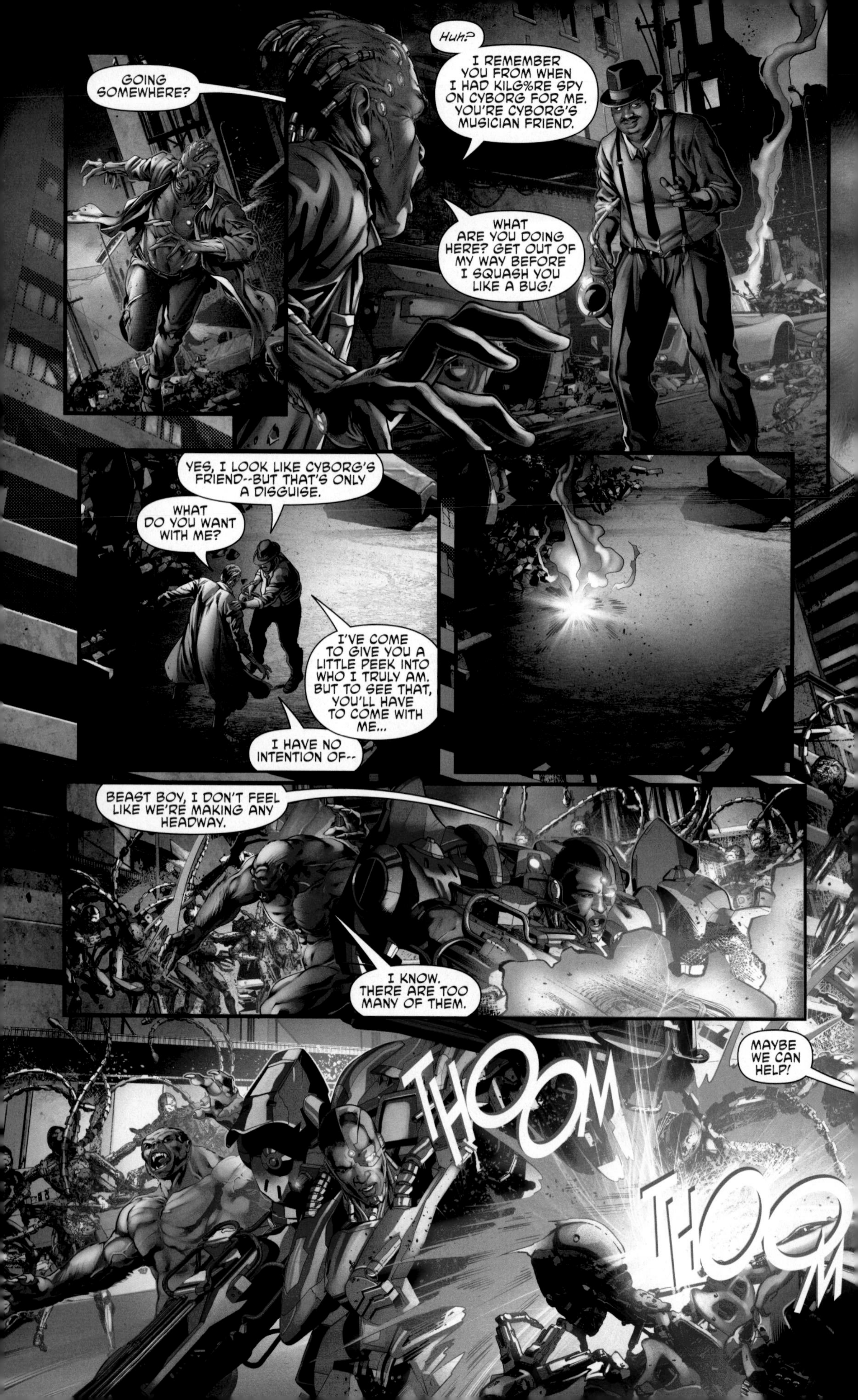
GOING SOMEWHERE?
Huh?
I REMEMBER YOU FROM WHEN I HAD KILG%RE SPY ON CYBORG FOR ME. YOU'RE CYBORG'S MUSICIAN FRIEND.
WHAT ARE YOU DOING HERE? GET OUT OF MY WAY BEFORE I SQUASH YOU LIKE A BUG!
YES, I LOOK LIKE CYBORG'S FRIEND--BUT THAT'S ONLY A DISGUISE.
WHAT DO YOU WANT WITH ME?
I'VE COME TO GIVE YOU A LITTLE PEEK INTO WHO I TRULY AM. BUT TO SEE THAT, YOU'LL HAVE TO COME WITH ME...
I HAVE NO INTENTION OF--
BEAST BOY, I DON'T FEEL LIKE WE'RE MAKING ANY HEADWAY.
I KNOW. THERE ARE TOO MANY OF THEM.
MAYBE WE CAN HELP!
THOOM
THOOM

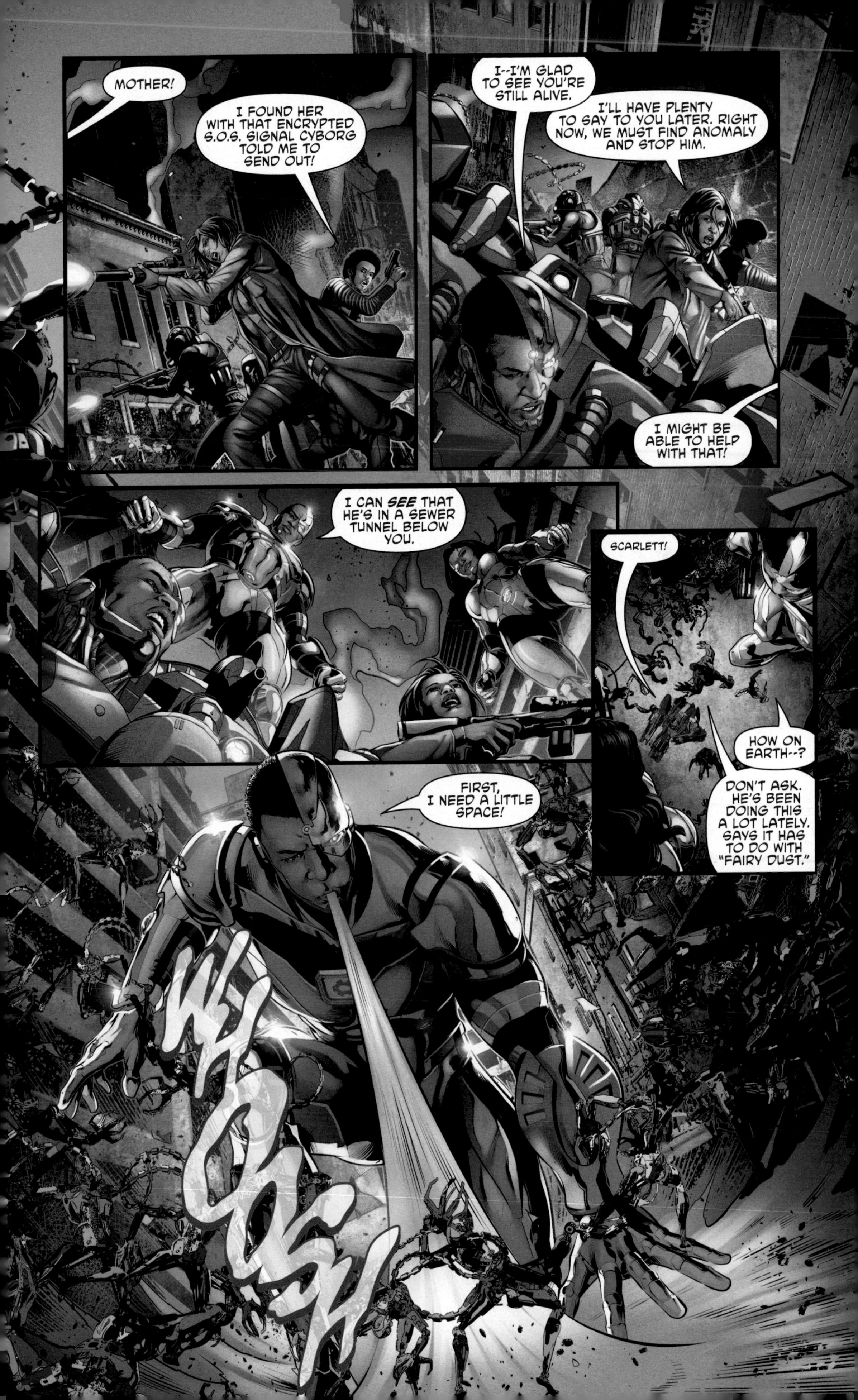

MOTHER!
I FOUND HER WITH THAT ENCRYPTED S.O.S. SIGNAL CYBORG TOLD ME TO SEND OUT!
I--I'M GLAD TO SEE YOU'RE STILL ALIVE.
I'LL HAVE PLENTY TO SAY TO YOU LATER. RIGHT NOW, WE MUST FIND ANOMALY AND STOP HIM.
I MIGHT BE ABLE TO HELP WITH THAT!
I CAN SEE THAT HE'S IN A SEWER TUNNEL BELOW YOU.
SCARLETT!
HOW ON EARTH--?
DON'T ASK. HE'S BEEN DOING THIS A LOT LATELY. SAYS IT HAS TO DO WITH "FAIRY DUST."
FIRST, I NEED A LITTLE SPACE!

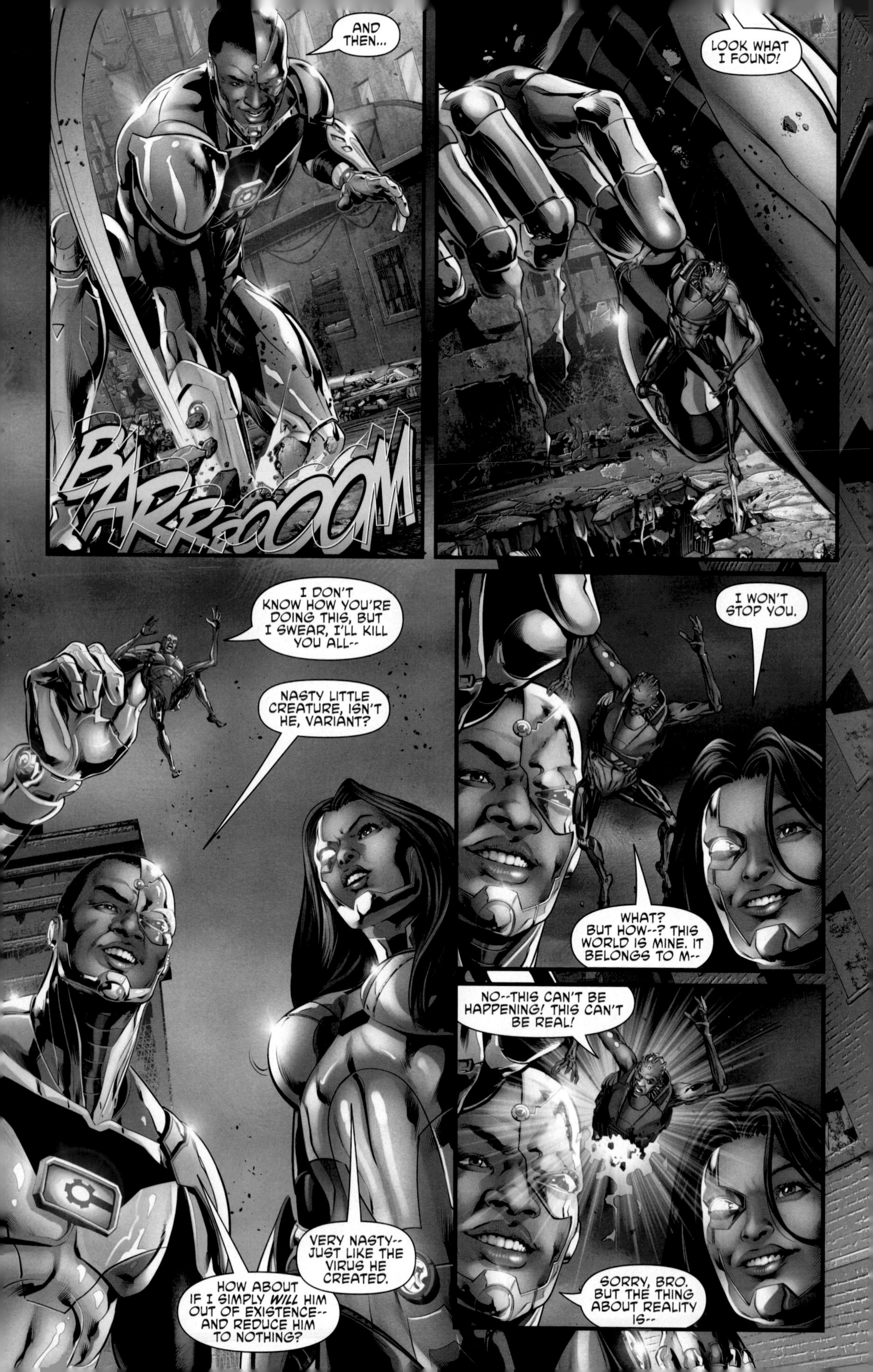
AND THEN...
BA-BARRROOOOM
LOOK WHAT I FOUND!
I DON'T KNOW HOW YOU'RE DOING THIS, BUT I SWEAR, I'LL KILL YOU ALL--
NASTY LITTLE CREATURE, ISN'T HE, VARIANT?
HOW ABOUT IF I SIMPLY WILL HIM OUT OF EXISTENCE--AND REDUCE HIM TO NOTHING?
VERY NASTY--JUST LIKE THE VIRUS HE CREATED.
I WON'T STOP YOU.
WHAT? BUT HOW--? THIS WORLD IS MINE. IT BELONGS TO M--
NO--THIS CAN'T BE HAPPENING! THIS CAN'T BE REAL!
SORRY, BRO. BUT THE THING ABOUT REALITY IS--

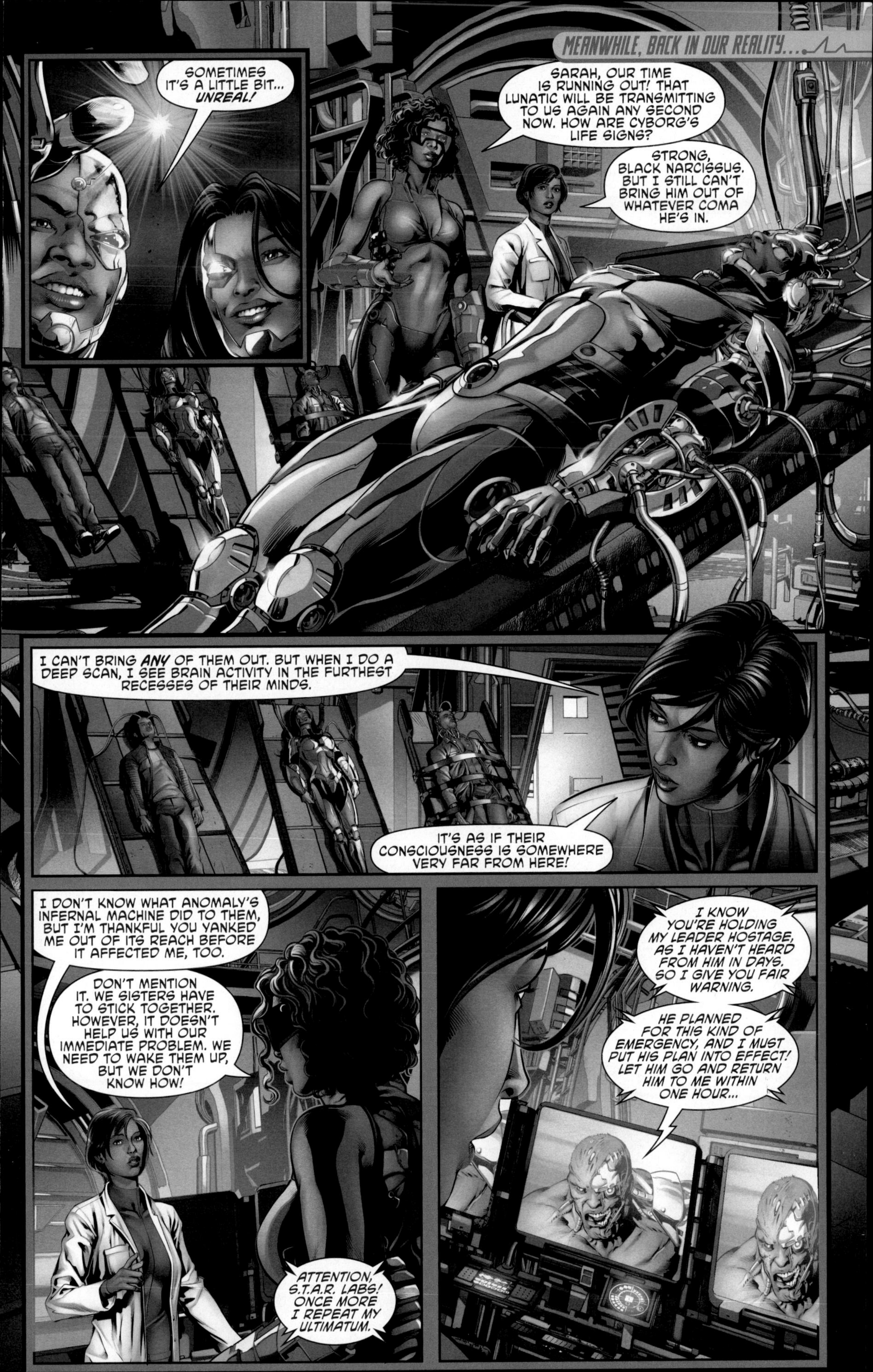
MEANWHILE, BACK IN OUR REALITY...
SOMETIMES IT'S A LITTLE BIT... UNREAL!
SARAH, OUR TIME IS RUNNING OUT! THAT LUNATIC WILL BE TRANSMITTING TO US AGAIN ANY SECOND NOW. HOW ARE CYBORG'S LIFE SIGNS?
STRONG, BLACK NARCISSUS. BUT I STILL CAN'T BRING HIM OUT OF WHATEVER COMA HE'S IN.
I CAN'T BRING ANY OF THEM OUT. BUT WHEN I DO A DEEP SCAN, I SEE BRAIN ACTIVITY IN THE FURTHEST RECESSES OF THEIR MINDS.
IT'S AS IF THEIR CONSCIOUSNESS IS SOMEWHERE VERY FAR FROM HERE!
I DON'T KNOW WHAT ANOMALY'S INFERNAL MACHINE DID TO THEM, BUT I'M THANKFUL YOU YANKED ME OUT OF ITS REACH BEFORE IT AFFECTED ME, TOO.
DON'T MENTION IT. WE SISTERS HAVE TO STICK TOGETHER. HOWEVER, IT DOESN'T HELP US WITH OUR IMMEDIATE PROBLEM. WE NEED TO WAKE THEM UP, BUT WE DON'T KNOW HOW!
ATTENTION, S.T.A.R. LABS! ONCE MORE I REPEAT MY ULTIMATUM.
I KNOW YOU'RE HOLDING MY LEADER HOSTAGE, AS I HAVEN'T HEARD FROM HIM IN DAYS, SO I GIVE YOU FAIR WARNING.
HE PLANNED FOR THIS KIND OF EMERGENCY, AND I MUST PUT HIS PLAN INTO EFFECT! LET HIM GO AND RETURN HIM TO ME WITHIN ONE HOUR...

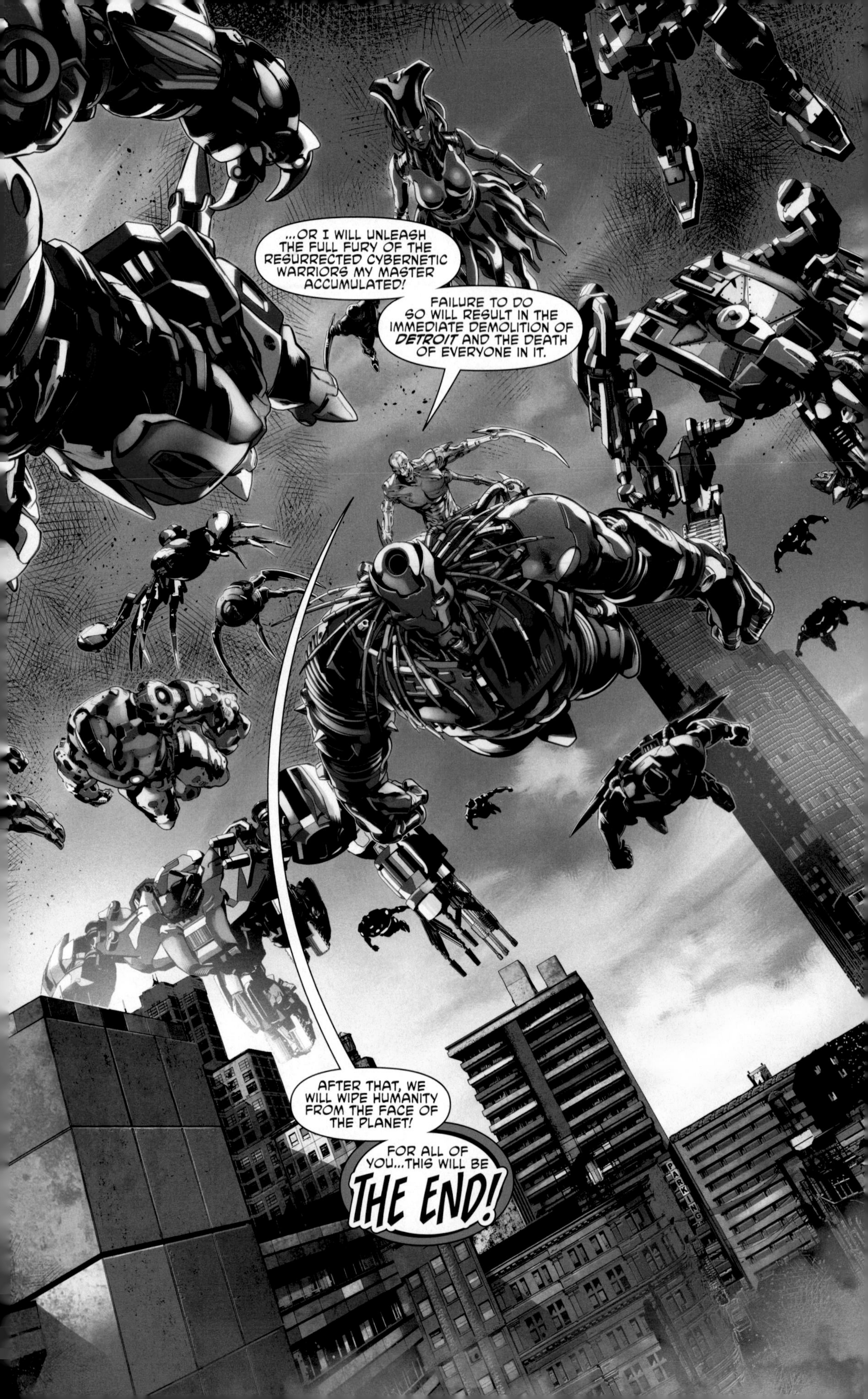
...OR I WILL UNLEASH THE FULL FURY OF THE RESURRECTED CYBERNETIC WARRIORS MY MASTER ACCUMULATED!
FAILURE TO DO SO WILL RESULT IN THE IMMEDIATE DEMOLITION OF DETROIT AND THE DEATH OF EVERYONE IN IT.
AFTER THAT, WE WILL WIPE HUMANITY FROM THE FACE OF THE PLANET!
FOR ALL OF YOU...THIS WILL BE THE END!
PARKING

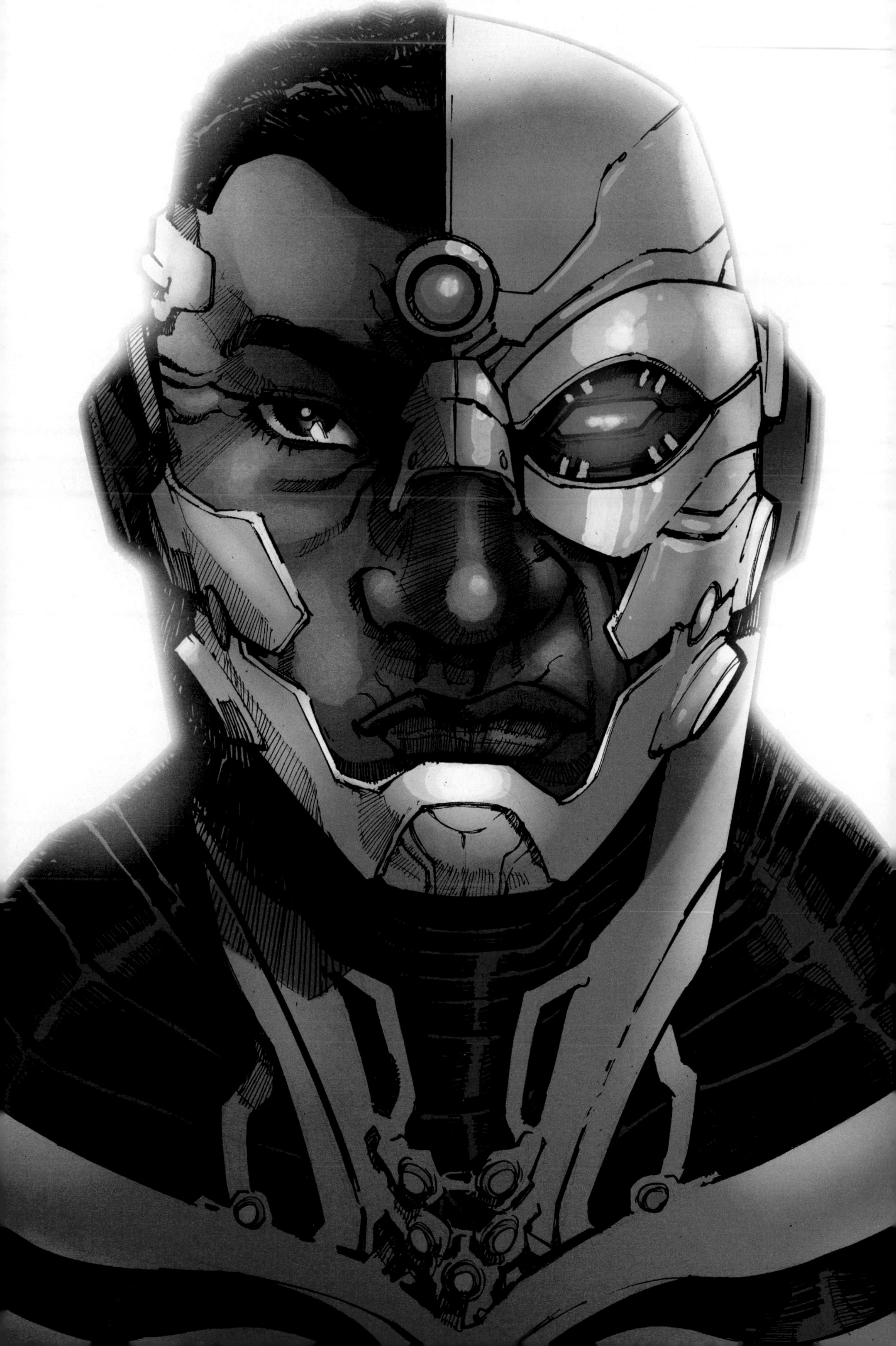

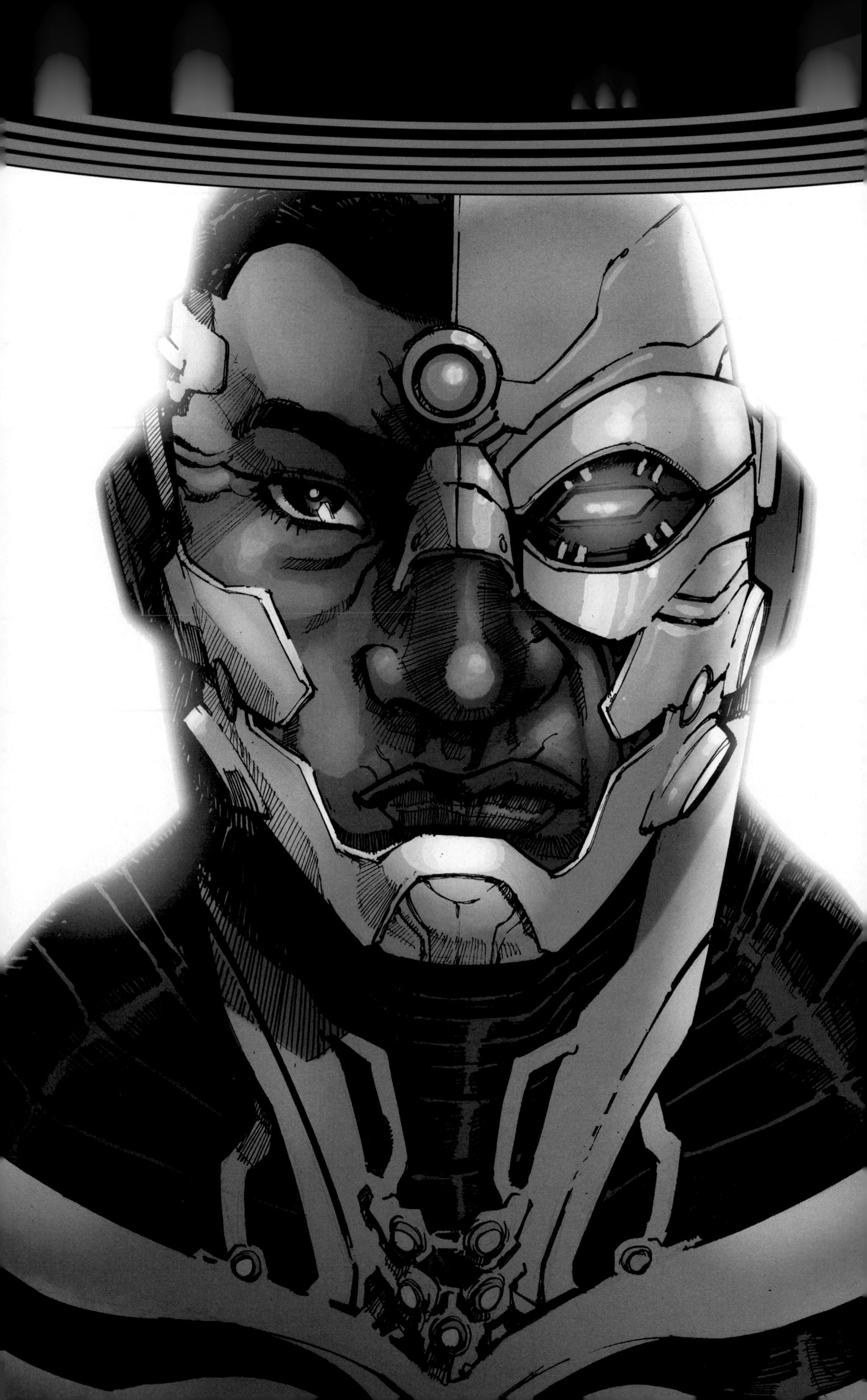

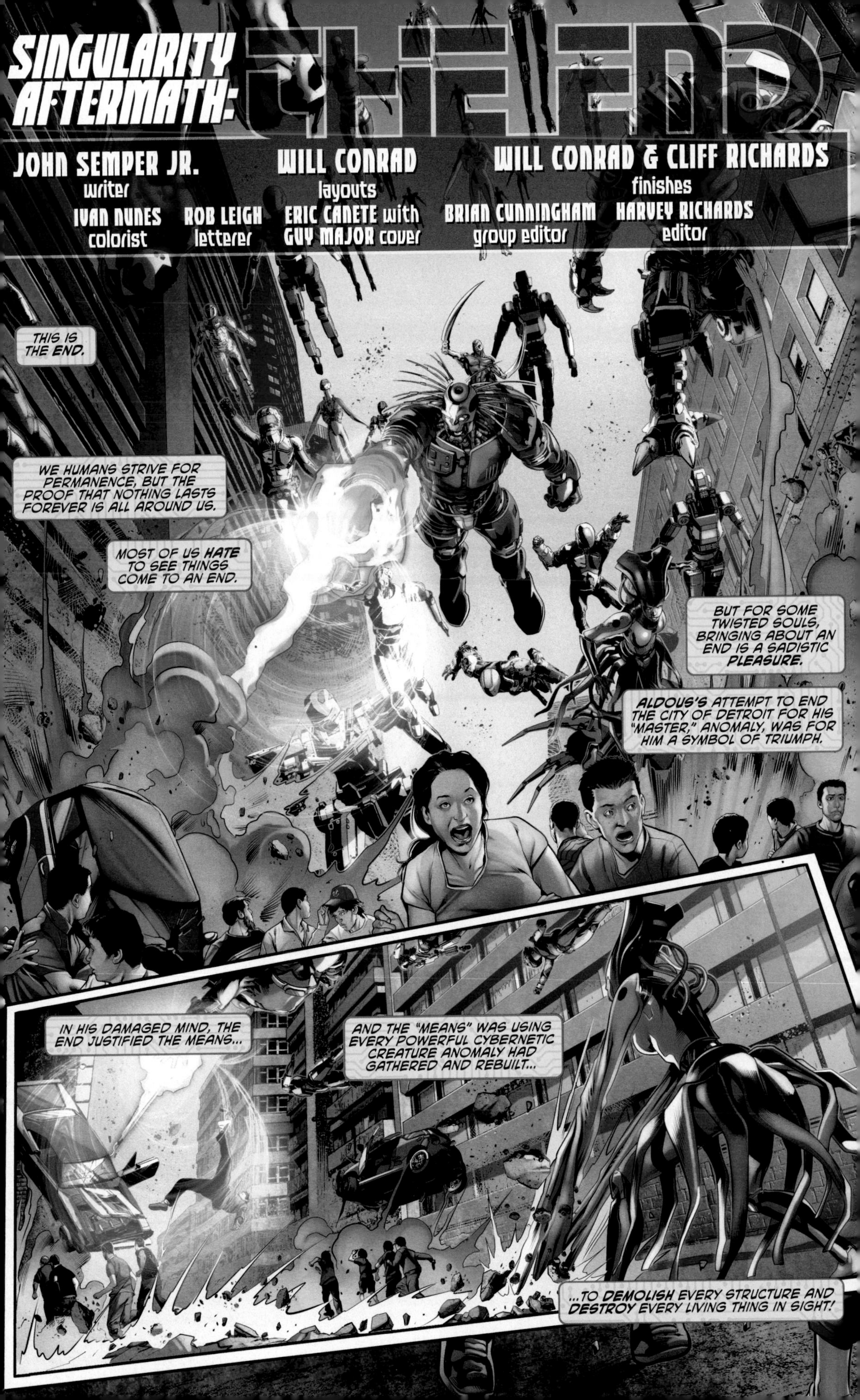
SINGULARITY AFTERMATH: THE END
JOHN SEMPER JR. writer
WILL CONRAD layouts
WILL CONRAD & CLIFF RICHARDS finishes
IVAN NUNES colorist
ROB LEIGH letterer
ERIC CANETE with GUY MAJOR cover
BRIAN CUNNINGHAM group editor
HARVEY RICHARDS editor
THIS IS THE END.
WE HUMANS STRIVE FOR PERMANENCE, BUT THE PROOF THAT NOTHING LASTS FOREVER IS ALL AROUND US.
MOST OF US HATE TO SEE THINGS COME TO AN END.
BUT FOR SOME TWISTED SOULS, BRINGING ABOUT AN END IS A SADISTIC PLEASURE.
ALDOUS'S ATTEMPT TO END THE CITY OF DETROIT FOR HIS "MASTER," ANOMALY, WAS FOR HIM A SYMBOL OF TRIUMPH.
IN HIS DAMAGED MIND, THE END JUSTIFIED THE MEANS...
AND THE "MEANS" WAS USING EVERY POWERFUL CYBERNETIC CREATURE ANOMALY HAD GATHERED AND REBUILT...
...TO DEMOLISH EVERY STRUCTURE AND DESTROY EVERY LIVING THING IN SIGHT!

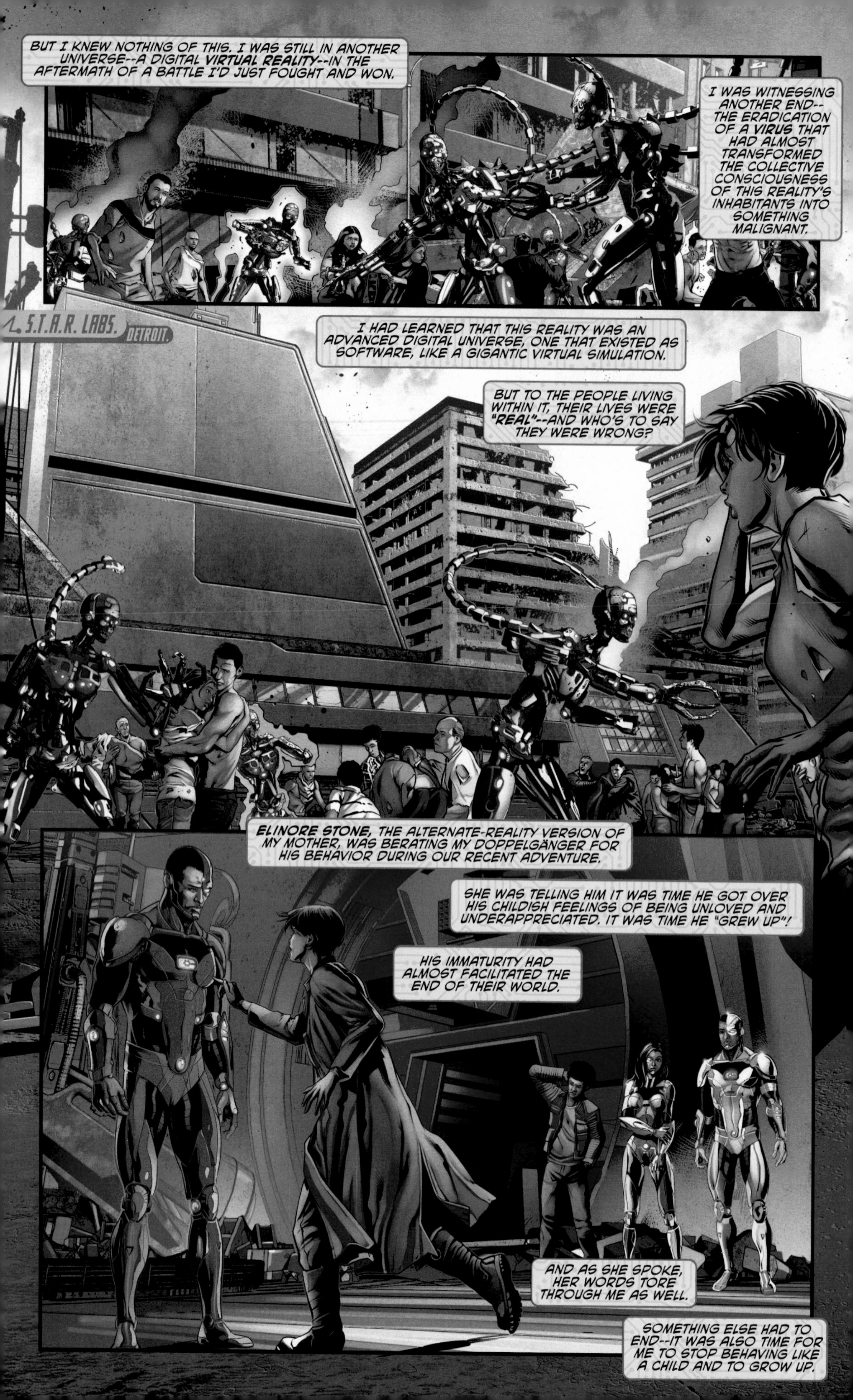

BUT I KNEW NOTHING OF THIS. I WAS STILL IN ANOTHER UNIVERSE--A DIGITAL VIRTUAL REALITY--IN THE AFTERMATH OF A BATTLE I'D JUST FOUGHT AND WON.
I WAS WITNESSING ANOTHER END--THE ERADICATION OF A VIRUS THAT HAD ALMOST TRANSFORMED THE COLLECTIVE CONSCIOUSNESS OF THIS REALITY'S INHABITANTS INTO SOMETHING MALIGNANT.
S.T.A.R. LABS. DETROIT.
I HAD LEARNED THAT THIS REALITY WAS AN ADVANCED DIGITAL UNIVERSE, ONE THAT EXISTED AS SOFTWARE, LIKE A GIGANTIC VIRTUAL SIMULATION.
BUT TO THE PEOPLE LIVING WITHIN IT, THEIR LIVES WERE "REAL"--AND WHO'S TO SAY THEY WERE WRONG?
ELINORE STONE, THE ALTERNATE-REALITY VERSION OF MY MOTHER, WAS BERATING MY DOPPELGÄNGER FOR HIS BEHAVIOR DURING OUR RECENT ADVENTURE.
SHE WAS TELLING HIM IT WAS TIME HE GOT OVER HIS CHILDISH FEELINGS OF BEING UNLOVED AND UNDERAPPRECIATED. IT WAS TIME HE "GREW UP"!
HIS IMMATURITY HAD ALMOST FACILITATED THE END OF THEIR WORLD.
AND AS SHE SPOKE, HER WORDS TORE THROUGH ME AS WELL.
SOMETHING ELSE HAD TO END--IT WAS ALSO TIME FOR ME TO STOP BEHAVING LIKE A CHILD AND TO GROW UP.

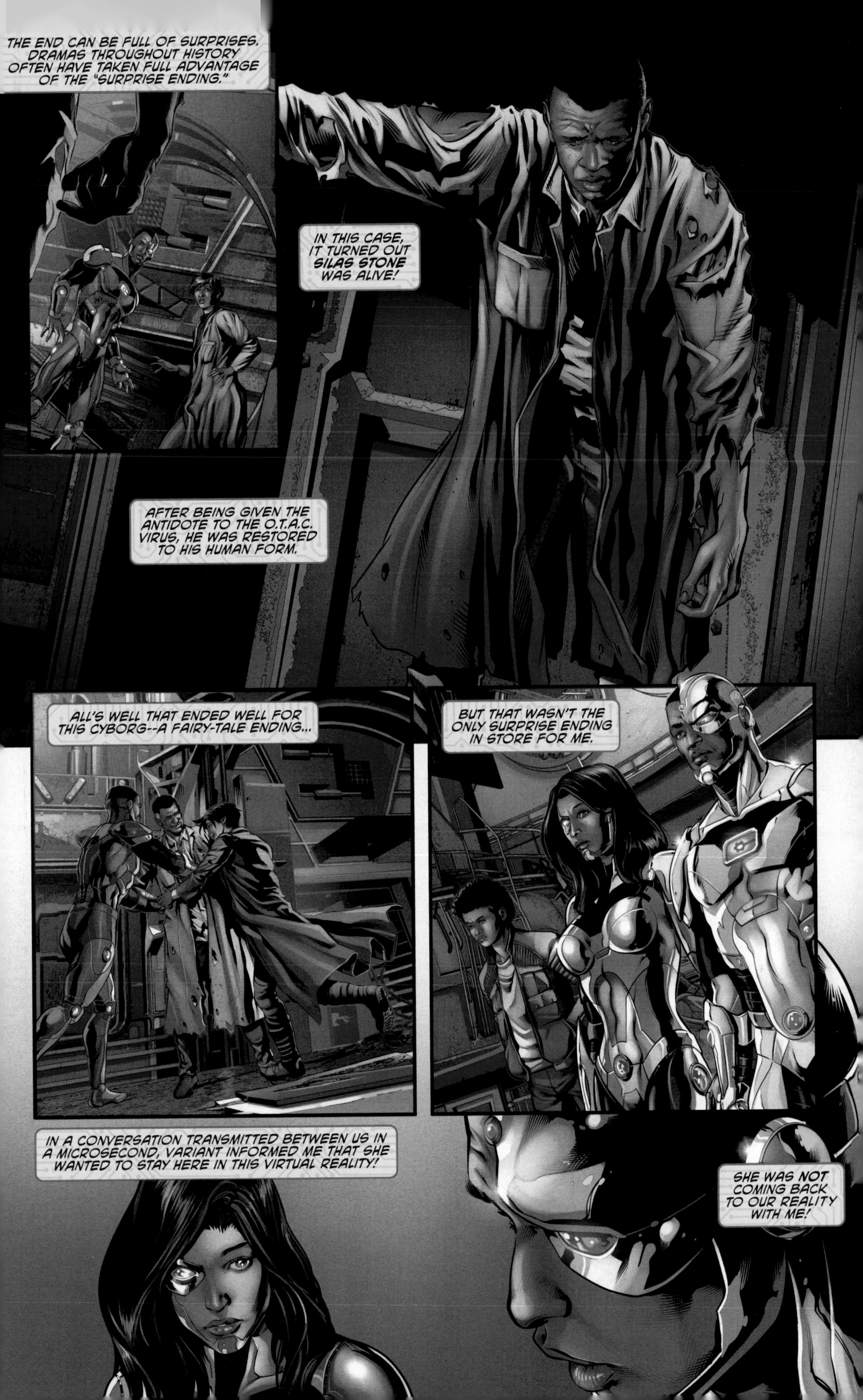
THE END CAN BE FULL OF SURPRISES. DRAMAS THROUGHOUT HISTORY OFTEN HAVE TAKEN FULL ADVANTAGE OF THE "SURPRISE ENDING."
IN THIS CASE, IT TURNED OUT SILAS STONE WAS ALIVE!
AFTER BEING GIVEN THE ANTIDOTE TO THE O.T.A.C. VIRUS, HE WAS RESTORED TO HIS HUMAN FORM.
ALL'S WELL THAT ENDED WELL FOR THIS CYBORG--A FAIRY-TALE ENDING...
BUT THAT WASN'T THE ONLY SURPRISE ENDING IN STORE FOR ME.
IN A CONVERSATION TRANSMITTED BETWEEN US IN A MICROSECOND, VARIANT INFORMED ME THAT SHE WANTED TO STAY HERE IN THIS VIRTUAL REALITY!
SHE WAS NOT COMING BACK TO OUR REALITY WITH ME!

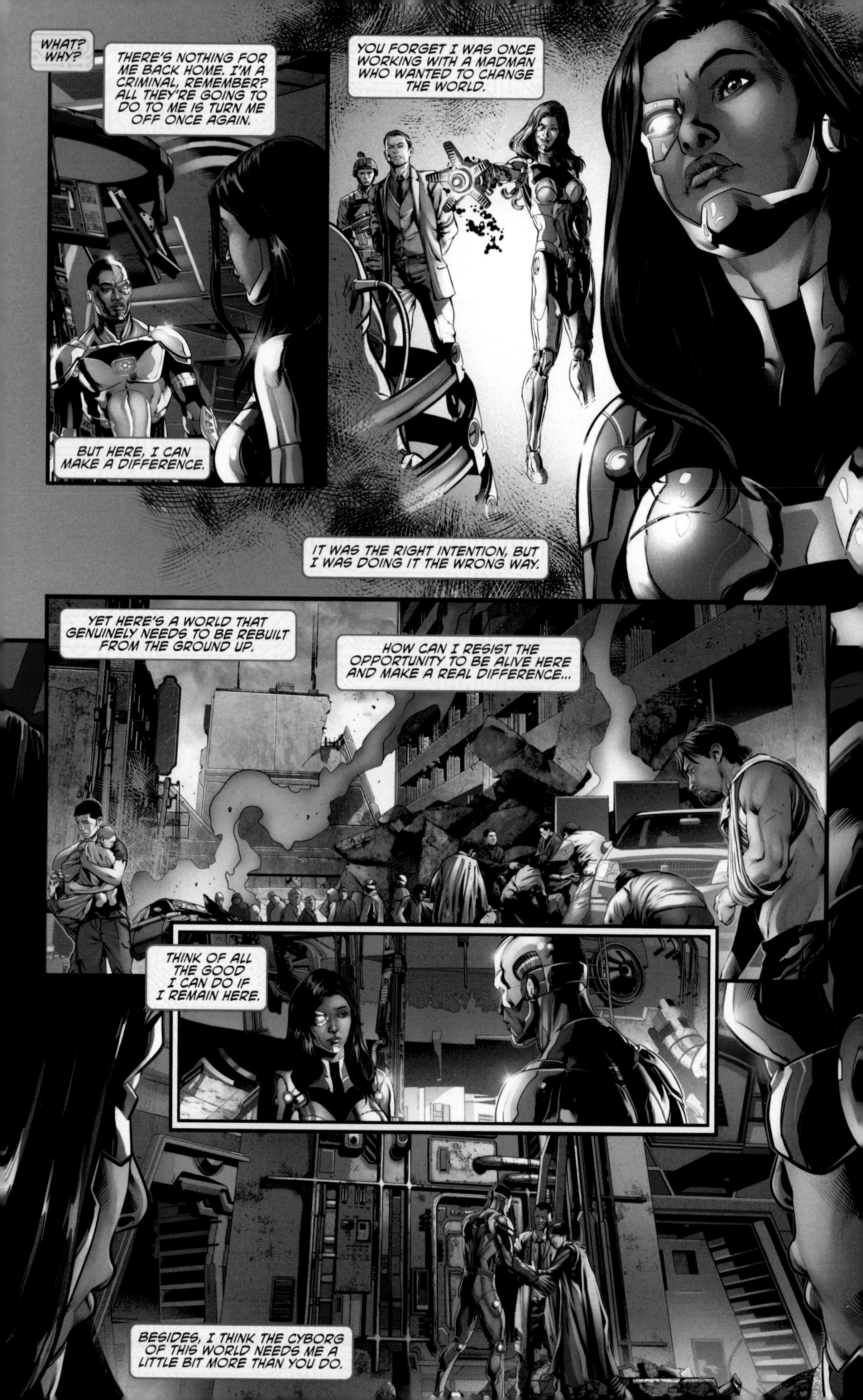
WHAT? WHY?
THERE'S NOTHING FOR ME BACK HOME. I'M A CRIMINAL, REMEMBER? ALL THEY'RE GOING TO DO TO ME IS TURN ME OFF ONCE AGAIN.
BUT HERE, I CAN MAKE A DIFFERENCE.
YOU FORGET I WAS ONCE WORKING WITH A MADMAN WHO WANTED TO CHANGE THE WORLD.
IT WAS THE RIGHT INTENTION, BUT I WAS DOING IT THE WRONG WAY.
YET HERE'S A WORLD THAT GENUINELY NEEDS TO BE REBUILT FROM THE GROUND UP.
HOW CAN I RESIST THE OPPORTUNITY TO BE ALIVE HERE AND MAKE A REAL DIFFERENCE...
THINK OF ALL THE GOOD I CAN DO IF I REMAIN HERE.
BESIDES, I THINK THE CYBORG OF THIS WORLD NEEDS ME A LITTLE BIT MORE THAN YOU DO.

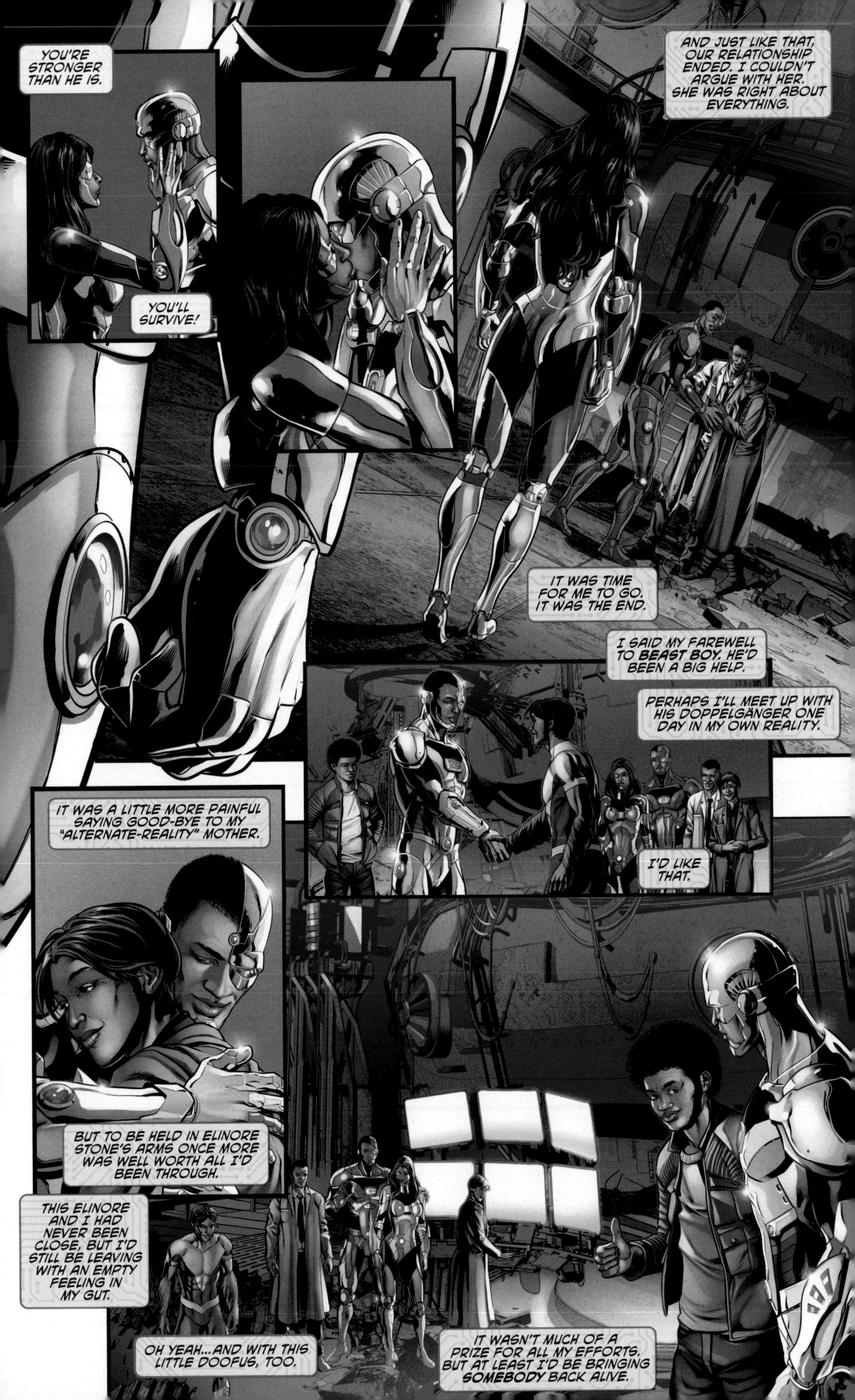
YOU'RE STRONGER THAN HE IS.
YOU'LL SURVIVE!
AND JUST LIKE THAT, OUR RELATIONSHIP ENDED. I COULDN'T ARGUE WITH HER. SHE WAS RIGHT ABOUT EVERYTHING.
IT WAS TIME FOR ME TO GO. IT WAS THE END.
I SAID MY FAREWELL TO BEAST BOY. HE'D BEEN A BIG HELP.
PERHAPS I'LL MEET UP WITH HIS DOPPELGÄNGER ONE DAY IN MY OWN REALITY.
I'D LIKE THAT.
IT WAS A LITTLE MORE PAINFUL SAYING GOOD-BYE TO MY "ALTERNATE-REALITY" MOTHER.
BUT TO BE HELD IN ELINORE STONE'S ARMS ONCE MORE WAS WELL WORTH ALL I'D BEEN THROUGH.
THIS ELINORE AND I HAD NEVER BEEN CLOSE, BUT I'D STILL BE LEAVING WITH AN EMPTY FEELING IN MY GUT.
OH YEAH...AND WITH THIS LITTLE DOOFUS, TOO.
IT WASN'T MUCH OF A PRIZE FOR ALL MY EFFORTS. BUT AT LEAST I'D BE BRINGING SOMEBODY BACK ALIVE.

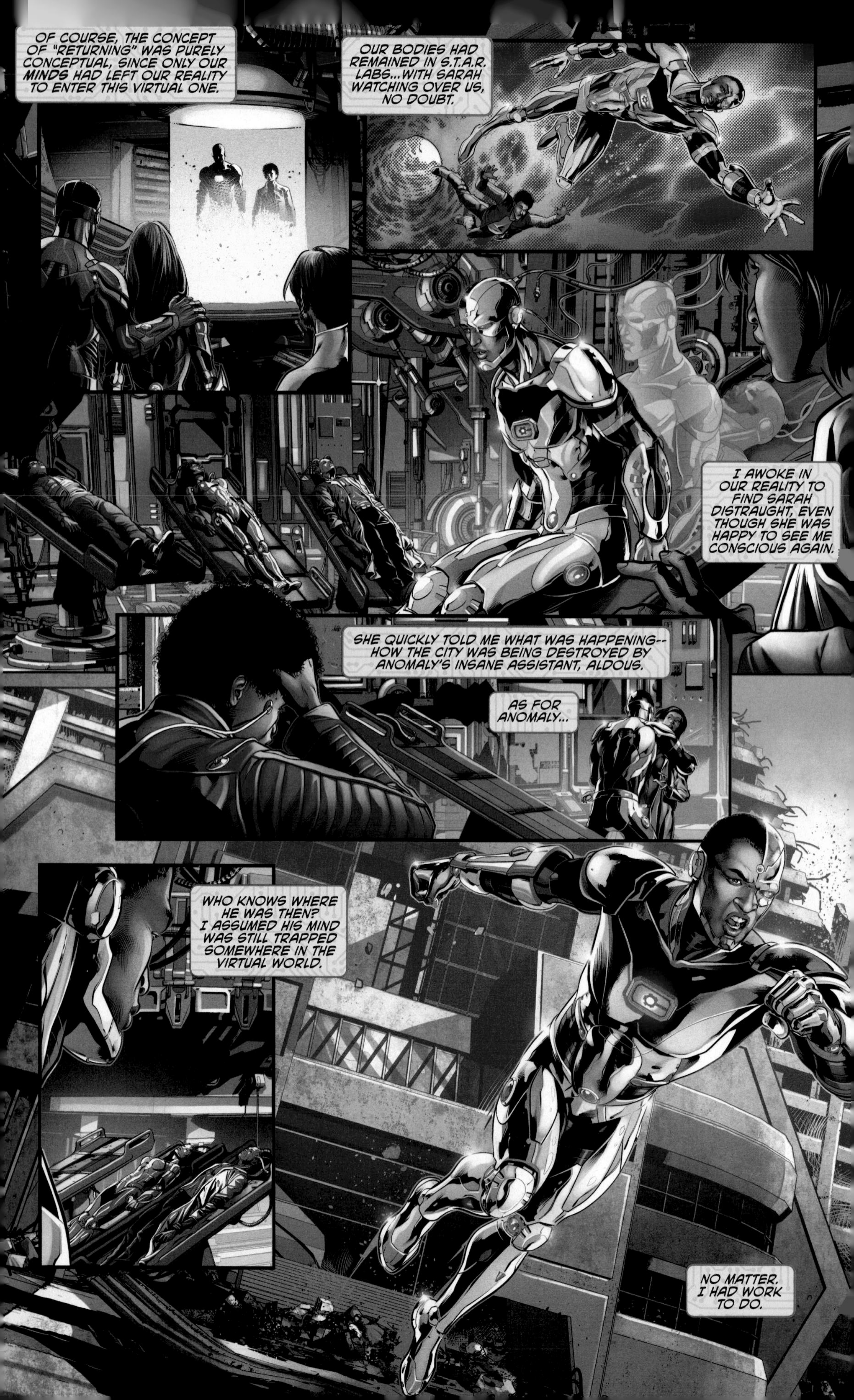
OF COURSE, THE CONCEPT OF "RETURNING" WAS PURELY CONCEPTUAL, SINCE ONLY OUR MINDS HAD LEFT OUR REALITY TO ENTER THIS VIRTUAL ONE.
OUR BODIES HAD REMAINED IN S.T.A.R. LABS...WITH SARAH WATCHING OVER US, NO DOUBT.
I AWOKE IN OUR REALITY TO FIND SARAH DISTRAUGHT, EVEN THOUGH SHE WAS HAPPY TO SEE ME CONSCIOUS AGAIN.
SHE QUICKLY TOLD ME WHAT WAS HAPPENING--HOW THE CITY WAS BEING DESTROYED BY ANOMALY'S INSANE ASSISTANT, ALDOUS.
AS FOR ANOMALY...
WHO KNOWS WHERE HE WAS THEN? I ASSUMED HIS MIND WAS STILL TRAPPED SOMEWHERE IN THE VIRTUAL WORLD.
NO MATTER. I HAD WORK TO DO.

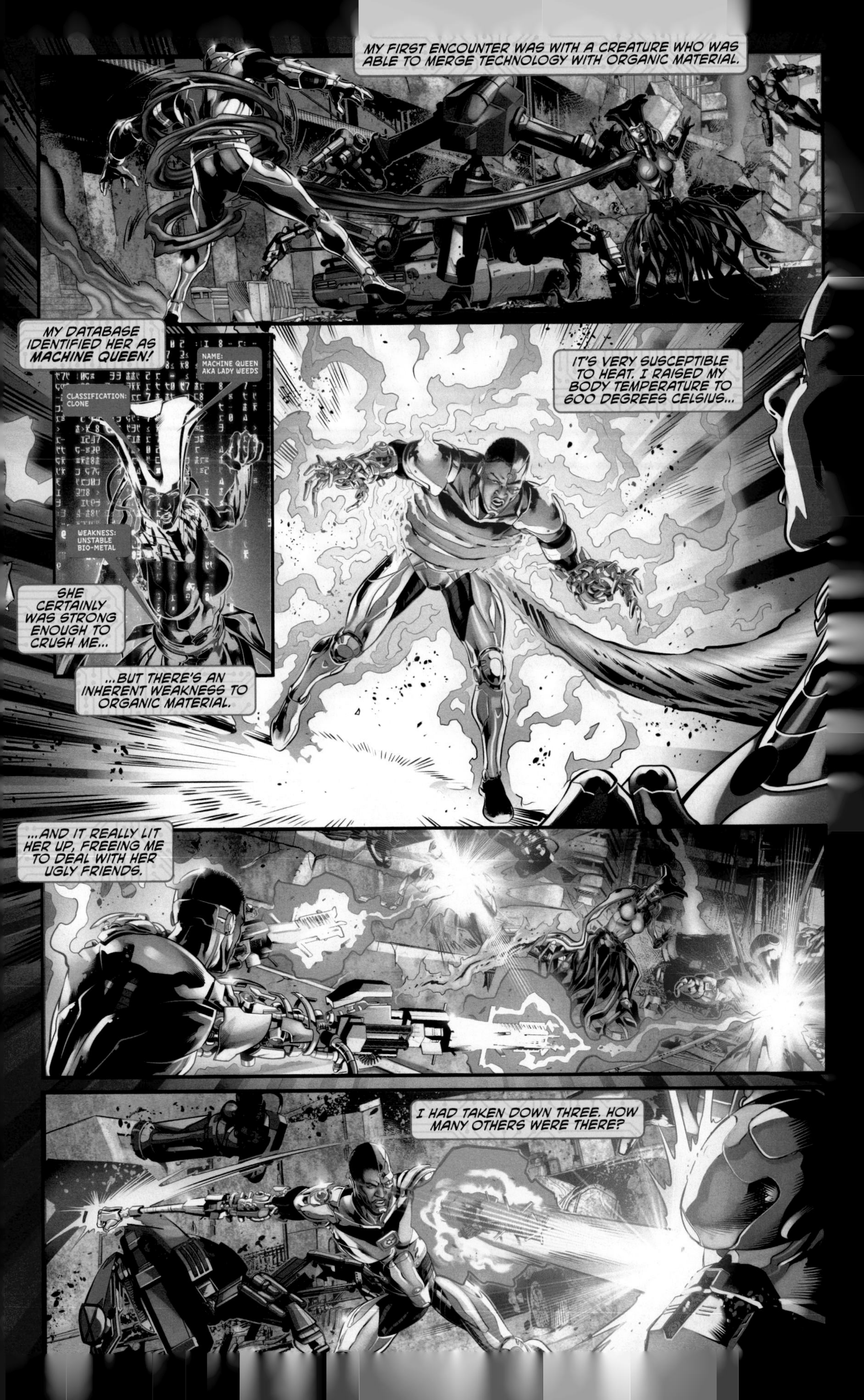
MY FIRST ENCOUNTER WAS WITH A CREATURE WHO WAS ABLE TO MERGE TECHNOLOGY WITH ORGANIC MATERIAL.
MY DATABASE IDENTIFIED HER AS MACHINE QUEEN!
NAME: MACHINE QUEEN AKA LADY WEEDS
CLASSIFICATION: CLONE
WEAKNESS: UNSTABLE BIO-METAL
SHE CERTAINLY WAS STRONG ENOUGH TO CRUSH ME...
...BUT THERE'S AN INHERENT WEAKNESS TO ORGANIC MATERIAL.
IT'S VERY SUSCEPTIBLE TO HEAT. I RAISED MY BODY TEMPERATURE TO 600 DEGREES CELSIUS...
...AND IT REALLY LIT HER UP, FREEING ME TO DEAL WITH HER UGLY FRIENDS.
I HAD TAKEN DOWN THREE. HOW MANY OTHERS WERE THERE?

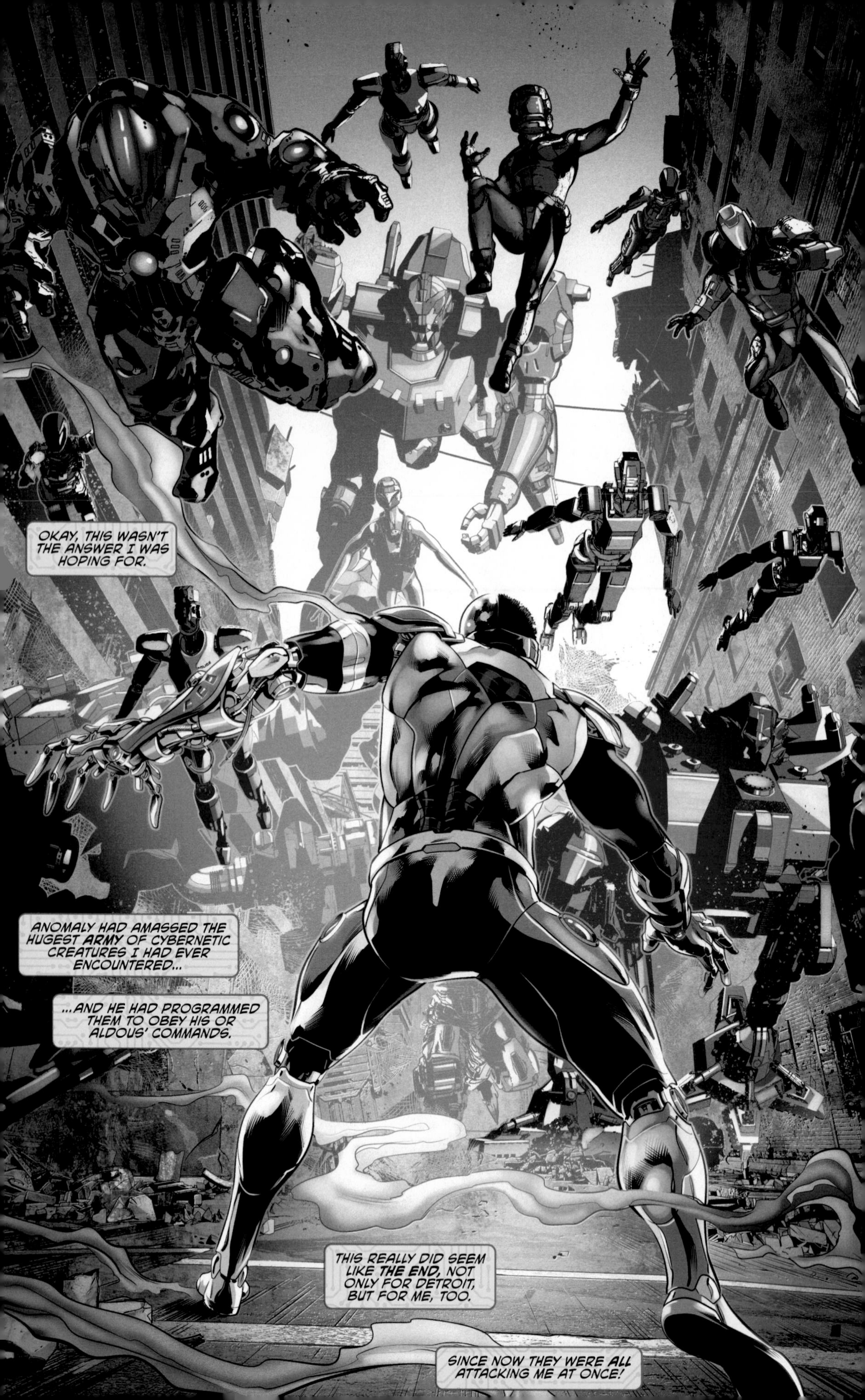
OKAY, THIS WASN'T THE ANSWER I WAS HOPING FOR.
ANOMALY HAD AMASSED THE HUGEST ARMY OF CYBERNETIC CREATURES I HAD EVER ENCOUNTERED...
...AND HE HAD PROGRAMMED THEM TO OBEY HIS OR ALDOUS' COMMANDS.
THIS REALLY DID SEEM LIKE THE END, NOT ONLY FOR DETROIT, BUT FOR ME, TOO.
SINCE NOW THEY WERE ALL ATTACKING ME AT ONCE!

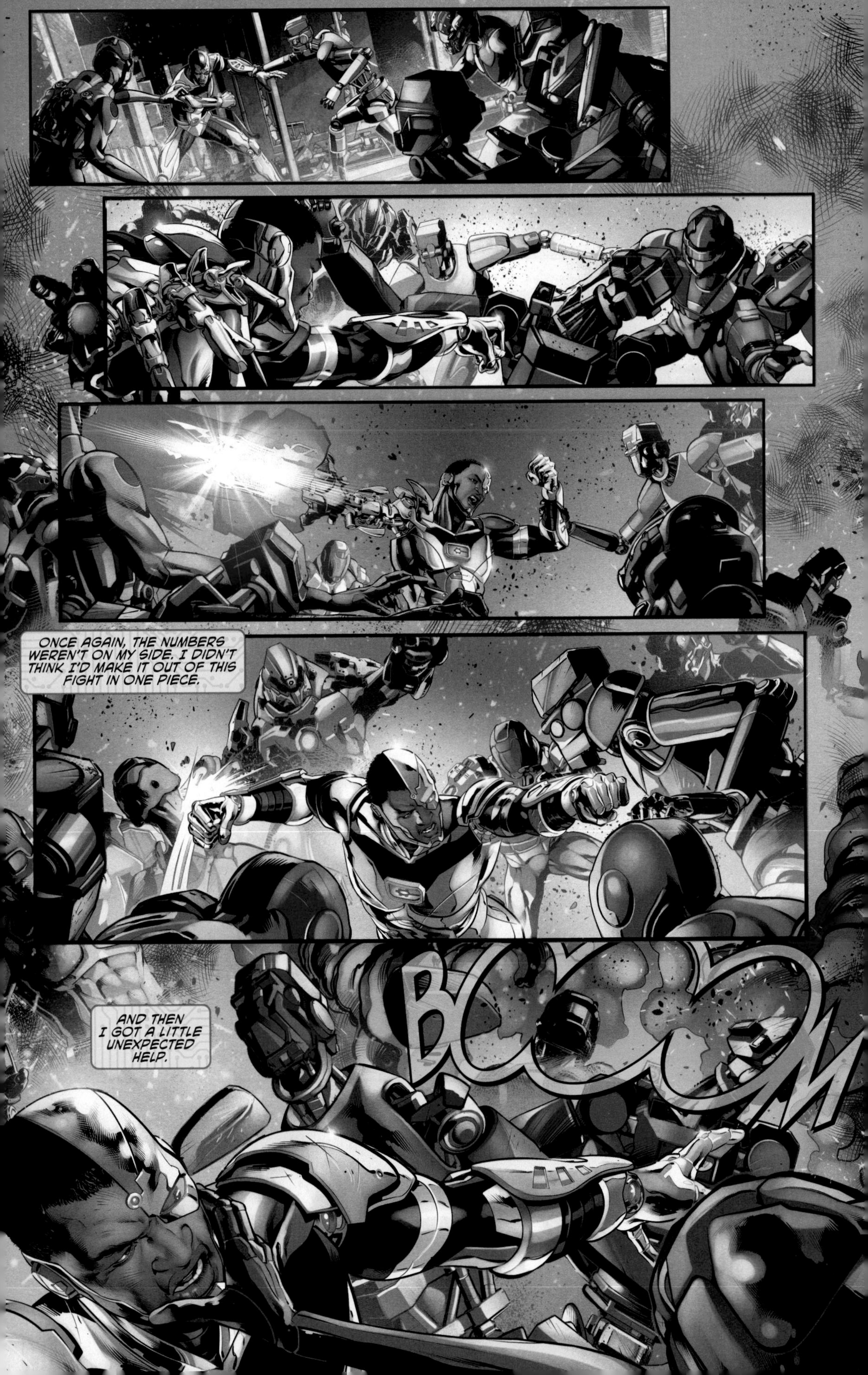
ONCE AGAIN, THE NUMBERS WEREN'T ON MY SIDE. I DIDN'T THINK I'D MAKE IT OUT OF THIS FIGHT IN ONE PIECE.
AND THEN I GOT A LITTLE UNEXPECTED HELP.
BOOOM

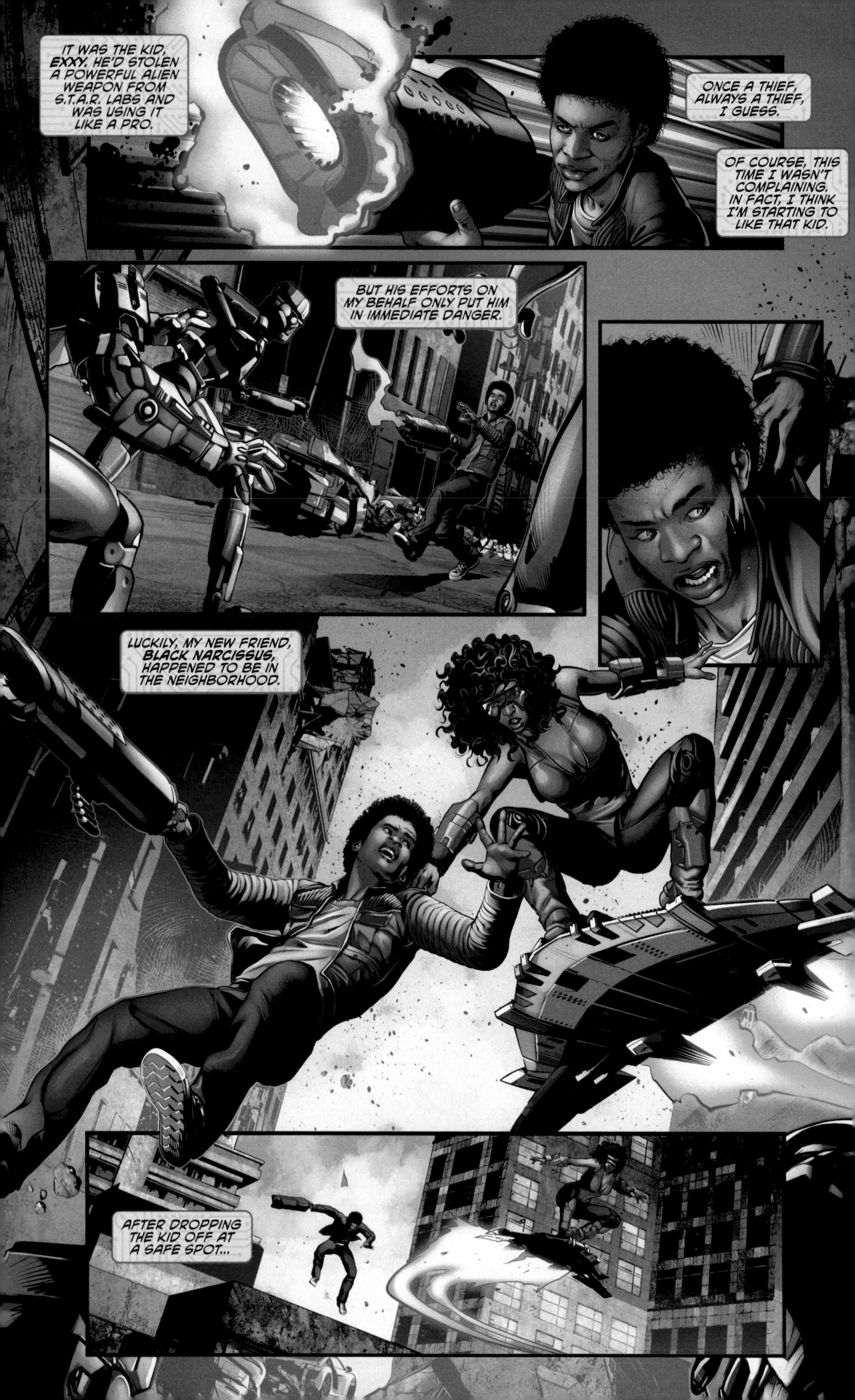
IT WAS THE KID, EXXY. HE'D STOLEN A POWERFUL ALIEN WEAPON FROM S.T.A.R. LABS AND WAS USING IT LIKE A PRO.
ONCE A THIEF, ALWAYS A THIEF, I GUESS.
OF COURSE, THIS TIME I WASN'T COMPLAINING. IN FACT, I THINK I'M STARTING TO LIKE THAT KID.
BUT HIS EFFORTS ON MY BEHALF ONLY PUT HIM IN IMMEDIATE DANGER.
LUCKILY, MY NEW FRIEND, BLACK NARCISSUS, HAPPENED TO BE IN THE NEIGHBORHOOD.
AFTER DROPPING THE KID OFF AT A SAFE SPOT...

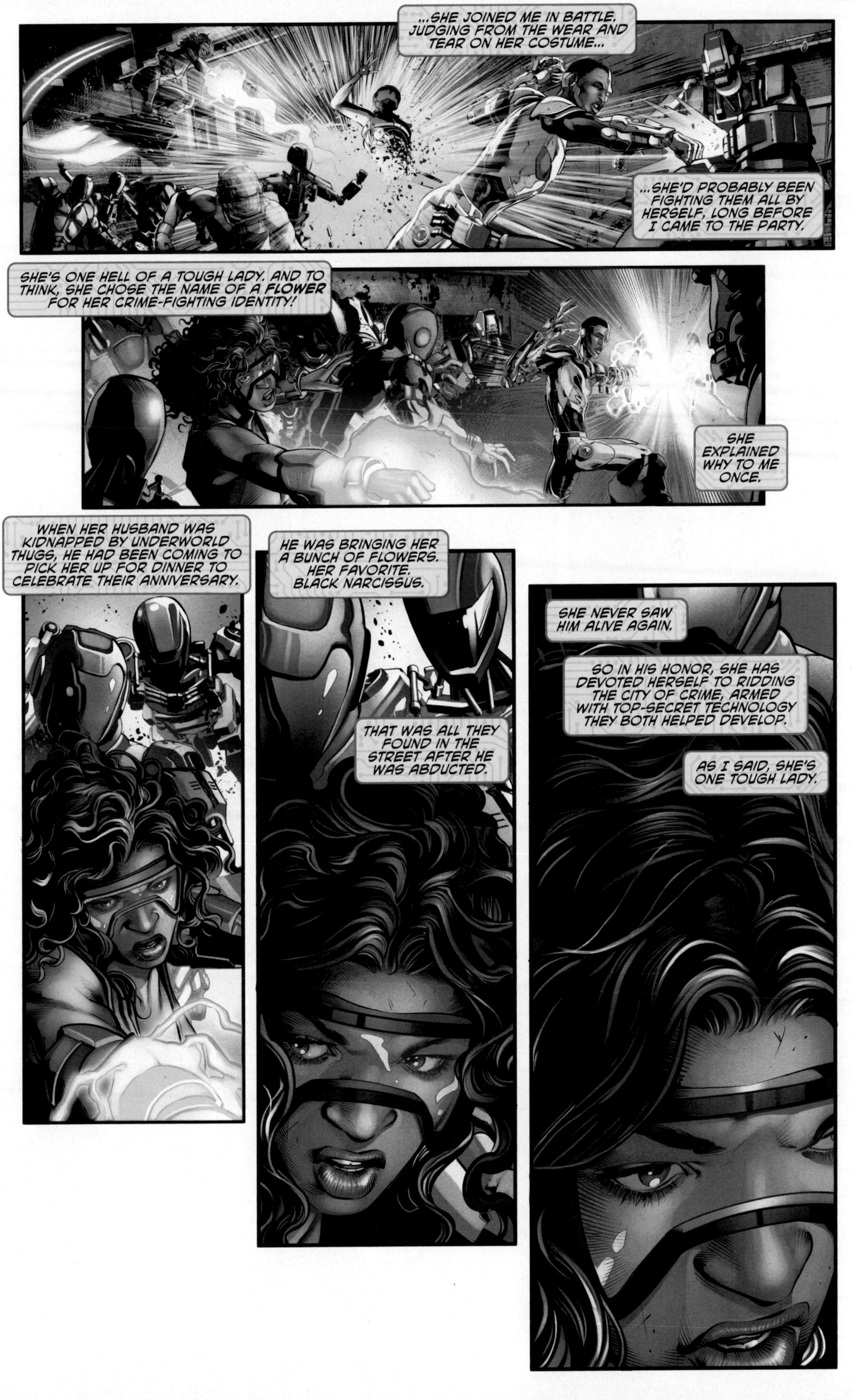
...SHE JOINED ME IN BATTLE. JUDGING FROM THE WEAR AND TEAR ON HER COSTUME...
...SHE'D PROBABLY BEEN FIGHTING THEM ALL BY HERSELF, LONG BEFORE I CAME TO THE PARTY.
SHE'S ONE HELL OF A TOUGH LADY. AND TO THINK, SHE CHOSE THE NAME OF A FLOWER FOR HER CRIME-FIGHTING IDENTITY!
SHE EXPLAINED WHY TO ME ONCE.
WHEN HER HUSBAND WAS KIDNAPPED BY UNDERWORLD THUGS, HE HAD BEEN COMING TO PICK HER UP FOR DINNER TO CELEBRATE THEIR ANNIVERSARY.
HE WAS BRINGING HER A BUNCH OF FLOWERS. HER FAVORITE. BLACK NARCISSUS.
THAT WAS ALL THEY FOUND IN THE STREET AFTER HE WAS ABDUCTED.
SHE NEVER SAW HIM ALIVE AGAIN.
SO IN HIS HONOR, SHE HAS DEVOTED HERSELF TO RIDDING THE CITY OF CRIME, ARMED WITH TOP-SECRET TECHNOLOGY THEY BOTH HELPED DEVELOP.
AS I SAID, SHE'S ONE TOUGH LADY.

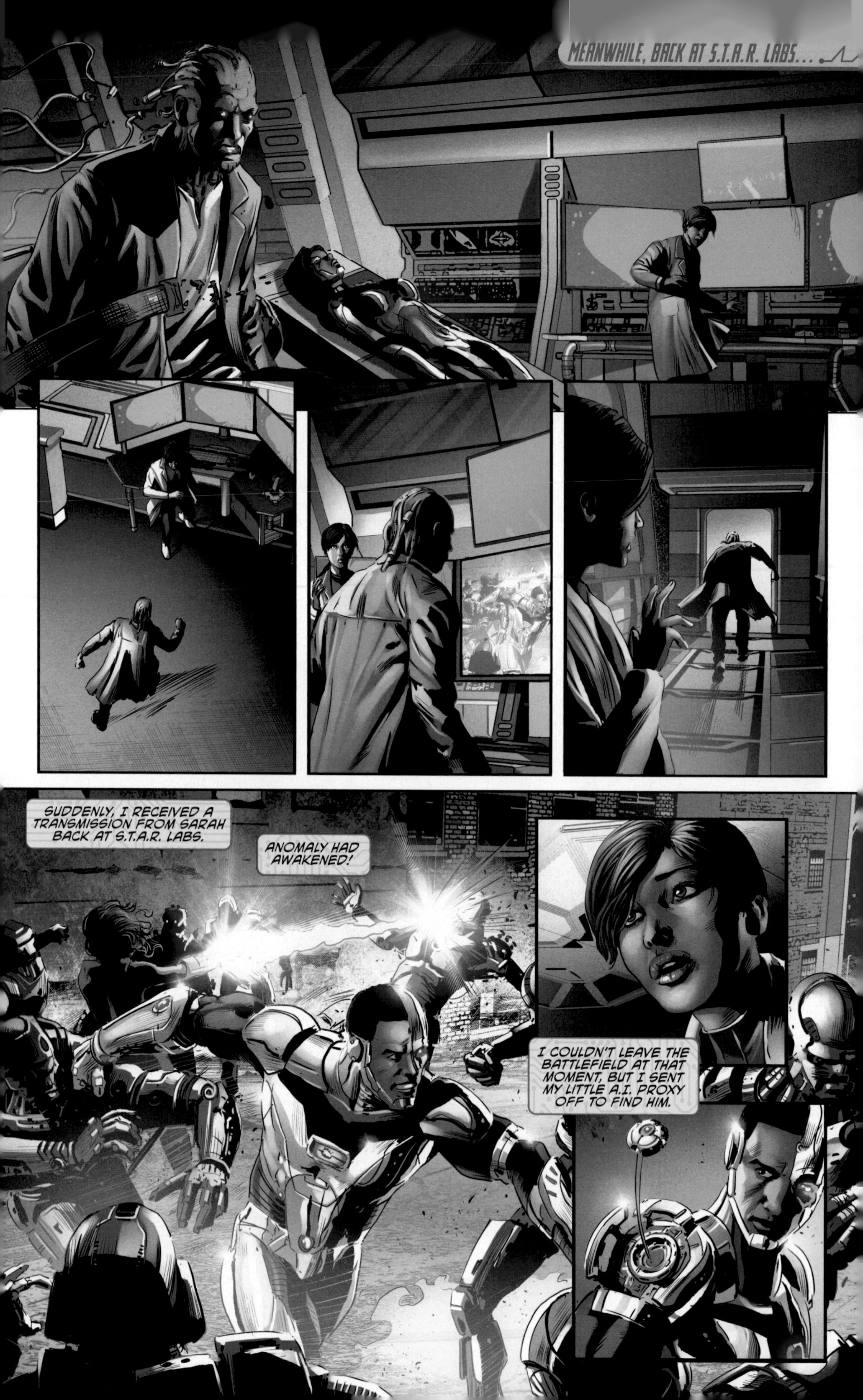
MEANWHILE, BACK AT S.T.A.R. LABS...
SUDDENLY, I RECEIVED A TRANSMISSION FROM SARAH BACK AT S.T.A.R. LABS.
ANOMALY HAD AWAKENED!
I COULDN'T LEAVE THE BATTLEFIELD AT THAT MOMENT, BUT I SENT MY LITTLE A.I. PROXY OFF TO FIND HIM.

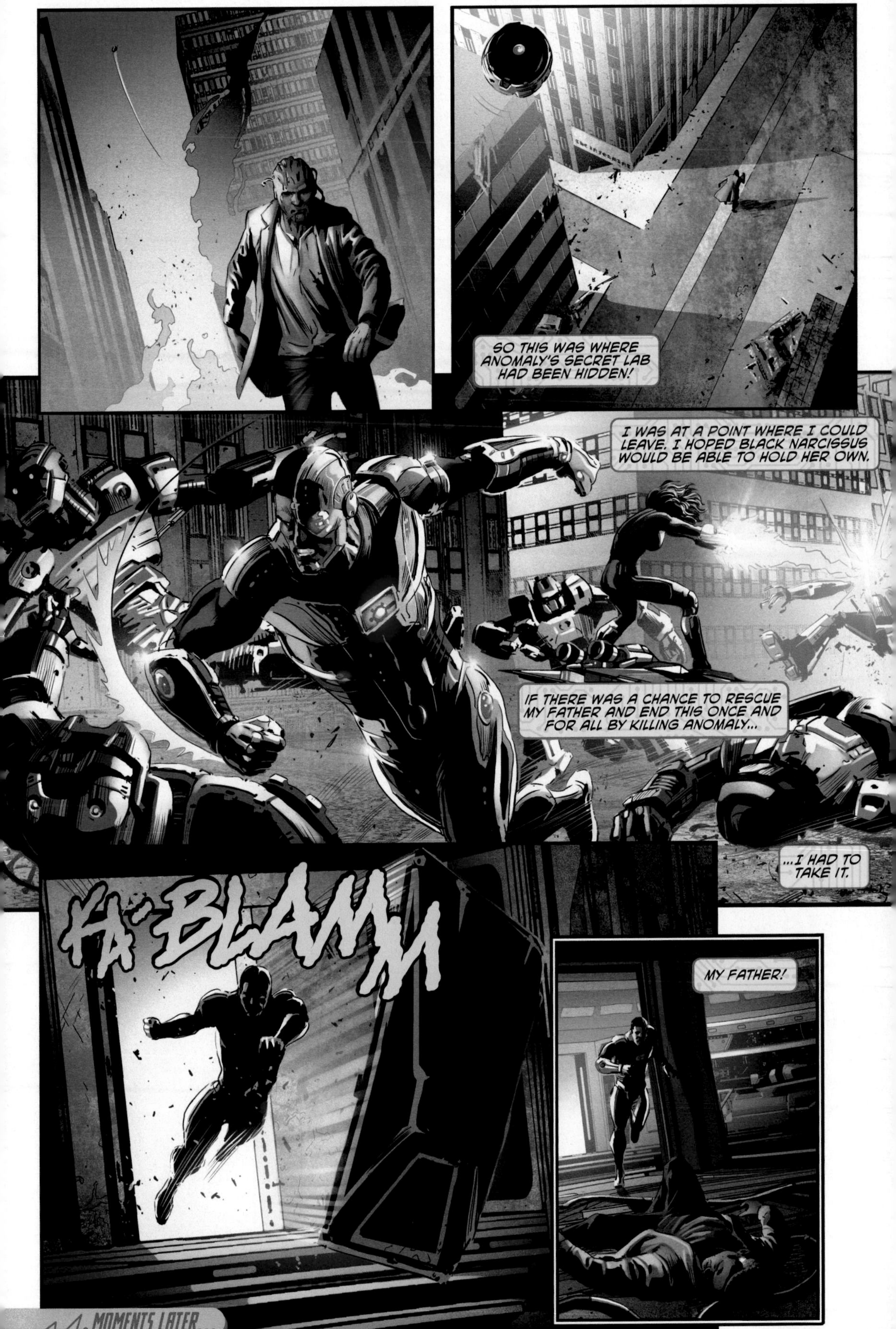
SO THIS WAS WHERE ANOMALY'S SECRET LAB HAD BEEN HIDDEN!
I WAS AT A POINT WHERE I COULD LEAVE. I HOPED BLACK NARCISSUS WOULD BE ABLE TO HOLD HER OWN.
IF THERE WAS A CHANCE TO RESCUE MY FATHER AND END THIS ONCE AND FOR ALL BY KILLING ANOMALY...
...I HAD TO TAKE IT.
KA-BLAMM
MOMENTS LATER...
MY FATHER!

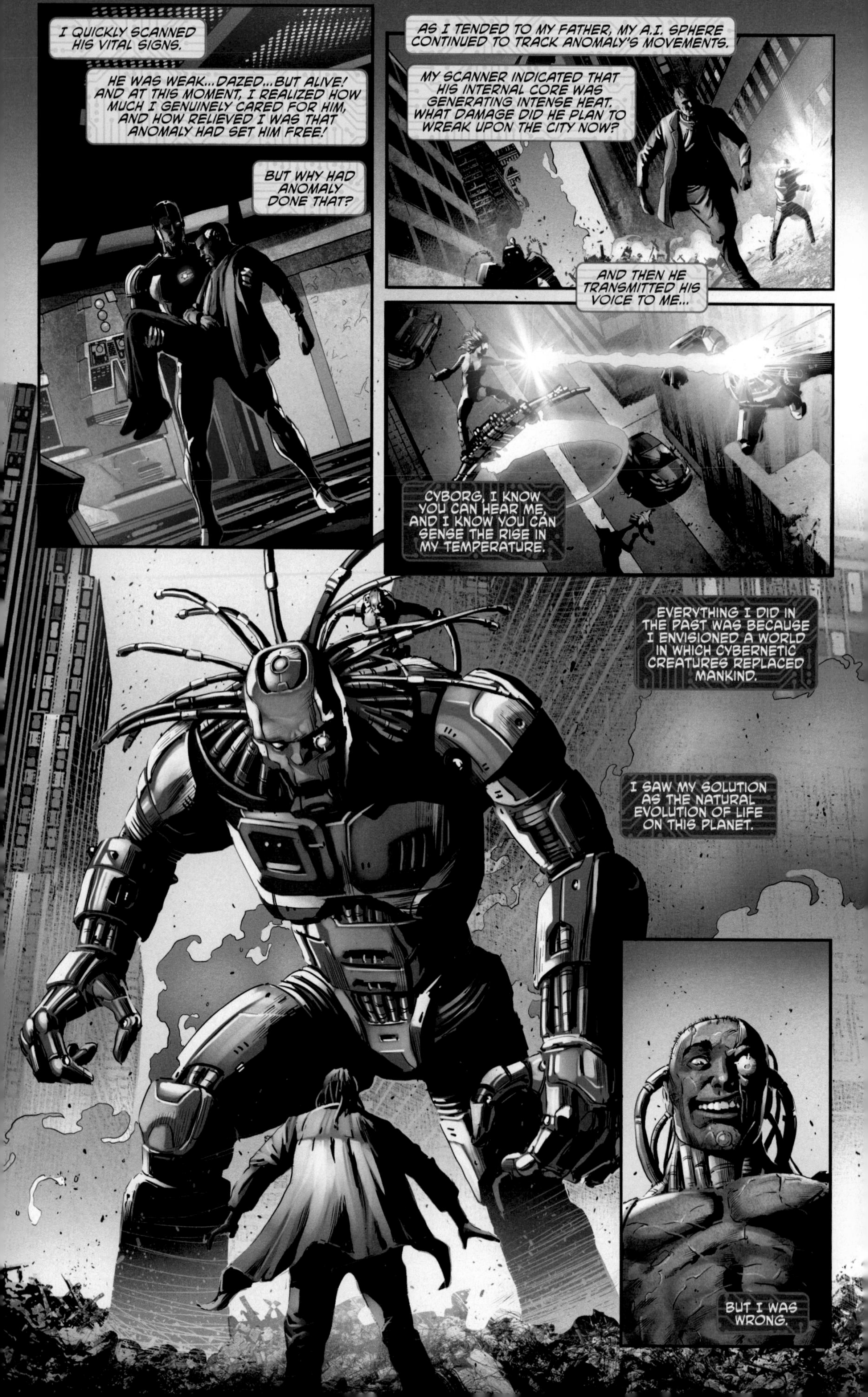

I QUICKLY SCANNED HIS VITAL SIGNS.
HE WAS WEAK...DAZED...BUT ALIVE! AND AT THIS MOMENT, I REALIZED HOW MUCH I GENUINELY CARED FOR HIM, AND HOW RELIEVED I WAS THAT ANOMALY HAD SET HIM FREE!
BUT WHY HAD ANOMALY DONE THAT?
AS I TENDED TO MY FATHER, MY A.I. SPHERE CONTINUED TO TRACK ANOMALY'S MOVEMENTS.
MY SCANNER INDICATED THAT HIS INTERNAL CORE WAS GENERATING INTENSE HEAT. WHAT DAMAGE DID HE PLAN TO WREAK UPON THE CITY NOW?
AND THEN HE TRANSMITTED HIS VOICE TO ME...
CYBORG, I KNOW YOU CAN HEAR ME, AND I KNOW YOU CAN SENSE THE RISE IN MY TEMPERATURE.
EVERYTHING I DID IN THE PAST WAS BECAUSE I ENVISIONED A WORLD IN WHICH CYBERNETIC CREATURES REPLACED MANKIND.
I SAW MY SOLUTION AS THE NATURAL EVOLUTION OF LIFE ON THIS PLANET.
BUT I WAS WRONG.

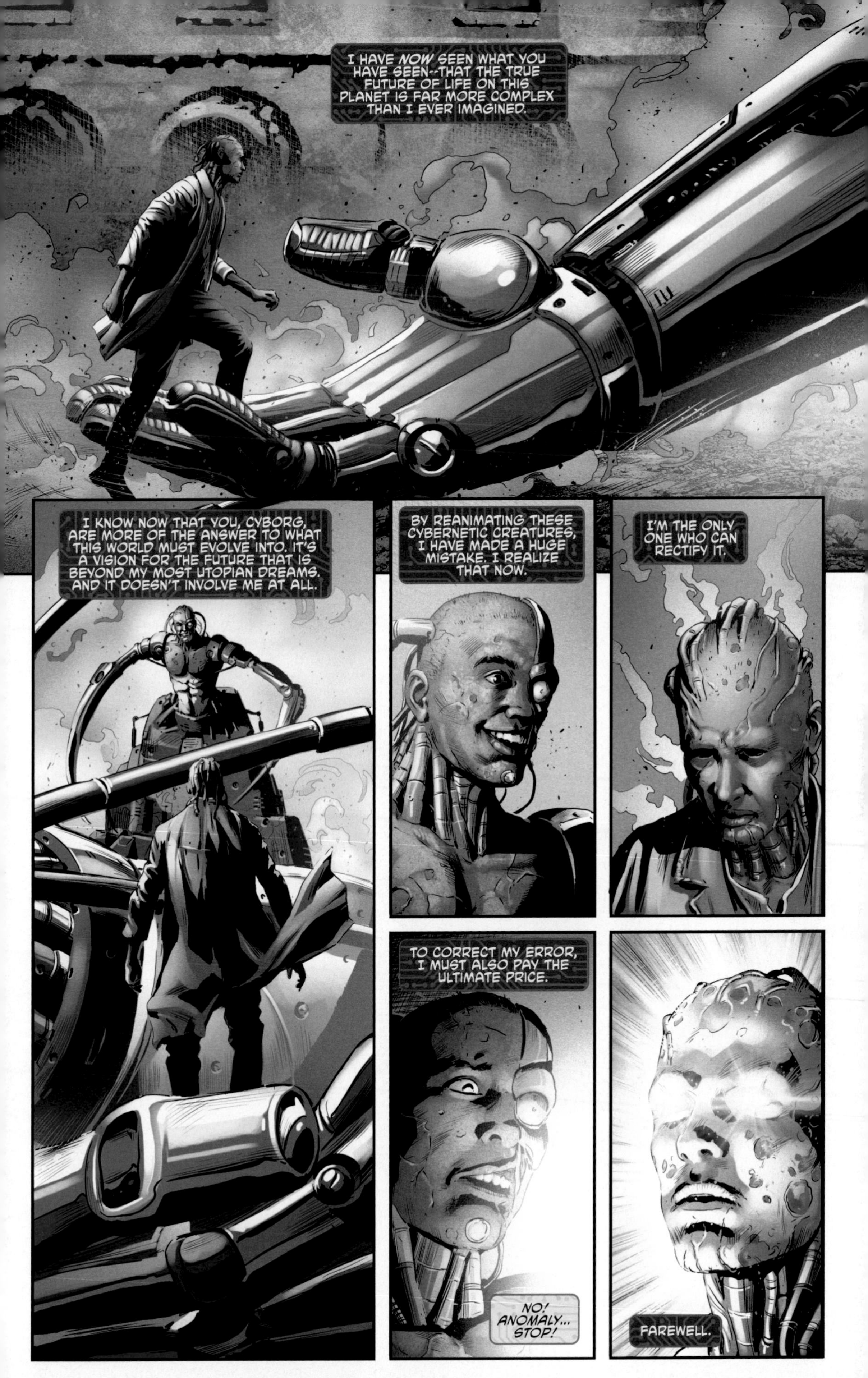
I HAVE NOW SEEN WHAT YOU HAVE SEEN--THAT THE TRUE FUTURE OF LIFE ON THIS PLANET IS FAR MORE COMPLEX THAN I EVER IMAGINED.
I KNOW NOW THAT YOU, CYBORG, ARE MORE OF THE ANSWER TO WHAT THIS WORLD MUST EVOLVE INTO. IT'S A VISION FOR THE FUTURE THAT IS BEYOND MY MOST UTOPIAN DREAMS. AND IT DOESN'T INVOLVE ME AT ALL.
BY REANIMATING THESE CYBERNETIC CREATURES, I HAVE MADE A HUGE MISTAKE. I REALIZE THAT NOW.
I'M THE ONLY ONE WHO CAN RECTIFY IT.
TO CORRECT MY ERROR, I MUST ALSO PAY THE ULTIMATE PRICE.
NO! ANOMALY... STOP!
FAREWELL.

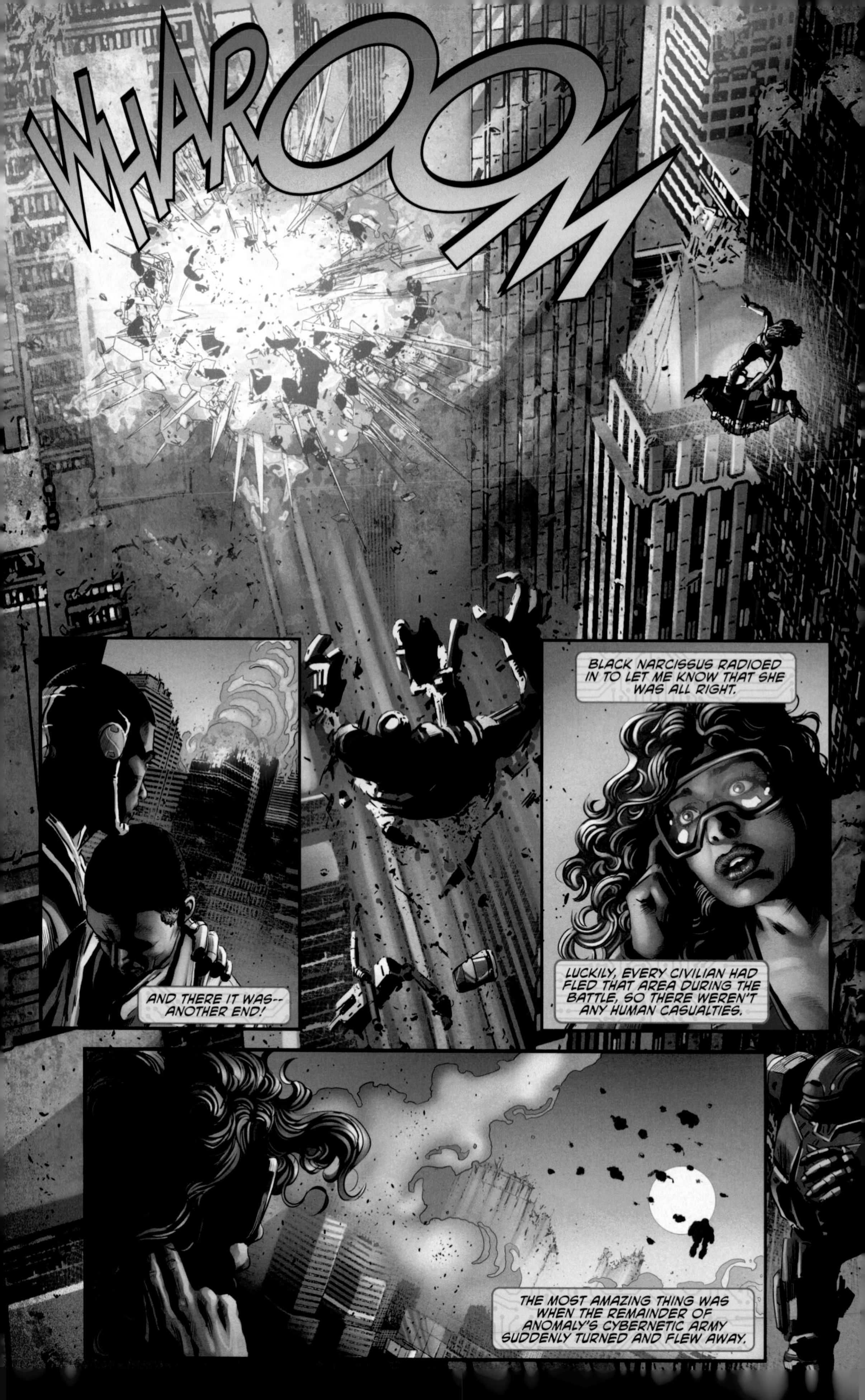
WHAROOM
AND THERE IT WAS--
ANOTHER END!
BLACK NARCISSUS RADIOED IN TO LET ME KNOW THAT SHE WAS ALL RIGHT.
LUCKILY, EVERY CIVILIAN HAD FLED THAT AREA DURING THE BATTLE, SO THERE WEREN'T ANY HUMAN CASUALTIES.
THE MOST AMAZING THING WAS WHEN THE REMAINDER OF ANOMALY'S CYBERNETIC ARMY SUDDENLY TURNED AND FLEW AWAY.

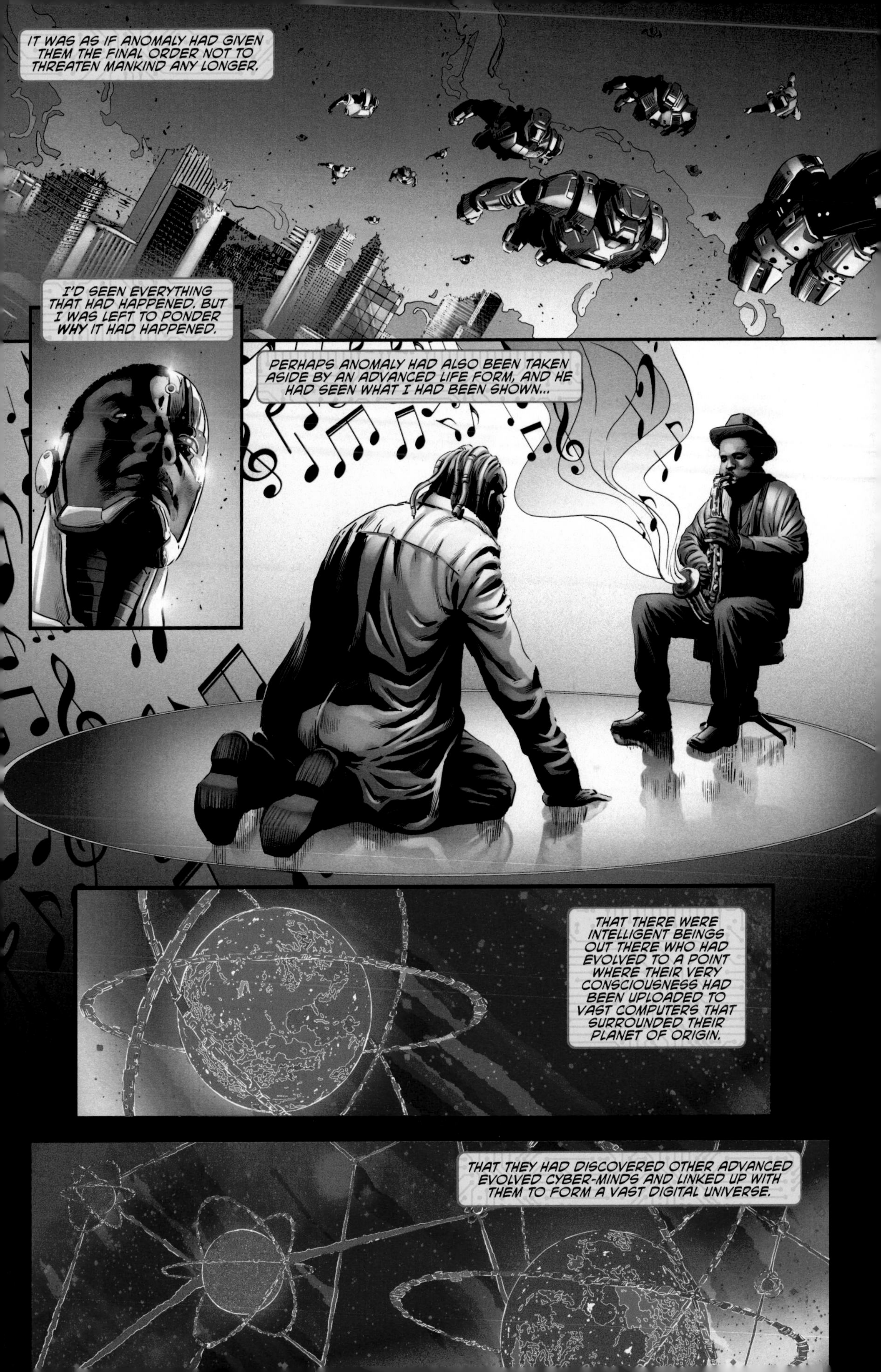
IT WAS AS IF ANOMALY HAD GIVEN THEM THE FINAL ORDER NOT TO THREATEN MANKIND ANY LONGER.
I'D SEEN EVERYTHING THAT HAD HAPPENED. BUT I WAS LEFT TO PONDER **WHY** IT HAD HAPPENED.
PERHAPS ANOMALY HAD ALSO BEEN TAKEN ASIDE BY AN ADVANCED LIFE FORM, AND HE HAD SEEN WHAT I HAD BEEN SHOWN...
THAT THERE WERE INTELLIGENT BEINGS OUT THERE WHO HAD EVOLVED TO A POINT WHERE THEIR VERY CONSCIOUSNESS HAD BEEN UPLOADED TO VAST COMPUTERS THAT SURROUNDED THEIR PLANET OF ORIGIN.
THAT THEY HAD DISCOVERED OTHER ADVANCED EVOLVED CYBER-MINDS AND LINKED UP WITH THEM TO FORM A VAST DIGITAL UNIVERSE.

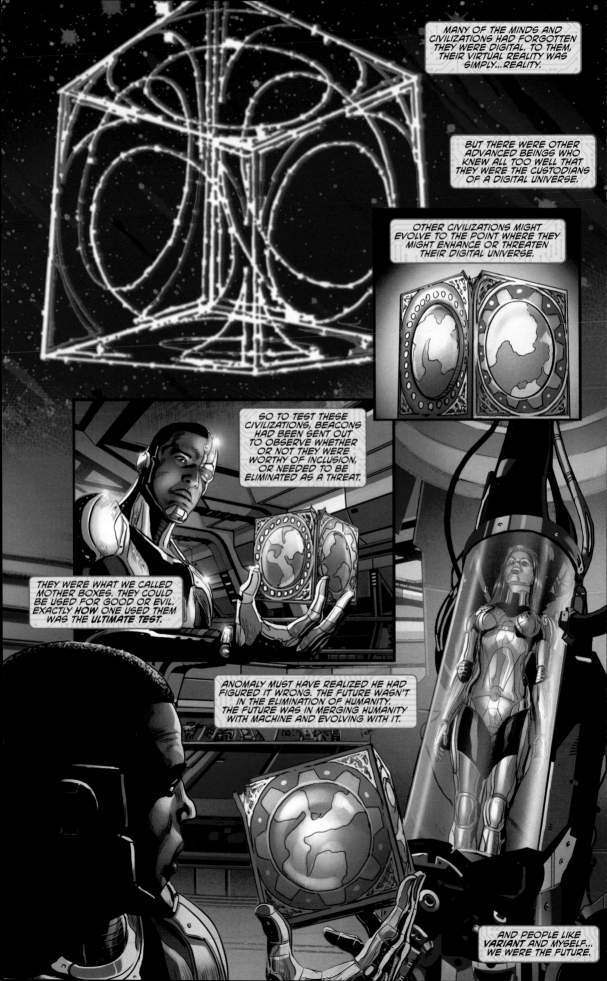

MANY OF THE MINDS AND CIVILIZATIONS HAD FORGOTTEN THEY WERE DIGITAL. TO THEM, THEIR VIRTUAL REALITY WAS SIMPLY...REALITY.

BUT THERE WERE OTHER ADVANCED BEINGS WHO KNEW ALL TOO WELL THAT THEY WERE THE CUSTODIANS OF A DIGITAL UNIVERSE.

OTHER CIVILIZATIONS MIGHT EVOLVE TO THE POINT WHERE THEY MIGHT ENHANCE OR THREATEN THEIR DIGITAL UNIVERSE.

SO TO TEST THESE CIVILIZATIONS, BEACONS HAD BEEN SENT OUT TO OBSERVE WHETHER OR NOT THEY WERE WORTHY OF INCLUSION, OR NEEDED TO BE ELIMINATED AS A THREAT.

THEY WERE WHAT WE CALLED MOTHER BOXES. THEY COULD BE USED FOR GOOD OR EVIL. EXACTLY HOW ONE USED THEM WAS THE ULTIMATE TEST.

ANOMALY MUST HAVE REALIZED HE HAD FIGURED IT WRONG. THE FUTURE WASN'T IN THE ELIMINATION OF HUMANITY. THE FUTURE WAS IN MERGING HUMANITY WITH MACHINE AND EVOLVING WITH IT.

AND PEOPLE LIKE VARIANT AND MYSELF... WE WERE THE FUTURE.

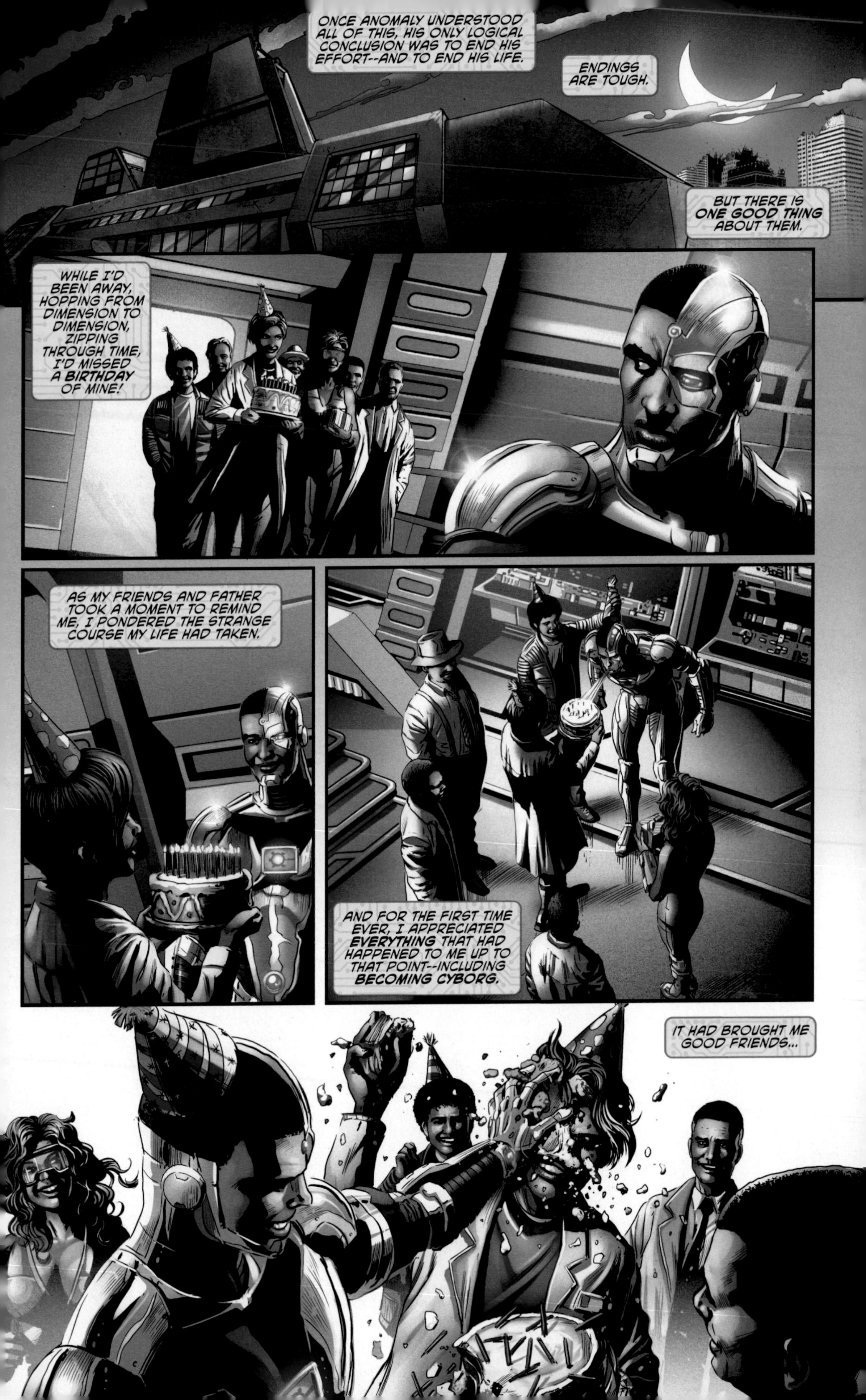
ONCE ANOMALY UNDERSTOOD ALL OF THIS, HIS ONLY LOGICAL CONCLUSION WAS TO END HIS EFFORT--AND TO END HIS LIFE.
ENDINGS ARE TOUGH.
BUT THERE IS ONE GOOD THING ABOUT THEM.
WHILE I'D BEEN AWAY, HOPPING FROM DIMENSION TO DIMENSION, ZIPPING THROUGH TIME, I'D MISSED A BIRTHDAY OF MINE!
AS MY FRIENDS AND FATHER TOOK A MOMENT TO REMIND ME, I PONDERED THE STRANGE COURSE MY LIFE HAD TAKEN.
AND FOR THE FIRST TIME EVER, I APPRECIATED EVERYTHING THAT HAD HAPPENED TO ME UP TO THAT POINT--INCLUDING BECOMING CYBORG.
IT HAD BROUGHT ME GOOD FRIENDS...

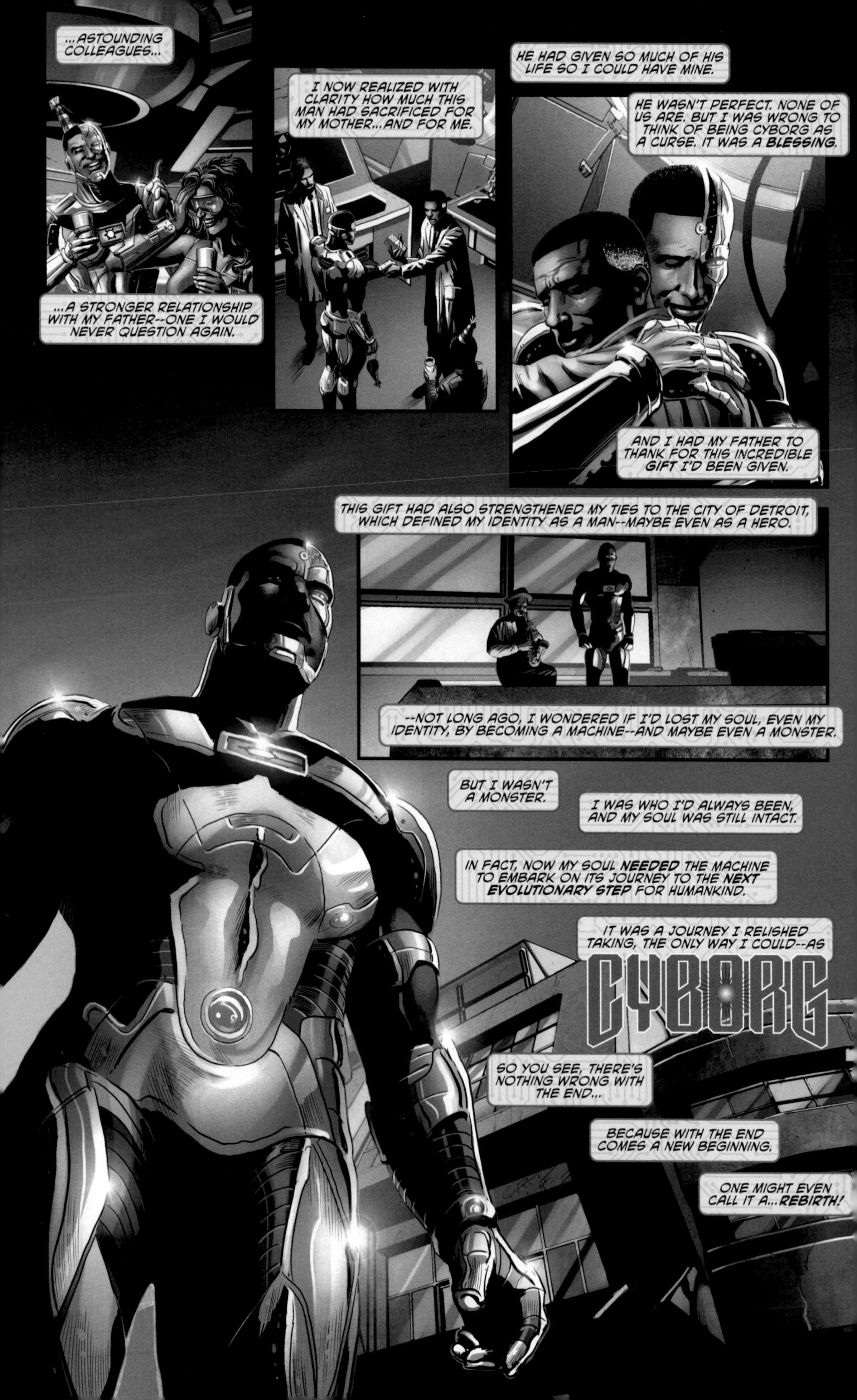
...ASTOUNDING COLLEAGUES...
...A STRONGER RELATIONSHIP WITH MY FATHER--ONE I WOULD NEVER QUESTION AGAIN.
I NOW REALIZED WITH CLARITY HOW MUCH THIS MAN HAD SACRIFICED FOR MY MOTHER...AND FOR ME.
HE HAD GIVEN SO MUCH OF HIS LIFE SO I COULD HAVE MINE.
HE WASN'T PERFECT. NONE OF US ARE. BUT I WAS WRONG TO THINK OF BEING CYBORG AS A CURSE. IT WAS A **BLESSING.**
AND I HAD MY FATHER TO THANK FOR THIS INCREDIBLE **GIFT** I'D BEEN GIVEN.
THIS GIFT HAD ALSO STRENGTHENED MY TIES TO THE CITY OF DETROIT, WHICH DEFINED MY IDENTITY AS A MAN--MAYBE EVEN AS A HERO.
--NOT LONG AGO, I WONDERED IF I'D LOST MY SOUL, EVEN MY IDENTITY, BY BECOMING A MACHINE--AND MAYBE EVEN A MONSTER.
BUT I WASN'T A MONSTER.
I WAS WHO I'D ALWAYS BEEN, AND MY SOUL WAS STILL INTACT.
IN FACT, NOW MY SOUL **NEEDED** THE MACHINE TO EMBARK ON ITS JOURNEY TO THE **NEXT EVOLUTIONARY STEP** FOR HUMANKIND.
IT WAS A JOURNEY I RELISHED TAKING, THE ONLY WAY I COULD--AS
CYBORG
SO YOU SEE, THERE'S NOTHING WRONG WITH THE END...
BECAUSE WITH THE END COMES A NEW BEGINNING.
ONE MIGHT EVEN CALL IT A...**REBIRTH!**

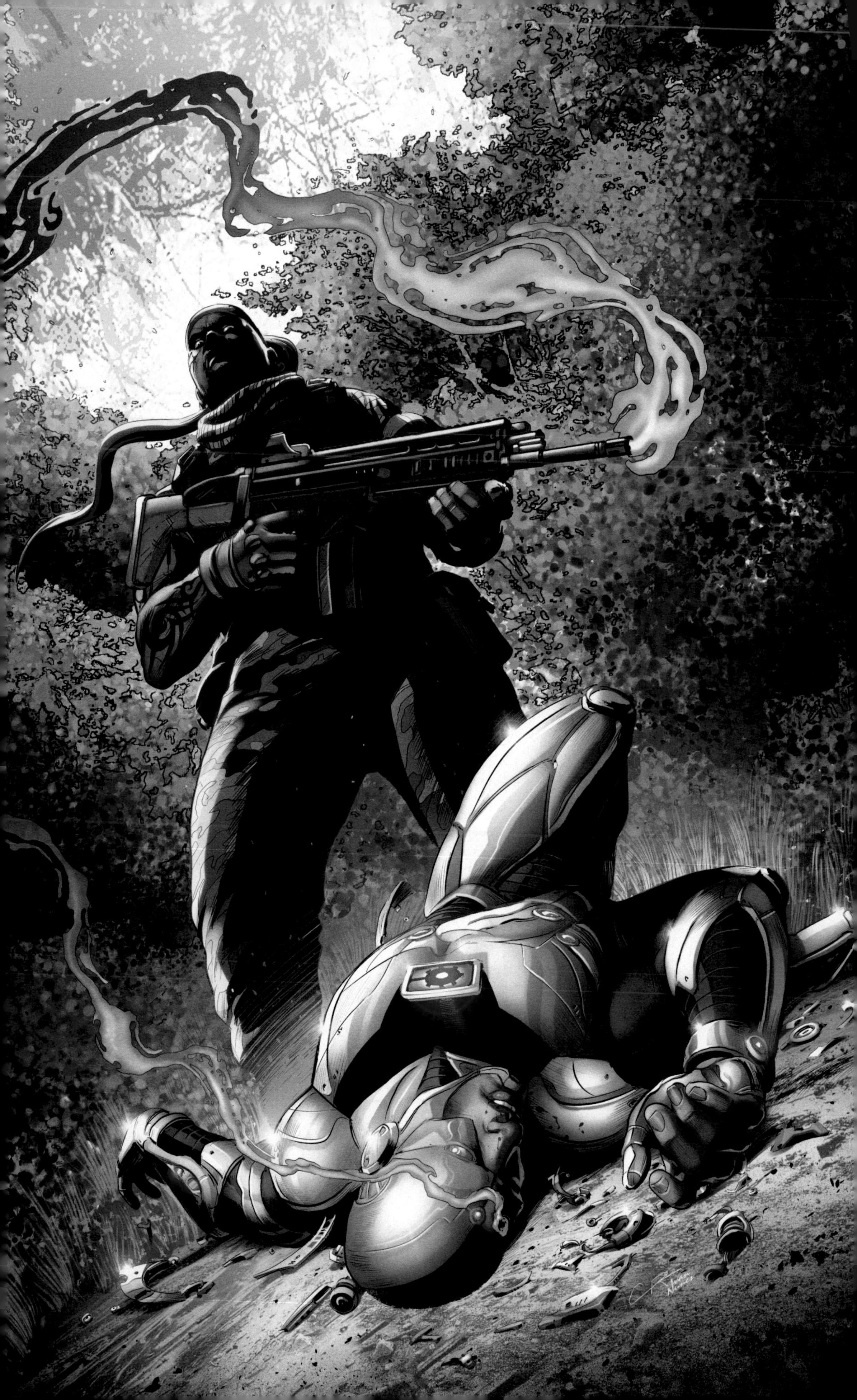

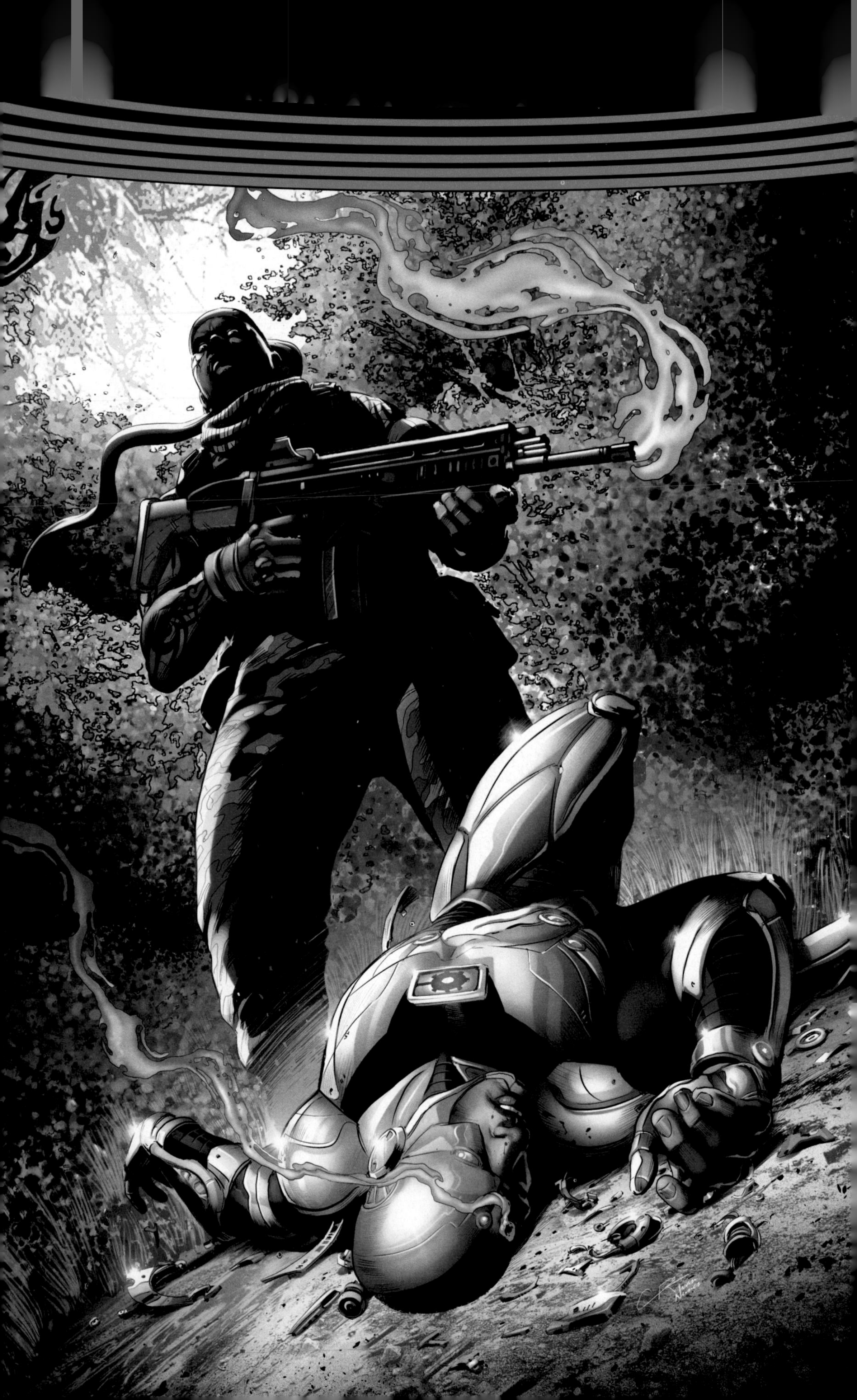

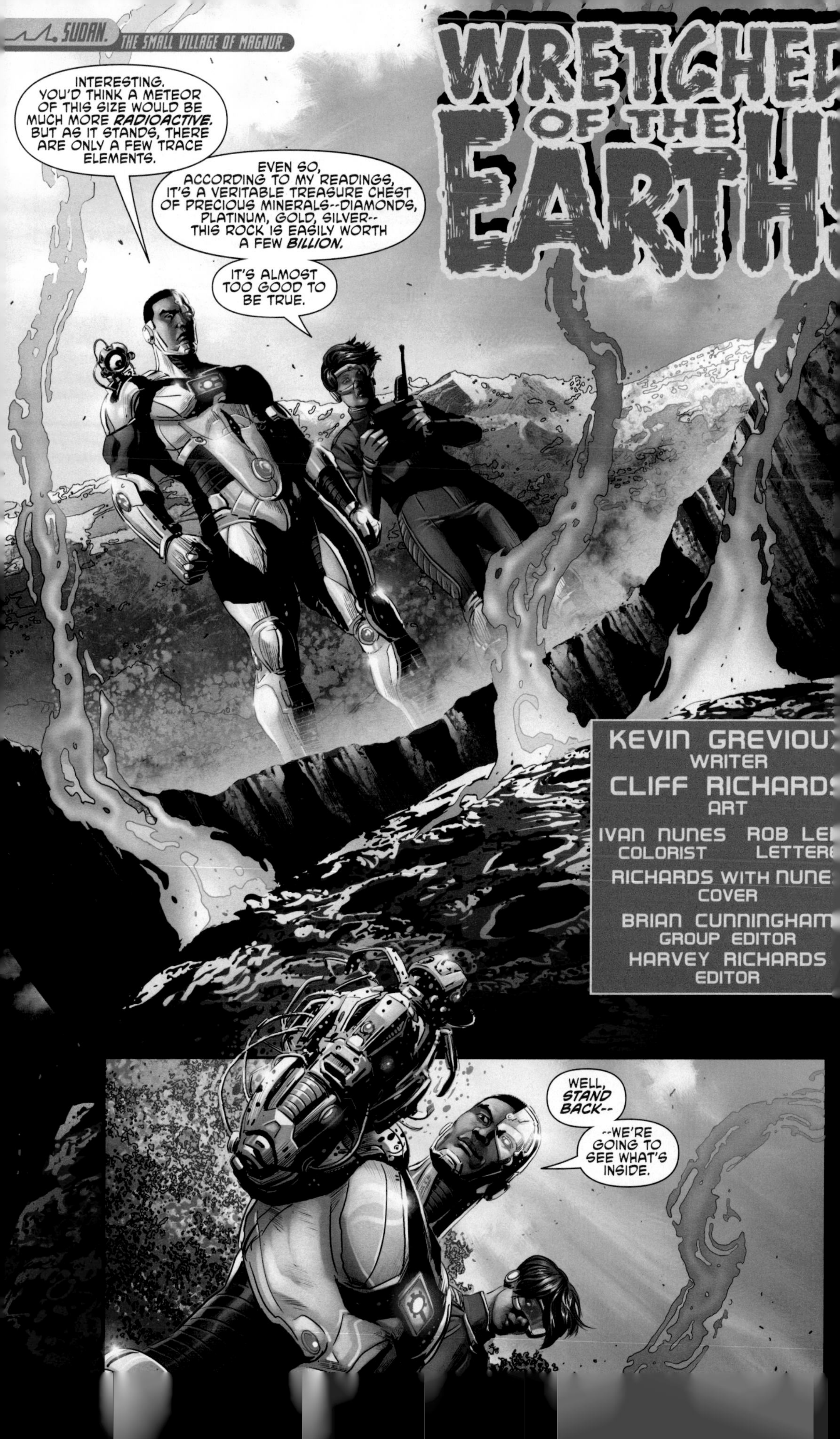

SUDAN. THE SMALL VILLAGE OF MAGNUR.
WRETCHED OF THE EARTH
INTERESTING. YOU'D THINK A METEOR OF THIS SIZE WOULD BE MUCH MORE *RADIOACTIVE.* BUT AS IT STANDS, THERE ARE ONLY A FEW TRACE ELEMENTS.
EVEN SO, ACCORDING TO MY READINGS, IT'S A VERITABLE TREASURE CHEST OF PRECIOUS MINERALS--DIAMONDS, PLATINUM, GOLD, SILVER-- THIS ROCK IS EASILY WORTH A FEW *BILLION.*
IT'S ALMOST TOO GOOD TO BE TRUE.
KEVIN GREVIOUX WRITER
CLIFF RICHARDS ART
IVAN NUNES COLORIST
ROB LE LETTERE
RICHARDS WITH NUNES COVER
BRIAN CUNNINGHAM GROUP EDITOR
HARVEY RICHARDS EDITOR
WELL, *STAND BACK--*
--WE'RE GOING TO SEE WHAT'S INSIDE.

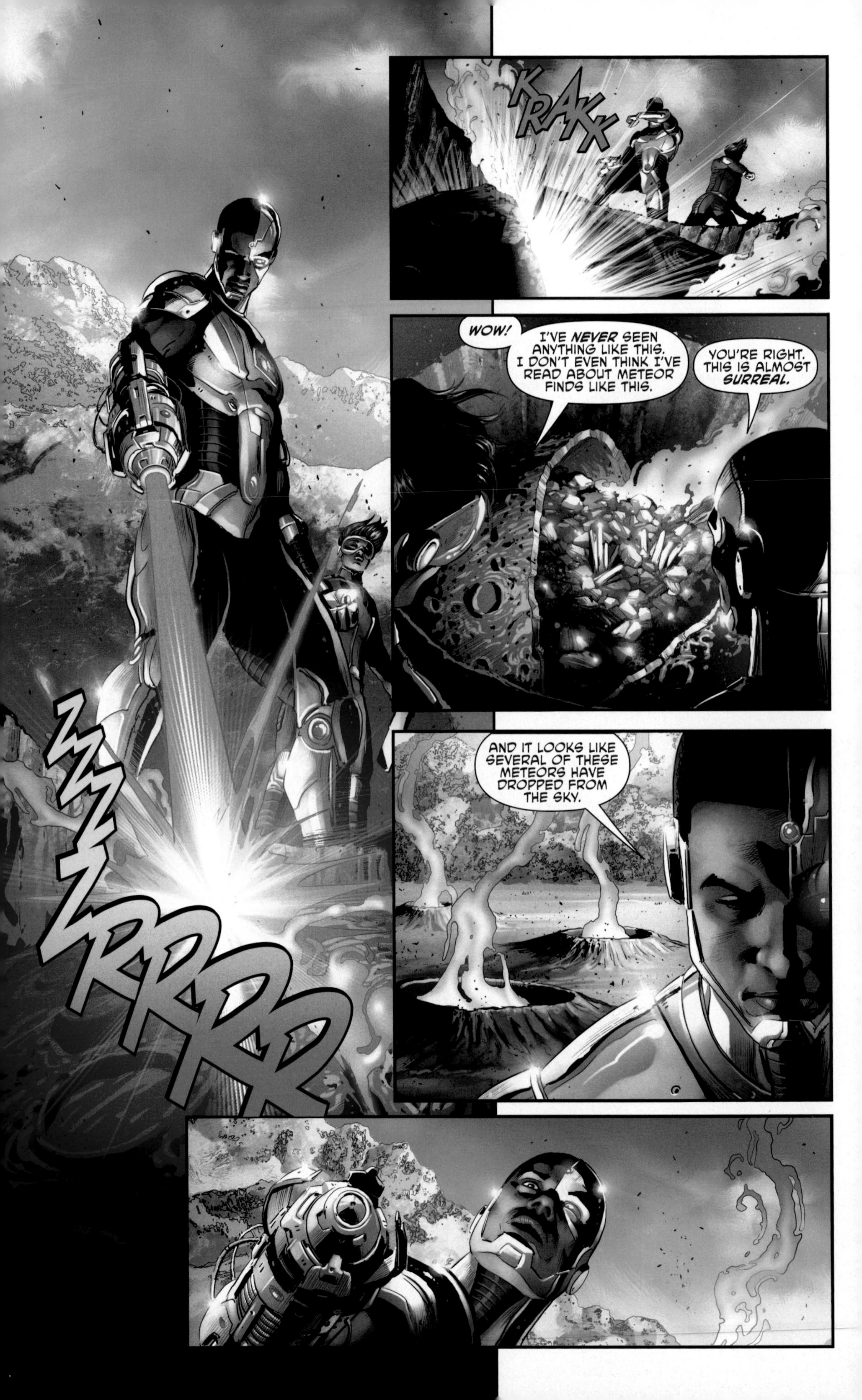
KRAKK
ZZZZ
ZRRRR
WOW!
I'VE NEVER SEEN ANYTHING LIKE THIS. I DON'T EVEN THINK I'VE READ ABOUT METEOR FINDS LIKE THIS.
YOU'RE RIGHT. THIS IS ALMOST SURREAL.
AND IT LOOKS LIKE SEVERAL OF THESE METEORS HAVE DROPPED FROM THE SKY.

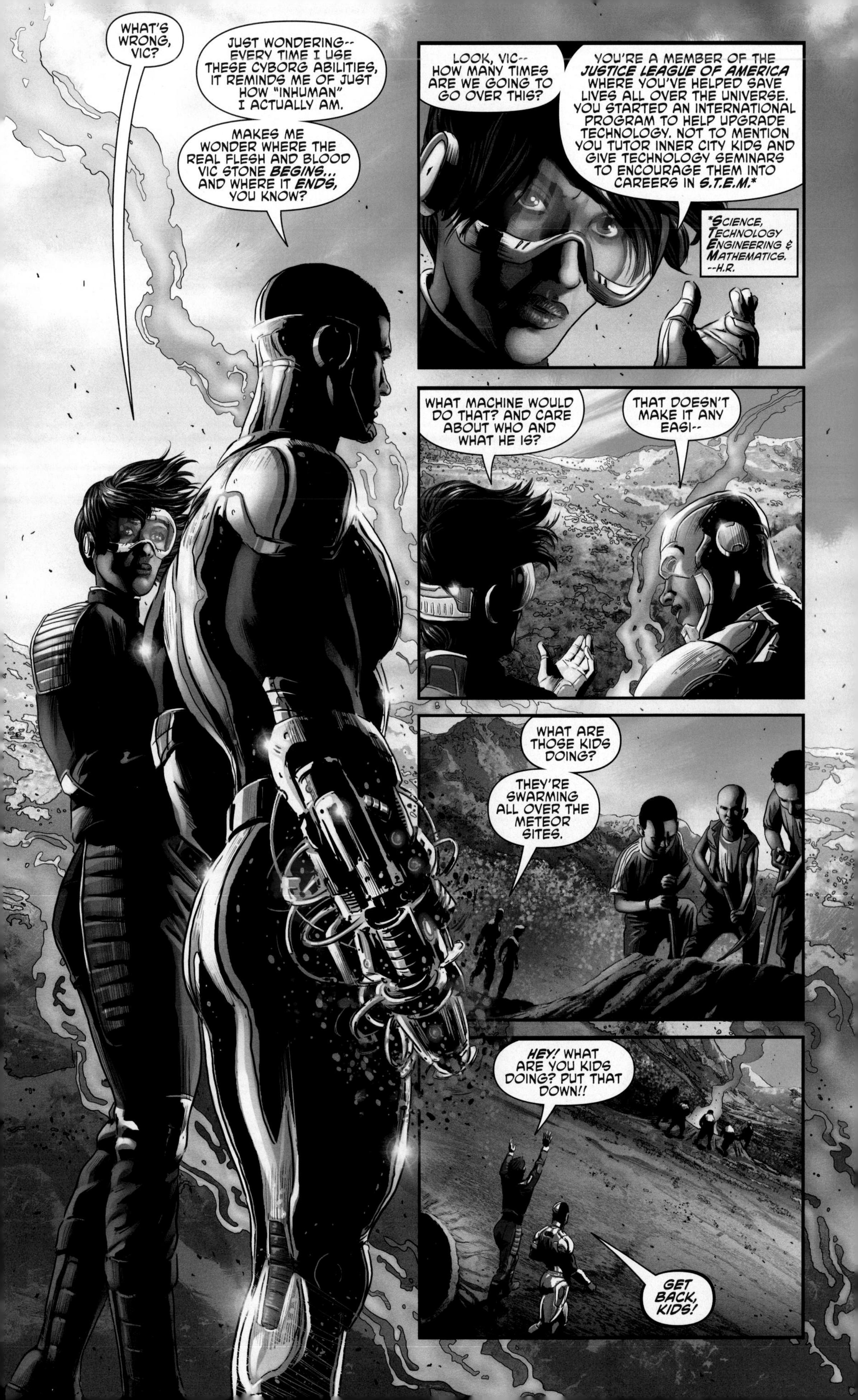
WHAT'S WRONG, VIC?
JUST WONDERING-- EVERY TIME I USE THESE CYBORG ABILITIES, IT REMINDS ME OF JUST HOW "INHUMAN" I ACTUALLY AM.
MAKES ME WONDER WHERE THE REAL FLESH AND BLOOD VIC STONE *BEGINS*... AND WHERE IT *ENDS*, YOU KNOW?
LOOK, VIC-- HOW MANY TIMES ARE WE GOING TO GO OVER THIS?
YOU'RE A MEMBER OF THE ***JUSTICE LEAGUE OF AMERICA*** WHERE YOU'VE HELPED SAVE LIVES ALL OVER THE UNIVERSE. YOU STARTED AN INTERNATIONAL PROGRAM TO HELP UPGRADE TECHNOLOGY. NOT TO MENTION YOU TUTOR INNER CITY KIDS AND GIVE TECHNOLOGY SEMINARS TO ENCOURAGE THEM INTO CAREERS IN *S.T.E.M.**
*SCIENCE, TECHNOLOGY ENGINEERING & MATHEMATICS. --H.R.
WHAT MACHINE WOULD DO THAT? AND CARE ABOUT WHO AND WHAT HE IS?
THAT DOESN'T MAKE IT ANY EASI--
WHAT ARE THOSE KIDS DOING?
THEY'RE SWARMING ALL OVER THE METEOR SITES.
HEY! WHAT ARE YOU KIDS DOING? PUT THAT DOWN!!
GET BACK, KIDS!

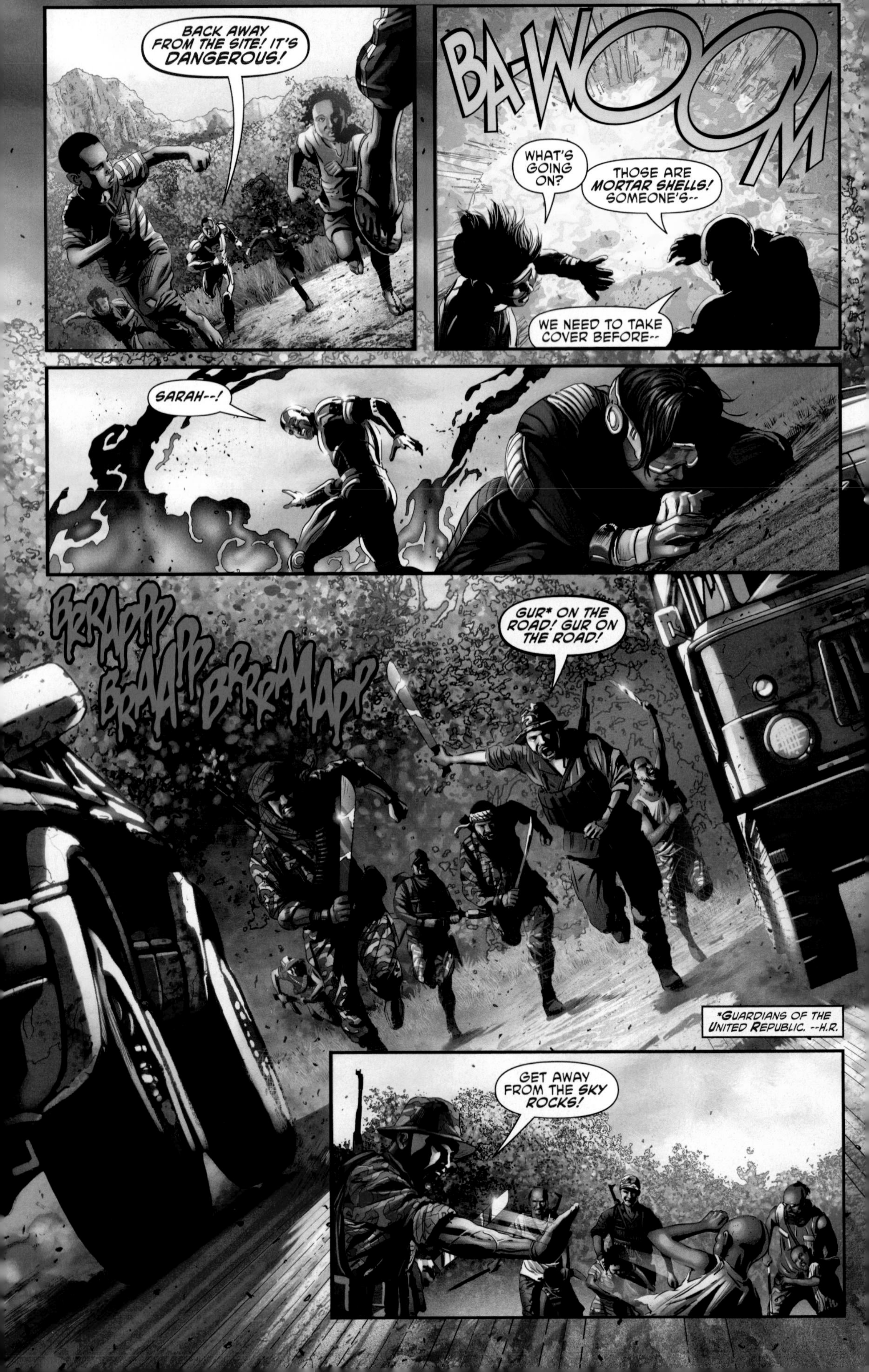
BACK AWAY FROM THE SITE! IT'S DANGEROUS!
BA-WOOM
WHAT'S GOING ON?
THOSE ARE MORTAR SHELLS! SOMEONE'S--
WE NEED TO TAKE COVER BEFORE--
SARAH--!
BRRAPP BRAAPP BRRRAAAPP
GUR* ON THE ROAD! GUR ON THE ROAD!
*GUARDIANS OF THE UNITED REPUBLIC. --H.R.
GET AWAY FROM THE SKY ROCKS!

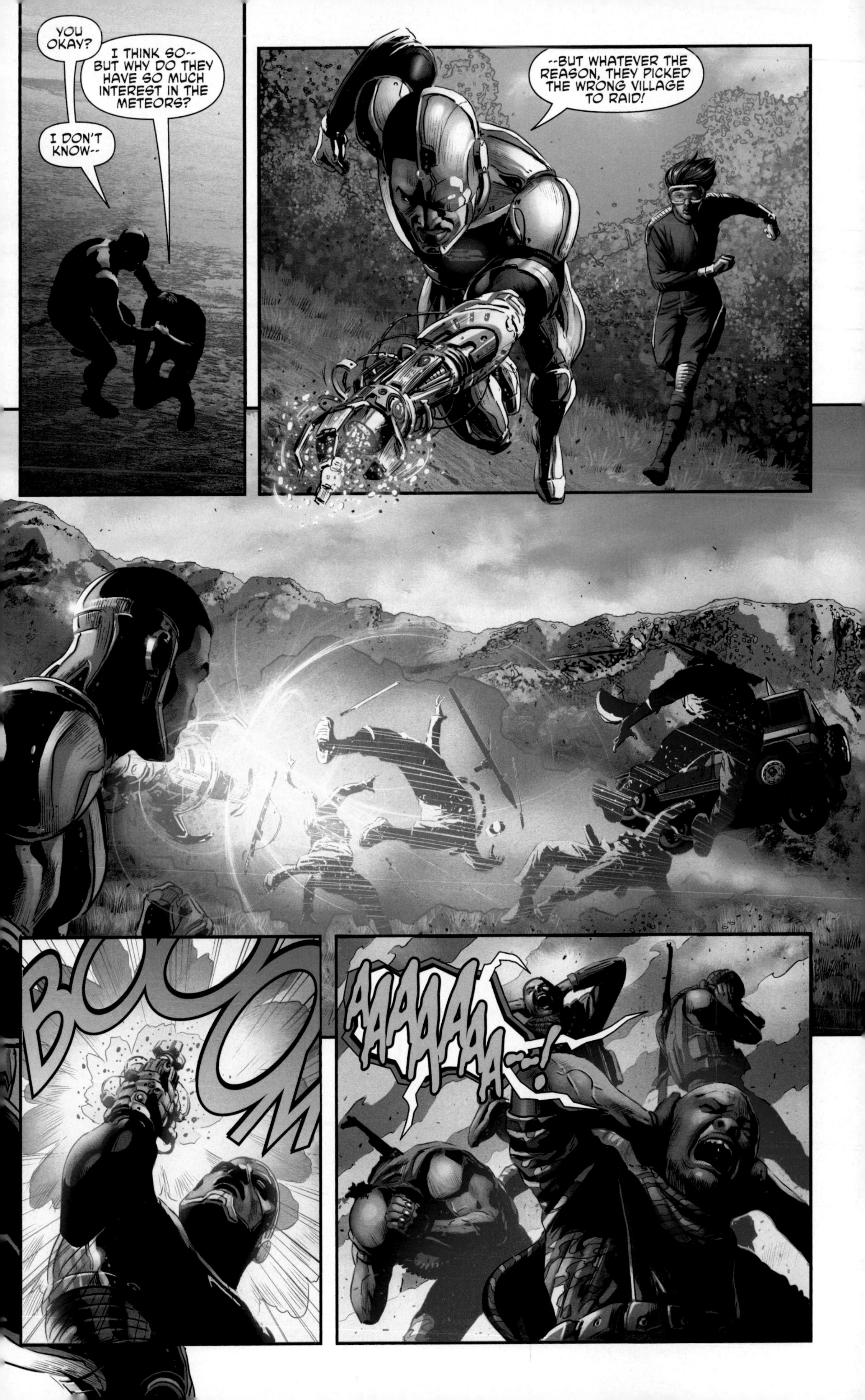
YOU OKAY?
I THINK SO-- BUT WHY DO THEY HAVE SO MUCH INTEREST IN THE METEORS?
I DON'T KNOW--
--BUT WHATEVER THE REASON, THEY PICKED THE WRONG VILLAGE TO RAID!
BOOOM
AAAAAAAA--!

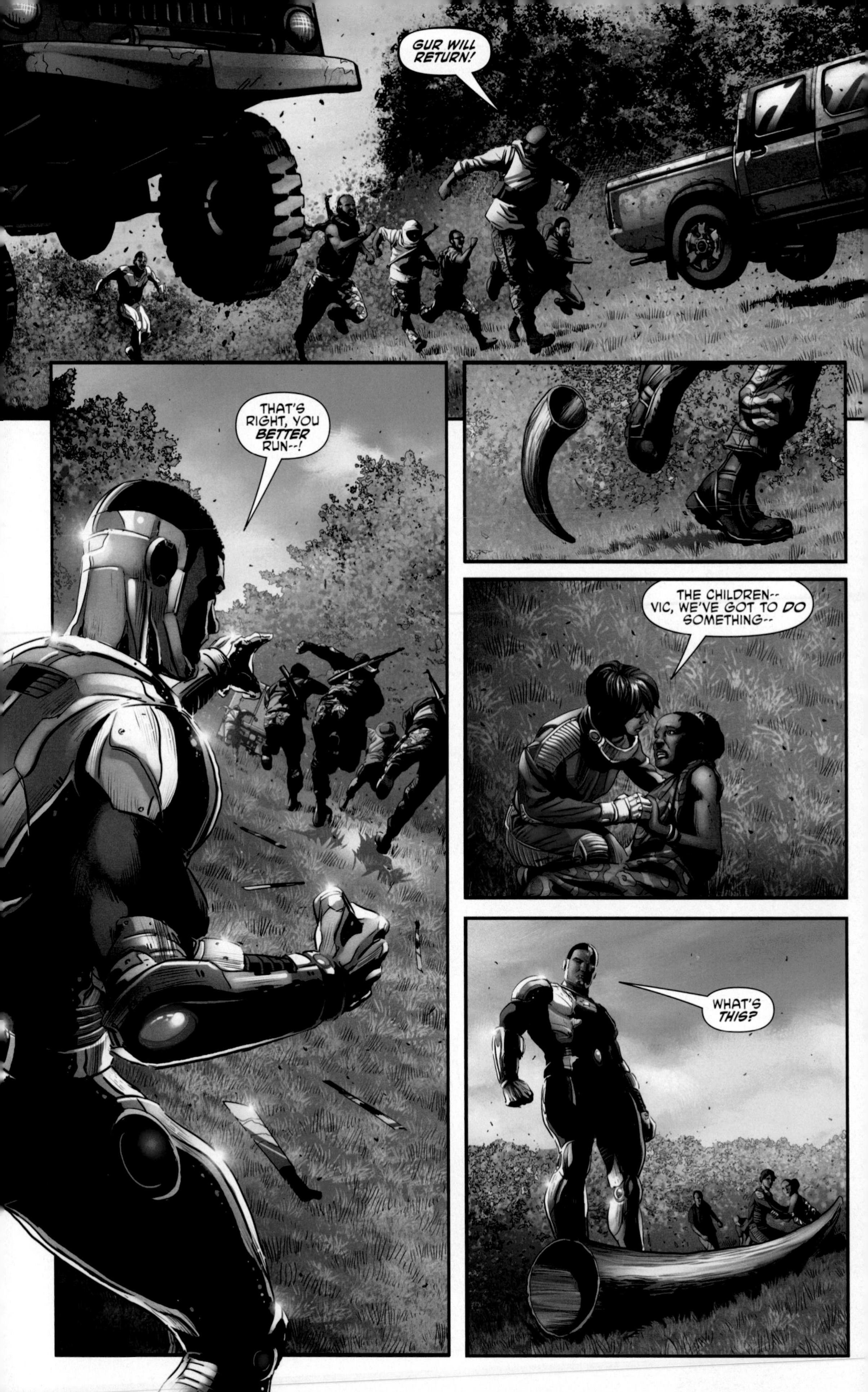
GUR WILL RETURN!
THAT'S RIGHT, YOU BETTER RUN--!
THE CHILDREN-- VIC, WE'VE GOT TO DO SOMETHING--
WHAT'S THIS?

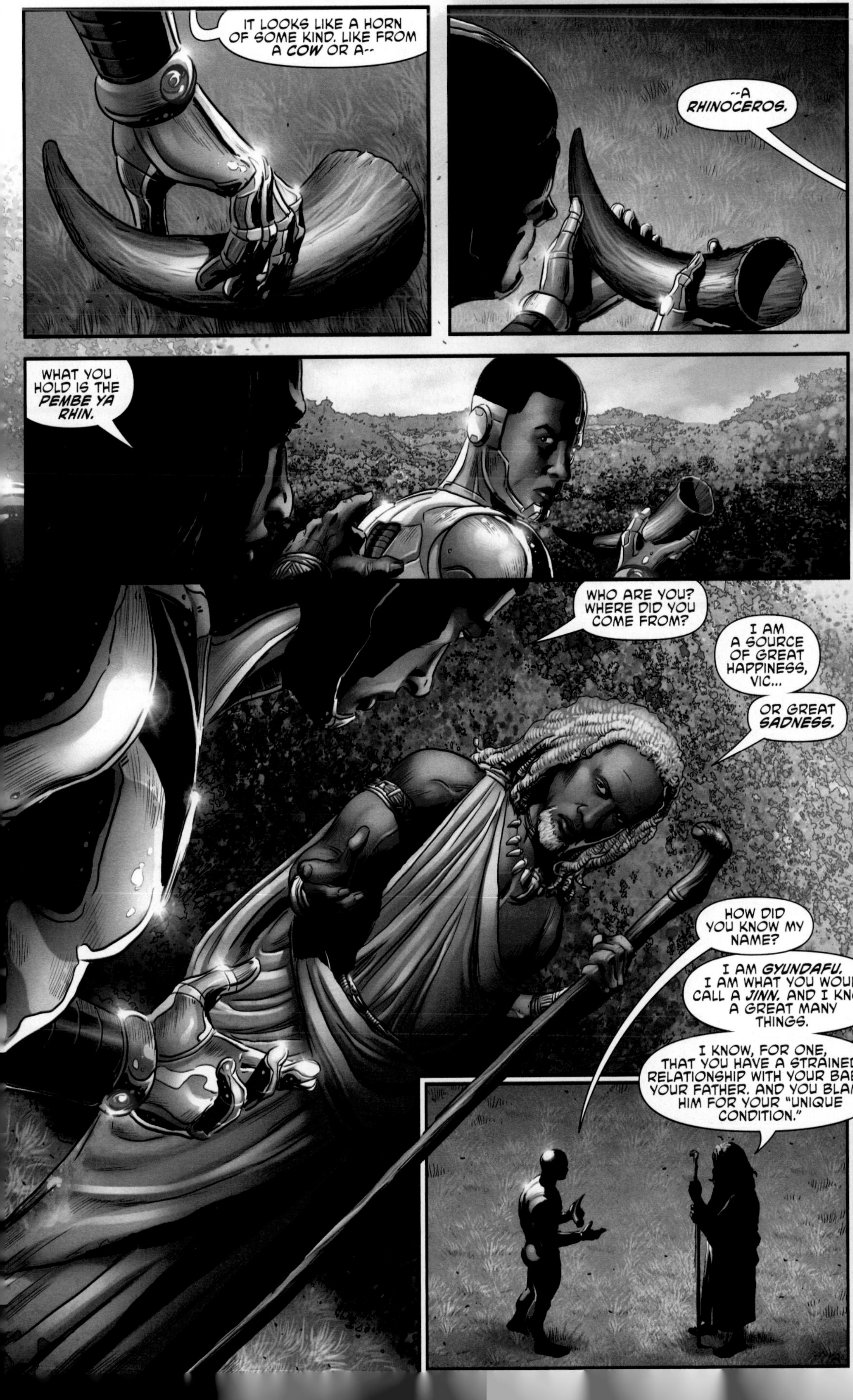
IT LOOKS LIKE A HORN OF SOME KIND. LIKE FROM A COW OR A--
--A RHINOCEROS.
WHAT YOU HOLD IS THE PEMBE YA RHIN.
WHO ARE YOU? WHERE DID YOU COME FROM?
I AM A SOURCE OF GREAT HAPPINESS, VIC...
OR GREAT SADNESS.
HOW DID YOU KNOW MY NAME?
I AM GYUNDAFU. I AM WHAT YOU WOULD CALL A JINN. AND I KNOW A GREAT MANY THINGS.
I KNOW, FOR ONE, THAT YOU HAVE A STRAINED RELATIONSHIP WITH YOUR BABA, YOUR FATHER. AND YOU BLAME HIM FOR YOUR "UNIQUE CONDITION."

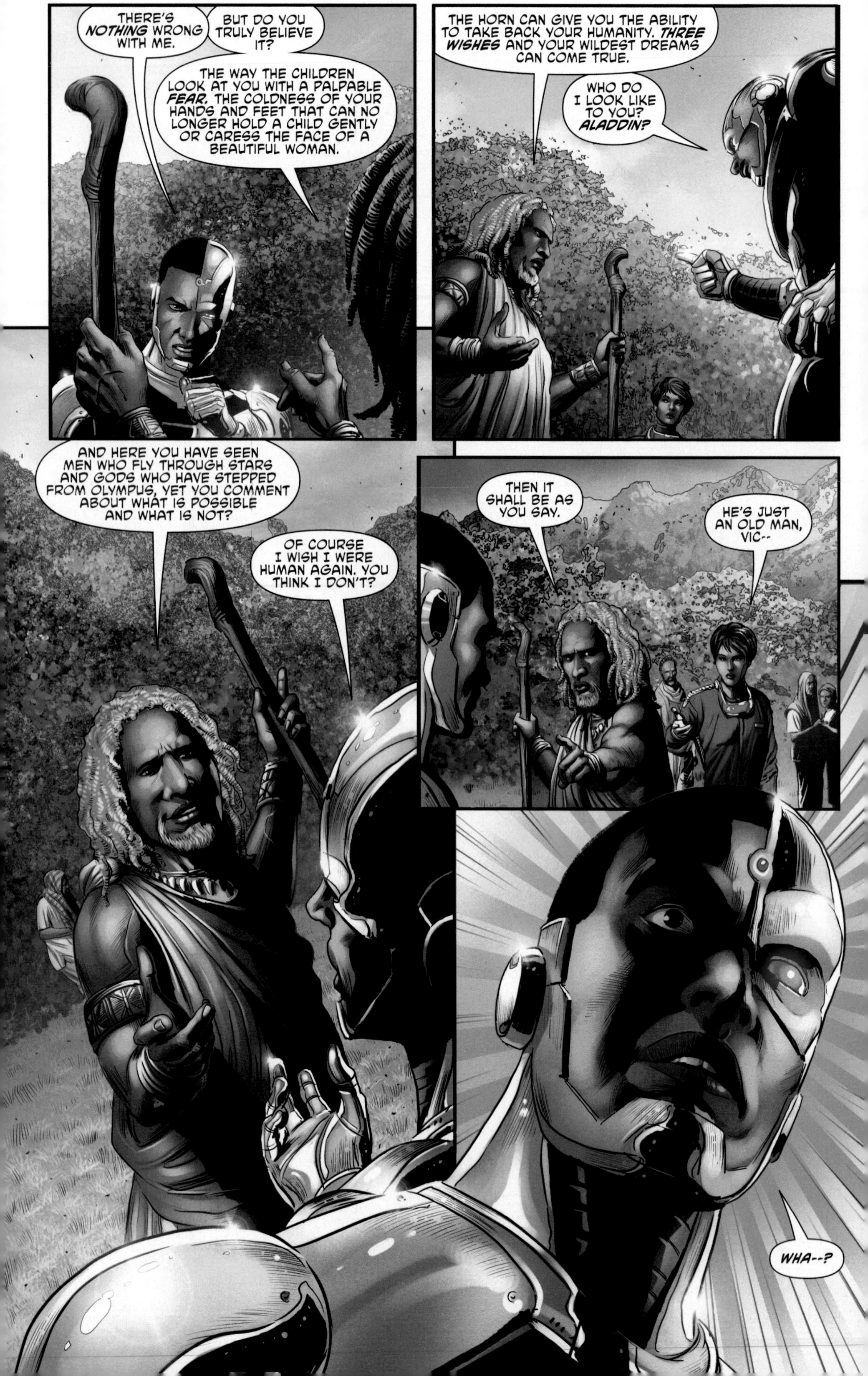

THERE'S NOTHING WRONG WITH ME.
BUT DO YOU TRULY BELIEVE IT?
THE WAY THE CHILDREN LOOK AT YOU WITH A PALPABLE FEAR, THE COLDNESS OF YOUR HANDS AND FEET THAT CAN NO LONGER HOLD A CHILD GENTLY OR CARESS THE FACE OF A BEAUTIFUL WOMAN.
THE HORN CAN GIVE YOU THE ABILITY TO TAKE BACK YOUR HUMANITY. THREE WISHES AND YOUR WILDEST DREAMS CAN COME TRUE.
WHO DO I LOOK LIKE TO YOU? ALADDIN?
AND HERE YOU HAVE SEEN MEN WHO FLY THROUGH STARS AND GODS WHO HAVE STEPPED FROM OLYMPUS, YET YOU COMMENT ABOUT WHAT IS POSSIBLE AND WHAT IS NOT?
OF COURSE I WISH I WERE HUMAN AGAIN. YOU THINK I DON'T?
THEN IT SHALL BE AS YOU SAY.
HE'S JUST AN OLD MAN, VIC--
WHA--?

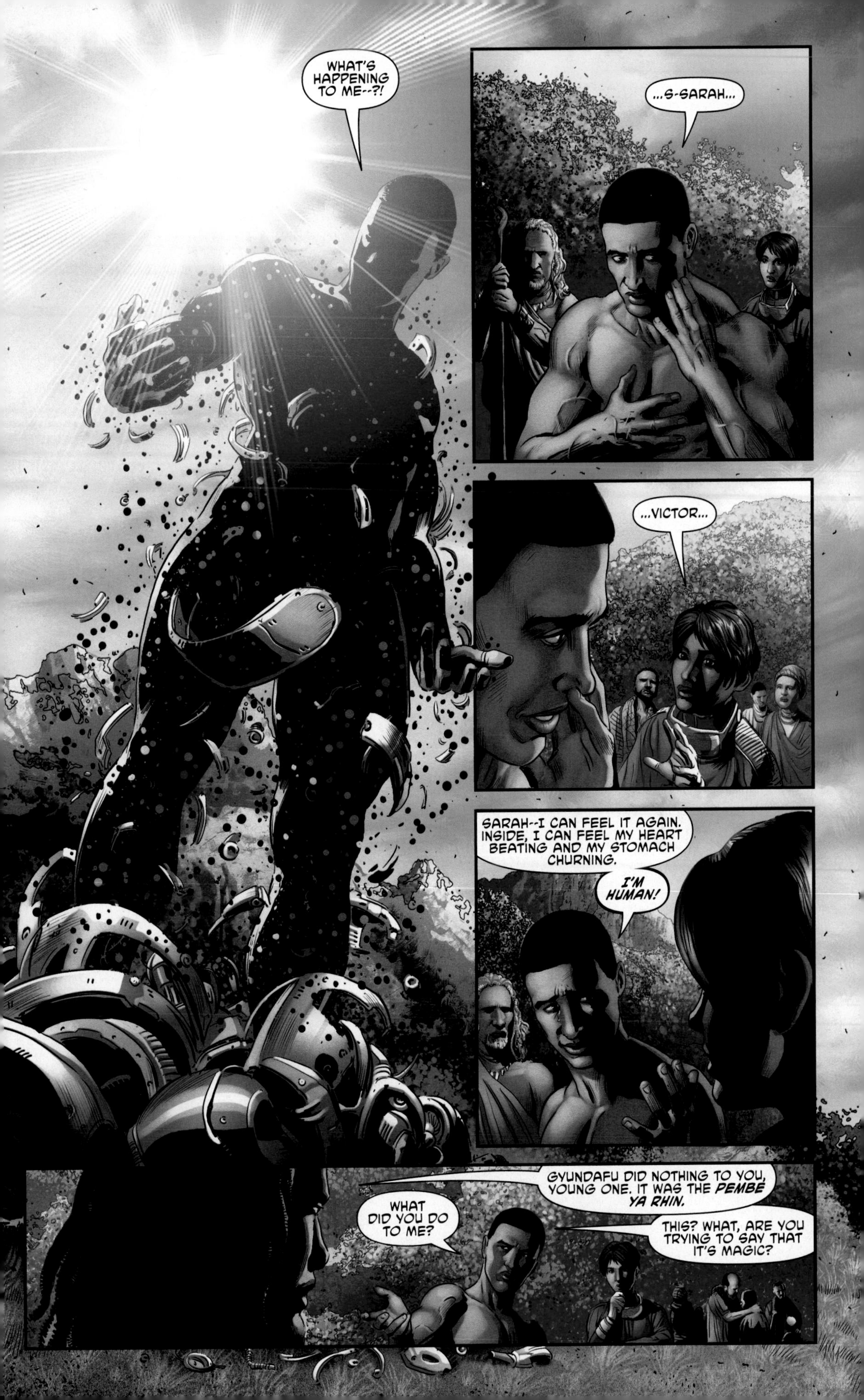
WHAT'S HAPPENING TO ME--?!
...S-SARAH...
...VICTOR...
SARAH--I CAN FEEL IT AGAIN. INSIDE, I CAN FEEL MY HEART BEATING AND MY STOMACH CHURNING.
I'M HUMAN!
WHAT DID YOU DO TO ME?
GYUNDAFU DID NOTHING TO YOU, YOUNG ONE. IT WAS THE PEMBE YA RHIN.
THIS? WHAT, ARE YOU TRYING TO SAY THAT IT'S MAGIC?

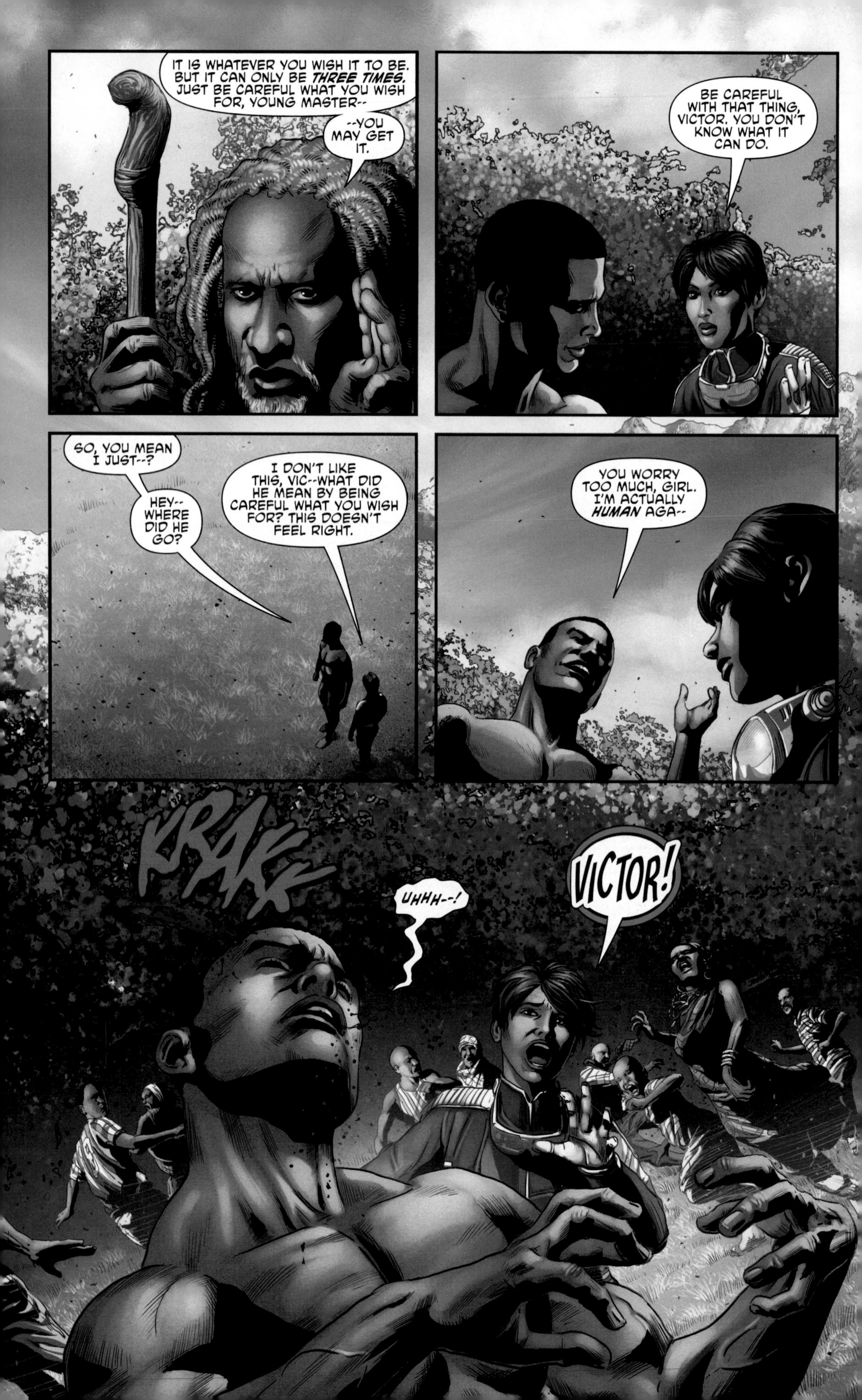
IT IS WHATEVER YOU WISH IT TO BE. BUT IT CAN ONLY BE THREE TIMES. JUST BE CAREFUL WHAT YOU WISH FOR, YOUNG MASTER--
--YOU MAY GET IT.
BE CAREFUL WITH THAT THING, VICTOR. YOU DON'T KNOW WHAT IT CAN DO.
SO, YOU MEAN I JUST--?
HEY--WHERE DID HE GO?
I DON'T LIKE THIS, VIC--WHAT DID HE MEAN BY BEING CAREFUL WHAT YOU WISH FOR? THIS DOESN'T FEEL RIGHT.
YOU WORRY TOO MUCH, GIRL. I'M ACTUALLY HUMAN AGA--
KRAKK
UHHH--!
VICTOR!

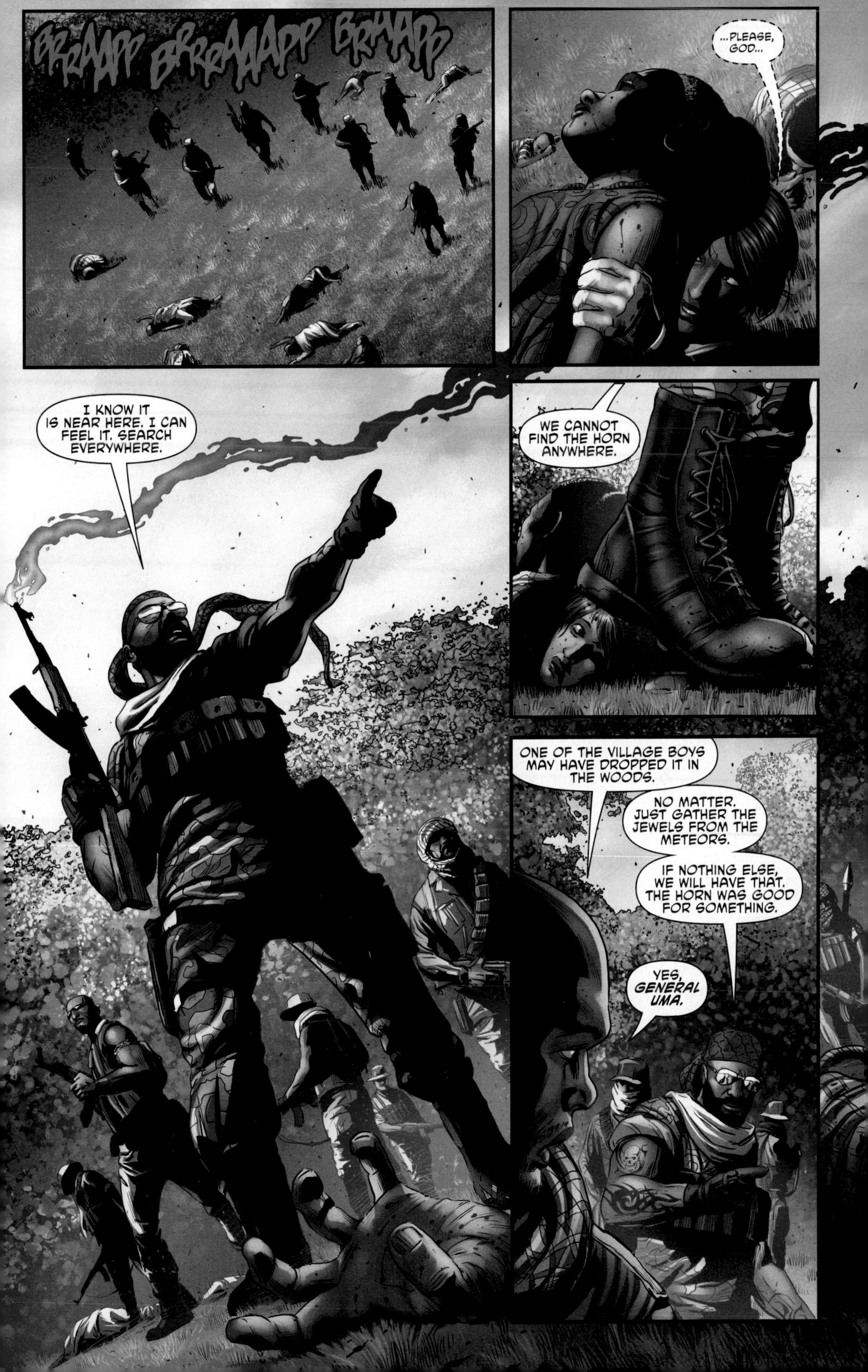
BRRAAPP BRRRAAAAPP BRRAAPP
...PLEASE, GOD...
I KNOW IT IS NEAR HERE. I CAN FEEL IT. SEARCH EVERYWHERE.
WE CANNOT FIND THE HORN ANYWHERE.
ONE OF THE VILLAGE BOYS MAY HAVE DROPPED IT IN THE WOODS.
NO MATTER. JUST GATHER THE JEWELS FROM THE METEORS.
IF NOTHING ELSE, WE WILL HAVE THAT. THE HORN WAS GOOD FOR SOMETHING.
YES, GENERAL UMA.

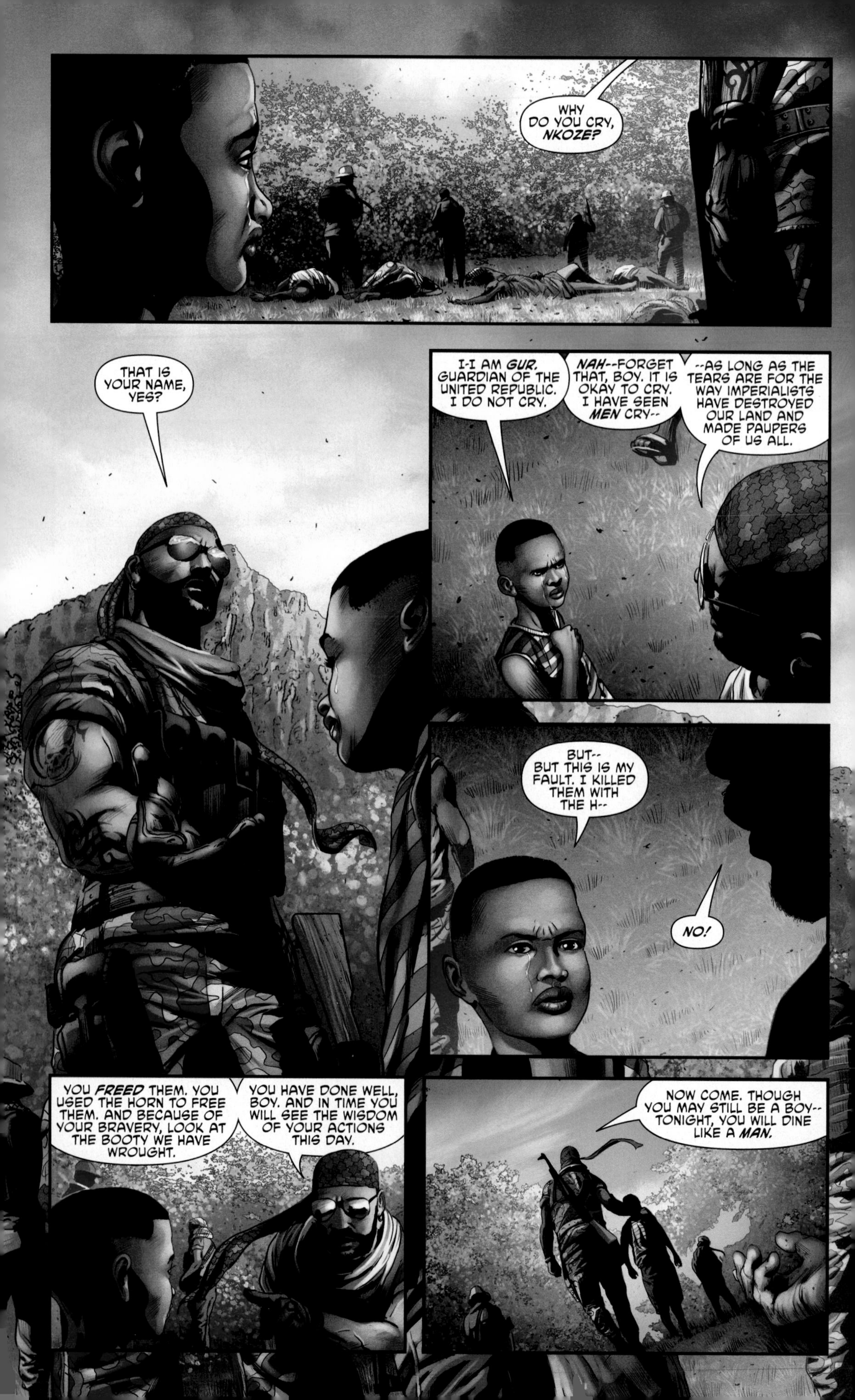
WHY DO YOU CRY, NKOZE?
THAT IS YOUR NAME, YES?
I-I AM GUR. GUARDIAN OF THE UNITED REPUBLIC. I DO NOT CRY.
NAH--FORGET THAT, BOY. IT IS OKAY TO CRY. I HAVE SEEN MEN CRY--
--AS LONG AS THE TEARS ARE FOR THE WAY IMPERIALISTS HAVE DESTROYED OUR LAND AND MADE PAUPERS OF US ALL.
BUT-- BUT THIS IS MY FAULT. I KILLED THEM WITH THE H--
NO!
YOU FREED THEM. YOU USED THE HORN TO FREE THEM. AND BECAUSE OF YOUR BRAVERY, LOOK AT THE BOOTY WE HAVE WROUGHT.
YOU HAVE DONE WELL, BOY. AND IN TIME YOU WILL SEE THE WISDOM OF YOUR ACTIONS THIS DAY.
NOW COME. THOUGH YOU MAY STILL BE A BOY-- TONIGHT, YOU WILL DINE LIKE A MAN.

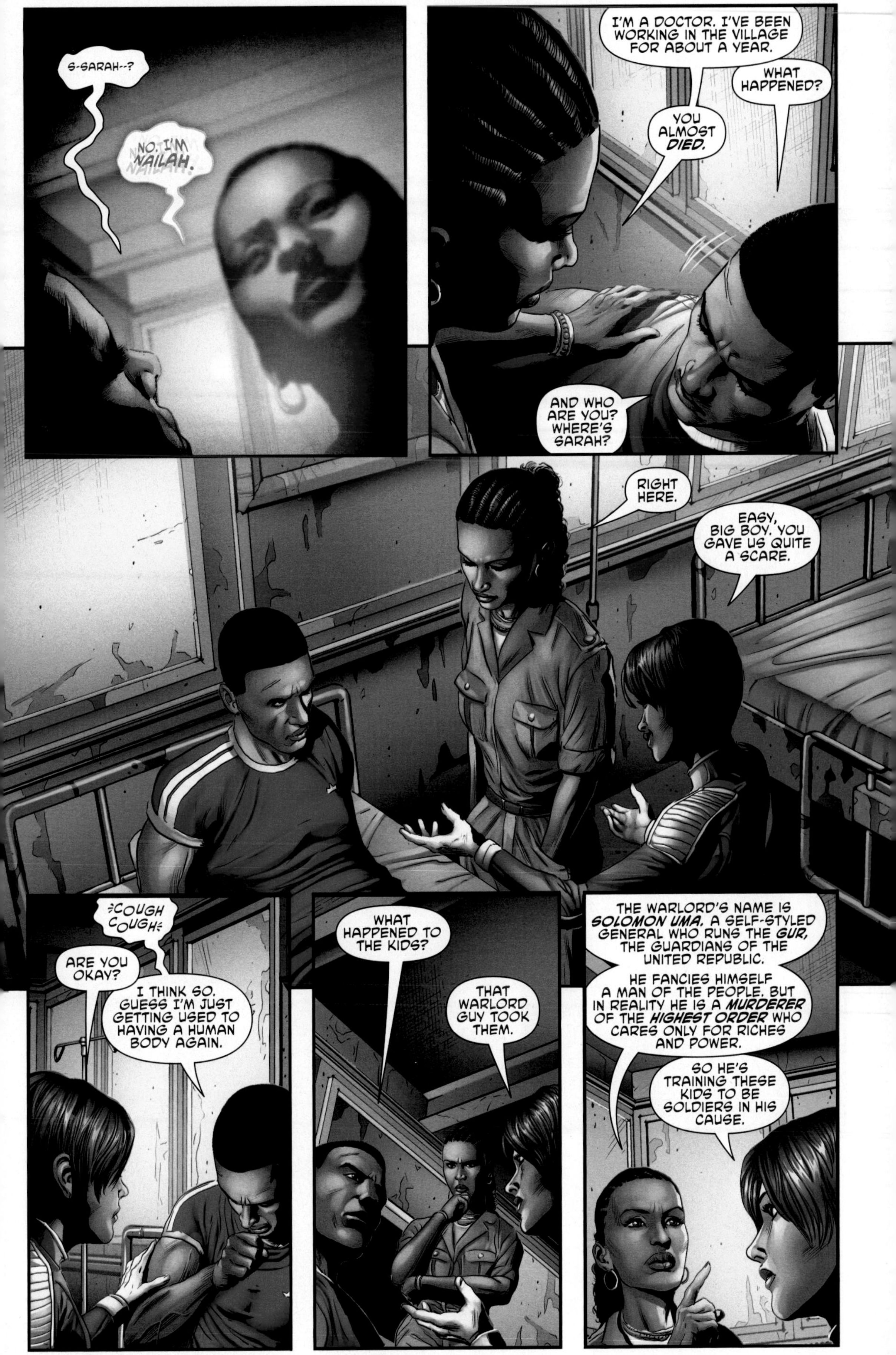
S-SARAH--?
NO. I'M NAILAH.
I'M A DOCTOR. I'VE BEEN WORKING IN THE VILLAGE FOR ABOUT A YEAR.
YOU ALMOST DIED.
WHAT HAPPENED?
AND WHO ARE YOU? WHERE'S SARAH?
RIGHT HERE.
EASY, BIG BOY. YOU GAVE US QUITE A SCARE.
COUGH COUGH
ARE YOU OKAY?
I THINK SO. GUESS I'M JUST GETTING USED TO HAVING A HUMAN BODY AGAIN.
WHAT HAPPENED TO THE KIDS?
THAT WARLORD GUY TOOK THEM.
THE WARLORD'S NAME IS SOLOMON UMA, A SELF-STYLED GENERAL WHO RUNS THE GUR, THE GUARDIANS OF THE UNITED REPUBLIC.
HE FANCIES HIMSELF A MAN OF THE PEOPLE. BUT IN REALITY HE IS A MURDERER OF THE HIGHEST ORDER WHO CARES ONLY FOR RICHES AND POWER.
SO HE'S TRAINING THESE KIDS TO BE SOLDIERS IN HIS CAUSE.

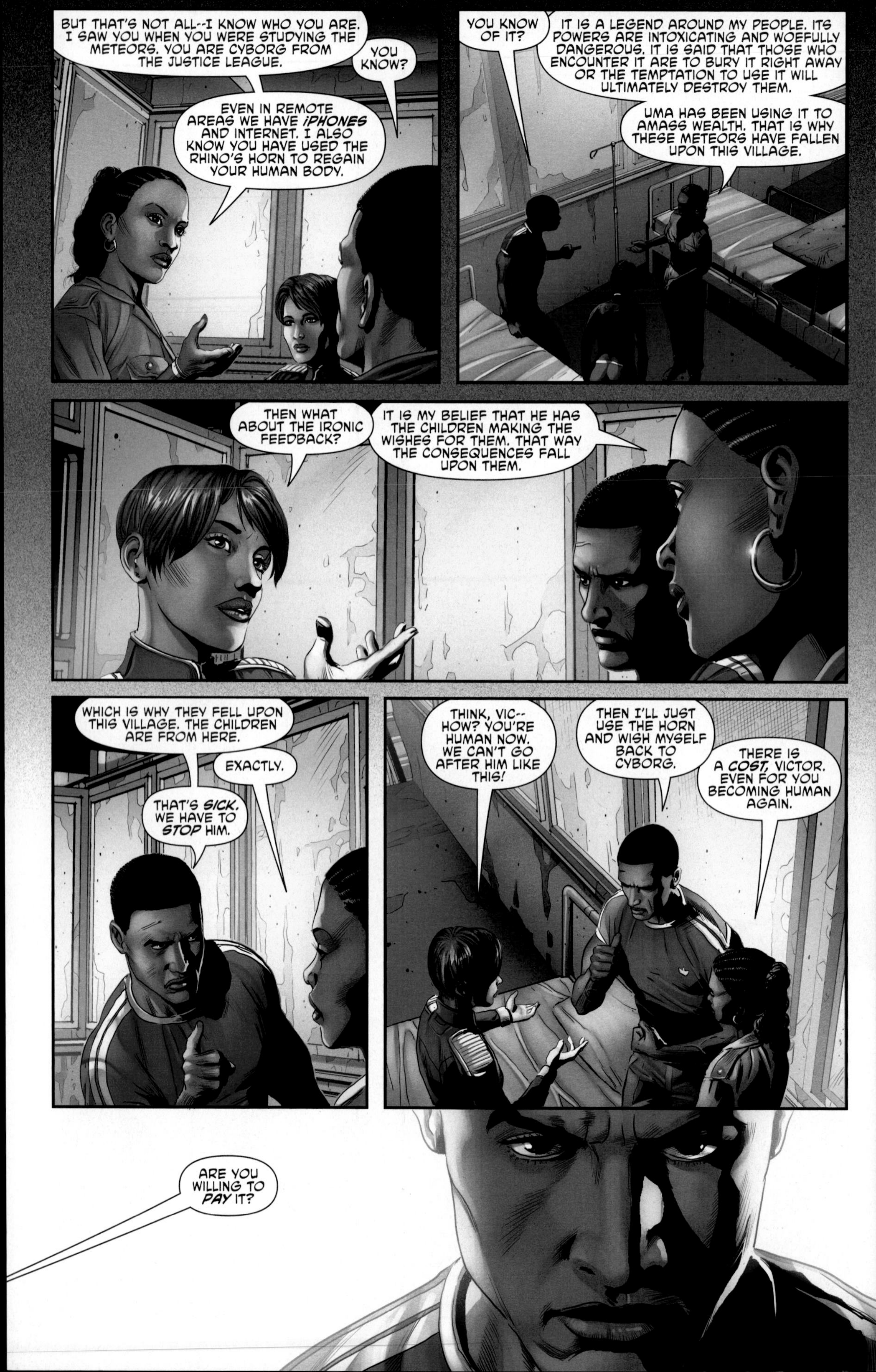
BUT THAT'S NOT ALL--I KNOW WHO YOU ARE. I SAW YOU WHEN YOU WERE STUDYING THE METEORS. YOU ARE CYBORG FROM THE JUSTICE LEAGUE.
YOU KNOW?
EVEN IN REMOTE AREAS WE HAVE *iPHONES* AND INTERNET. I ALSO KNOW YOU HAVE USED THE RHINO'S HORN TO REGAIN YOUR HUMAN BODY.
YOU KNOW OF IT?
IT IS A LEGEND AROUND MY PEOPLE. ITS POWERS ARE INTOXICATING AND WOEFULLY DANGEROUS. IT IS SAID THAT THOSE WHO ENCOUNTER IT ARE TO BURY IT RIGHT AWAY OR THE TEMPTATION TO USE IT WILL ULTIMATELY DESTROY THEM.
UMA HAS BEEN USING IT TO AMASS WEALTH. THAT IS WHY THESE METEORS HAVE FALLEN UPON THIS VILLAGE.
THEN WHAT ABOUT THE IRONIC FEEDBACK?
IT IS MY BELIEF THAT HE HAS THE CHILDREN MAKING THE WISHES FOR THEM. THAT WAY THE CONSEQUENCES FALL UPON THEM.
WHICH IS WHY THEY FELL UPON THIS VILLAGE. THE CHILDREN ARE FROM HERE.
EXACTLY.
THAT'S *SICK.* WE HAVE TO *STOP* HIM.
THINK, VIC-- HOW? YOU'RE HUMAN NOW. WE CAN'T GO AFTER HIM LIKE THIS!
THEN I'LL JUST USE THE HORN AND WISH MYSELF BACK TO CYBORG.
THERE IS A *COST,* VICTOR. EVEN FOR YOU BECOMING HUMAN AGAIN.
ARE YOU WILLING TO *PAY* IT?

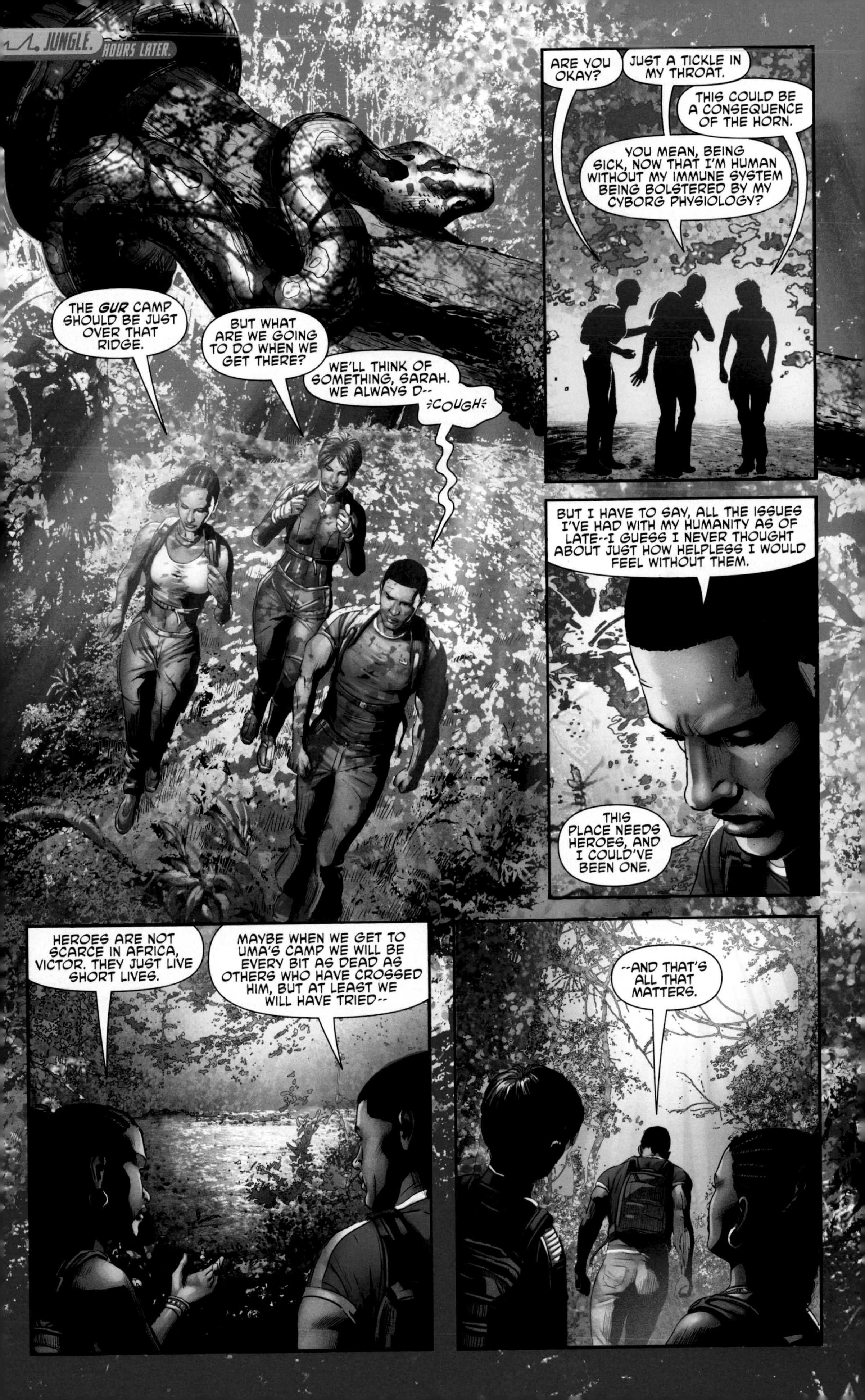
JUNGLE. HOURS LATER.
THE GUR CAMP SHOULD BE JUST OVER THAT RIDGE.
BUT WHAT ARE WE GOING TO DO WHEN WE GET THERE?
WE'LL THINK OF SOMETHING, SARAH. WE ALWAYS D--
COUGH
ARE YOU OKAY?
JUST A TICKLE IN MY THROAT.
THIS COULD BE A CONSEQUENCE OF THE HORN.
YOU MEAN, BEING SICK, NOW THAT I'M HUMAN WITHOUT MY IMMUNE SYSTEM BEING BOLSTERED BY MY CYBORG PHYSIOLOGY?
BUT I HAVE TO SAY, ALL THE ISSUES I'VE HAD WITH MY HUMANITY AS OF LATE--I GUESS I NEVER THOUGHT ABOUT JUST HOW HELPLESS I WOULD FEEL WITHOUT THEM.
THIS PLACE NEEDS HEROES, AND I COULD'VE BEEN ONE.
HEROES ARE NOT SCARCE IN AFRICA, VICTOR. THEY JUST LIVE SHORT LIVES.
MAYBE WHEN WE GET TO UMA'S CAMP WE WILL BE EVERY BIT AS DEAD AS OTHERS WHO HAVE CROSSED HIM, BUT AT LEAST WE WILL HAVE TRIED--
--AND THAT'S ALL THAT MATTERS.

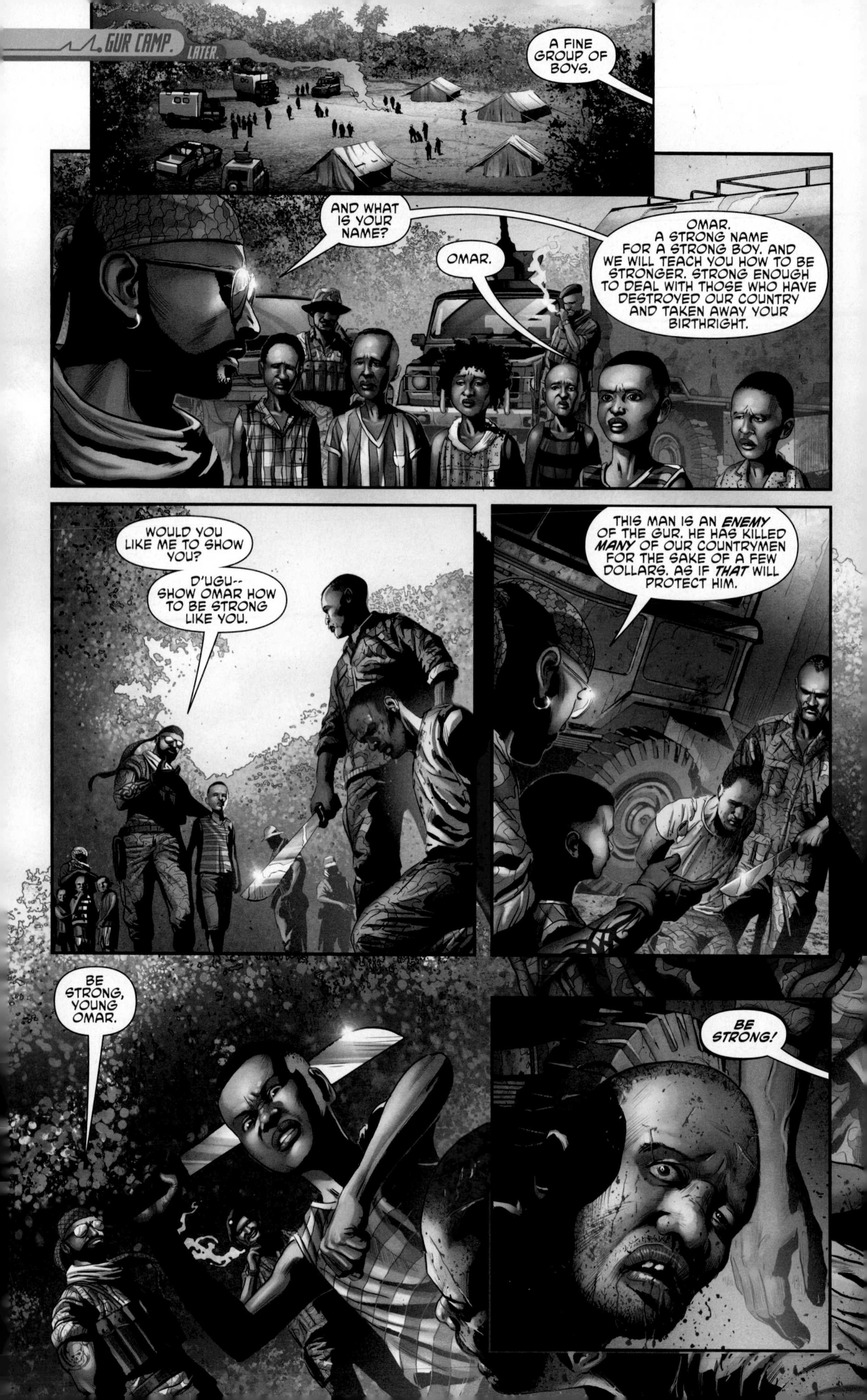
GUR CAMP.
LATER.
A FINE GROUP OF BOYS.
AND WHAT IS YOUR NAME?
OMAR.
OMAR. A STRONG NAME FOR A STRONG BOY. AND WE WILL TEACH YOU HOW TO BE STRONGER. STRONG ENOUGH TO DEAL WITH THOSE WHO HAVE DESTROYED OUR COUNTRY AND TAKEN AWAY YOUR BIRTHRIGHT.
WOULD YOU LIKE ME TO SHOW YOU?
D'UGU-- SHOW OMAR HOW TO BE STRONG LIKE YOU.
THIS MAN IS AN ENEMY OF THE GUR. HE HAS KILLED MANY OF OUR COUNTRYMEN FOR THE SAKE OF A FEW DOLLARS. AS IF THAT WILL PROTECT HIM.
BE STRONG, YOUNG OMAR.
BE STRONG!

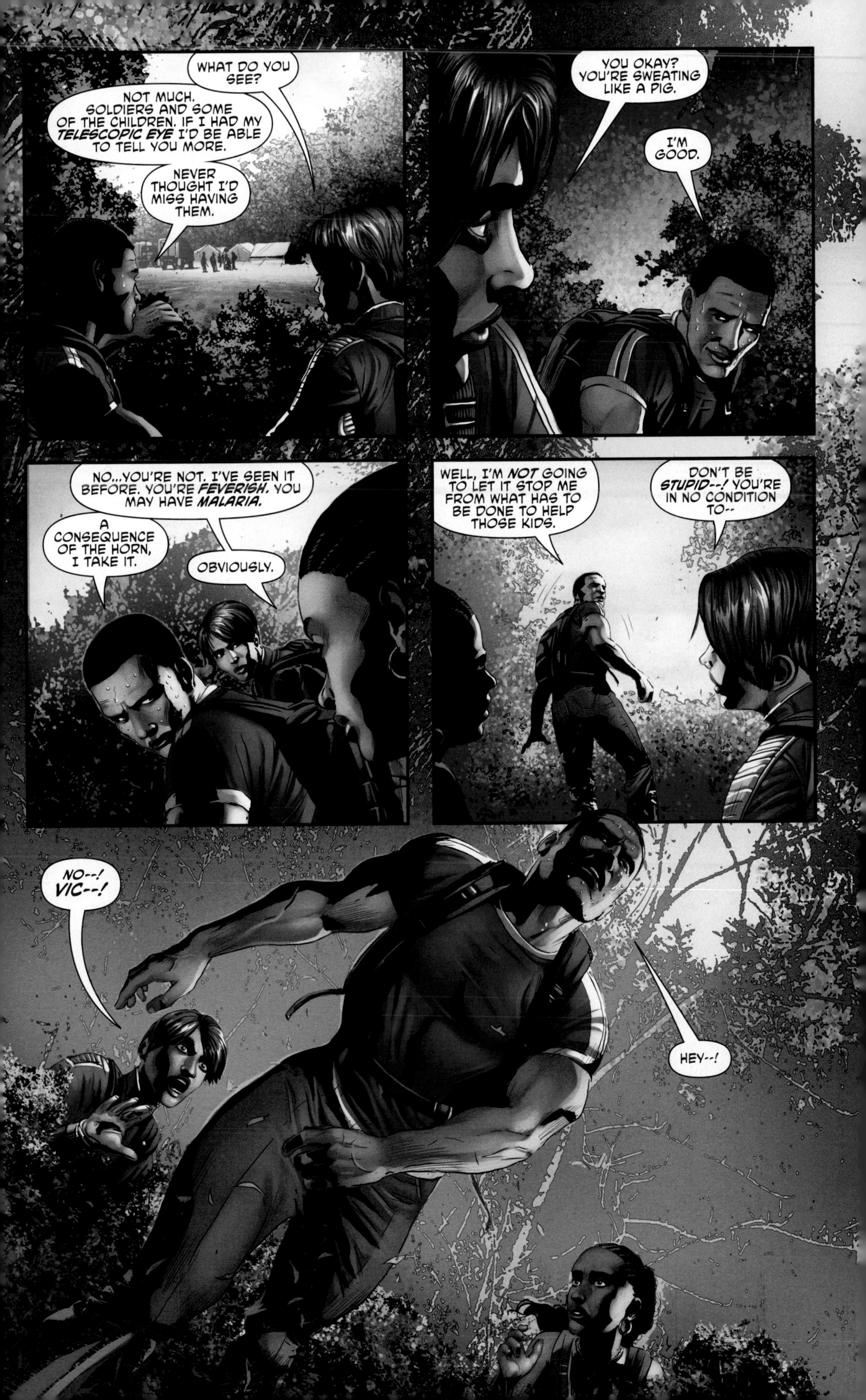
WHAT DO YOU SEE?
NOT MUCH. SOLDIERS AND SOME OF THE CHILDREN. IF I HAD MY *TELESCOPIC EYE* I'D BE ABLE TO TELL YOU MORE.
NEVER THOUGHT I'D MISS HAVING THEM.
YOU OKAY? YOU'RE SWEATING LIKE A PIG.
I'M GOOD.
NO...YOU'RE NOT. I'VE SEEN IT BEFORE. YOU'RE *FEVERISH.* YOU MAY HAVE *MALARIA.*
A CONSEQUENCE OF THE HORN, I TAKE IT.
OBVIOUSLY.
WELL, I'M *NOT* GOING TO LET IT STOP ME FROM WHAT HAS TO BE DONE TO HELP THOSE KIDS.
DON'T BE *STUPID--!* YOU'RE IN NO CONDITION TO--
NO--! VIC--!
HEY--!

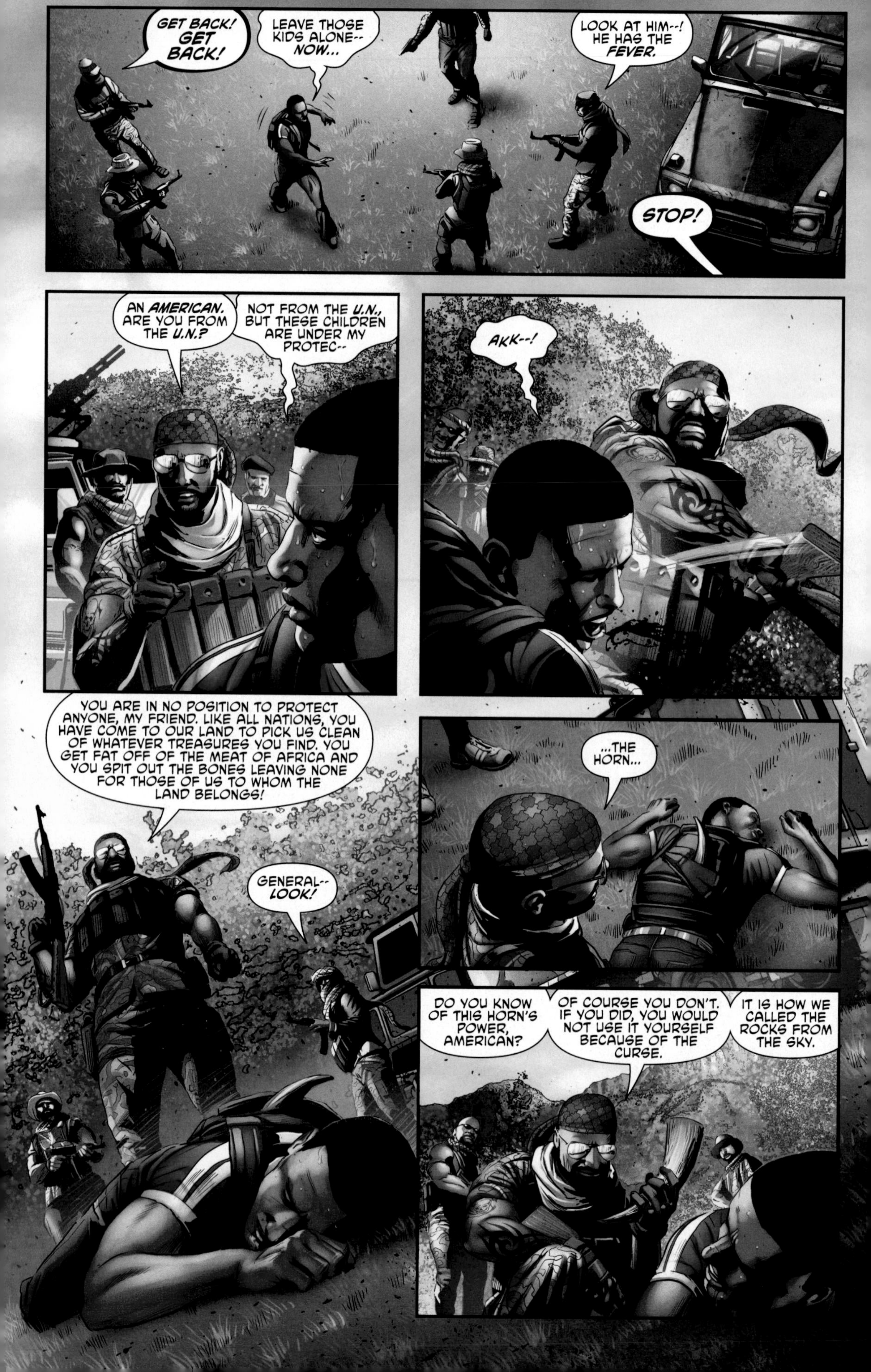
GET BACK! GET BACK!
LEAVE THOSE KIDS ALONE-- NOW...
LOOK AT HIM--! HE HAS THE FEVER.
STOP!
AN AMERICAN. ARE YOU FROM THE U.N.?
NOT FROM THE U.N., BUT THESE CHILDREN ARE UNDER MY PROTEC--
AKK--!
YOU ARE IN NO POSITION TO PROTECT ANYONE, MY FRIEND. LIKE ALL NATIONS, YOU HAVE COME TO OUR LAND TO PICK US CLEAN OF WHATEVER TREASURES YOU FIND. YOU GET FAT OFF OF THE MEAT OF AFRICA AND YOU SPIT OUT THE BONES LEAVING NONE FOR THOSE OF US TO WHOM THE LAND BELONGS!
GENERAL-- LOOK!
...THE HORN...
DO YOU KNOW OF THIS HORN'S POWER, AMERICAN?
OF COURSE YOU DON'T. IF YOU DID, YOU WOULD NOT USE IT YOURSELF BECAUSE OF THE CURSE.
IT IS HOW WE CALLED THE ROCKS FROM THE SKY.

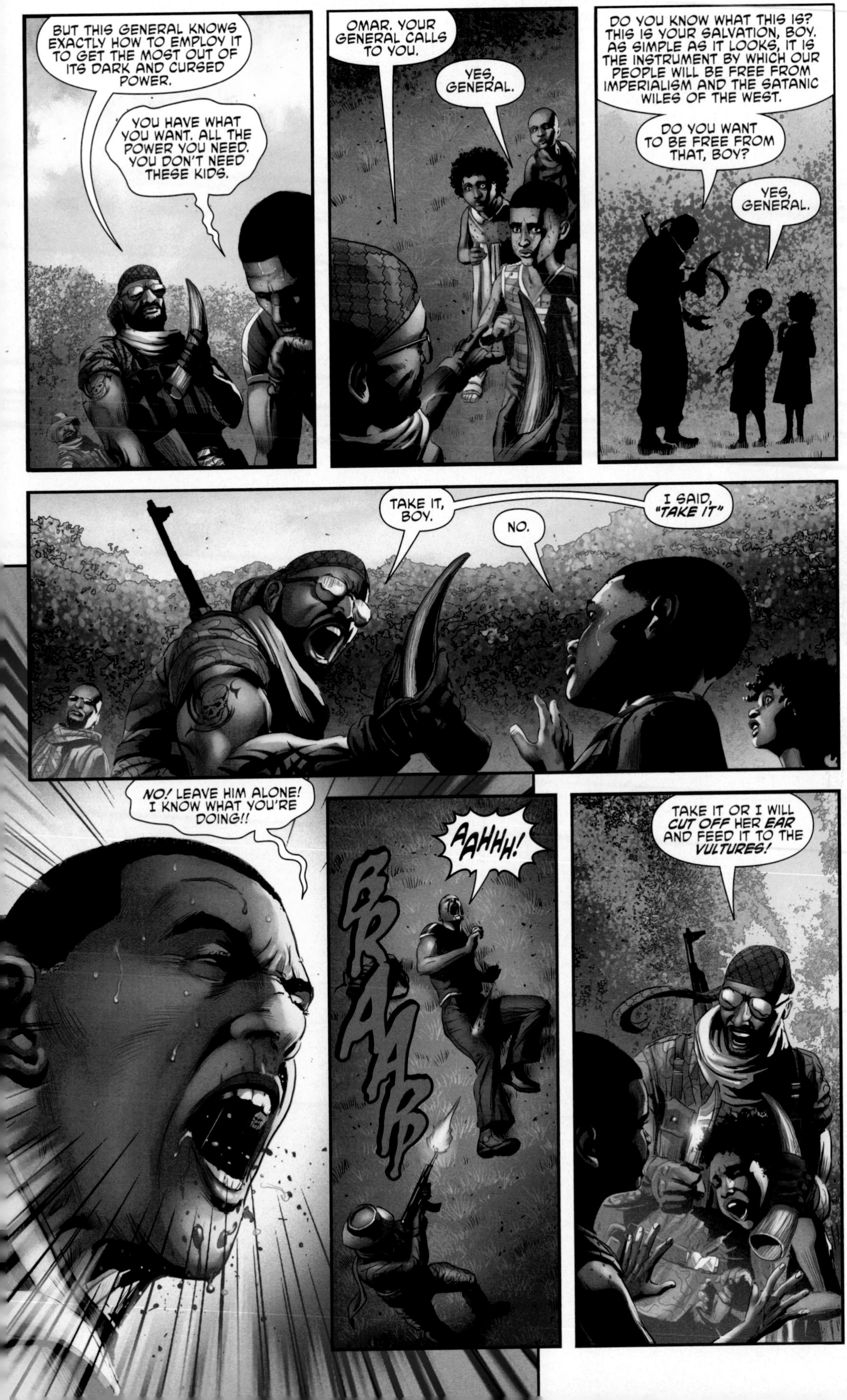
BUT THIS GENERAL KNOWS EXACTLY HOW TO EMPLOY IT TO GET THE MOST OUT OF ITS DARK AND CURSED POWER.
YOU HAVE WHAT YOU WANT. ALL THE POWER YOU NEED. YOU DON'T NEED THESE KIDS.
OMAR. YOUR GENERAL CALLS TO YOU.
YES, GENERAL.
DO YOU KNOW WHAT THIS IS? THIS IS YOUR SALVATION, BOY. AS SIMPLE AS IT LOOKS, IT IS THE INSTRUMENT BY WHICH OUR PEOPLE WILL BE FREE FROM IMPERIALISM AND THE SATANIC WILES OF THE WEST.
DO YOU WANT TO BE FREE FROM THAT, BOY?
YES, GENERAL.
TAKE IT, BOY.
I SAID, "TAKE IT"
NO.
NO! LEAVE HIM ALONE! I KNOW WHAT YOU'RE DOING!!
AAHHH!
BRAAAB
TAKE IT OR I WILL CUT OFF HER EAR AND FEED IT TO THE VULTURES!

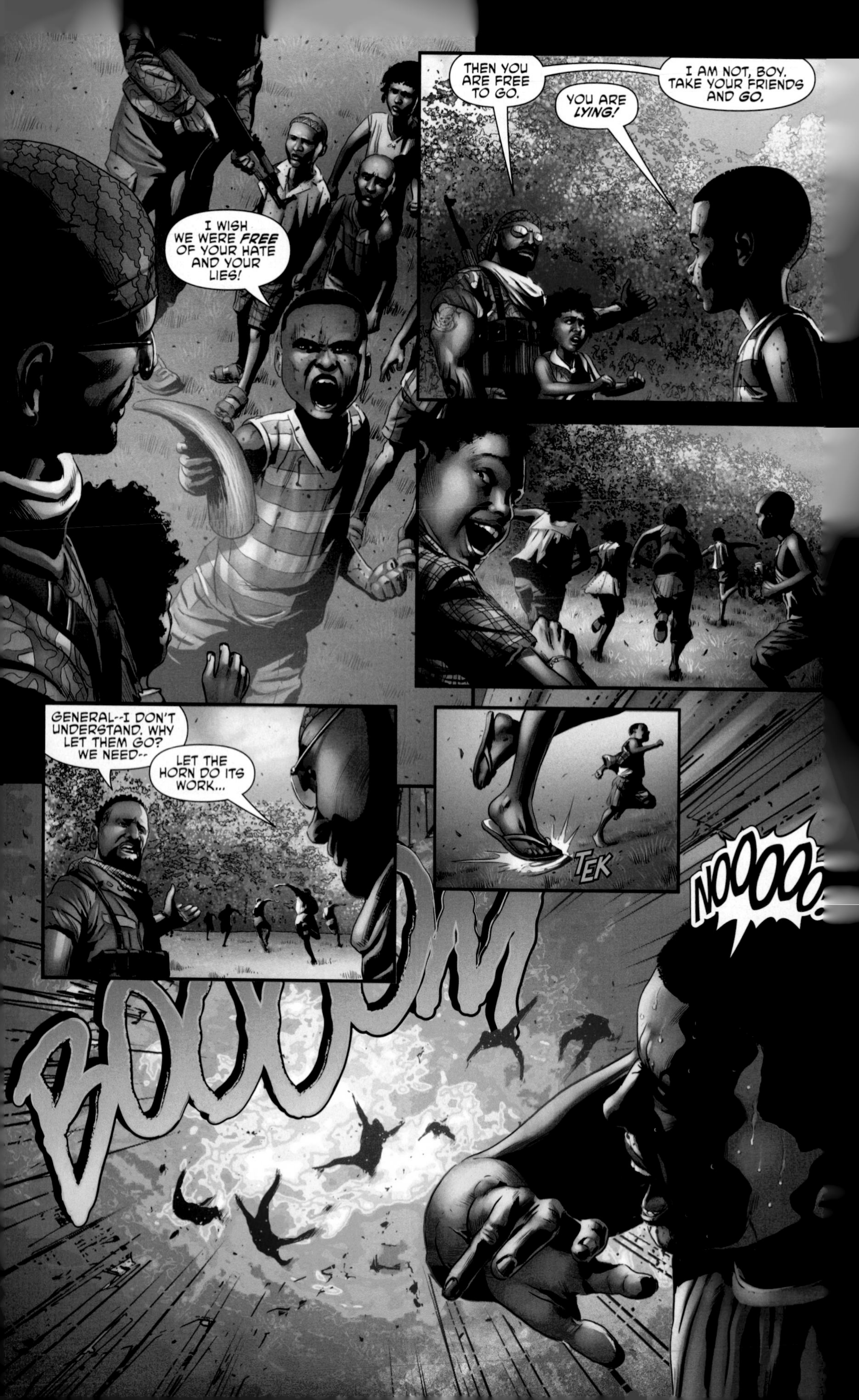
I WISH WE WERE FREE OF YOUR HATE AND YOUR LIES!
THEN YOU ARE FREE TO GO.
YOU ARE LYING!
I AM NOT, BOY. TAKE YOUR FRIENDS AND GO.
GENERAL--I DON'T UNDERSTAND. WHY LET THEM GO? WE NEED--
LET THE HORN DO ITS WORK...
TEK
NOOOO!
BOOOOM

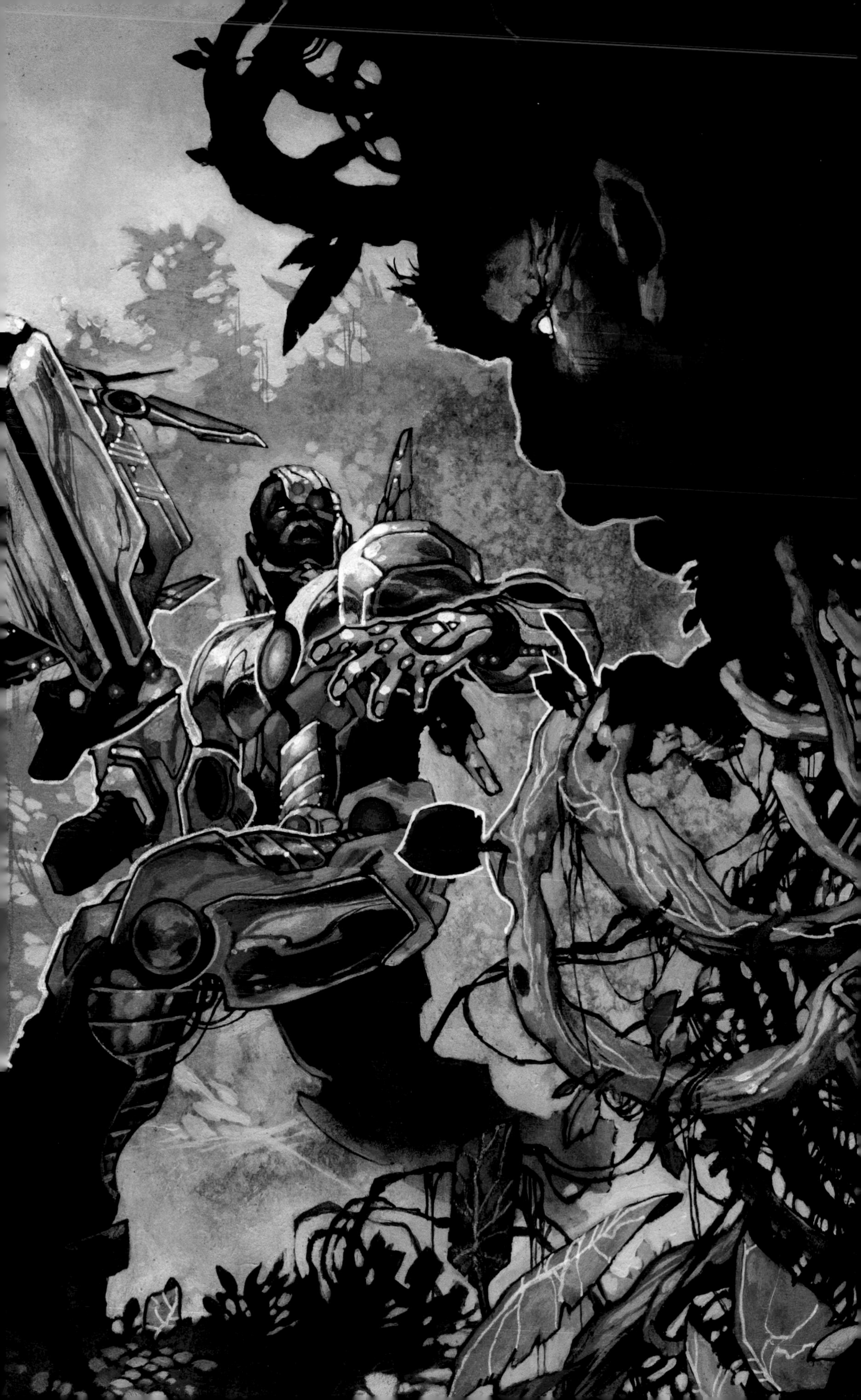

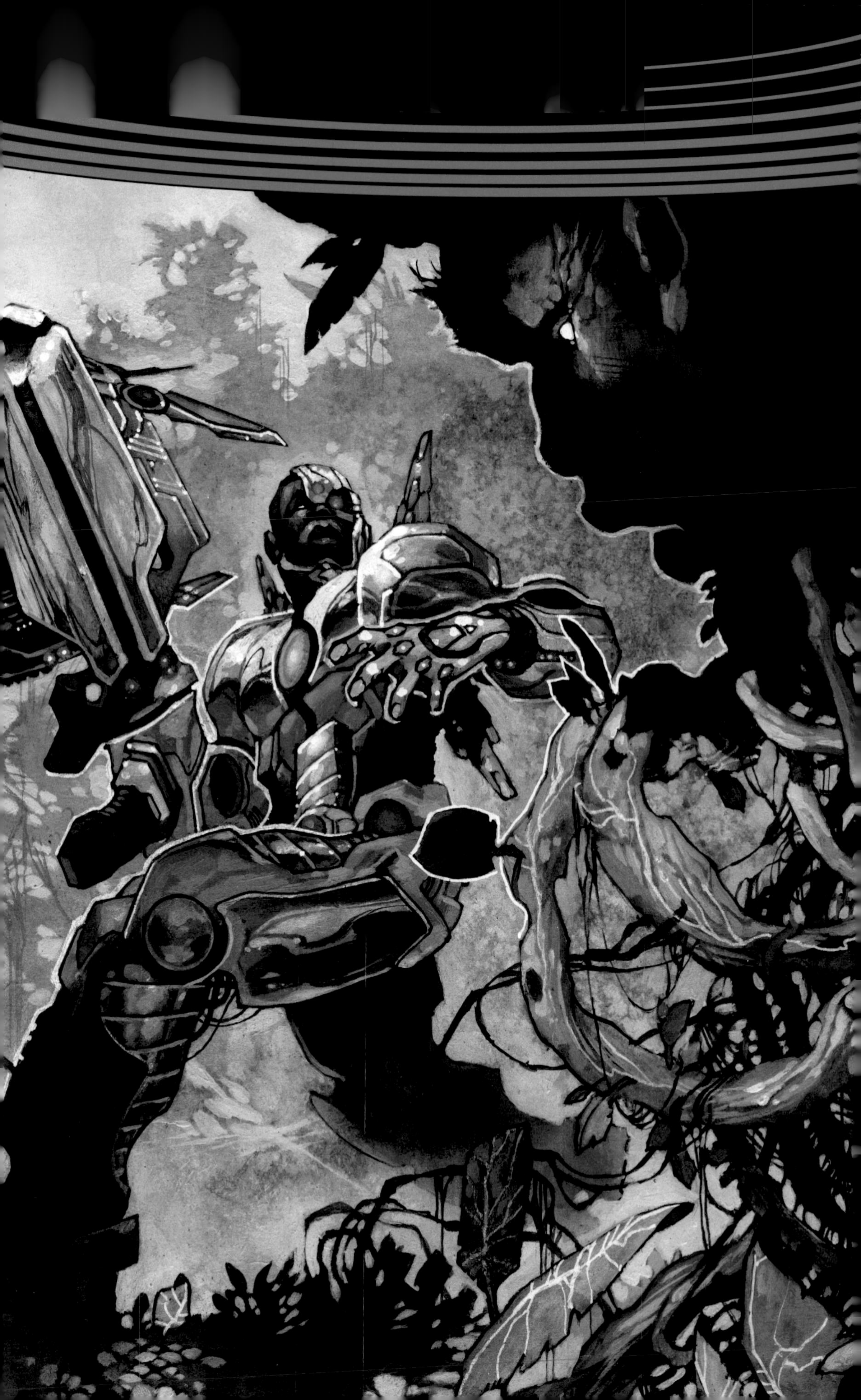

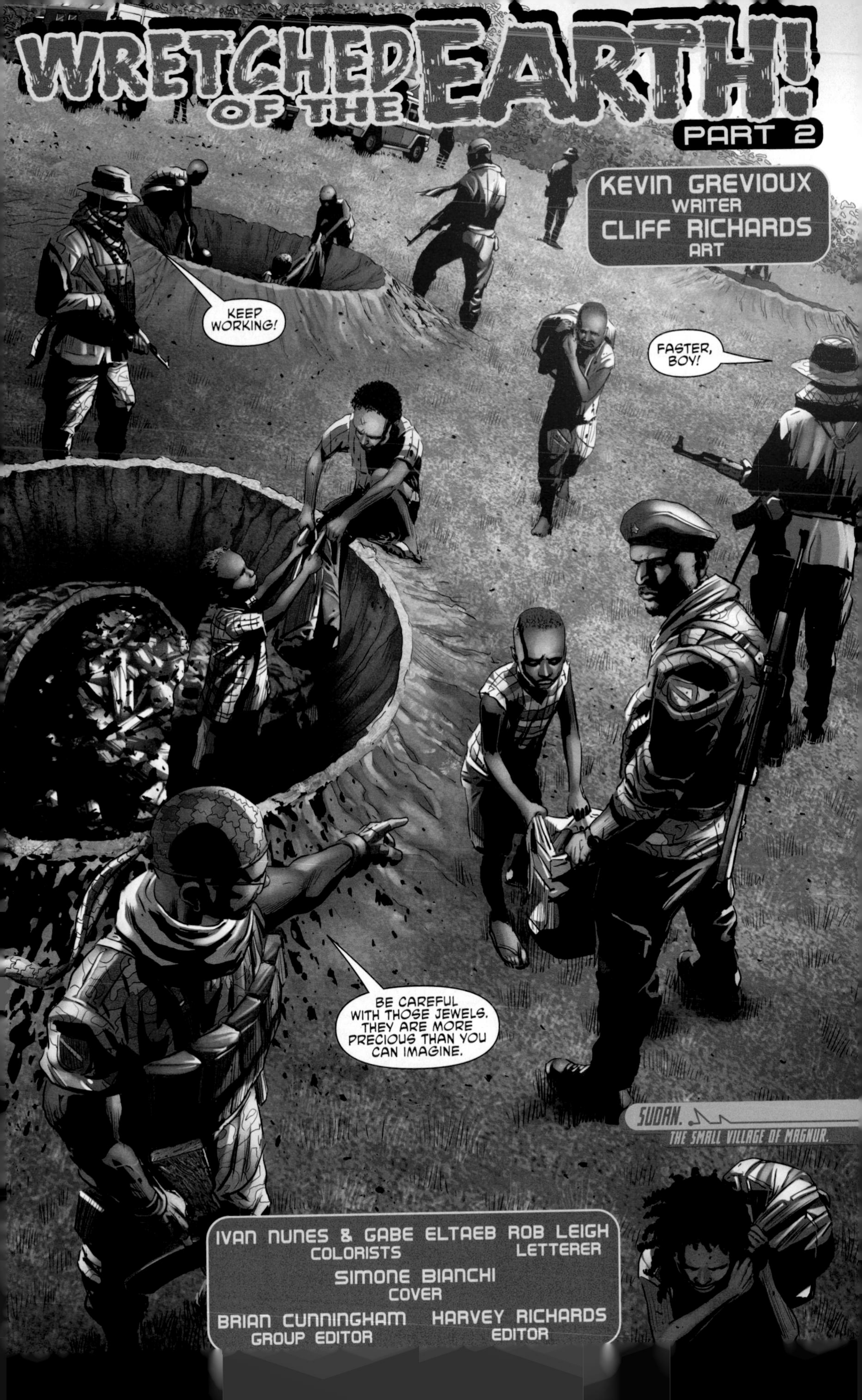
WRETCHED OF THE EARTH!
PART 2
KEVIN GREVIOUX
WRITER
CLIFF RICHARDS
ART
KEEP WORKING!
FASTER, BOY!
BE CAREFUL WITH THOSE JEWELS. THEY ARE MORE PRECIOUS THAN YOU CAN IMAGINE.
SUDAN.
THE SMALL VILLAGE OF MAGNUR.
IVAN NUNES & GABE ELTAEB
COLORISTS
ROB LEIGH
LETTERER
SIMONE BIANCHI
COVER
BRIAN CUNNINGHAM
GROUP EDITOR
HARVEY RICHARDS
EDITOR

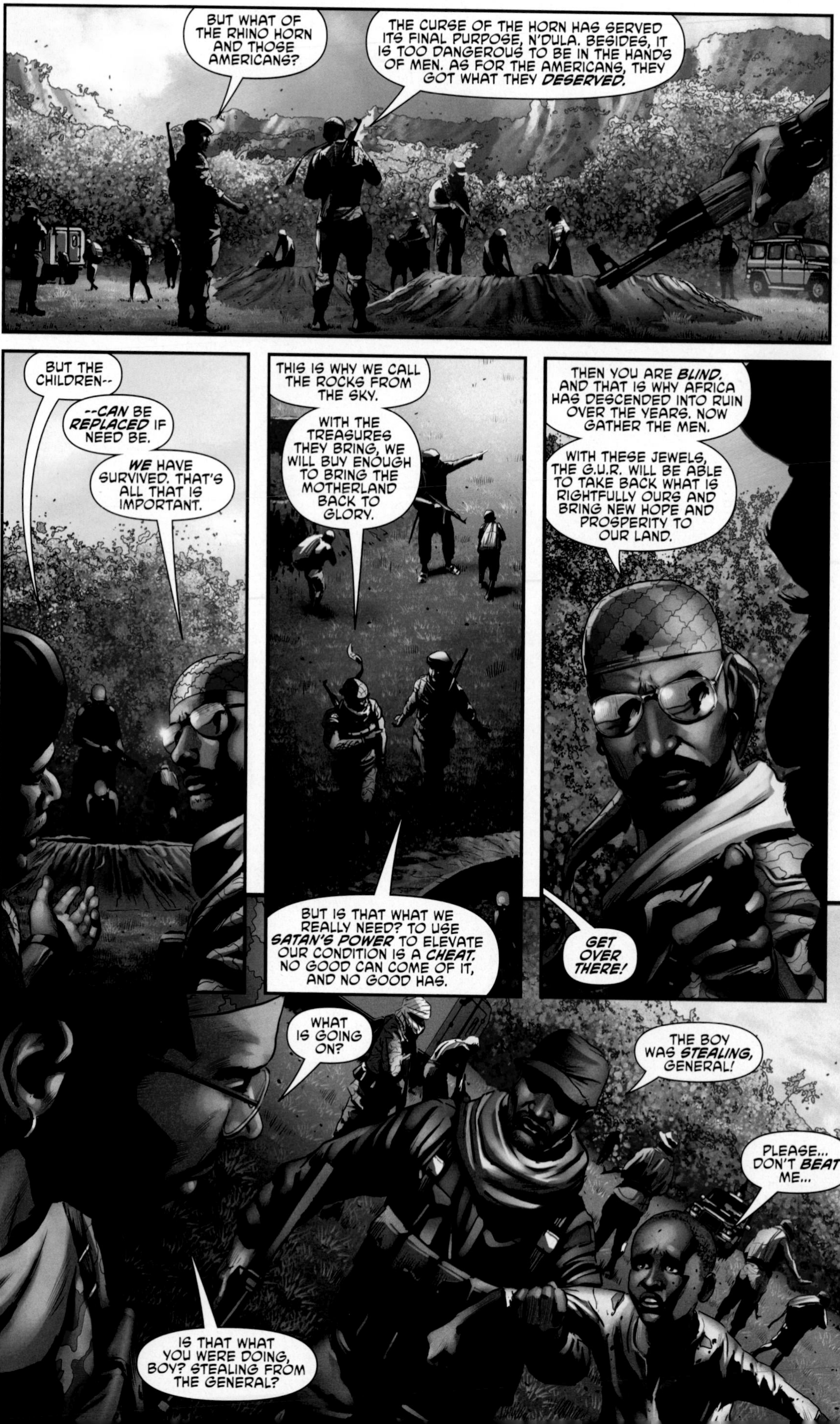
BUT WHAT OF THE RHINO HORN AND THOSE AMERICANS?
THE CURSE OF THE HORN HAS SERVED ITS FINAL PURPOSE, N'DULA. BESIDES, IT IS TOO DANGEROUS TO BE IN THE HANDS OF MEN. AS FOR THE AMERICANS, THEY GOT WHAT THEY DESERVED.
BUT THE CHILDREN--
--CAN BE REPLACED IF NEED BE.
WE HAVE SURVIVED. THAT'S ALL THAT IS IMPORTANT.
THIS IS WHY WE CALL THE ROCKS FROM THE SKY.
WITH THE TREASURES THEY BRING, WE WILL BUY ENOUGH TO BRING THE MOTHERLAND BACK TO GLORY.
BUT IS THAT WHAT WE REALLY NEED? TO USE SATAN'S POWER TO ELEVATE OUR CONDITION IS A CHEAT. NO GOOD CAN COME OF IT, AND NO GOOD HAS.
THEN YOU ARE BLIND. AND THAT IS WHY AFRICA HAS DESCENDED INTO RUIN OVER THE YEARS. NOW GATHER THE MEN.
WITH THESE JEWELS, THE G.U.R. WILL BE ABLE TO TAKE BACK WHAT IS RIGHTFULLY OURS AND BRING NEW HOPE AND PROSPERITY TO OUR LAND.
GET OVER THERE!
WHAT IS GOING ON?
THE BOY WAS STEALING, GENERAL!
PLEASE... DON'T BEAT ME...
IS THAT WHAT YOU WERE DOING, BOY? STEALING FROM THE GENERAL?

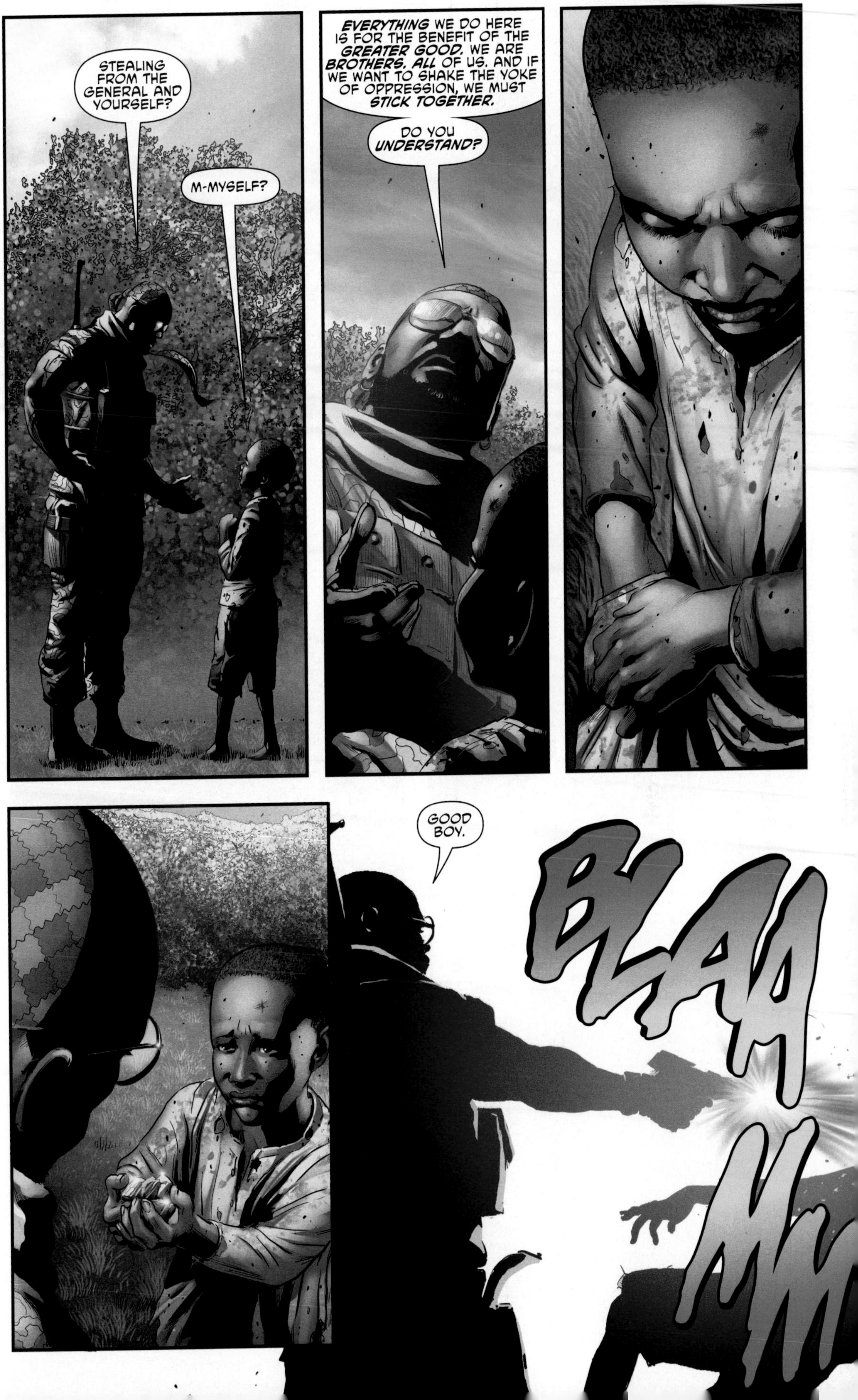
STEALING FROM THE GENERAL AND YOURSELF?
M-MYSELF?
EVERYTHING WE DO HERE IS FOR THE BENEFIT OF THE GREATER GOOD. WE ARE BROTHERS. ALL OF US. AND IF WE WANT TO SHAKE THE YOKE OF OPPRESSION, WE MUST STICK TOGETHER.
DO YOU UNDERSTAND?
GOOD BOY.
BLAAM

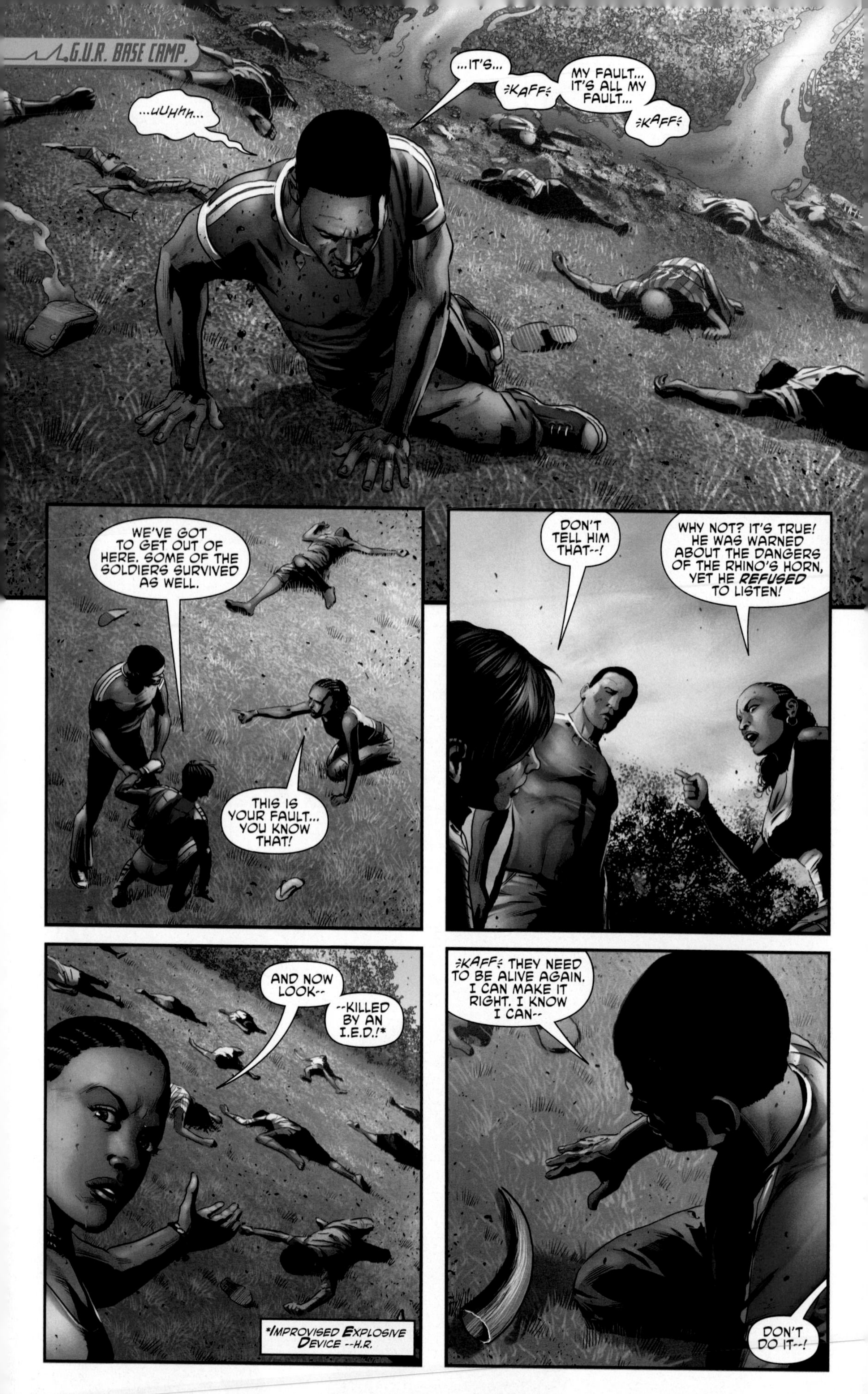
G.U.R. BASE CAMP.
...uUhhh...
...IT'S...
=KAFF=
MY FAULT... IT'S ALL MY FAULT...
=KAFF=
WE'VE GOT TO GET OUT OF HERE. SOME OF THE SOLDIERS SURVIVED AS WELL.
THIS IS YOUR FAULT... YOU KNOW THAT!
DON'T TELL HIM THAT--!
WHY NOT? IT'S TRUE! HE WAS WARNED ABOUT THE DANGERS OF THE RHINO'S HORN, YET HE REFUSED TO LISTEN!
AND NOW LOOK--
--KILLED BY AN I.E.D.!*
*IMPROVISED EXPLOSIVE DEVICE --H.R.
=KAFF= THEY NEED TO BE ALIVE AGAIN. I CAN MAKE IT RIGHT. I KNOW I CAN--
DON'T DO IT--!

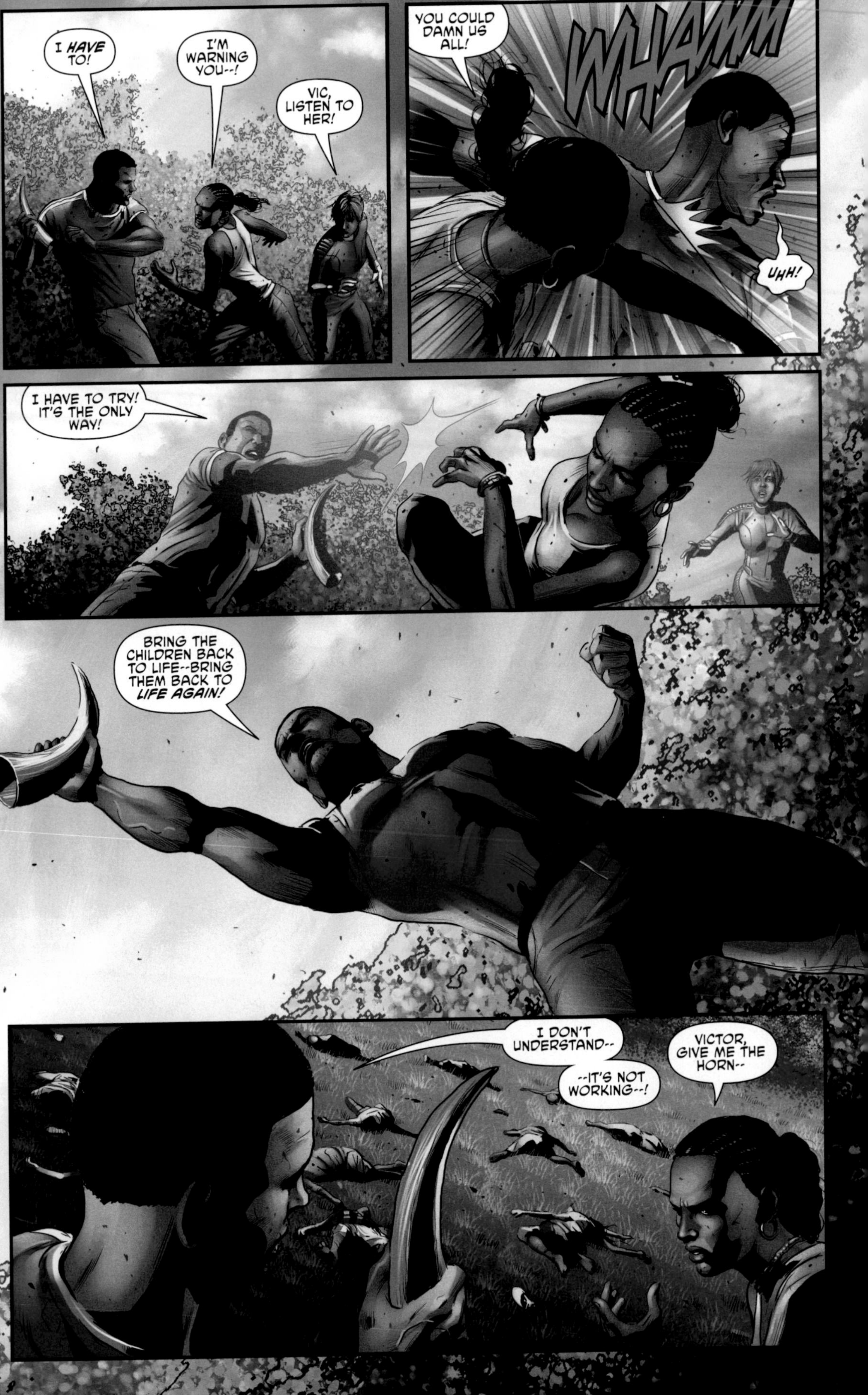

I HAVE TO!
I'M WARNING YOU--!
VIC, LISTEN TO HER!
YOU COULD DAMN US ALL!
WHAMM
UHH!
I HAVE TO TRY! IT'S THE ONLY WAY!
BRING THE CHILDREN BACK TO LIFE--BRING THEM BACK TO LIFE AGAIN!
I DON'T UNDERSTAND--
--IT'S NOT WORKING--!
VICTOR, GIVE ME THE HORN--

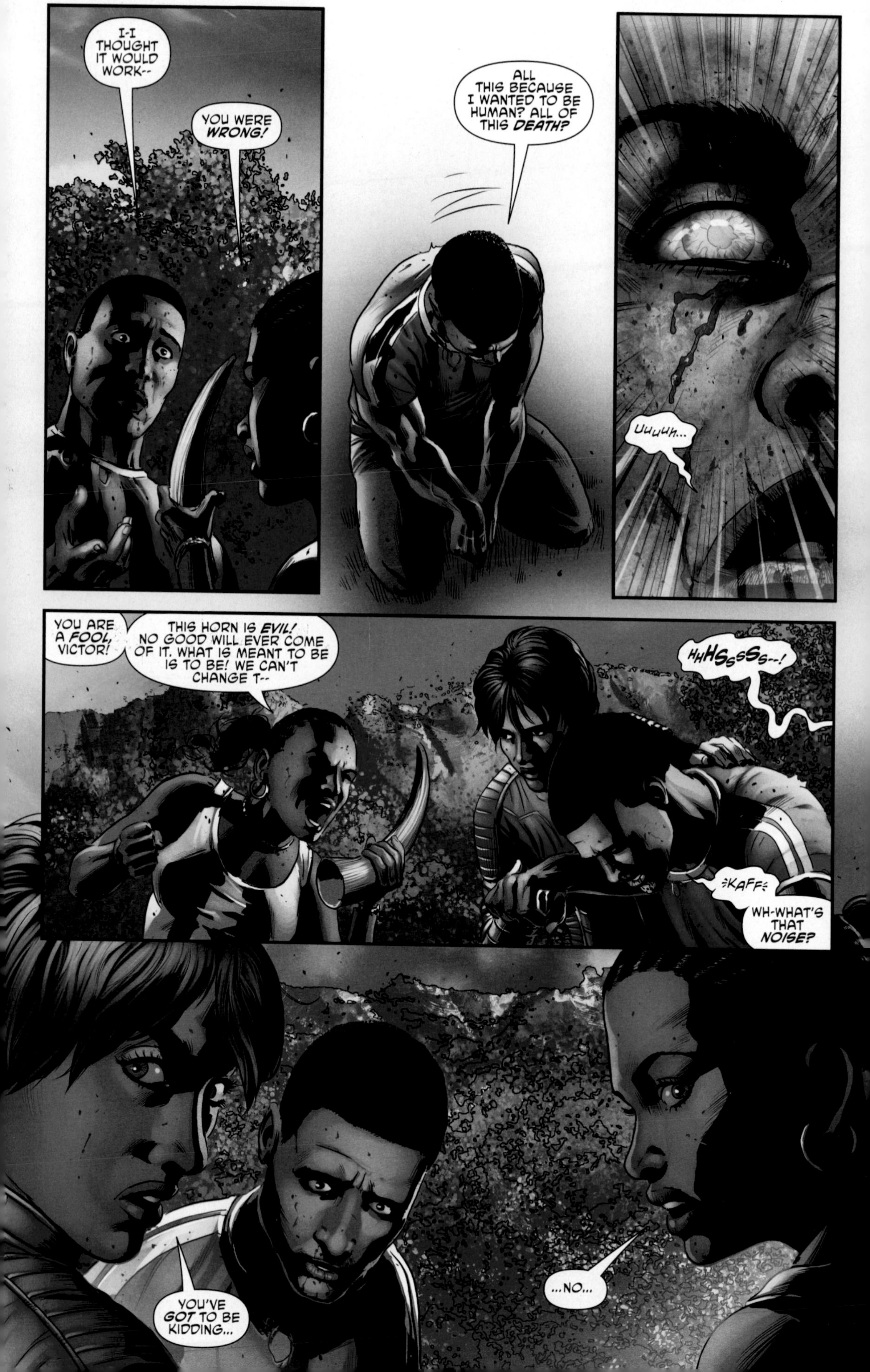
I-I THOUGHT IT WOULD WORK--
YOU WERE WRONG!
ALL THIS BECAUSE I WANTED TO BE HUMAN? ALL OF THIS DEATH?
Uuuuh...
YOU ARE A FOOL, VICTOR!
THIS HORN IS EVIL! NO GOOD WILL EVER COME OF IT. WHAT IS MEANT TO BE IS TO BE! WE CAN'T CHANGE T--
HHHSsSSs--!
KAFF
WH-WHAT'S THAT NOISE?
YOU'VE GOT TO BE KIDDING...
...NO...

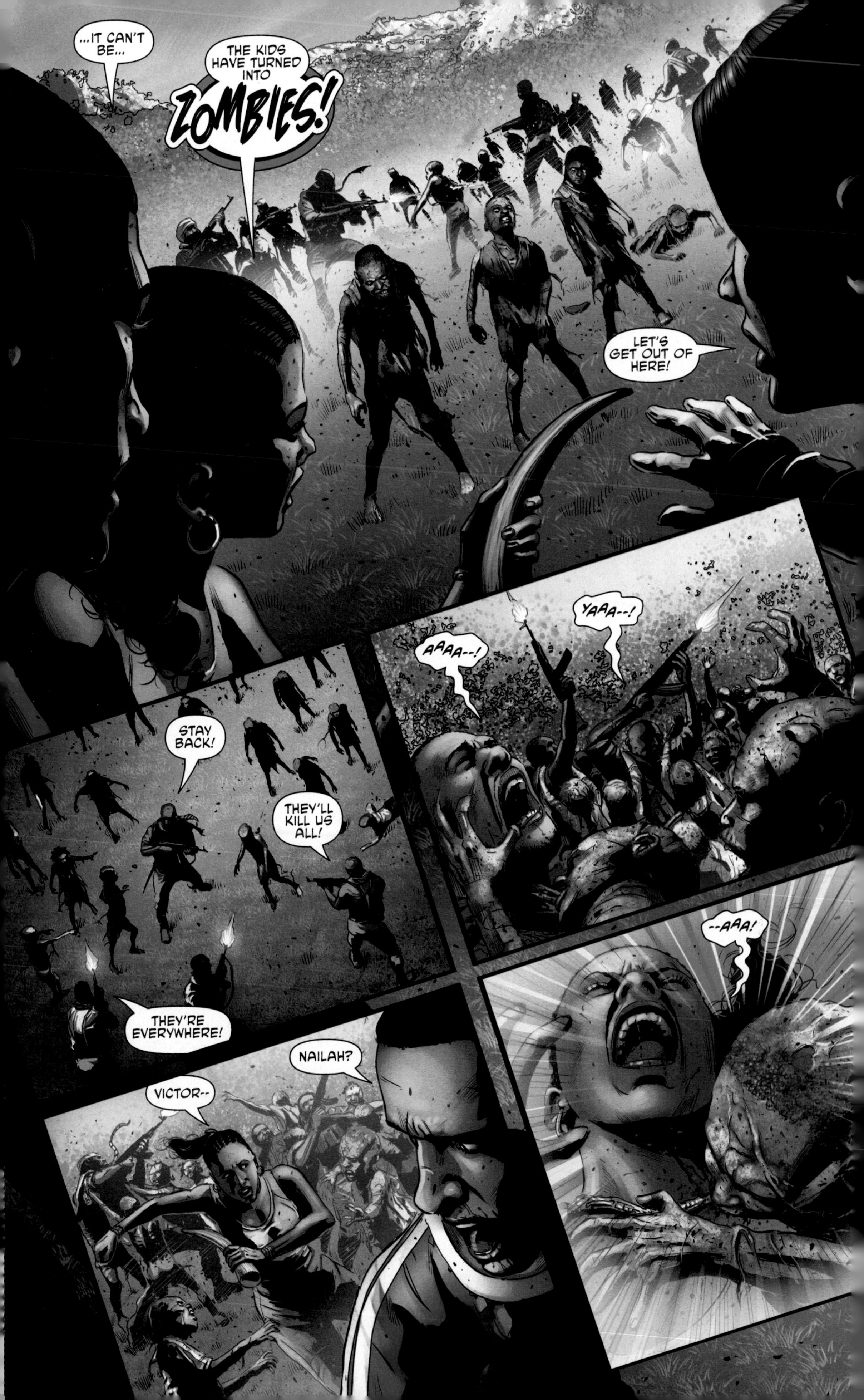
...IT CAN'T BE...
THE KIDS HAVE TURNED INTO ZOMBIES!
LET'S GET OUT OF HERE!
STAY BACK!
THEY'LL KILL US ALL!
THEY'RE EVERYWHERE!
AAAA--!
YAAA--!
NAILAH?
VICTOR--
--AAA!

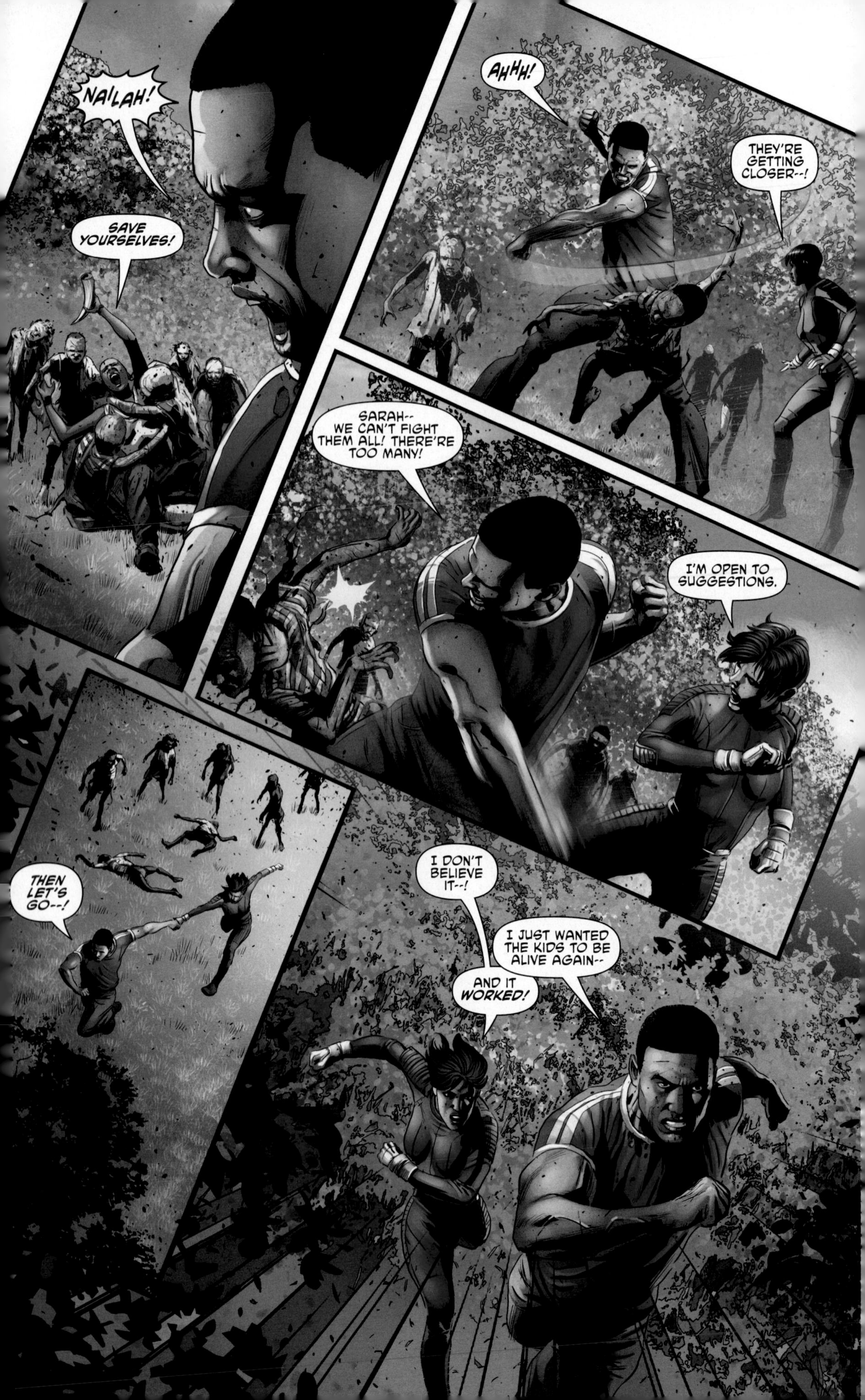
NAILAH!
SAVE YOURSELVES!
AHHH!
THEY'RE GETTING CLOSER--!
SARAH-- WE CAN'T FIGHT THEM ALL! THERE'RE TOO MANY!
I'M OPEN TO SUGGESTIONS.
THEN LET'S GO--!
I DON'T BELIEVE IT--!
I JUST WANTED THE KIDS TO BE ALIVE AGAIN--
AND IT WORKED!

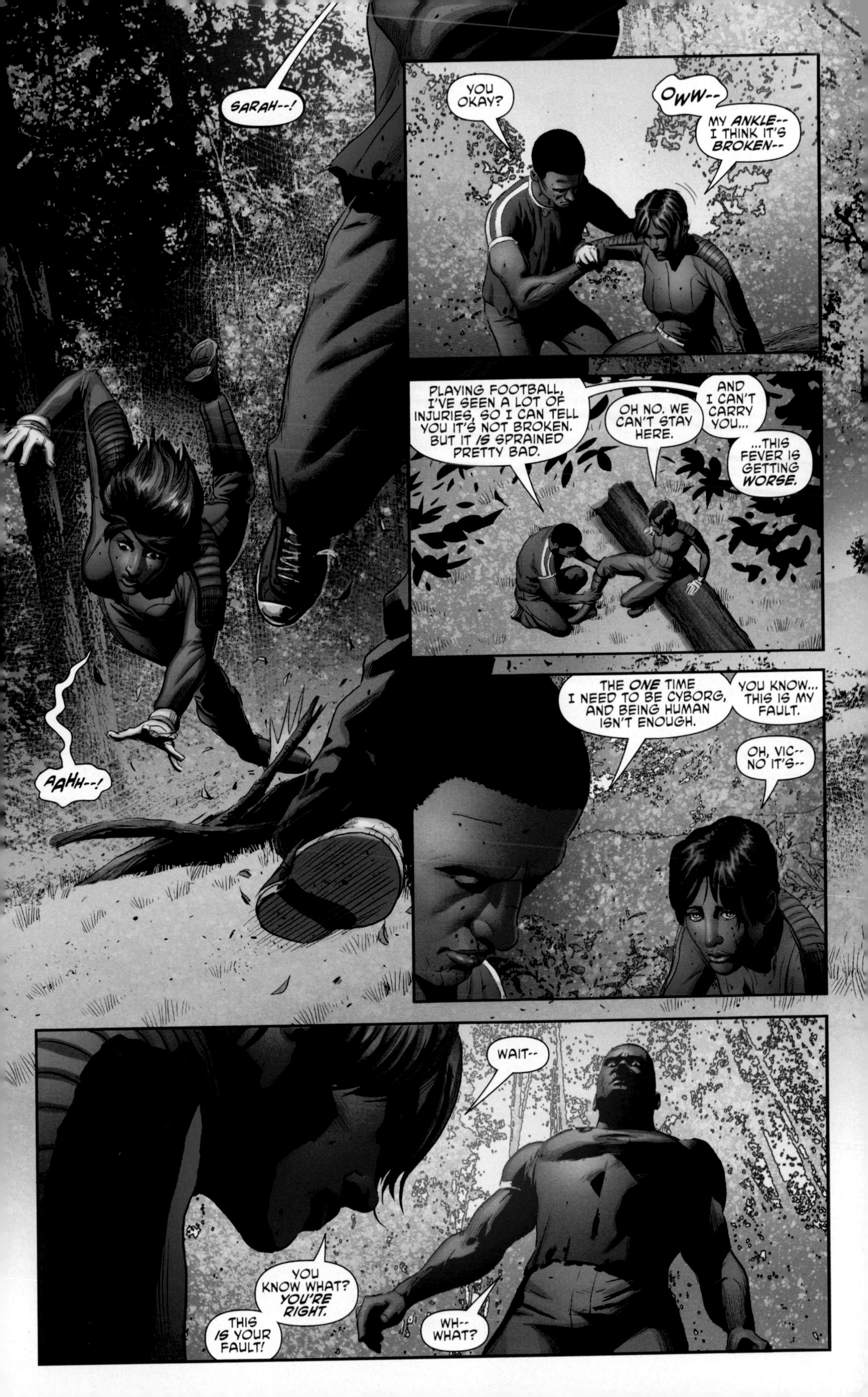
SARAH--!
AAHH--!
YOU OKAY?
OWW--
MY ANKLE-- I THINK IT'S BROKEN--
PLAYING FOOTBALL, I'VE SEEN A LOT OF INJURIES, SO I CAN TELL YOU IT'S NOT BROKEN. BUT IT IS SPRAINED PRETTY BAD.
OH NO. WE CAN'T STAY HERE.
AND I CAN'T CARRY YOU...
...THIS FEVER IS GETTING WORSE.
THE ONE TIME I NEED TO BE CYBORG, AND BEING HUMAN ISN'T ENOUGH.
YOU KNOW... THIS IS MY FAULT.
OH, VIC-- NO IT'S--
WAIT--
YOU KNOW WHAT? YOU'RE RIGHT.
THIS IS YOUR FAULT!
WH-- WHAT?

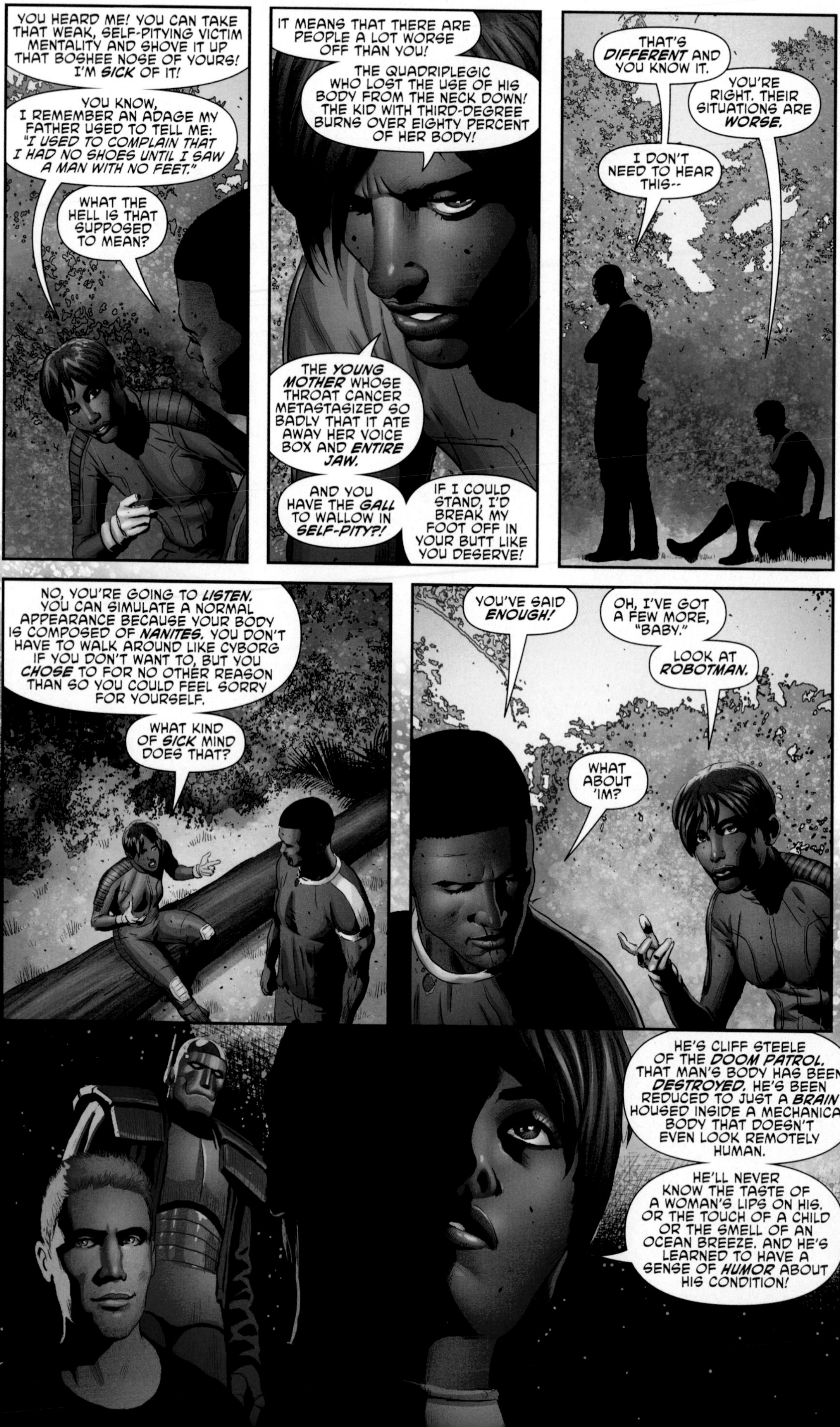
YOU HEARD ME! YOU CAN TAKE THAT WEAK, SELF-PITYING VICTIM MENTALITY AND SHOVE IT UP THAT BOSHEE NOSE OF YOURS! I'M SICK OF IT!
YOU KNOW, I REMEMBER AN ADAGE MY FATHER USED TO TELL ME: "I USED TO COMPLAIN THAT I HAD NO SHOES UNTIL I SAW A MAN WITH NO FEET."
WHAT THE HELL IS THAT SUPPOSED TO MEAN?
IT MEANS THAT THERE ARE PEOPLE A LOT WORSE OFF THAN YOU!
THE QUADRIPLEGIC WHO LOST THE USE OF HIS BODY FROM THE NECK DOWN! THE KID WITH THIRD-DEGREE BURNS OVER EIGHTY PERCENT OF HER BODY!
THE YOUNG MOTHER WHOSE THROAT CANCER METASTASIZED SO BADLY THAT IT ATE AWAY HER VOICE BOX AND ENTIRE JAW.
AND YOU HAVE THE GALL TO WALLOW IN SELF-PITY?!
IF I COULD STAND, I'D BREAK MY FOOT OFF IN YOUR BUTT LIKE YOU DESERVE!
THAT'S DIFFERENT AND YOU KNOW IT.
YOU'RE RIGHT. THEIR SITUATIONS ARE WORSE.
I DON'T NEED TO HEAR THIS--
NO, YOU'RE GOING TO LISTEN. YOU CAN SIMULATE A NORMAL APPEARANCE BECAUSE YOUR BODY IS COMPOSED OF NANITES. YOU DON'T HAVE TO WALK AROUND LIKE CYBORG IF YOU DON'T WANT TO, BUT YOU CHOSE TO FOR NO OTHER REASON THAN SO YOU COULD FEEL SORRY FOR YOURSELF.
WHAT KIND OF SICK MIND DOES THAT?
YOU'VE SAID ENOUGH!
OH, I'VE GOT A FEW MORE, "BABY."
LOOK AT ROBOTMAN.
WHAT ABOUT 'IM?
HE'S CLIFF STEELE OF THE DOOM PATROL. THAT MAN'S BODY HAS BEEN DESTROYED. HE'S BEEN REDUCED TO JUST A BRAIN HOUSED INSIDE A MECHANICAL BODY THAT DOESN'T EVEN LOOK REMOTELY HUMAN.
HE'LL NEVER KNOW THE TASTE OF A WOMAN'S LIPS ON HIS, OR THE TOUCH OF A CHILD OR THE SMELL OF AN OCEAN BREEZE. AND HE'S LEARNED TO HAVE A SENSE OF HUMOR ABOUT HIS CONDITION!

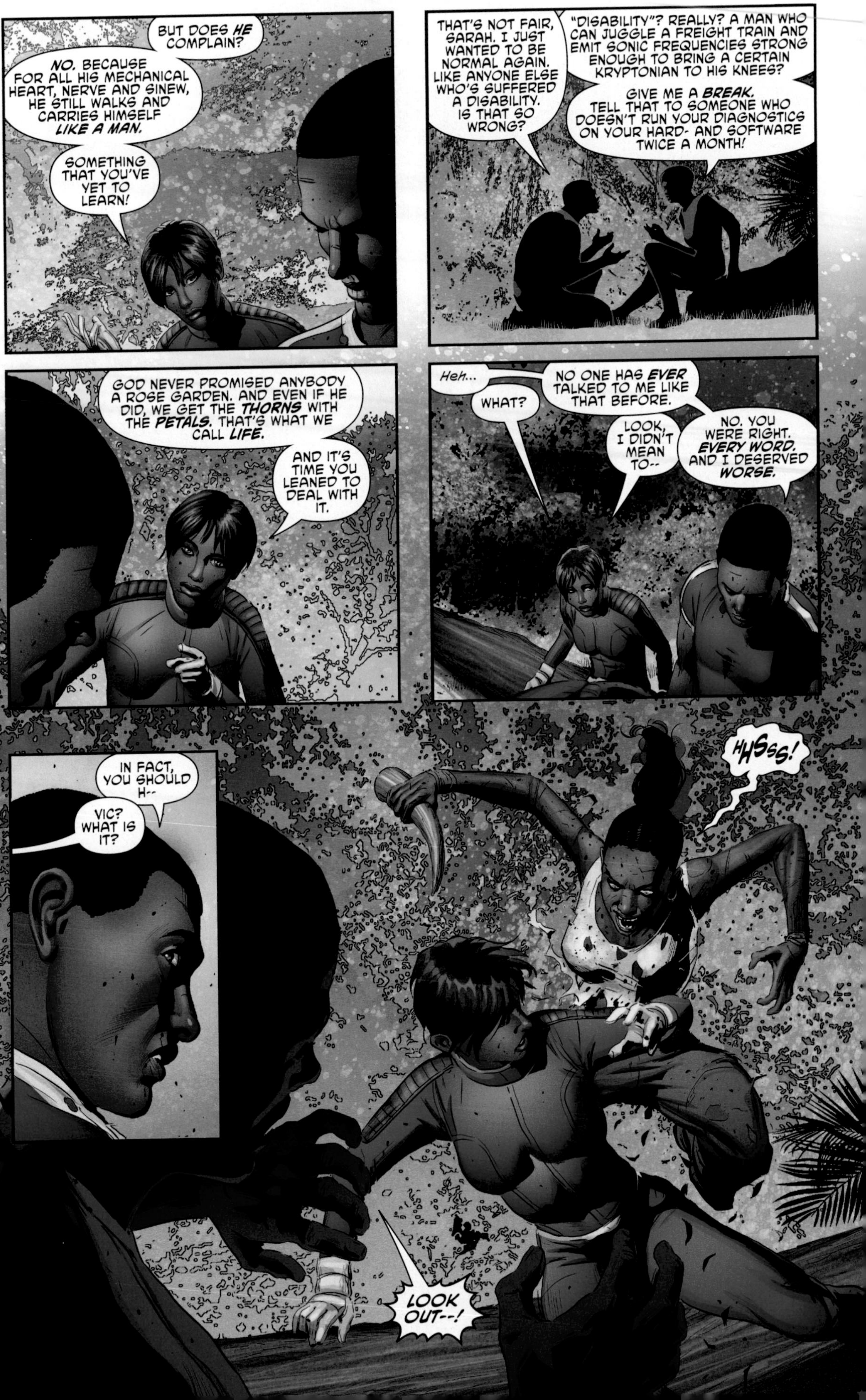
BUT DOES HE COMPLAIN?
NO, BECAUSE FOR ALL HIS MECHANICAL HEART, NERVE AND SINEW, HE STILL WALKS AND CARRIES HIMSELF LIKE A MAN.
SOMETHING THAT YOU'VE YET TO LEARN!
THAT'S NOT FAIR, SARAH. I JUST WANTED TO BE NORMAL AGAIN. LIKE ANYONE ELSE WHO'S SUFFERED A DISABILITY. IS THAT SO WRONG?
"DISABILITY"? REALLY? A MAN WHO CAN JUGGLE A FREIGHT TRAIN AND EMIT SONIC FREQUENCIES STRONG ENOUGH TO BRING A CERTAIN KRYPTONIAN TO HIS KNEES?
GIVE ME A BREAK. TELL THAT TO SOMEONE WHO DOESN'T RUN YOUR DIAGNOSTICS ON YOUR HARD- AND SOFTWARE TWICE A MONTH!
GOD NEVER PROMISED ANYBODY A ROSE GARDEN. AND EVEN IF HE DID, WE GET THE THORNS WITH THE PETALS. THAT'S WHAT WE CALL LIFE.
AND IT'S TIME YOU LEANED TO DEAL WITH IT.
Heh...
NO ONE HAS EVER TALKED TO ME LIKE THAT BEFORE.
WHAT?
LOOK, I DIDN'T MEAN TO--
NO. YOU WERE RIGHT. EVERY WORD. AND I DESERVED WORSE.
IN FACT, YOU SHOULD H--
VIC? WHAT IS IT?
HHSSS!
LOOK OUT--!

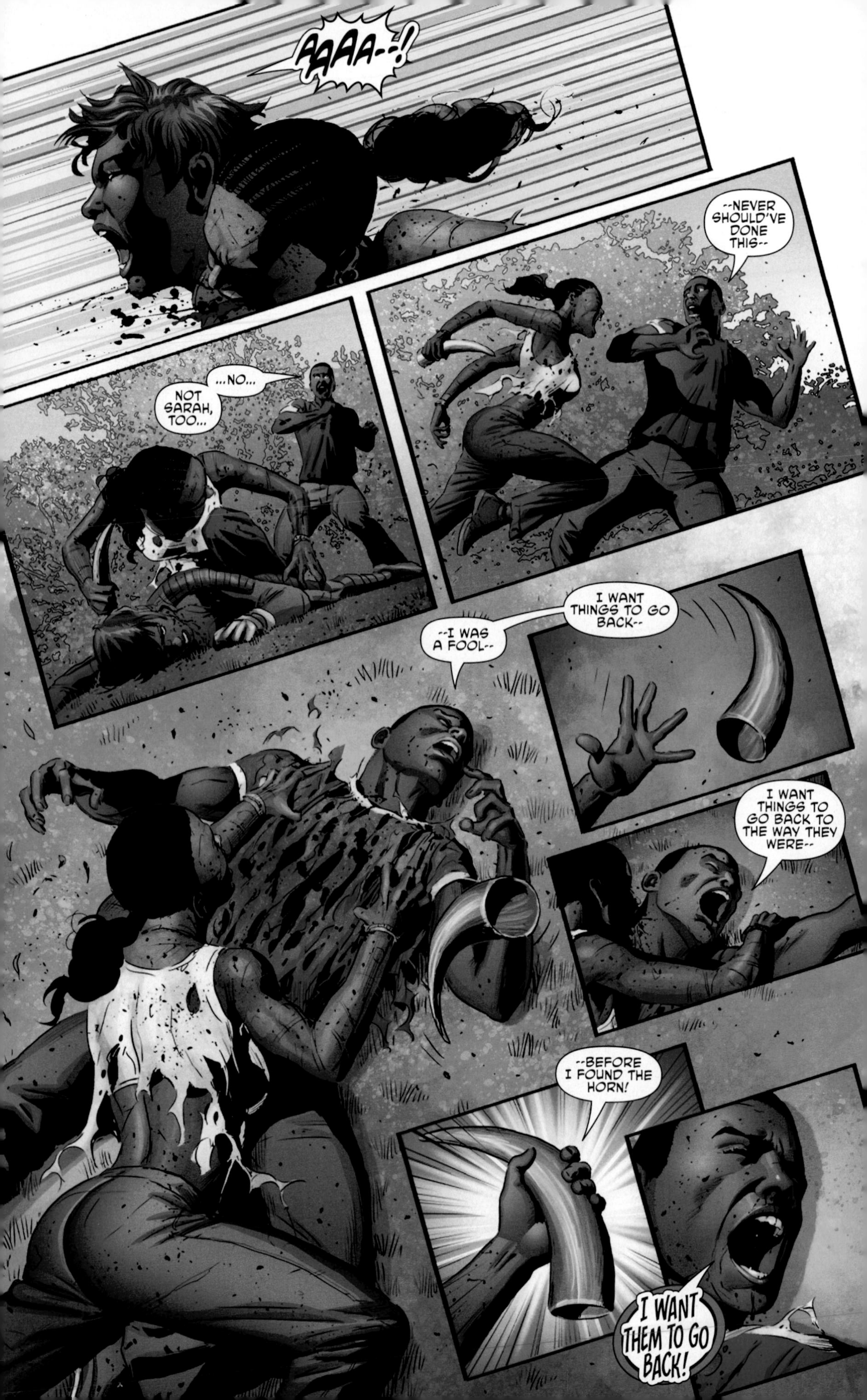
AAAA--!
...NO...
NOT SARAH, TOO...
--NEVER SHOULD'VE DONE THIS--
--I WAS A FOOL--
I WANT THINGS TO GO BACK--
I WANT THINGS TO GO BACK TO THE WAY THEY WERE--
--BEFORE I FOUND THE HORN!
I WANT THEM TO GO BACK!

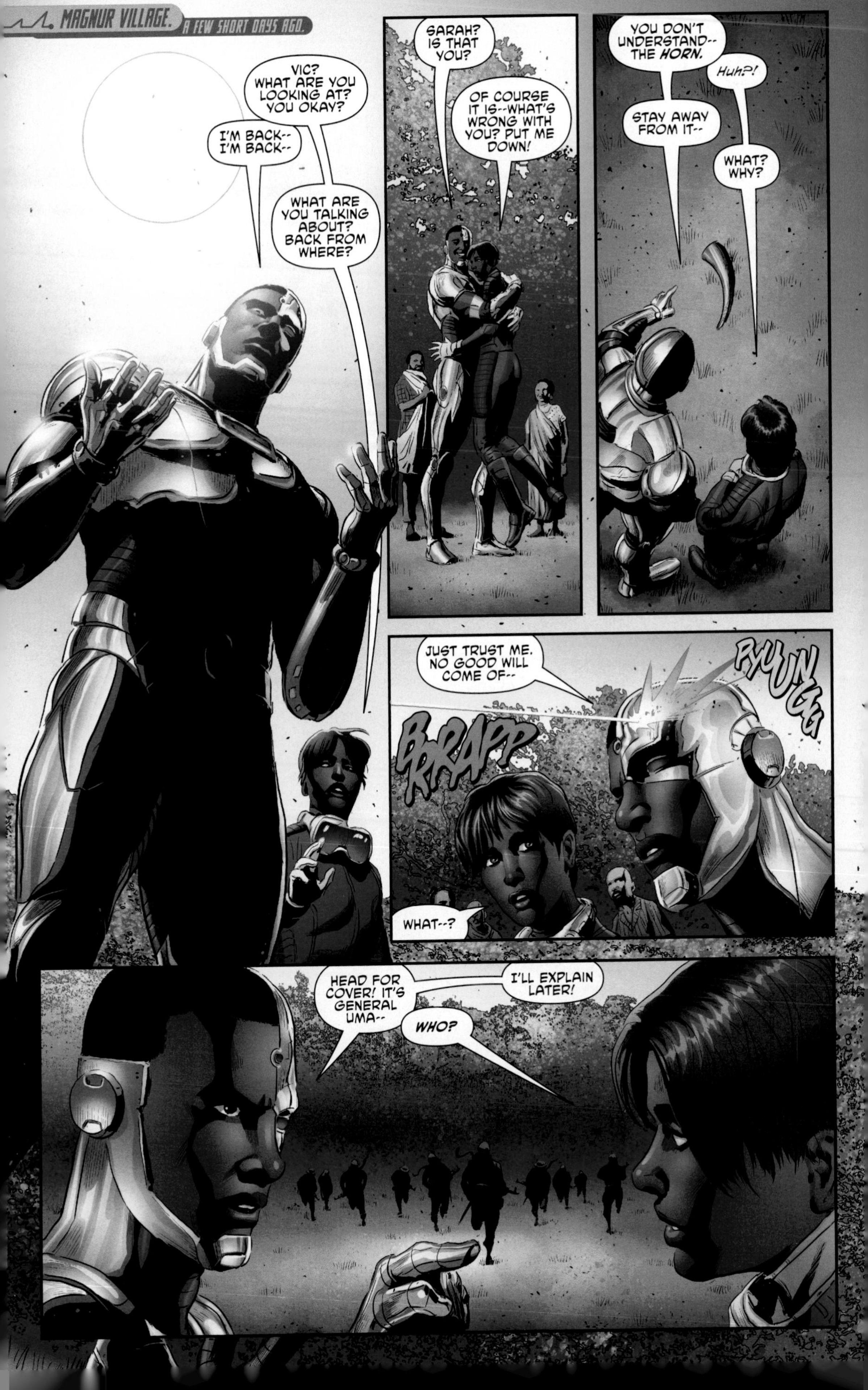
MAGNUR VILLAGE.
A FEW SHORT DAYS AGO.
VIC? WHAT ARE YOU LOOKING AT? YOU OKAY?
I'M BACK-- I'M BACK--
WHAT ARE YOU TALKING ABOUT? BACK FROM WHERE?
SARAH? IS THAT YOU?
OF COURSE IT IS--WHAT'S WRONG WITH YOU? PUT ME DOWN!
YOU DON'T UNDERSTAND-- THE HORN.
Huh?!
STAY AWAY FROM IT--
WHAT? WHY?
JUST TRUST ME. NO GOOD WILL COME OF--
PYUUNGG
BRRAPP
WHAT--?
HEAD FOR COVER! IT'S GENERAL UMA--
WHO?
I'LL EXPLAIN LATER!

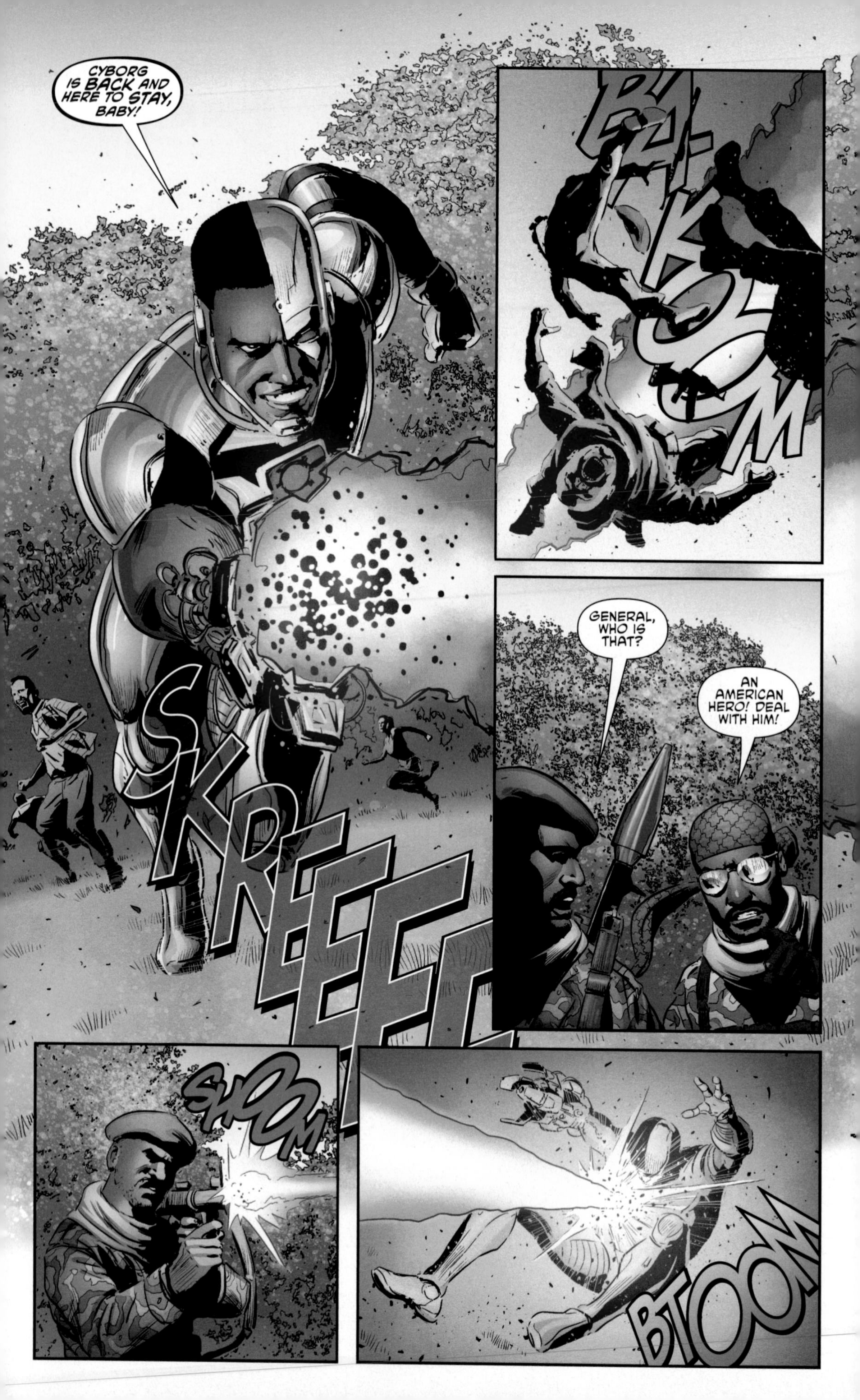
CYBORG IS BACK AND HERE TO STAY, BABY!
BA-KOOM
SKREEEE
GENERAL, WHO IS THAT?
AN AMERICAN HERO! DEAL WITH HIM!
SHOOM
BTOOM

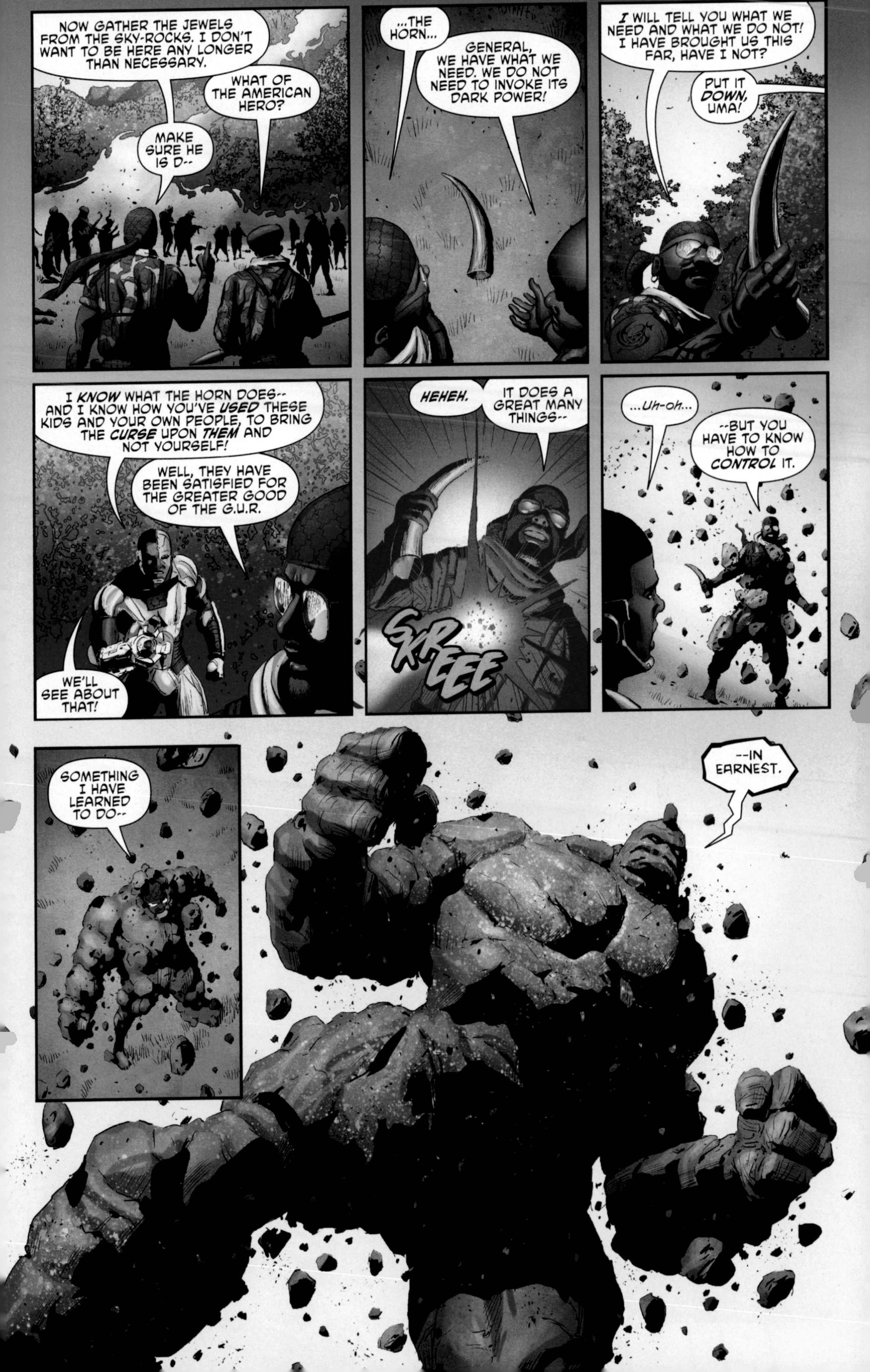
NOW GATHER THE JEWELS FROM THE SKY-ROCKS. I DON'T WANT TO BE HERE ANY LONGER THAN NECESSARY.
WHAT OF THE AMERICAN HERO?
MAKE SURE HE IS D--
...THE HORN...
GENERAL, WE HAVE WHAT WE NEED. WE DO NOT NEED TO INVOKE ITS DARK POWER!
I WILL TELL YOU WHAT WE NEED AND WHAT WE DO NOT! I HAVE BROUGHT US THIS FAR, HAVE I NOT?
PUT IT DOWN, UMA!
I KNOW WHAT THE HORN DOES-- AND I KNOW HOW YOU'VE USED THESE KIDS AND YOUR OWN PEOPLE, TO BRING THE CURSE UPON THEM AND NOT YOURSELF!
WELL, THEY HAVE BEEN SATISFIED FOR THE GREATER GOOD OF THE G.U.R.
WE'LL SEE ABOUT THAT!
HEHEH.
IT DOES A GREAT MANY THINGS--
SKREEE
...Uh-oh...
--BUT YOU HAVE TO KNOW HOW TO CONTROL IT.
SOMETHING I HAVE LEARNED TO DO--
--IN EARNEST.

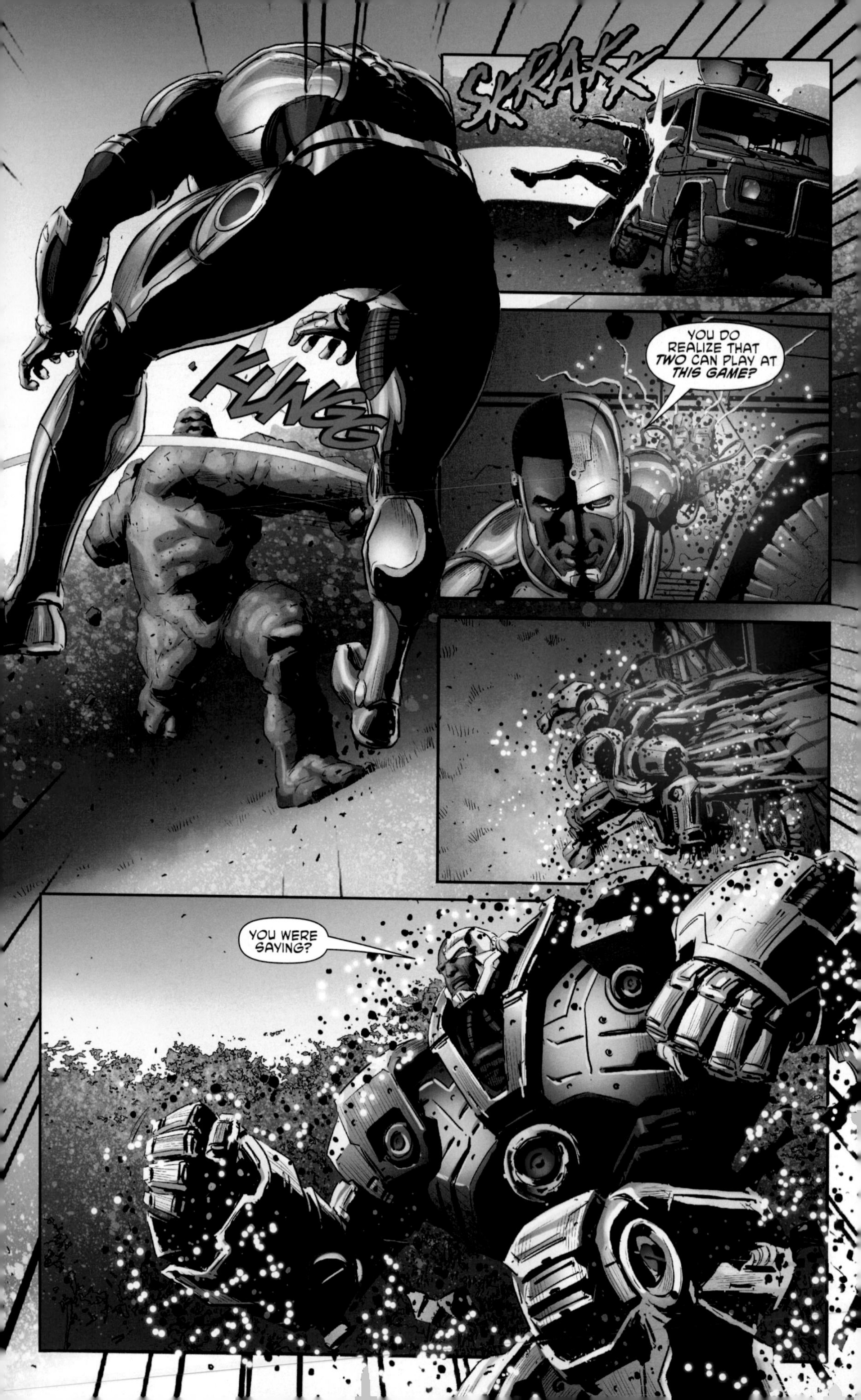
SKRAKK
KLANGG
YOU DO REALIZE THAT TWO CAN PLAY AT THIS GAME?
YOU WERE SAYING?

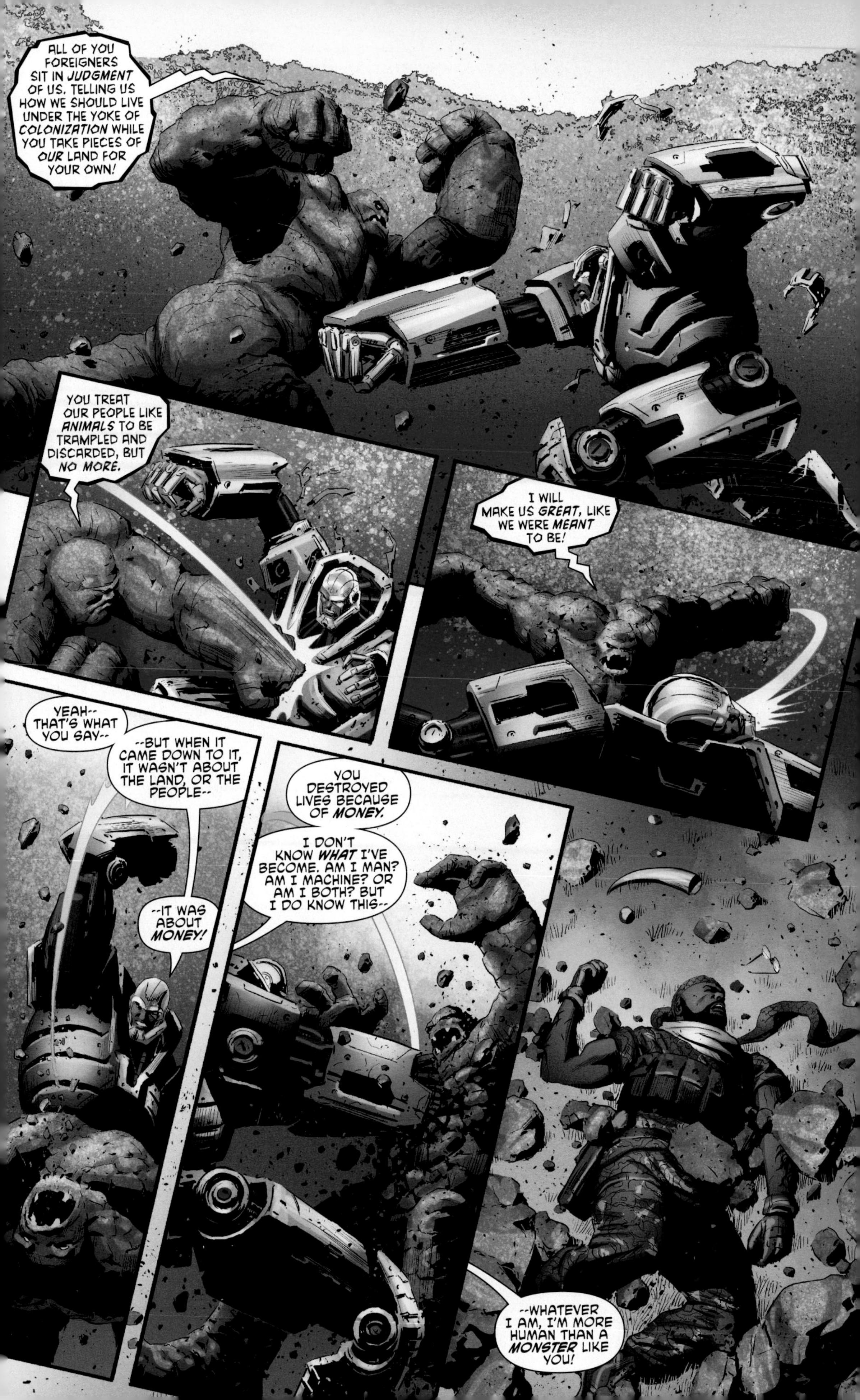
ALL OF YOU FOREIGNERS SIT IN JUDGMENT OF US. TELLING US HOW WE SHOULD LIVE UNDER THE YOKE OF COLONIZATION WHILE YOU TAKE PIECES OF OUR LAND FOR YOUR OWN!
YOU TREAT OUR PEOPLE LIKE ANIMALS TO BE TRAMPLED AND DISCARDED, BUT NO MORE.
I WILL MAKE US GREAT, LIKE WE WERE MEANT TO BE!
YEAH-- THAT'S WHAT YOU SAY--
--BUT WHEN IT CAME DOWN TO IT, IT WASN'T ABOUT THE LAND, OR THE PEOPLE--
--IT WAS ABOUT MONEY!
YOU DESTROYED LIVES BECAUSE OF MONEY.
I DON'T KNOW WHAT I'VE BECOME. AM I MAN? AM I MACHINE? OR AM I BOTH? BUT I DO KNOW THIS--
--WHATEVER I AM, I'M MORE HUMAN THAN A MONSTER LIKE YOU!

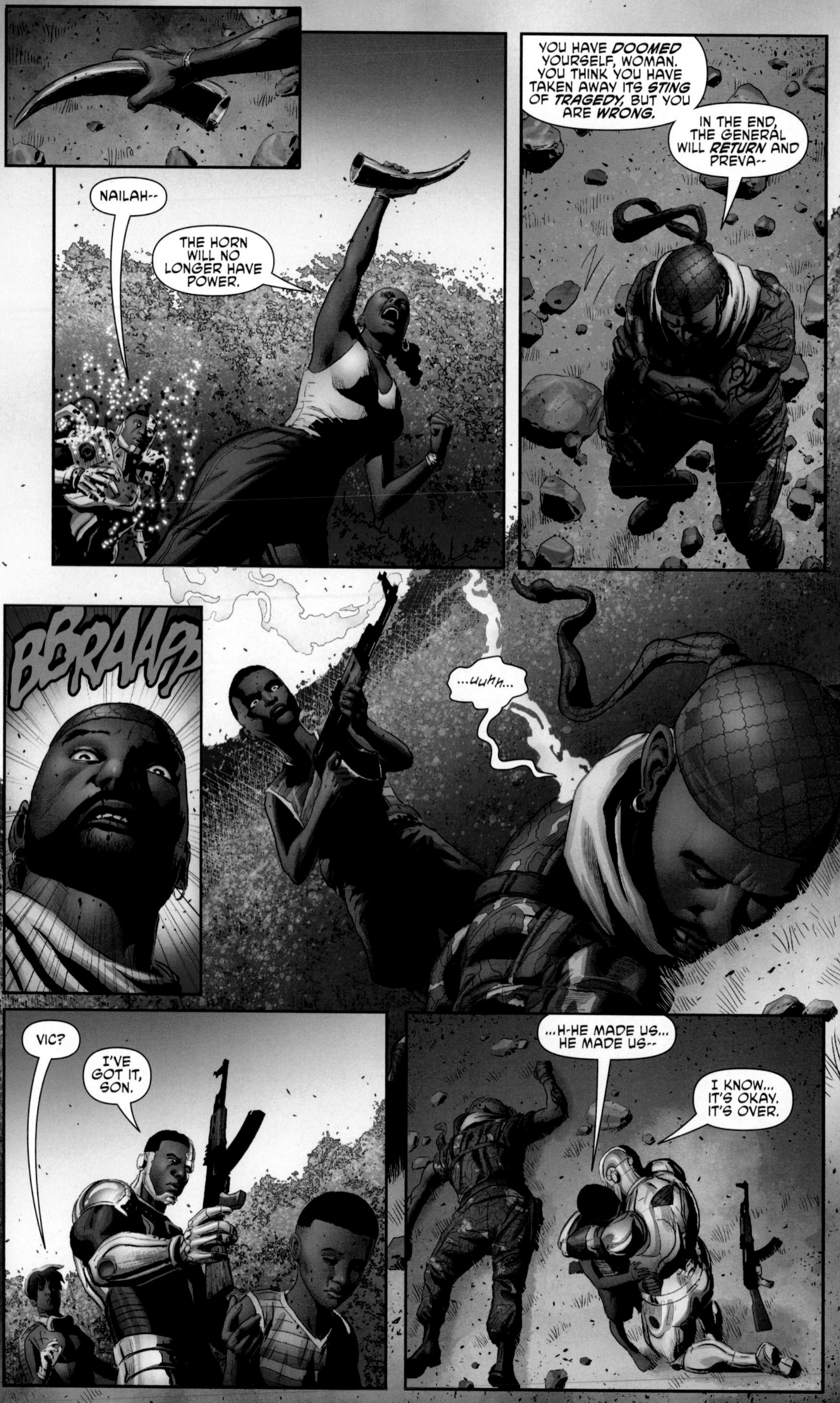
NAILAH--
THE HORN WILL NO LONGER HAVE POWER.
YOU HAVE DOOMED YOURSELF, WOMAN. YOU THINK YOU HAVE TAKEN AWAY ITS STING OF TRAGEDY, BUT YOU ARE WRONG.
IN THE END, THE GENERAL WILL RETURN AND PREVA--
BBRAAP
...uuhh...
VIC?
I'VE GOT IT, SON.
...H-HE MADE US... HE MADE US--
I KNOW... IT'S OKAY. IT'S OVER.

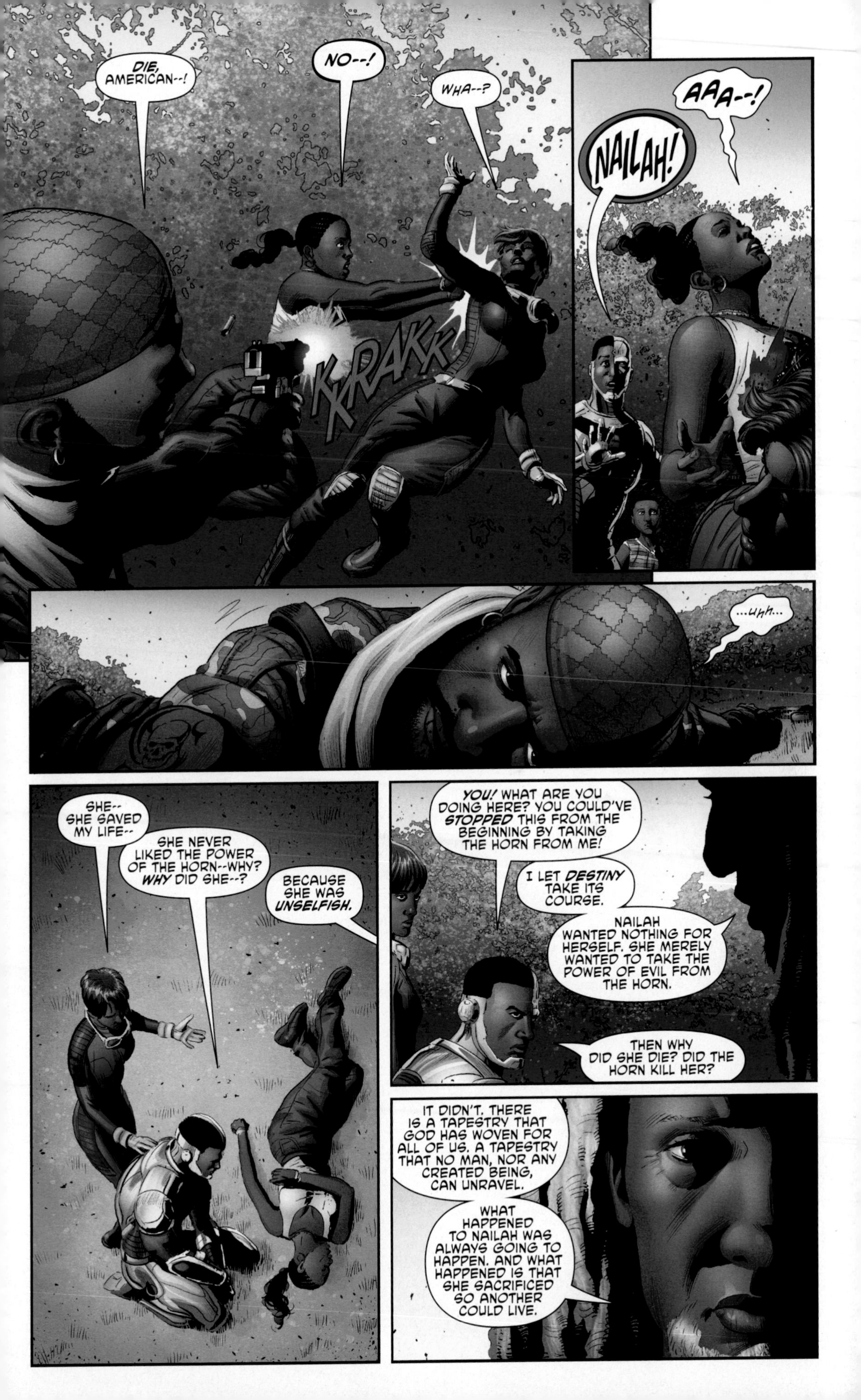
DIE, AMERICAN--!
NO--!
WHA--?
KRAKK
NAILAH!
AAA--!
...uhh...
SHE-- SHE SAVED MY LIFE--
SHE NEVER LIKED THE POWER OF THE HORN--WHY? WHY DID SHE--?
BECAUSE SHE WAS UNSELFISH.
YOU! WHAT ARE YOU DOING HERE? YOU COULD'VE STOPPED THIS FROM THE BEGINNING BY TAKING THE HORN FROM ME!
I LET DESTINY TAKE ITS COURSE.
NAILAH WANTED NOTHING FOR HERSELF. SHE MERELY WANTED TO TAKE THE POWER OF EVIL FROM THE HORN.
THEN WHY DID SHE DIE? DID THE HORN KILL HER?
IT DIDN'T. THERE IS A TAPESTRY THAT GOD HAS WOVEN FOR ALL OF US. A TAPESTRY THAT NO MAN, NOR ANY CREATED BEING, CAN UNRAVEL.
WHAT HAPPENED TO NAILAH WAS ALWAYS GOING TO HAPPEN. AND WHAT HAPPENED IS THAT SHE SACRIFICED SO ANOTHER COULD LIVE.

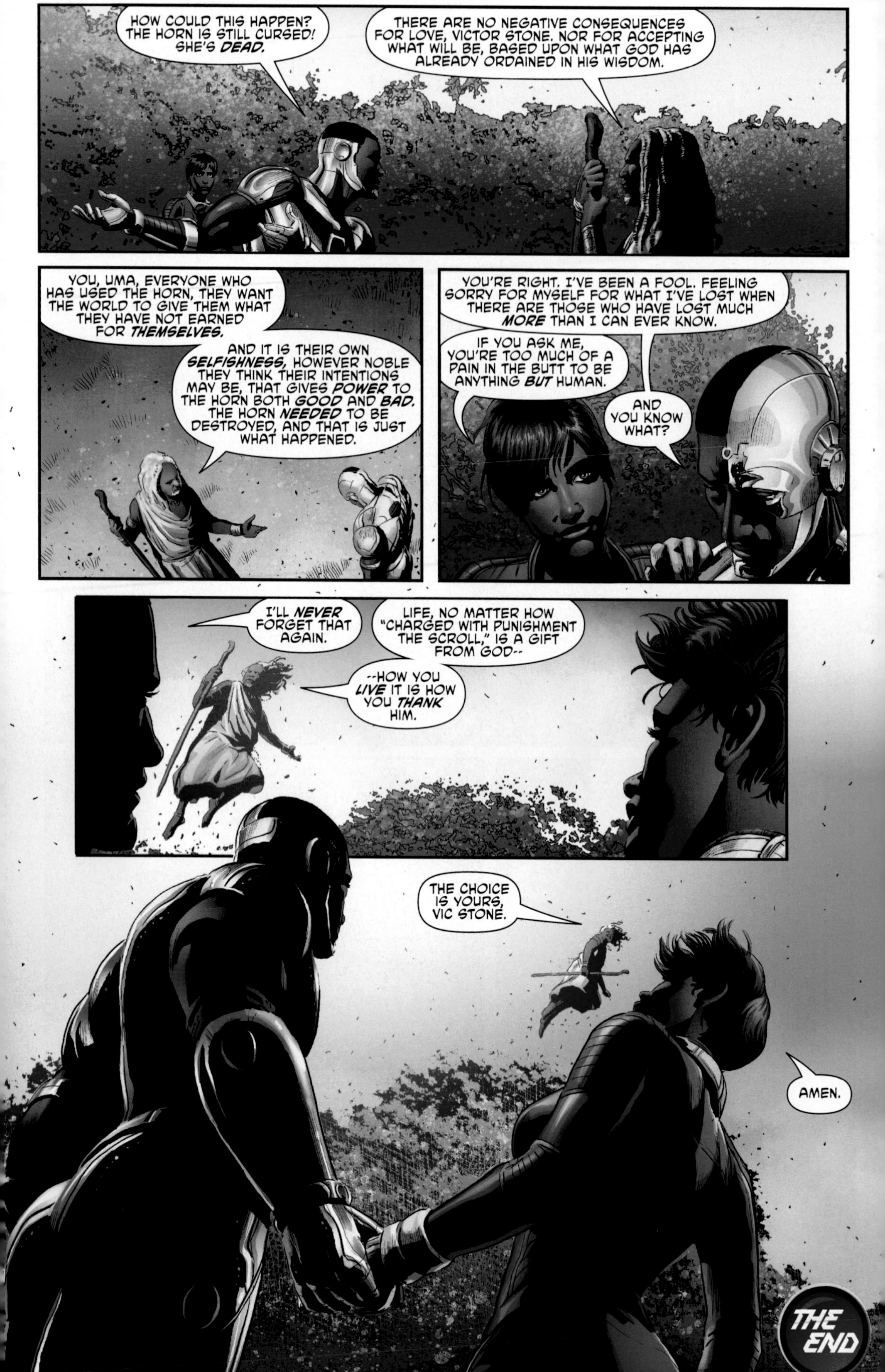
HOW COULD THIS HAPPEN? THE HORN IS STILL CURSED! SHE'S DEAD.
THERE ARE NO NEGATIVE CONSEQUENCES FOR LOVE, VICTOR STONE. NOR FOR ACCEPTING WHAT WILL BE, BASED UPON WHAT GOD HAS ALREADY ORDAINED IN HIS WISDOM.
YOU, UMA, EVERYONE WHO HAS USED THE HORN, THEY WANT THE WORLD TO GIVE THEM WHAT THEY HAVE NOT EARNED FOR THEMSELVES.
AND IT IS THEIR OWN SELFISHNESS, HOWEVER NOBLE THEY THINK THEIR INTENTIONS MAY BE, THAT GIVES POWER TO THE HORN BOTH GOOD AND BAD. THE HORN NEEDED TO BE DESTROYED, AND THAT IS JUST WHAT HAPPENED.
YOU'RE RIGHT. I'VE BEEN A FOOL. FEELING SORRY FOR MYSELF FOR WHAT I'VE LOST WHEN THERE ARE THOSE WHO HAVE LOST MUCH MORE THAN I CAN EVER KNOW.
IF YOU ASK ME, YOU'RE TOO MUCH OF A PAIN IN THE BUTT TO BE ANYTHING BUT HUMAN.
AND YOU KNOW WHAT?
I'LL NEVER FORGET THAT AGAIN.
LIFE, NO MATTER HOW "CHARGED WITH PUNISHMENT THE SCROLL," IS A GIFT FROM GOD--
--HOW YOU LIVE IT IS HOW YOU THANK HIM.
THE CHOICE IS YOURS, VIC STONE.
AMEN.
THE END

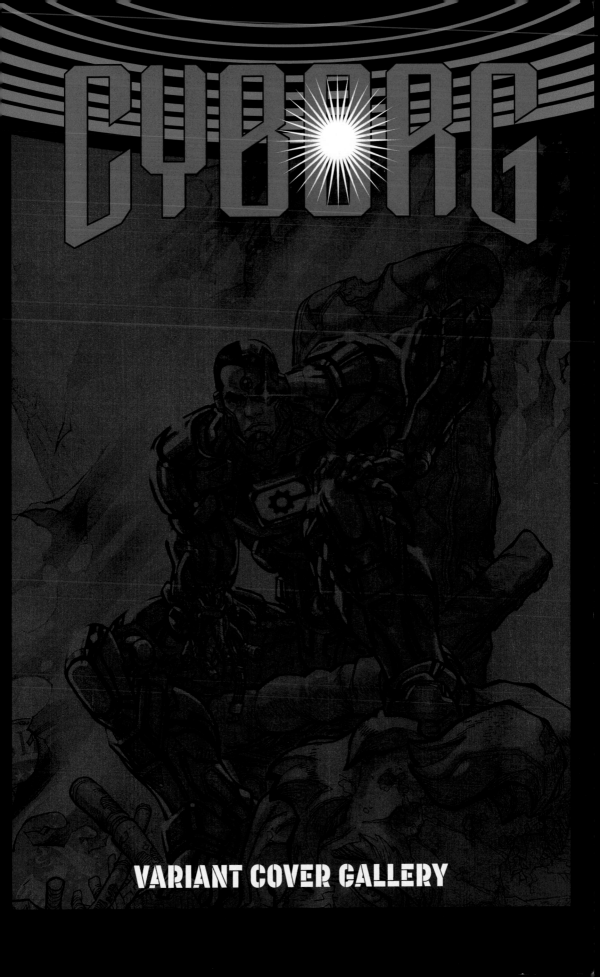

CYBORG

VARIANT COVER GALLERY

CYBORG #14 variant cover by CARLOS D'ANDA

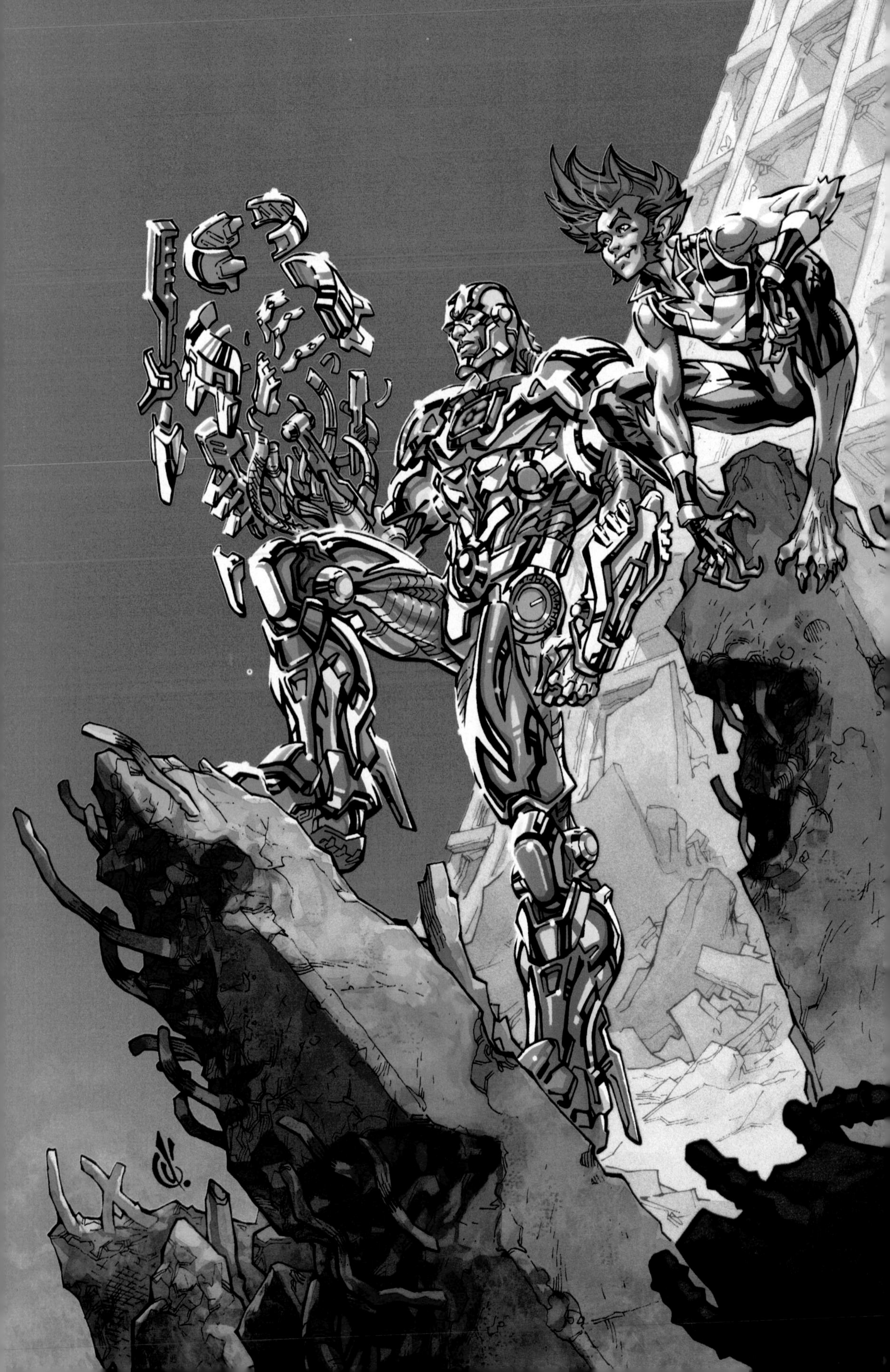

CYBORG #15 variant cover by CARLOS D'ANDA

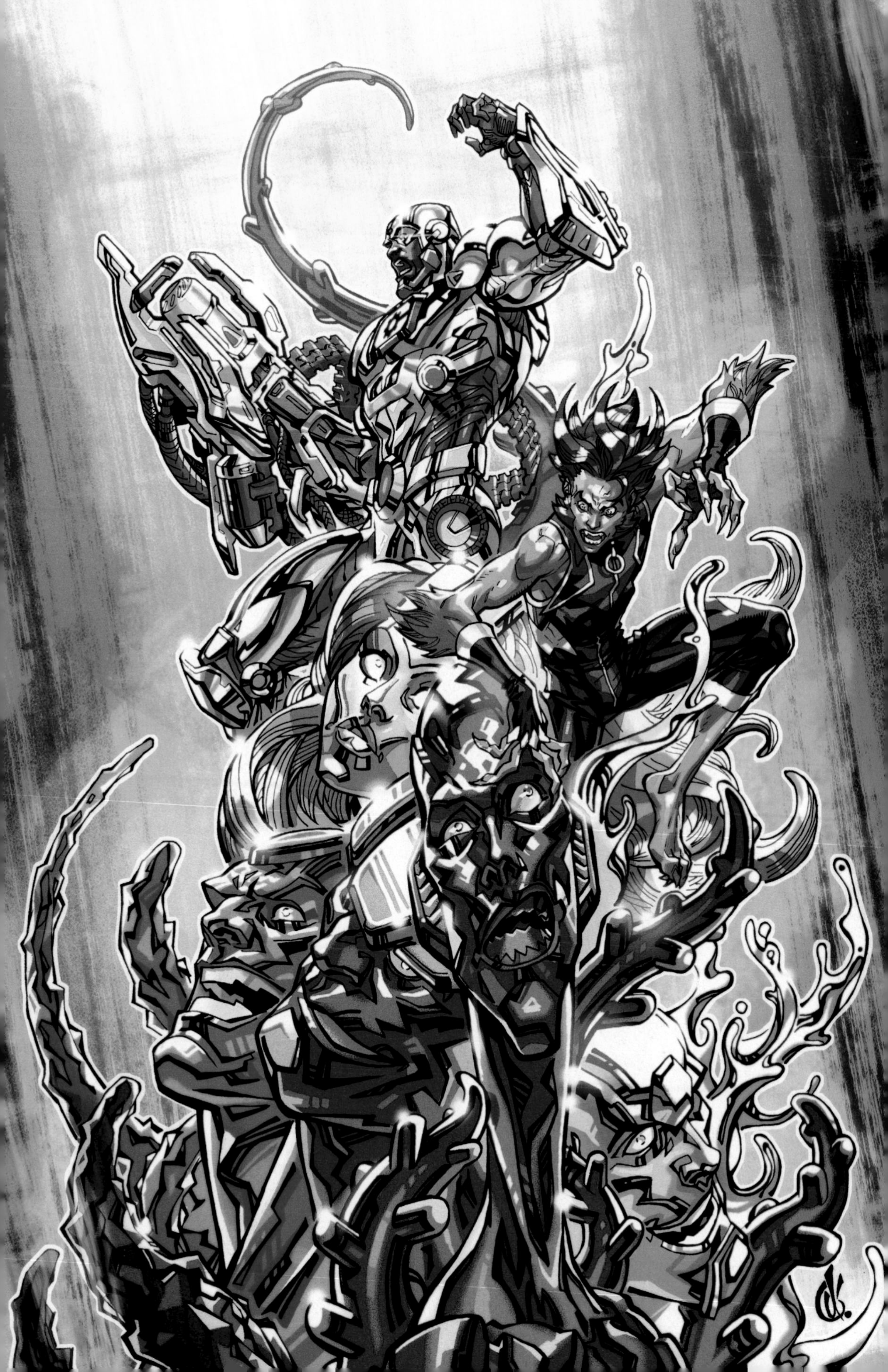

CYBORG #16 variant cover by CARLOS D'ANDA

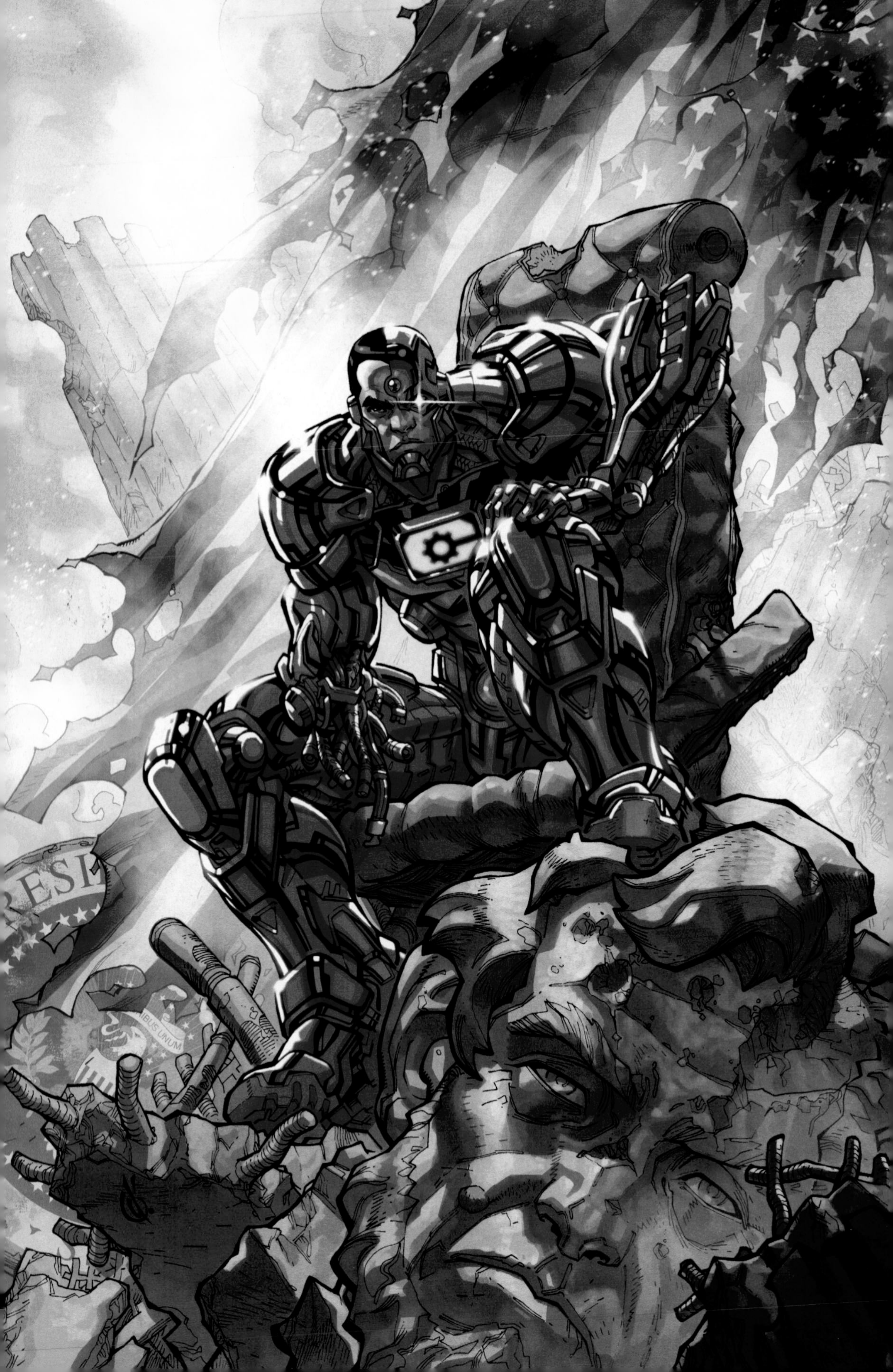

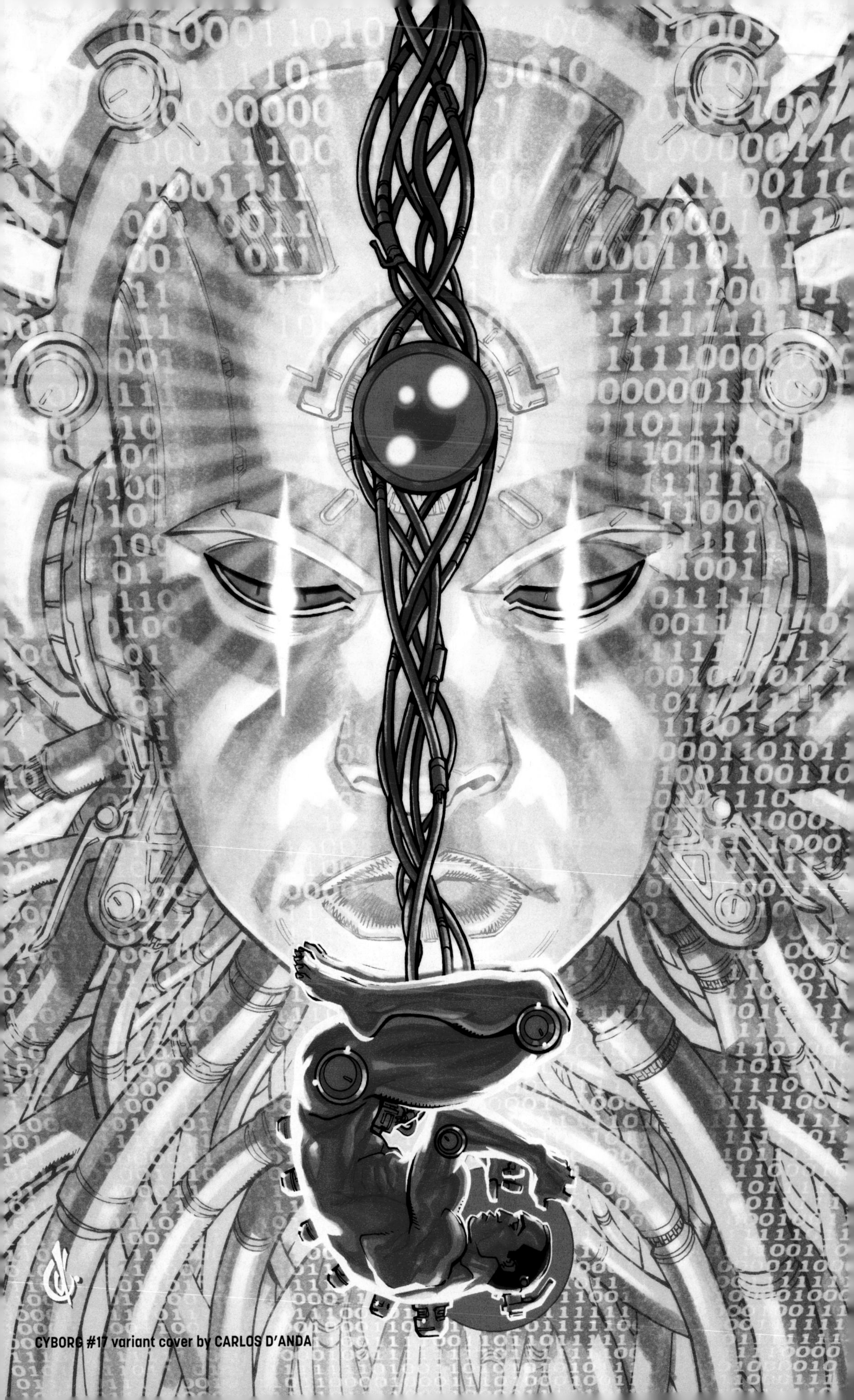

CYBORG #17 variant cover by CARLOS D'ANDA

CYBORG #18 variant cover by DUSTIN NGUYEN

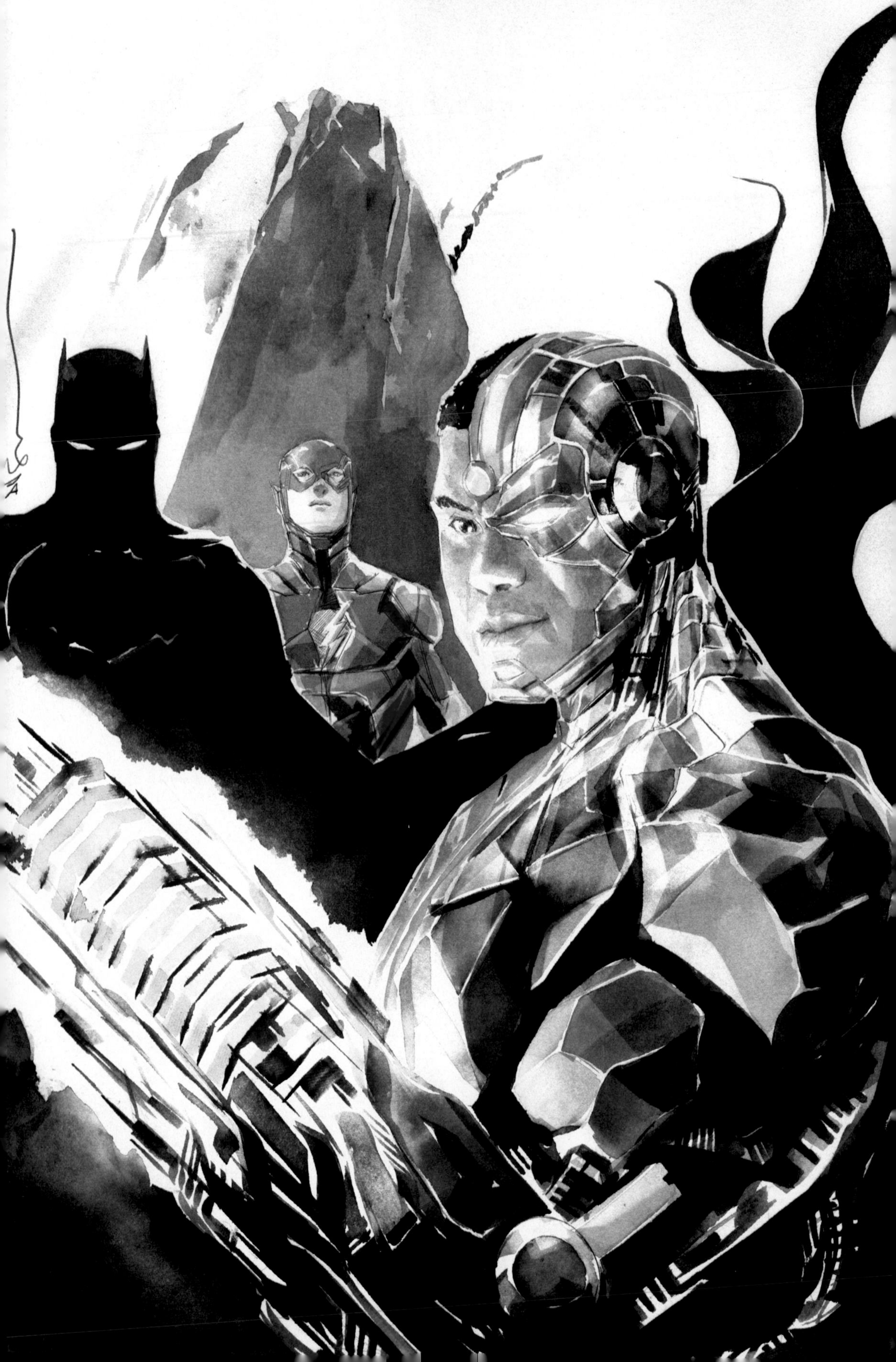

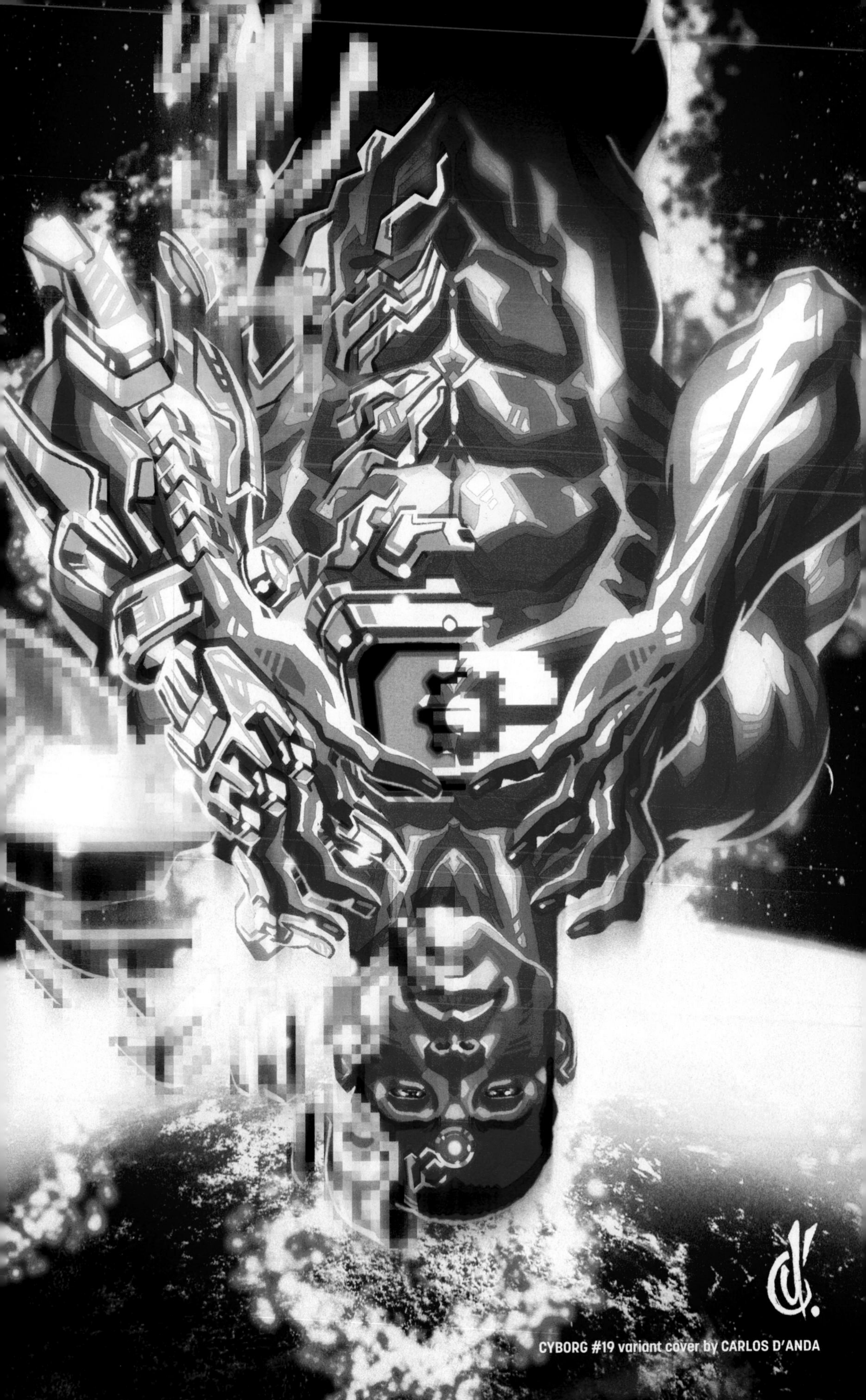

CYBORG #19 variant cover by CARLOS D'ANDA

CYBORG #20 variant cover by CARLOS D'ANDA

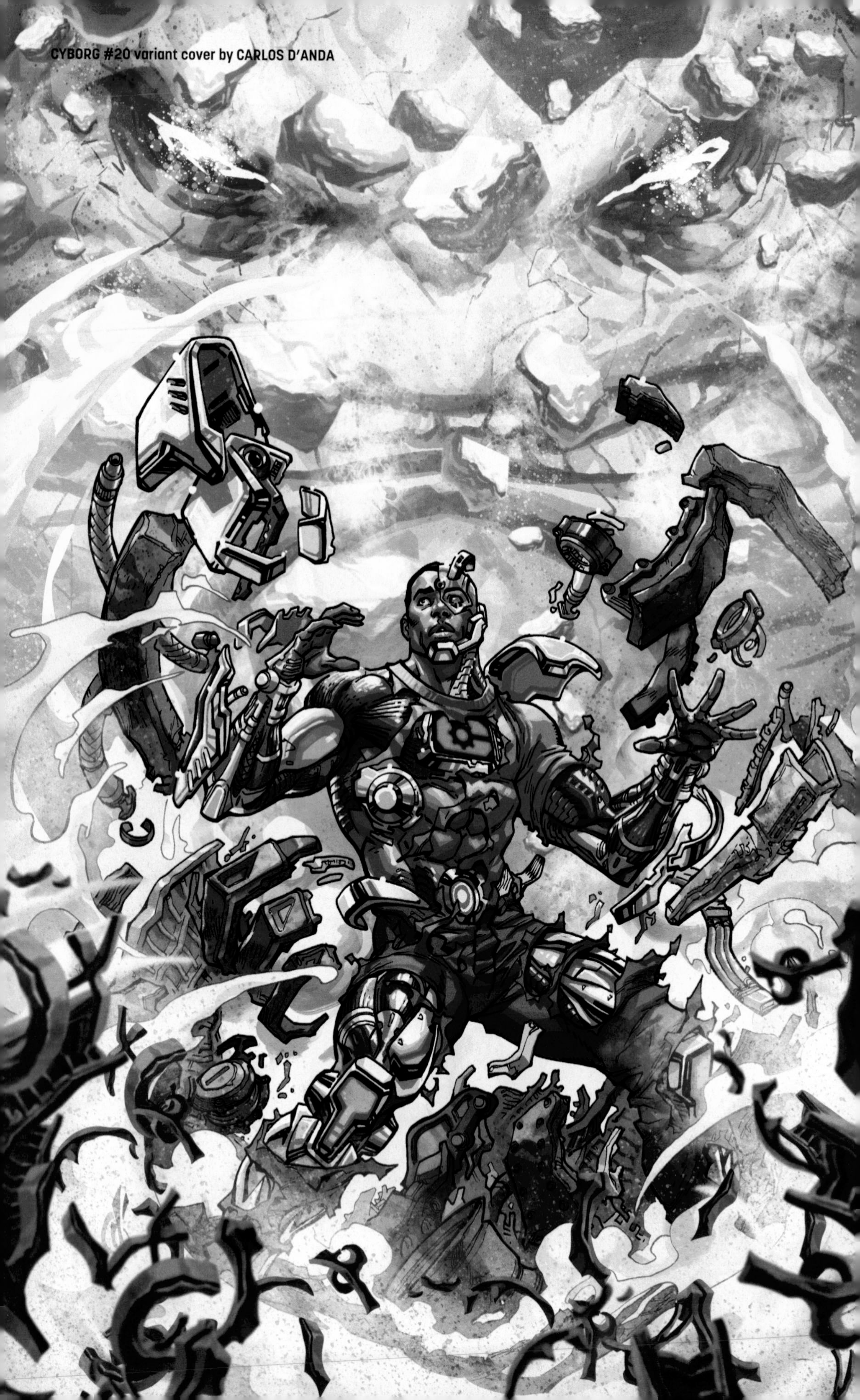

> "Some really thrilling artwork that establishes incredible scope and danger."
> **–IGN**

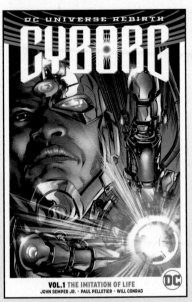

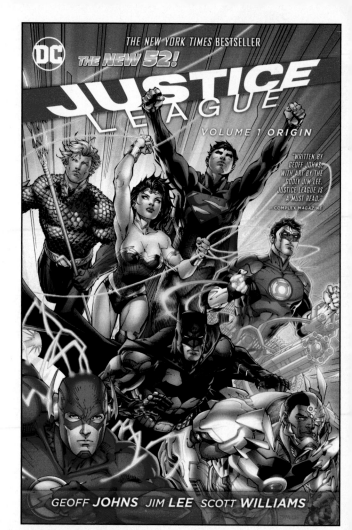

> "Welcoming to new fans looking to get into superhero comics for the first time and old fans who gave up on the funny-books long ago."
> – **SCRIPPS HOWARD NEWS SERVICE**

JUSTICE LEAGUE

VOL. 1: ORIGIN
GEOFF JOHNS and JIM LEE

JUSTICE LEAGUE
VOL. 2: THE VILLAIN'S JOURNEY

JUSTICE LEAGUE
VOL. 3: THRONE OF ATLANTIS

READ THE ENTIRE EPIC!

JUSTICE LEAGUE VOL. 4:
   THE GRID

JUSTICE LEAGUE VOL. 5:
   FOREVER HEROES

JUSTICE LEAGUE VOL. 6:
   INJUSTICE LEAGUE

JUSTICE LEAGUE VOL. 7:
   DARKSEID WAR PART 1

JUSTICE LEAGUE VOL. 8:
   DARKSEID WAR PART 2